MCE
Microsoft® Certified Expert
Cybersecurity Architect
Study Guide

MCE

Microsoft® Certified Expert Cybersecurity Architect Study Guide

Exam SC-100

Kathiravan Udayakumar

Puthiyavan Udayakumar

SYBEX®
A Wiley Brand

To the Wiley team for this opportunity and all their support to complete this book.
—*Kathiravan Udayakumar*

I am grateful to my mother and father for all you have done for me.
I am deeply thankful to my better half for helping me thrive in our life journey.
To my dearest brother and mentor, my sincere gratitude.
To the Wiley team, thanks for creating this opportunity.
—*Puthiyavan Udayakumar*

Acknowledgments

We want to express our sincere thanks to Sybex for continuing to support this project.

Although this book bears our name as authors, numerous people contributed to its design and development of the content. They helped make this book possible, or at best, it would be in a lesser form without them. Kenyon Brown was the acquisitions editor and so helped get the book started. Pete Gaughan, the managing editor, oversaw the book as it progressed through all its stages. Jon Buhagiar was the technical editor who checked the text for technical errors and omissions—but any remaining mistakes are our own. Patrick Walsh, the project editor, helped keep the text grammatical and understandable. Archana Pragash, content refinement specialist, and others from her team helped check the text for typos and shaped the content.

About the Authors

Kathiravan Udayakumar is Head of Delivery and Chief Architect for Oracle Technologies & Analytics (Europe Practice) at Cognizant covering various elements of technology services in on-prem and cloud. He has more than 19 years of experience in architecture, design, implementation, administration, and integration with greenfield IT systems, ERP, and cloud platforms and solutions across various business domains and industries. He is passionate about networking from his undergraduate studies and is a Cisco Certified Network Associate (CCNA). He has also proposed, in his undergraduate thesis protocols for optimal routings in complex networks, using the Differential Routing Information Protocol (DRIP) to avoid pinhole congestion.

Puthiyavan Udayakumar is an infrastructure architect with more than 14 years of experience in modernizing and securing IT infrastructure, including the cloud. He has been writing technical books for more than 10 years on various infrastructure and security domains. He has designed, deployed, and secured IT infrastructure out of and on-premises and on the cloud, including virtual servers, networks, storage, and desktops for various industries such as pharmaceutical, banking, healthcare, aviation, federal entities, and so on. He is an Open Group Certified Master Certified Architect.

About the Technical Editor

Jon Buhagiar (Network+, A+, CCNA, MCSA, MCSE, BS/ITM) is an information technology professional with two decades of experience in higher education. During the past 23 years he has been responsible for network operations at Pittsburgh Technical College and has led several projects, such as virtualization (server and desktop), VoIP, Microsoft 365, and many other projects supporting the quality of education at the college. He has achieved several certifications from Cisco, CompTIA, and Microsoft, and has taught many of the certification paths. He is the author of several books, including Sybex's *CompTIA Network+ Review Guide: Exam N10-008* (Sybex, 2021) and *CCNA Certification Practice Tests: Exam 200-301* (Sybex, 2020).

Contents at a Glance

Contents

Introduction

Welcome to *MCE Microsoft® Certified Expert Cybersecurity Architect Study Guide: Exam SC-100*. This book offers a firm grounding for Microsoft's Exam SC-100. This introduction provides a basic overview of this book and the Microsoft Certified Architect SC-100 exam.

What Is Azure?

The Microsoft Azure cloud platform consists of more than 200 IT products and services designed to help you bring new IT solutions to life to solve today's challenges and create the future. You can build, run, and manage applications across multiple clouds, on-premises, and at the edge, with the tools and frameworks of your choice.

Organizations worldwide can become more digitally connected with Microsoft Azure, and cybersecurity strategy can transform their security. In a cloud environment, security as a service provides security strategies for data, applications, identity, and infrastructure to customers. The Cybersecurity Architect role continues to evolve in the cloud landscape as professionals secure the workloads to the cloud, manage hybrid security, secure remote workers, and support strategic scenario-led digital transformations.

About the SC-100 Certification Exam

The SC-100 certification exam tests your knowledge and understanding of the Microsoft Azure Cybersecurity Architect role. Specifically, the certification aims to validate your expertise in securing Azure workloads, including data, applications, access management, identity, infrastructure compliance, governance risk compliance, and privacy access to Azure services.

You will be tested on your capabilities to translate requirements into secure, scalable, and reliable cybersecurity design and deployment of cybersecurity solutions.

The exam tests your deep understanding of all aspects of enterprise architecture and the Microsoft Cybersecurity Architect's role to design and evolve a cybersecurity strategy that protects a company's mission and business processes. In addition to GRC technical strategies, your skills as a Cybersecurity Architect in creating Zero Trust security strategies for data, applications, access management, identity, and infrastructure, as well as designing Zero Trust architectures and evaluating security operations strategies, will be validated in this SC-100 exam.

Why Become a Certified Microsoft Azure Cybersecurity Architect?

Would you like to demonstrate your Microsoft Azure cybersecurity skills and experience to your company or clients by planning, designing, deploying, and managing their Azure cybersecurity solutions?

Because Microsoft certification is a globally recognized and industry-endorsed proof of mastering real-world skills, those with such a certification are known to be more productive and efficient. Microsoft certifications differentiate you by proving your broad skills and experience with current Microsoft network solutions.

A Microsoft certification exam is a great way to demonstrate your expertise and build your résumé. You can validate your product knowledge and experience by taking Microsoft certification SC-100 exams.

 During and following the COVID-19 pandemic that began in 2020, many testing organizations changed their on-site testing procedures, some even offering remote exam proctoring. In light of this, be sure you check with Microsoft's website and the provider where you plan to take the exam prior to registration and again prior to exam day for the latest, up-to-the-minute changes in exam site procedures.

Preparing to Become a Certified Microsoft Cybersecurity Architect

To plan and implement an organization's cybersecurity strategy, a Cybersecurity Architect collaborates continuously with IT security, privacy, and other organizational roles.

This exam requires advanced knowledge and experience in several security engineering areas, including identity and access, platform protection, security operations, and data and application security. Additionally, you should be familiar with hybrid and cloud implementations.

To earn the Microsoft Cybersecurity Architect Expert certification, candidates must pass one of the following exams: SC-200, SC-300, AZ-500, or MS-500. Microsoft strongly recommends that you do this before taking the SC-100 exam.

The best preparation for the exam is through studying and hands-on practice. Studying this book will give you the necessary information and skills to prepare for the Microsoft Cybersecurity Architect Certification SC-100.

We recommend spending 10 weeks or so of intensive study for the MCE SC-100 exam. The following are some recommendations to maximize your learning time. You can modify this list as necessary based on your own learning experiences.

- Get hands-on experience with the Azure Portal daily, read articles about Azure, and learn Azure cybersecurity terminology.

- Take one or two evenings to read each chapter in this book and work through its review materials.

- Answer all the review questions and take the practice exam provided on the book's website.

- Review the Microsoft Azure SC-100 skills measured on Microsoft's page for this exam.

    learn.microsoft.com/en-us/certifications/exams/sc-100

    - You'll find a "skills measured" section on every exam and Microsoft certification page. The following are the primary skills that will be assessed for the SC-100 exam. A detailed outline can be downloaded from the Microsoft site for this exam.

        - Design a Zero Trust strategy and architecture.
        - Evaluate governance risk compliance technical strategies and security operations strategies.
        - Design security for infrastructure.
        - Design a strategy for data and applications.
        - Recommend security best practices and priorities.

- Use the flashcards included with the online study tools for this book to reinforce your understanding of concepts.

- Take free hands-on learning courses on Microsoft Learn.

    learn.microsoft.com/en-gb/certifications/exams/sc-100

- Read the Microsoft Azure documentation.

    docs.microsoft.com/en-us/azure/?product=popular

How to Become a Certified Microsoft Cybersecurity Architect

You can register for your exam from the Microsoft certification Exam SC-100 details page once you are ready.

    learn.microsoft.com/en-gb/certifications/exams/sc-100

On the certification detail pages, you'll find the choice to register in the "Schedule Exam" section.

Azure security engineers with previous Azure certifications in security, compliance, and identity will be tested for this exam. Security engineers should have advanced expertise and knowledge in various security engineering fields, including identity and access, platform protection, security operations, data security, and applications. A hybrid or cloud-based implementation should also be familiar to them. Those just starting should take SC-900: Microsoft Security, Compliance, and Identity Fundamentals instead.

You can take the exam online or at a local testing center, so you need to choose a test center or use online proctoring. There are advantages to each. Local test centers provide a secure environment. By taking your exam online, you can take it almost anywhere at any time. However, a reliable connection and a secure browser are required. When you take your test online, your system will first be checked to be sure it meets the requirements.

Who Should Buy This Book

Anybody who wants to pass the Microsoft SC-100 exam will benefit from reading this book. If you're new to Azure cybersecurity, this book covers the material you will need to learn, starting from the basics. It continues by providing the knowledge you need to be proficient enough to pass the SC-100 exams. If you're already familiar with Azure cybersecurity, this book can serve as a review and a refresher course for the information you might not be entirely aware of. Reading this book will help you pass the Microsoft SC-100 exams in either case.

This book is written assuming that you know at least a little about Azure and have essential cybersecurity experience and knowledge in a wide range of security engineering areas, including identity and access, platform protection, security operations, securing data, and securing applications. If you have experience with hybrid and cloud implementations, it will be a great value to add to kick-start your journey with SC-100.

How This Book Is Organized

This book covers four areas: Zero Trust, governance risk compliance (GRC), security operations (SecOps), and data and applications. In addition, students will be able to design and architect solutions using Zero Trust principles and specify security requirements for cloud infrastructure in multiple service models (SaaS, PaaS, IaaS).

This book consists of nine chapters plus supplementary information. The chapters are organized as follows:

Chapter 1: Define and Implement an Overall Security Strategy and Architecture This chapter covers the basics of cloud and cybersecurity, getting started with Zero Trust, designing integration points in an architecture, designing security needs based on business goals, decoding security needs' technical abilities, designing security for a resiliency approach, identifying the security risks associated with hybrid and multi-tenant environments, and planning traffic filtering and segmentation of technical and governance strategies.

Chapter 2: Define a Security Operations Strategy   Chapter 2 covers designing a logging and auditing security strategy, developing security operations for hybrid and multi-cloud environments, designing a strategy for security information and event management (SIEM) & security orchestration, automation, and response (SOAR), evaluating security workflows, reviewing security strategies for incident management, evaluating security operations for technical threat intelligence, monitoring sources for insights on threats and mitigations, and developing integration points in an architecture.

Chapter 3: Define an Identity Security Strategy   This chapter covers the design of a strategy for access to cloud resources, recommending an identity store (tenants, B2B, B2C, hybrid), recommending an authentication strategy, recommending an authorization strategy, designing a system for conditional access, designing a strategy for role assignment and delegation, designing a security strategy for privileged role access to infrastructure including identity-based firewall rules, using Azure PIM, and designing a security strategy for privileged activities including PAM, entitlement management, cloud tenant administration.

Chapter 4: Identify a Regulatory Compliance Strategy   Chapter 4 covers getting started with a regulatory compliance strategy, assessing the technical capabilities of compliance requirements, assessing infrastructure compliance with Microsoft Defender for Cloud, identifying compliance issues and recommending actions to resolve them, developing and validating Azure policies, designing data residency requirements, and converting privacy requirements into security requirements.

Chapter 5: Identify Security Posture and Recommend Technical Strategies to Manage Risk   This chapter covers analyzing security postures using benchmarks, analyzing security postures using Microsoft Defender for Cloud, assessing security postures using Secure Scores, evaluating cloud workload security, planning and design security for an Azure landing zone, identifying technical threats, recommending mitigation measures, and providing recommendations for reducing identified risks through the use of security controls.

Chapter 6: Define a Strategy for Securing Infrastructure   Chapter 6 covers planning and deploying a security strategy across teams, establishing a process for proactive and continuous evolution of a security strategy, specifying security baselines for server and client endpoints, specifying security baselines for servers, and specifying security requirements for mobile devices and clients, including endpoint protection, hardening, and configuration. It also includes specifying requirements for securing Active Directory Domain Services; designing a strategy to manage secrets, keys, and certificates; designing a strategy for secure remote access; and designing a strategy for securing privileged access.

Chapter 7: Define a Strategy and Requirements for Securing PaaS, IaaS, and SaaS Services   This chapter covers establishing PaaS security baselines, establishing security baselines for IaaS services, establishing SaaS security baselines, establishing security requirements for IoT workloads, establishing data security requirements, defining the security requirements for web workloads, determining the security requirements for storage workloads, defining container security requirements, and providing a security specification for container orchestration.

Chapter 8: Define a Strategy and Requirements for Applications and Data   Chapter 8 covers specifying priorities for mitigating threats to applications, defining a security standard for onboarding a new application, defining a security strategy for applications and APIs, identifying sensitive data and protecting it, designing a strategy to mitigate threats to data, and defining the encryption standard for data at rest and in motion.

Chapter 9: Recommend Security Best Practices and Priorities   This chapter covers best practices for several areas, including cybersecurity capabilities and controls, insider and external attacks, Zero Trust security, Zero Trust rapid modernization plans, DevSecOps processes, and asset protection. It also covers strategies for managing and minimizing risk, planning for ransomware protection and extortion-based attacks, protecting assets from ransomware attacks, and recommending Microsoft ransomware best practices.

Chapter Features

Each chapter begins with a list of the Microsoft Cybersecurity Architect SC-100 exam objectives covered in that chapter. Note that the book doesn't cover the goals in order. Thus, you shouldn't be alarmed at some of the odd ordering of the objectives within the book.

The examples within each chapter are intended to reinforce the content just learned. We have listed a few elements you can use to prepare for the exam for each chapter:

Exam Essentials   This section in each chapter provides an overview of the critical information presented in the chapter. It should be possible for you to complete each task or convey the information requested.

Review Questions   There are 20 review questions at the end of each chapter. The answers to these questions are provided in the appendix at the back of the book; you can check your answers there. You should review the chapter or the sections you are having trouble understanding if you can't answer at least 80 percent of these questions correctly.

The review questions, assessment test, and other testing elements included in this book are *not* derived from the SC-100 exam questions, so don't memorize the answers to these questions and assume that doing so will enable you to pass the exam. You should learn the underlying topic, as described in the text of the book. This will let you answer the questions provided with this book *and* pass the exam. Learning the underlying topic is also the approach that will serve you best in the workplace—the goal of a certification like SC-100.

To get the most out of this book, you should read each chapter from start to finish and then check your memory and understanding with the chapter-end elements. Even if you're already familiar with a topic, you should skim the chapter; Azure cybersecurity is complex enough that there are often multiple ways to accomplish a task, so you may learn something even if you're already competent in an area.

Bonus Digital Contents

We've put together some great online tools to help you pass the SC-100 exam. The interactive online learning environment that accompanies *MCE Microsoft® Certified Expert Cybersecurity Architect Study Guide: Exam SC-100* provides a test bank and study tools to help you prepare for the exam.

Items available among these companion files include the following:

Practice Tests   All of the questions in this book appear in our proprietary digital test engine—including the 30-question assessment test at the end of this introduction, a 65-question practice exam, and the 180 questions that make up the review question sections at the end of each chapter. In addition, there is a 30-question bonus exam.

Electronic Flashcards   The digital companion files include 100 questions in flashcard format (a question followed by a single correct answer). You can use these to review your knowledge of the SC-100 exam objectives.

Glossary   The key terms from this book, and their definitions, are available as a fully searchable PDF.

Interactive Online Learning Environment and Test Bank

You can access all these resources at www.wiley.com/go/sybextestprep. Once there, select your book from the list, complete the registration including the question to show you own the book, and you will be emailed your personal PIN code. When you receive the PIN code, follow the directions in the email or go to www.wiley.com/go/sybextestprep where you will activate the PIN code and sign up for an account or add your new book to an existing account.

Like all exams, the Exam SC-100: Microsoft Cybersecurity Architect is updated periodically and may eventually be retired or replaced. At some point after Microsoft is no longer offering this exam, the old editions of our books and online tools will be retired. If you have purchased this book after the exam was retired or are attempting to register in the Sybex online learning environment after the exam was retired, please know that we make no guarantees that this exam's online Sybex tools will be available once the exam is no longer available.

Conventions Used in This Book

This book uses certain typographic styles to help you quickly identify important information and to avoid confusion over the meaning of words such as on-screen prompts. In particular, look for the following styles:

- A `monospaced font` indicates the contents of configuration files, messages displayed at a text-mode Linux shell prompt, filenames, text-mode command names, and Internet URLs.

In addition to these text conventions, which can apply to individual words or entire paragraphs, a few conventions highlight segments of text.

A tip provides information that can save you time or frustration and that may not be entirely obvious. A tip might describe how to get around a limitation or how to use a feature to perform an unusual task.

A note indicates information that's useful or interesting or provides additional relevant information that's somewhat peripheral to the main text.

Sidebars

A sidebar is like a note but longer. The information in a sidebar is useful, but it doesn't fit into the main flow of the text.

Using This Book

To get the most out of this book, all you need are an Azure subscription (paid) and a connection to the Internet, which is required to use and practice the online exercises for this book.

In addition to its web-based console, the Azure Portal is available for desktop, tablet, and mobile devices. JavaScript must be enabled on your browser to use the Azure Portal. Make sure you use the latest browser for your operating system.

There are detailed explanations of real-world examples and scenarios included in this book covering all SC-100 Cybersecurity Architect exam objectives. With this exam reference, IT security professionals will learn the critical thinking and decision-making skills they need to succeed at the Microsoft Certified Expert level.

While we have made every effort to ensure this book is as accurate as possible, Azure is constantly changing. In this book, some screenshots referring to the Azure Portal may look different from what you see on your monitor because the Azure Portal is different now than it was when the book was published. Additionally, minor interface changes, a name change, and so on, might have taken place as well.

As a Cybersecurity Architect, your responsibilities include designing and deploying Azure cybersecurity solutions. You're expected to maintain security, privacy, and compliance with cybersecurity solutions. This book will help you design, deploy and manage cybersecurity solutions using the Azure References Framework, architecture, security baselines, and best practices.

While this book covers all the topics found on the exam, you won't find every question that might appear in the real exam. We cannot cover specific questions because only Microsoft examination team members have access to exam questions, and Microsoft continuously adds new exam questions. So view this book as a complement to your related real-world experience and other study materials.

Technology Requirements

In addition to a paid Azure subscription and a connection to the Internet, the following are good to have for going through the book easily:

- **An Azure subscription (must have):** You can sign up by visiting azure .microsoft.com.

- **PowerShell:** Run $PSVersionTable.PSVersion to check which version of PowerShell you have installed. You must have PowerShell 7.0.6 LTS or PowerShell 7.1.3 or higher.

- **Azure PowerShell module:** Download the latest PowerShell module for Azure Security modules. You will not have it all by default.

- **Azure PowerShell:** To run PowerShell, a Windows 10 or 11 machine with 4 GB of RAM is sufficient.

SC-100 Exam Objectives

The structure of this book is based on Microsoft's published "Exam SC-100: Microsoft Cybersecurity Architect–Skills Measured" document (available at query.prod.cms .rt.microsoft.com/cms/api/am/binary/RWVbXN).

SC-100 covers the following five major topic areas:

Subject Area	% of Exam
Design a Zero Trust strategy and architecture	30%–35%
Evaluate Governance Risk Compliance (GRC) technical strategies and security operations strategies	10%–15%
Design security for infrastructure	10%–15%
Design a strategy for data and applications	15%–20%
Recommend security best practices and priorities	20%–15%

The book's nine chapters are mapped to each Azure skill measured. The following tables indicate where in the book the topics are covered.

Skill Measured: Design a Zero Trust Strategy and Architecture

Exam Objective	Chapter
Define and implement an overall security strategy and architecture	1
Define a security operations strategy	2
Define an identity security strategy	3

Skill Measured: Evaluate Governance Risk Compliance (GRC) Technical Strategies and Security Operations Strategies

Exam Objective	Chapter
Design a regulatory compliance strategy	4
Evaluate security posture and recommend technical strategies to manage risk	5

Skill Measured: Design Security for Infrastructure

Exam Objective	Chapter
Define a strategy for securing server and client endpoints	6
Define a strategy and requirements for securing PaaS, IaaS, and SaaS services	7

Skill Measured: Design a Strategy for Data and Applications

Exam Objective	Chapter
Define a strategy and requirements for applications	8
Define a strategy and requirements for securing data	8

Skill Measured: Recommend Security Best Practices and Priorities

Exam Objective	Chapter
Recommend security best practices by using the Microsoft Cybersecurity Reference Architecture (MCRA) and Azure Security Benchmarks	9
Recommend a secure methodology by using the Cloud Adoption Framework (CAF)	9
Recommend a ransomware strategy by using Microsoft Security Best Practices	9

Microsoft reserves the right to change exam domains and objectives without prior notice. The most up-to-date information can be found on the Microsoft website at query.prod.cms.rt.microsoft.com/cms/api/am/binary/RWVbXN.

How to Contact the Publisher

If you believe you've found a mistake in this book, please bring it to our attention. At John Wiley & Sons, we understand how important it is to provide our customers with accurate content, but even with our best efforts an error may occur.

To submit your possible errata, please email it to our Customer Service Team at wileysupport@wiley.com with the subject line "Possible Book Errata Submission."

Assessment Test

1. Who is responsible for designing, building, and maintaining the security functions of an organization's IT environment?

   A. Infrastructure architect

   B. Application architect

   C. Security analyst

   D. Cybersecurity Architect

2. Sybex wants a new security model that effectively adapts to the complexity of the modern environment; embraces the mobile workforce; and protects people, devices, applications, and data wherever they're located. Which of the following meets these requirements?

   A. Zero Trust

   B. DMZ firewall

   C. Internal firewall

   D. None of the above

3. The company wants to establish a secure communication tunnel between its remote offices. Which of the following technologies CANNOT be used?

   A. Site-to-site VPN

   B. Point-to-site VPN

   C. ExpressRoute

   D. Implicit FTP over SSL

4. Azure resource logs provide insight into operations that your resource performed using which integrated Azure service?

   A. Azure Monitor

   B. Graph API

   C. Network Watcher

   D. All of the above

5. True or False: The Azure Active Directory (Azure AD) activity logs do not include audit logs, which provide an overview of every logged event.

   A. True

   B. False

6. True or False: The Microsoft 365 admin center does not provide access to activity logs for Microsoft 365.

   A. True

   B. False

7. What measures might be implemented as part of a company's in-depth security methodology?

   A. Multifactor authentication for all users

   B. Domain username and password

   C. Anonymous login

   D. None of the above

8. A company is launching a new app for its end users. End users will use a sign-in screen customized with the company's brand identity. Which Azure external identity solution should the organization use?

   A. Azure AD B2B

   B. Azure AD B2C

   C. Azure AD hybrid identities

   D. None of the above

9. Your company has finished a full migration to the cloud and has purchased devices for all its end users. End users log into the device through a company account configured in Azure AD. Select the option that best describes how these devices are configured in Azure AD.

   A. Devices are connected to Azure AD.

   B. Devices are connected to On-Premises AD joined.

   C. Devices are connected to external cloud joined.

   D. None of the above.

10. A Sybex developer wants an application to connect Azure resources that support Azure AD authentication without incurring additional costs. What is the best way to describe the identity type of the application?

   A. Third-party identity

   B. Managed identity

   C. Hybrid identity

   D. None of the above

11. True or False: With single sign-on, a user logs in only once and can then access a wide array of applications or resources.

   A. True

   B. False

12. True or False: By enabling admins to understand and improve their compliance score, Microsoft Purview Compliance Manager helps organizations improve their compliance posture, stay compliant, mitigate data protection risks, implement controls, and stay current with regulations and certifications.

   A. True

   B. False

13. True or False: You can enforce your privacy requirements with Azure Policy, deeply integrated into Azure Resource Manager, which allows your organization to enforce policies across resources.

    A. True

    B. False

14. Customers can utilize various Microsoft options to secure data in transit internally within the Azure network and externally across the Internet; which of the following is valid?

    A. VPNs (encrypted with IPsec/IKE)

    B. TLS 1.2 or later (via Azure components such as Azure Front Door or Application Gateway)

    C. Using Windows IPsec or SMB directly on the Azure virtual machines and other protocols

    D. All of the above

15. True or False: Every customer should consider security when designing and implementing an Azure landing zone.

    A. True

    B. False

16. True or False: Through Microsoft Defender for Cloud, the Azure Security Benchmark OS baseline is available as Windows or Linux security recommendations.

    A. True

    B. False

17. Providing remote access to VMs, Azure offers different technologies. Which of the following are they? (Choose three.)

    A. Just in Time

    B. Azure Bastion

    C. VPN and Express Route

    D. Azure Resource Manager

18. Your company has deployed Microsoft 365 applications to all employees. Based on the shared responsibility model, who is responsible for these employees' accounts and identities?

    A. You

    B. Microsoft

    C. Another cloud service provided

    D. None of the above

19. True or False: Credentials do not need to access APIs, because container clusters cannot span several Azure regions.

    A. True

    B. False

20. Which Azure service is a cloud-native solution that improves, monitors, and maintains the security of clusters, containers, and their applications?

A. Azure Monitor

B. Azure Insights

C. Microsoft Defender for Cloud

D. Microsoft Defender for Containers

21. Defender for Containers protects your Kubernetes clusters while they are running in which of the following environments? (Choose three.)

A. Azure Kubernetes Service

B. Kubernetes on-premises/IaaS

C. Amazon EKS

D. Azure Insights

22. True or False: When you assign permissions through Azure RBAC to an Azure AD security principal, keep the principle of least privilege in mind.

A. True

B. False

23. Which tool allows software architects to identify and mitigate potential security issues early when they're relatively easy and cost-effective to resolve?

A. OWASP

B. STRIDE

C. Microsoft Threat Modeling Tool

D. All of the above

24. True or False: Consistently authenticate with identity services, preferably with cryptographic keys when available.

A. True

B. False

25. Which security mechanism would you use to ensure that employee data is encrypted?

A. Data at rest

B. Data in transit

C. Data in motion

D. All of the above

26. What is the best way to describe the concept of data sovereignty?

A. Trust no one, verify everything.

B. All data, especially personal data, must adhere to the laws and regulations of the country or region where they are stored, processed, or collected.

C. Regulations governing data storage locations.

D. None of the above.

27. True or False: As per Microsoft's recommendation for web applications, ensure that sensitive content is cached on the browser.

    A. True

    B. False

28. True or False: The Zero Trust rapid modernization plan (RaMP) is not included in the Microsoft Cybersecurity Reference Architecture (MCRA).

    A. True

    B. False

29. You company has moved to the cloud. Which of the following responsibilities can transfer to the cloud provider?

    A. Physical hardware firmware updates

    B. Host virtualization solution

    C. Storage virtualization solution

    D. A and B

30. Your company needs responsive detection and remediation of common attacks on endpoints, emails, and identities; needs high-quality alerts; and wants to minimize friction and manual steps during response. Which of the Azure services should you adopt?

    A. Extended Detection and Response (XDR) tools like Microsoft 365 Defender

    B. Azure Monitor

    C. Azure Sentinel

    D. None of the above

Answers to Assessment Test

1. D. Cybersecurity Architects are responsible for designing, building, and maintaining the security functions of an organization's IT environment.

2. A. Today, organizations need a new security model that effectively adapts to the complexity of the modern environment, embraces the mobile workforce, and protects people, devices, applications, and data wherever they're located. This is offered by Zero Trust.

3. D. FTP over SSL can't be used to deploy a secure communication tunnel.

4. A. Azure resource logs provide insight into operations that your resource itself performed using integration with Azure Monitor.

5. B. Changes to applications, groups, users, and licenses are all reflected in the Azure Active Directory audit logs, which comprehensively report the logged events in Azure AD.

6. B. Microsoft 365 activity logs can be viewed only in the Microsoft 365 admin center, even though Microsoft 365 activity logs and Azure AD activity logs share many directory resources.

7. A. Multifactor authentication is an example of defense in depth at the identity and access layer.

8. B. Azure AD B2C is a customer authentication solution that you can customize with your brand identity.

9. A. An Azure AD joined device is joined to Azure AD through an organizational account, which is then used to sign into the device. Devices are generally owned by Azure AD, which joined the organization.

10. A. Managed identities are a kind of service principal instantly collected in Azure AD and eradicate the demand for developers to manage credentials.

11. A. Using single sign-on (SSO), users can access multiple applications using only one set of login credentials, such as a username and password.

12. A. A feature within the Microsoft Purview compliance portal, Microsoft Purview Compliance Manager enables your organization to manage its multi-cloud compliance requirements more conveniently and quickly. Using Compliance Manager, you can take inventory of your data protection risks, implement controls, stay current with regulations and certifications, and report to auditors throughout your compliance journey.

13. A. You can enforce your privacy requirements using Azure Policy. Azure Policy is deeply integrated into Azure Resource Manager, so your organization can enforce policies across all resources. By defining Azure Policy at the organizational level, you can prevent developers from allocating resources violating those policies.

14. D. Customers can utilize various Microsoft options such as VPN, TLS 1.2 or later, Windows IPsec, or SMB Azure VM (and much more) to secure data in transit internally within the Azure network and externally across the Internet.

15. True. Designing and deploying security controls and processes to protect your cloud environments is an essential factor.

16. A. Microsoft Defender for Cloud provides security recommendations for Linux and Windows servers based on the Azure Security Benchmark (ASB) OS baseline.

17. A, B, C. For remote access to VMs, Azure offers the following technologies: Azure Bastion, hybrid connectivity options including Azure ExpressRoute and VPNs, and just in time (JIT).

18. A. Using a shared responsibility model, the customer organization is responsible for their data, including employee, device, account, and identity information.

19. B. Credentials needed to access APIs and logins must be secured, such as passwords and tokens, because container clusters may span several Azure regions.

20. D. The Microsoft Defender for Containers cloud-native solution improves, monitors, and maintains the security of clusters, containers, and their applications.

21. A, B, C. Azure Kubernetes Service, Kubernetes on-premises/IaaS, and Amazon EKS protect your Kubernetes clusters.

22. True. In configuring your Azure Storage Account, Microsoft recommends considering the principle of least privilege when assigning permissions to an Azure AD security principal through Azure RBAC.

23. C. The Microsoft Threat Modeling Tool is critical to the Microsoft Security Development Lifecycle (SDL). It allows software architects to identify and mitigate potential security issues early in development.

24. A. Rather than starting from zero, organizations should use guidance and automation to secure cloud applications; one of the key recommendations is to always authenticate with identity services preferably with cryptographic keys when available.

25. A. An employee data security strategy could include encryption at rest.

26. B. Data sovereignty is closely related to data security, cloud computing, network, and technological sovereignty. Data sovereignty is the principle that data is subject to the laws and governance structures of the nation where they are collected.

27. B. Microsoft does not recommend caching sensitive content on the browser.

28. B. The Zero Trust rapid modernization plan is included in the Microsoft Cybersecurity Reference Architecture and outlines best practices that aid you to prioritize security modernization.

29. D. Cloud computing allows many responsibilities to be transferred to the cloud provider, including updating firmware and virtualization solutions.

30. A. Microsoft 365 Defender delivers comprehensive alerts and minimizes variance and manual steps during responsive detection and remediation of common attacks on endpoints, emails, and identities.

Chapter

1

Define and Implement an Overall Security Strategy and Architecture

---

THE MICROSOFT AZ-700 EXAM OBJECTIVES COVERED IN THIS CHAPTER INCLUDE:

✓ Introduction to Cybersecurity

✓ Getting started with Zero Trust

✓ Identify the integration points in an architecture by using Microsoft Cybersecurity Reference Architecture (MCRA)

✓ Translate business goals into security requirements

✓ Translate security requirements into technical capabilities, including security services, security products, and security processes

✓ Design security for a resiliency strategy

✓ Integrate a hybrid or multi-tenant environment into a security strategy

✓ Develop a technical governance strategy for security

In Chapter 1, we will focus on prerequisites for SC-100 preparation. You will read about the basics of cloud and cybersecurity. You will learn how to design and deploy an overall security strategy and architecture.

Microsoft Azure provides infrastructure as a service, platform as a service, and software as a service through its cloud computing service. Azure's cloud computing services include the ability to add virtual networks, storage, compute resources, database services, analytics reporting, security services, and many more. With Azure, you can access various operating systems, programming languages, frameworks, tools, databases, and devices. JavaScript, Python, .NET, PHP, Java, and Node.js apps can be built, along with back ends for iOS, Android, and Windows devices.

Microsoft Azure public cloud services support the same solutions that millions of developers and IT professionals already count on. Organizations rely on a public cloud service provider to protect their applications and data with the services and controls needed to manage the security of cloud-based assets when organizations build on or migrate IT assets to the cloud service. Organizations can meet their security requirements using Azure's secure infrastructure, designed to host millions of customers simultaneously.

By the end of this chapter, you will have read about the basics of cloud and cybersecurity and getting started with Zero Trust. You will learn about designing integration points in an architecture, designing security needs to be based on business goals, decoding security requirements against available Azure technical capabilities, designing security for a resiliency approach, identifying the security risks associated with hybrid and multi-tenant environments, and planning traffic filtering and segmentation technical and governance strategies.

Basics of Cloud Computing

Let's get started with a basics of cloud computing and cybersecurity. Information technology (IT) resources are delivered via the Internet on demand on a pay-per-use basis through cloud computing. Rather than building and maintaining physical data centers, an organization can rent IT resources from a cloud service provider like Microsoft Azure and access technology services in real time as needed.

Despite cloud computing's profound impact on IT, real transformational opportunities are still to come. Cloud-first cultures have emerged in companies of all sizes in recent years, as more resources are dedicated to following a cloud-first strategy.

When comparing cloud computing to traditional on-premises IT, and depending on the cloud services organization chosen, cloud computing helps lower IT costs, increases agility and time-to-value, and scales more efficiently and cheaply.

Cloud computing is defined by the National Institute of Standards and Technology (NIST) as follows:

> Cloud computing is a model for enabling ubiquitous, convenient, on-demand network access to a shared pool of configurable computing resources (for example, networks, servers, storage, applications, and services) that can be rapidly provisioned and released with minimal management effort or service provider interaction. (nvlpubs.nist.gov/nistpubs/Legacy/SP/nistspecialpublication800-145.pdf)

In simple terms, with cloud computing, you can instantly access computing services including servers, storage, databases, networking, software, analytics, and intelligence via the Internet to innovate more rapidly, adapt resources more efficiently, and achieve economies of scale. Typically, you pay only for the cloud services you use, allowing you to reduce your operating costs, run your infrastructure more efficiently, and scale as your business needs change.

The Need for the Cloud

Businesses can use cloud computing to maximize efficiencies, flexibility, and strategic advantages. A cloud-based computing environment allows businesses to scale their computing resources, reducing the cost of acquiring and maintaining them. Organizations pay as they go for these resources, meaning they pay only for the resources they use. This has proven significantly cheaper than acquiring and managing the resources alone.

Organization-owned IT infrastructures are experiencing abnormal wear and tear to meet expectations for speedy, secure, and stable services. Organizations often find that improving and managing a hardy, scalable, and secure IT foundation is prohibitively expensive as they strive to develop their IT systems' processing capabilities and storage capabilities.

For the modern digital era, cloud computing has become the standard approach to building and delivering applications in order to drive agility, differentiation, and speed-to-market. Businesses with fluctuating workloads should consider cloud computing since cloud infrastructure scales to meet organizations' needs. With cloud computing capabilities, people from different places can collaborate on business projects without meeting in person.

Cloud service providers acquire and control underlying cloud infrastructure, boosting businesses to concentrate on their efforts on managing core business operations. Modern digital transformation and cloud computing offer the following processes, services, and tools to empower and focus on core business operations.

DevOps By combining cultural philosophies, practices, and tools, development and operations (DevOps) increase an organization's capability to produce applications and services quickly. DevOps allows organizations to develop and improve products more rapidly than traditional software development and infrastructure management processes, which enables organizations to serve their customers better and compete more effectively.

DevSecOps   A development, security, and operations (DevSecOps) approach combines development, security, and operations to integrate security across the entire IT life cycle as a shared responsibility.

SRE   Site reliability engineering (SRE) IT operations are managed through site reliability engineering software, which SRE teams use to solve problems, automate operations, and manage systems.

DevOps, DevSecOps, and SRE engineers can converge on what matters most with cloud computing and withdraw undifferentiated trades, such as procurement, support, and retention planning. The adoption of cloud computing has led to numerous distinct models and deployment strategies tailored to fit the specific needs of users. Cloud service and deployment organizations offer consumers varying control, flexibility, and management.

Cloud Service Models

Various cloud computing service models are available, each meeting a unique business need. The NIST defines three types of cloud deployment: infrastructure as a service (IaaS), platform as a service (PaaS), software as a service (SaaS).

Software as a Service (SaaS)   The capability provided to the consumer is to use the provider's applications running on a cloud infrastructure. The applications are accessible from various client devices through either a thin client interface, such as a web browser (for example, web-based email), or a program interface. The consumer does not manage or control the underlying cloud infrastructure including network, servers, operating systems, storage, or even individual application capabilities, with the possible exception of limited user specific application configuration settings.

Infrastructure as a Service (IaaS)   The capability provided to the consumer is to provision processing, storage, networks, and other fundamental computing resources where the consumer is able to deploy and run arbitrary software, which can include operating systems and applications. The consumer does not manage or control the underlying cloud infrastructure but has control over operating systems, storage, and deployed applications; and possibly limited control of select networking components (for example, host firewalls).

Platform as a Service (PaaS)   The capability provided to the consumer is to deploy onto the cloud infrastructure consumer-created or acquired applications created using programming languages, libraries, services, and tools supported by the provider. The consumer does not manage or control the underlying cloud infrastructure, including networks, servers, operating systems, or storage, but has control over the deployed applications and possibly configuration settings for the application-hosting environment.

(nvlpubs.nist.gov/nistpubs/Legacy/SP/nistspecialpublication800-145.pdf)

Cloud Deployment Models

NIST defines four types of cloud deployment: public clouds, private clouds, community clouds, and hybrid clouds. Cloud deployment models are defined by where the infrastructure resides and who controls it. One of the most critical decisions IT organizations should make in cloud deployment is their deployment model.

Public Cloud   The cloud infrastructure is provisioned for open use by the general public. It may be owned, managed, and operated by a business, academic, or government organization, or some combination of them. It exists on the premises of the cloud provider.

Private Cloud   The cloud infrastructure is provisioned for exclusive use by a single organization comprising multiple consumers (for example, business units). It may be owned, managed, and operated by the organization, a third party, or some combination of them, and it may exist on or off premises.

Community Cloud   The cloud infrastructure is provisioned for exclusive use by a specific community of consumers from organizations that have shared concerns (for example, mission, security requirements, policy, and compliance considerations). It may be owned, managed, and operated by one or more of the organizations in the community, a third party, or some combination of them, and it may exist on or off premises.

Hybrid Cloud   The cloud infrastructure is a composition of two or more distinct cloud infrastructures (private, community, or public) that remain unique entities but that are bound together by standardized or proprietary technology that enables data and application portability (for example, cloud bursting for load balancing between clouds).

(nvlpubs.nist.gov/nistpubs/Legacy/SP/nistspecialpublication800-145.pdf)

Introduction to Cybersecurity

Cybersecurity guides the blend of people, processes, and technology employed to protect organizations, computer systems, networks, and individuals from theft, misdirection, and corruption of their data, hardware, and software. Cybersecurity aims to protect critical systems, networks, programs, and sensitive information from digital attacks. Cybersecurity measures, also known as IT security, protect networked systems and applications from external or internal threats.

Integrating technology and digital information into everyday work has made organizations far more vulnerable to cyber threats. The sophistication of the attacks that target critical infrastructure and information is also increasing.

An organization may experience operational, financial, reputational, and strategic consequences due to cyber-risk incidents. Because of this, existing measures have become less effective, requiring most organizations to beef up their cybersecurity efforts. The demand for cybersecurity professionals has never been more significant due to the unprecedented surge in cyberattacks.

Cybersecurity addresses preventing unauthorized access to and use of networked systems and data by individuals, organizations, and governments.

Individual level   Individual identity, data, and computing devices must be protected on a personal level. Any information that can identify users can be considered personal data and can exist either offline or online. Many people believe they do not have an online identity if they do not have any social media accounts or online accounts. Online identities are created by those who use the Internet.

Organizational level   Everyone who is part of an organization is responsible for protecting the organization's reputation, data, and customers.

Government level   Increasing amounts of digital information are being collected and shared by government entities, making data protection even more critical at the government level, where state, local, and federal security, economic stability, and public safety are concerned.

In spite of the fact that cybersecurity and information-security skills are becoming more similar, there are a few differences to note.

Cybersecurity involves stopping and preventing cyberattacks from inside or outside an organization. It protects and secures anything susceptible to hacks, attacks, or unauthorized access, including computers, devices, networks, servers, and programs.

Cybersecurity also pertains exclusively to protecting data that originates in a digital form—it's specific to digital files, which is a crucial way it differs from information security. So, when we talk about cybersecurity, we automatically discuss digital information, systems, and networks.

Information security provides confidentiality, integrity, and availability by preventing unauthorized access, modifications, and removal of information. Information security principally protects data's confidentiality, integrity, and availability, no matter its form.

The Need for Cybersecurity

With the development of digital technologies, an increase in devices and users, complex global supply chains, and an increase in data value, data will become increasingly important in the digital economy. A solid cybersecurity strategy is essential to the system and data security to minimize the risk of an attack.

Data breaches and cyberattacks affect individuals, governments, businesses, not-for-profit organizations, and educational institutions. Even when an organization has a security incident response plan, it can take more than six months to detect a breach. During this time, attackers may steal data, conduct surveillance, damage systems, or demand ransom.

In addition to protecting all enterprise assets, both on-premises and in the cloud, enterprise cybersecurity involves even more complex procedures than traditional information security.

Cybersecurity is essential to protect all types of data from theft and damage. The categories include sensitive data, personally identifiable information (PII), protected health information (PHI), personal information, and proprietary data.

Sensitive data The term *sensitive data* refers to any information that an organization needs to protect due to its value to the organization or to comply with existing laws and regulations. For instance, confidential, proprietary, and protected information can all fall under this category.

Personally identifiable information Any information that can be used to identify a particular individual is considered PII. Organizations are responsible for protecting PII, including information about their employees and customers. Many laws require organizations to inform individuals if PII is compromised due to a data breach.

Protected health information The United States HIPAA law protects protected health information. Some people think that PHI must be protected only by medical care providers, such as doctors and hospitals. However, HIPAA defines PHI much more broadly. Every employer providing or supplementing healthcare policies collects and handles PHI. The HIPAA Act applies to many organizations in the United States because they offer or increase healthcare policies.

Proprietary data An organization's proprietary data can include software code developed, technical plans for products, internal processes, intellectual property, trade secrets, and other information that helps it maintain its competitive advantage. An organization's primary mission can be seriously compromised if competitors gain access to proprietary data.

A level of protection is provided for proprietary data by copyright, patent, and trade secret laws, but it isn't always sufficient. Many criminals ignore these laws, while foreign entities have stolen substantial amounts of proprietary information.

Cybercriminals will take advantage of your organization's vulnerability if you lack a cybersecurity program, which makes your organization an irresistible target.

Because of the growing use of global connectivity and cloud services, such as Amazon Web Services, to store sensitive data and personal information, both inherent and residual risks are increasing. Cloud services are widely configured poorly, and cybercriminals are becoming increasingly sophisticated, increasing the likelihood of your organization being the victim of a successful cyberattack.

Cybercriminals are becoming more innovative and resilient in the face of conventional cyber defenses, so businesses can no longer rely on out-of-the-box cybersecurity solutions like antivirus software and firewalls. Protecting yourself from cyber threats requires covering all fields of cybersecurity.

Moreover, there are cyber threats at all levels of your organization. Cybersecurity awareness training must be provided in workplaces to educate employees about social engineering scams, phishing, ransomware attacks (think WannaCry), and malware designed to steal intellectual property.

Cybersecurity isn't just relevant for heavily regulated industries such as healthcare due to the proliferation of data breaches. Small organizations may be especially vulnerable if they don't have adequate resources for building robust cyber defenses. A data breach can cause irreparable reputational damage to a small organization. You should be concerned about cybersecurity risks if you aren't already. By 2025, cybercrime will cost the world $10.5 trillion, an increase of $6 trillion since 2021. To combat cybercrime, robust cybersecurity is essential.

In general, our society is more technologically dependent than ever, and this trend shows no sign of slowing down. The public disclosure of data leaks that may lead to identity theft has become commonplace on social media platforms. Cloud storage services like Dropbox or Google Drive store sensitive information, such as Social Security numbers, credit card numbers, and bank account numbers.

We all depend on computer systems, whether individuals, small businesses, or multinationals. In addition, cloud services are on the rise, cloud service security is poor, and smartphones are ubiquitous.

Governments worldwide are paying more attention to cybercrime; the General Data Protection Regulation (GDPR) is a great example. Because of EU regulations, data breaches have increased the reputational damage to organizations operating in the EU.

Europe is not the only region where public disclosure is on the rise. The United States does not have a national law overseeing data breach disclosure, but all 50 states have data breach laws. There are several things in common:

- The requirement to notify those affected as soon as possible
- The requirement to let the government know as quickly as possible
- The levying of fines

When a data breach occurs, those affected must be notified "without reasonable delay" or "immediately."

NIST has released frameworks to help organizations understand their security risks, improve cybersecurity, and prevent cyberattacks. For more information, refer to the following link: www.nist.gov/cyberframework/getting-started.

Advanced cyber defense programs and mechanisms to protect this data are crucial and in everyone's interest. Everyone relies on critical infrastructures such as hospitals and other healthcare institutions, financial service programs, and power plants.

Cybersecurity attacks can lead to identity theft and extortion attempts at an individual level, which can seriously damage that individual's life.

The safety of our data and personal information is necessary for all organizations, such as when logging into an application or filling out sensitive data in a digital healthcare system. We're talking about security through technology and policies in this sense. If these systems, networks, and infrastructures aren't adequately protected, our data might fall into the wrong hands.

The same goes for organizations and businesses, governments, the military, and other socially critical organizations. They store vast amounts of data in data warehouses, computers, and other devices, and much of this data includes sensitive information. The exposure of this information can, in many cases, negatively affect the trust of citizens in institutions, the competitiveness of businesses, the reputation of individuals, and the confidence of consumers in organizations.

Cybersecurity Domains

Several layers of protection are necessary to prevent cybercrime, including threats that can access, modify, or destroy data; extort IT resources from users; or disrupt normal business activities. Solutions should address the following:

Cloud security   To support customer privacy, business requirements, and regulatory compliance standards, trustworthy confidential computing encrypts cloud data at rest (at storage), in motion (at transition between services), and in use (during processing).

Azure offers built-in security services that can identify rapidly evolving threats early so you can respond quickly to protect your data, apps, and infrastructure. Make sure identity, data, hosts, and networks are all adequately protected by layered, defense-in-depth strategies. Hybrid cloud security management can be unified, and advanced threat protection enabled.

Critical infrastructure security   National security, economic health, and public safety depend on computer systems, networks, and other protected assets. NIST has created a cybersecurity framework, while the Homeland Security Department (DHS) provides additional guidance.

In most IaaS scenarios, Azure virtual machines (VMs) are the primary workload for organizations that use cloud computing. The following are factors to consider for VM workloads:

- Secure virtual machine by using IAM control.
- Use multiple VMs for better availability.
- Secure against malware.
- Manage your VM updates.
- Manage your VM security posture.
- Monitor VM performance.
- Encrypt your virtual hard disk files.
- Restrict direct Internet connectivity.

Network security   Your applications and services can connect to Microsoft Azure using a robust network infrastructure. Network connectivity is possible between Azure resources on-premises, Azure-hosted resources, and to and from the Internet and Azure. The Azure network infrastructure enables you to connect Azure resources with virtual networks (VNets) securely.

The Azure Firewall is a cloud-native and intelligent network firewall security service that protects your Azure workloads from threats. You get a fully stateful firewall that is highly available and scalable in the cloud using the Azure Firewall. Inspection is provided both east-west and north-south.

Network traffic on Azure Virtual Networks can be routed according to your custom routing preferences. Azure allows you to configure user-defined routes for this purpose.

Application security   These processes protect on-premises and cloud applications. Data handling, user authentication, and other security concerns should be considered when designing applications.

Security of Azure's infrastructure and platform is Azure's responsibility, but you are responsible for securing your application. Developing, deploying, and managing your application code and content securely is crucial. Without this, you are still vulnerable to your application code and content threats.

Azure web application firewalls (WAFs) provide centralized protection against common exploits and vulnerabilities for your web applications.

Storage security   To ensure data resilience, there should be several safeguards in place. The data copies must be immutable and isolated, as well as encrypted. Keeping these in the same pool enables them to be quickly restored in case of a cyberattack, minimizing the damage.

Identity management and data security   As part of data security, we implement robust information storage techniques that guarantee data security at rest and in transit. It is a framework, process, and activity that enables legitimate individuals to access information systems within an organization. Using Azure, you can manage user identities and credentials and control access to business and personal information.

Access to corporate data centers and cloud applications is protected with Microsoft identity and access management solutions, which enable multifactor authentication and conditional access policies. Advanced security reporting, auditing, and alerting make mitigating potential security issues easier. Through Azure Active Directory Premium, you can access thousands of cloud and web applications you run on your servers.

Azure RMS helps protect your files and emails by encrypting, authenticating, and authorizing them. With Azure RMS, you can protect both internal and external devices—phones, tablets, and PCs. Because Azure RMS adds a level of protection to data even when it leaves the boundaries of your organization, this capability is possible.

Mobile security   A secure mobile mail system, container app security, and app security for the end-user mobile workforce will help you manage and secure the mobile end-user workforce.

Data security   Data classification is a critical step in securing the data. Following the classification of data and assets, you must identify security requirements and security controls to implement them. Consider using Confidential/Proprietary, Private, Sensitive, and Public data labels for your organization. Management determines specific security controls to protect data in these categories based on a data security policy.

End-user education   To strengthen endpoint security, build security awareness throughout the organization. As a result of end-user education, end users become more aware of how to protect themselves and their organization's data from loss or attack by providing them with the right tools and skills. To be mindful of organizational weaknesses, system vulnerabilities, and security risks, employees need to receive periodic end-user education and reviews. Today's complex threat landscape makes it easy for cyberattackers to use employees as entry points into private organizations systems. The more employees are aware of cyberattacks, the easier it is for them to recognize them and keep themselves safe. Security awareness training is the most effective way to reduce cybersecurity risks and build a security-aware culture.

Disaster recovery/business continuity planning   Natural disasters, power outages, and cybersecurity incidents can be handled with minimal disruption to critical operations when unplanned events occur.

Security operations   Security operations primarily focus on detecting and protecting sensitive and business-critical information. Most Security Operations Center (SOC) positions will be located in this domain. To perform their job functions satisfactorily, they need to understand a threat hunter's duties, including incident response, threat intelligence, and forensic analysis.

Security architecture   The security architecture domain refers to a method and set of regulations that represent the security services that a system is required to provide to meet the requirements of its users, the system elements needed to deploy the services, and the performance levels as are necessary for the details to haggle with the threat environment.

Getting Started with Zero Trust

In this section, you will learn about the fundamentals of the Zero Trust model. In the modern world, organizations require a new security model that adapts effectively to the complexity of the contemporary environment, embraces the mobile workforce, and protects people, devices, applications, and data wherever they are.

Zero Trust presents a visionary, integrated approach to cybersecurity in the cloud estate. Zero Trust continuously verifies every transaction, asserts the least privilege, and relies on intelligence, advanced detection, and real-time response to threats.

The core of Zero Trust lies here: a Zero Trust model assumes a breach in the corporate firewall and verifies all requests as though they originated from an uncontrolled network. Zero Trust teaches us to "never trust, always verify" regardless of where or what resource a request accesses.

Zero Trust is a security framework that requires users to authenticate, authorize, and continuously validate their security configuration and posture before gaining or maintaining access to applications and data, whether inside or outside the organization's network. In Zero Trust, networks can be local, in the cloud, or hybrid with resources and workers anywhere; there is no traditional network edge.

Modern digital transformation requires securing infrastructure and data; Zero Trust provides that framework. The solution uniquely addresses security issues related to remote workers, hybrid cloud environments, and ransomware threats. Several organizations have developed standards to help you align Zero Trust with your organization, although many vendors have tried to create their definitions.

NIST Abstract Definition of Zero Trust

Zero Trust (ZT) is the term for an evolving set of cybersecurity paradigms that move defenses from static, network-based perimeters to focus on users, assets, and resources. A Zero Trust architecture (ZTA) uses Zero Trust principles to plan industrial and enterprise infrastructure and workflows. Zero Trust assumes there is no implicit trust granted to assets or user accounts based solely on their physical or network location (that is, local area networks versus the Internet) or based on asset ownership (enterprise or personally owned). Authentication and authorization (both subject and device) are discrete functions performed before a session to an enterprise resource is established. Zero Trust is a response to enterprise network trends that include remote users, bring your own device (BYOD), and cloud-based assets that are not located within an enterprise-owned network boundary. Zero Trust focuses on protecting resources (assets, services, workflows, network accounts, and so on), not network segments, as the network location is no longer seen as the prime component to the security posture of the resource. This Chapter contains an abstract definition of ZTA and gives general deployment models and use cases where Zero Trust could improve an enterprise's overall information technology security posture.

For more information, refer to nvlpubs.nist.gov/nistpubs/SpecialPublications/ NIST.SP.800-207.pdf.

An approach based on Zero Trust involves treating everything as an unknown—whether human or machine—to ensure responsible behavior within the context of a cybersecurity strategy.

Key Benefits of Zero Trust

The following are the key benefits of Zero Trust:

- Zero Trust is more effective than perimeter-based security. Perimeter-based security ensures that anyone inside the internal network can be trusted, while anyone outside the network cannot be trusted. Since this model was established as the leading cybersecurity model, more than two decades have passed. Zero Trust is based on the principle that Trust is verified first—to trust, one must first verify—Zero Trust eliminates the inherent Trust assumed within traditional internal networks.

- Cybersecurity within an enterprise can be more structured and risk-based using this approach.

- As a result, corporate assets and resources can be better understood and utilized, and the network and data are better protected this way.

- The Zero Trust approach assures that only authorized users, devices, and services can access specified resources on the corporate network. Cybersecurity regulations and standards can be met more effectively by improving situational awareness.

- Zero Trust can allow workers to access corporate resources and networks securely, whether on-site or off-site, as the workforce transitions toward hybrid working models.

Guiding Principles of Zero Trust

The maxim "Never trust, always verify" is perhaps best described as Zero Trust. However, the security model is often based on a broader collection of guiding principles, some of which are provided by the U.S. National Security Agency (SP 800-207). According to the U.S. National Security Agency best practices, organizations should analyze which contextual principles they should consider according to the feasibility of their implementation.

Zero Trust is an essential aspect of security. The following security principles describe how to design and implement them, not products or services. Microsoft defines Zero Trust as following these three fundamental principles:

- **Verify explicitly:** Use all available data points to authenticate and authorize, including user identity, location, device health, service or workload, data classification, and anomalies.

- **Apply least privilege access:** Provide just-in-time and just-enough-access (JIT/JEA), risk-based policies, and data protection to aid in securing both data and productivity.

- **Assume breach:** The blast radius should be minimized, and access should be segmented. Get visibility, detect threats, and improve defenses by verifying end-to-end encryption and analytics.

Zero Trust Architecture

A Zero Trust approach should spread throughout the cloud estate and serve as an integrated security philosophy and end-to-end strategy. Integrated policy enforcement and automation, threat intelligence, and threat protection are essential components of Zero Trust architecture. These integrated components operate upon telemetry across every pillar to inform determinations with real-time signals.

A Zero Trust approach is implemented across nine foundational elements. Figure 1.1 depicts Zero Trust architecture. Each element is a signal source, a control plane for enforcement, and a crucial resource to be defended.

FIGURE 1.1   Microsoft Zero Trust architecture

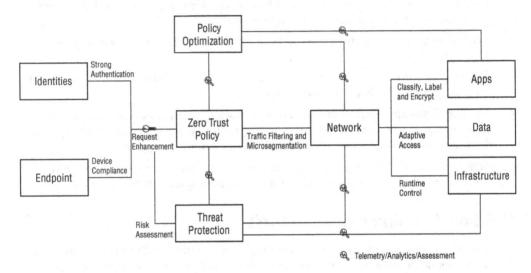

Microsoft's Zero Trust approach is organized around the following critical technological building blocks.

Secure identities with Zero Trust   A Zero Trust control plane consists of people, workloads, endpoints, and IoT devices. Microsoft recommends ensuring that when an identity attempts to access a resource, access is compliant and typical for that identity and that least privilege access principles are followed.

Secure endpoints with Zero Trust   Multiple identities can access data via various devices—from IoT devices to smartphones, BYOD to partner-managed devices, and on-premises workloads to cloud-hosted servers. For secure access, we must monitor and enforce device health and compliance due to this diversity.

Secure infrastructure with Zero Trust   A critical threat vector is an infrastructure (servers on-premises, virtual machines in the cloud, containers, or microservices). Harden defenses by assessing version, configuration, and JIT access, using telemetry to detect attacks and anomalies, and automatically blocking and flagging risky behavior.

Secure network with Zero Trust   The network infrastructure is ultimately responsible for providing access to all data. As a result of using networking controls, attackers can't move laterally across a network and can be more visible. Segmenting networks (including microsegmentation within the network) and employing real-time threat protection, end-to-end encryption, monitoring, and analytics are recommended.

Secure application with Zero Trust   To consume data, APIs and applications are used. The application can be a legacy application on-premises, a lift-and-shift cloud workload, or a modern SaaS application. Shadow IT should be discovered, appropriate permissions should be granted, real-time analytics should be used to gate access, abnormal behavior should be monitored, user actions should be controlled, and secure configuration options should be validated.

Secure Data with Zero Trust   Security teams are focused on protecting data. Data should remain secure even if devices, apps, infrastructure, and networks leave the organization's control. The classification, labeling, encryption, and restriction of access to data should be based on the attributes of that data.

Secure with policy optimization   Organization-specific security policies apply across all digital assets of an organization. The guidelines are optimized for business processes, governance, compliance, and the end-user experience.

Secure with Zero Trust policy   As a result of the Zero Trust policy, the request is intercepted, all six foundational elements are explicitly verified based on the policy configuration, and the least privileged access is enforced. A user's role, location, device compliance, data sensitivity, application sensitivity, and much more are all considered signals. A threat protection policy reacts automatically in real time to threats based on telemetry and state information and risk assessment from threat protection. The policy is enforced during access and continuously evaluated throughout the session.

Secure with threat protection   Microsoft Zero Trust architecture feeds telemetry and analytics from all six foundational elements fed into Microsoft's threat-protection system. By combining telemetry and analytics with threat intelligence, high-quality risk assessments can be generated that can be manually investigated or automatically performed. The risk assessment provides the policy engine for real-time automated threat protection.

Zero Trust replaces trust-by-default with trust-by-exception. An integrated capability to automatically manage exceptions and alerts is essential to find and detect threats, respond to them, and prevent or block undesired events across your organization more easily.

Design Integration Points in an Architecture

Microsoft developed Microsoft Cybersecurity Reference Architecture (MCRA). Microsoft's security capabilities are integrated with Microsoft services and applications, Microsoft cloud platforms like Azure and Microsoft 365, third-party apps like Salesforce and ServiceNow, and third-party platforms like Amazon Web Services (AWS) and Google Cloud Platform (GCP).

Microsoft Cybersecurity Reference Architecture (MCRA) is used for several purposes.

- An organization's cybersecurity capabilities are typically defined using this template as a starting point for a security architecture. In addition to encompassing capabilities across on-premises, mobile devices, multiple clouds, and IoT/Operations and Maintenance (O&M), this architecture is valuable to organizations because it covers a wide range of capabilities across the modern enterprise estate.

- Some organizations use MCRA to compare Microsoft's architecture recommendations with their own. Many organizations weren't aware of how much security architecture technology they already possess.

- MCRA assists architects and technical teams in identifying opportunities to use Microsoft's integration points.

- If you are new to cybersecurity, use this as a reference model to plan for greenfield deployment.

MCRA reference architecture provides high-level technical diagrams of Microsoft's cybersecurity capabilities, Zero Trust access to users, security operations, operational technology (OT), cross-platform and multi-cloud capabilities, attack chain coverage, Azure native security controls, and security organizational functions.

Figure 1.2 depicts MCRA.

FIGURE 1.2   High-level Microsoft Cybersecurity Reference Architecture

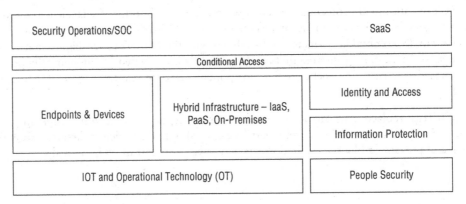

Also included in the MCRA is an overview of Zero Trust and a rapid modernization plan (RaMP) for Zero Trust. It has other essential information on security operations and critical endeavors such as protecting from human-operated ransomware, securing privileged access, moving beyond VPN, and much more.

Security Operations Center

An enterprise security operation monitors its environment for active attack operations to identify and remediate risk, sharing its insights and threat intelligence with other departments.

Figure 1.3 depicts the MCRA SOC building block.

FIGURE 1.3   High-level Microsoft Cybersecurity Reference Architecture SOC building block

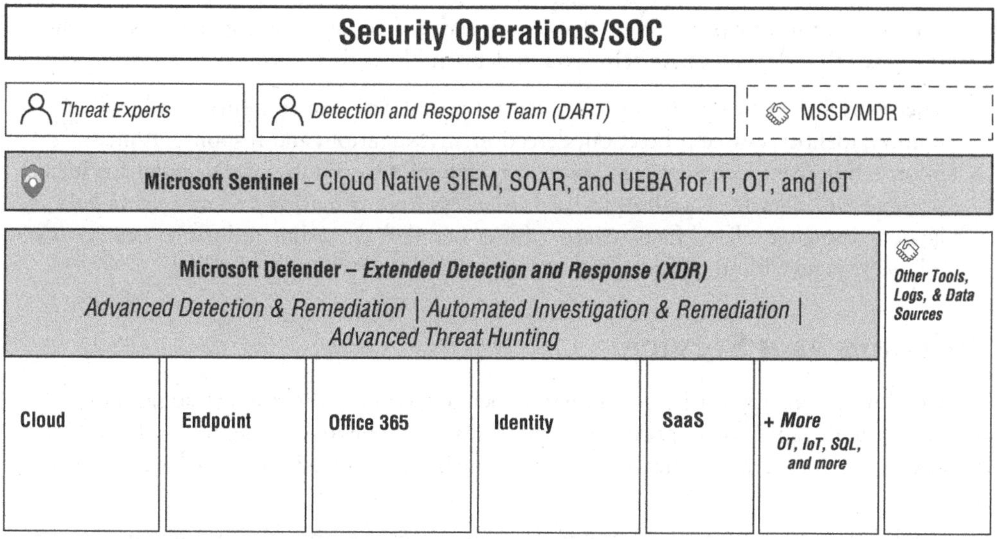

MCRA's SOC building block illustrates how key Microsoft technologies fit into the organization's security landscape.

Microsoft Sentinel   This solution combines security orchestration automated response (SOAR) and security information event management (SIEM). With Microsoft Sentinel, organizations can detect alerts, identify threats, hunt for threats, and respond to threats in a unified way.

Microsoft Defender for Cloud   Secure your hybrid workloads in the cloud and on-premises with a unified infrastructure security management method that supports the security posture of your data centers and delivers advanced threat protection.

Microsoft Defender for Identity   Using your Active Directory Domain Services signals, a cloud-based security solution can identify, detect, and investigate advanced threats, compromised identities, and malicious insider activities. Security professionals and SecOp analysts can detect advanced attacks in hybrid environments with Defender for Identity.

Microsoft Defender for Office 365   This provides protection against malicious email messages, links, and collaboration tools.

Microsoft Defender for Endpoint   Enterprise networks can prevent, detect, investigate, and respond to advanced threats with this endpoint protection platform.

App Governance Add-on to Microsoft Defender for Cloud Apps   The Microsoft Graph API allows apps to access Microsoft 365 data using OAuth-enabled apps.

Azure Monitor   This enhances the availability and performance of your applications and services by enabling you to collect, analyze, and act on telemetry from the cloud and on-premises. By proactively identifying issues affecting your applications and the resources they depend on, it helps you understand how they perform.

Microsoft 365 Defender Portal   In a central portal, you can combine email, collaboration, identity, device protection, detection, investigation, and response. It includes information from Defender for Office 365, Defender for Endpoint, Defender for Identity, and Defender for Cloud Apps for fast access to information and more detailed layouts, bringing related facts together for easier alert detection and threat detection visibility, proactive hunting, and incident response.

Software as a Service

In a cloud platform, applications and their associated data are the primary sources of business value. Despite the importance of platform components like identity and storage in the security environment, applications play an outsize role in business risks for the following reasons:

- Applications encapsulate and execute business processes, and services must be available and provided with high integrity.
- Application workloads store and process business data, which requires high assurances of confidentiality, integrity, and availability.

Figure 1.4 depicts the MCRA SaaS building block.

MCRA's SaaS building block illustrates how key Microsoft technologies fit into the organization's security landscape.

Microsoft Defender for Cloud Apps   Microsoft Defender for Cloud Apps is a Cloud Access Security Broker (CASB) that manages data travel across multiple clouds so you can identify and combat cyberthreats across all of your cloud services with rich visibility, control, and sophisticated analytics. CASBs operate across multiple cloud environments. It identifies and combats cyberthreats across all your cloud services through detailed visibility, data travel control, and sophisticated analytics.

As a CASB, Microsoft Defender for Cloud Apps supports a variety of deployment methods, including log collection, API connectors, and reverse proxies. With this solution, you can identify and combat cyberthreats across Microsoft and third-party cloud services with rich visibility, control over data travel, and sophisticated analytics.

Cybersecurity professionals benefit from Microsoft Defender for Cloud Apps, which integrates natively with Microsoft solutions and offers simple deployment, centralized management, and innovative automation features.

FIGURE 1.4   High-level Microsoft Cybersecurity Reference Architecture SaaS building block

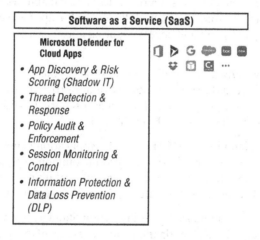

Hybrid Infrastructure—IaaS, PaaS, On-Premises

Fundamental to the success of any business is securing its hybrid infrastructure. As businesses worldwide struggle with the growth of an industrialized, organized, and highly economically motivated attacker ecosystem, multi-cloud and hybrid infrastructure and workload security have become increasingly urgent.

Figure 1.5 depicts the MCRA Hybrid Infrastructure building block.

What does a cybersecurity solution look like for multi-cloud, on-premises, and hybrid environments? An effective defense must be unified, simplified, and actionable, allowing digital transformation to be more manageable and not stifling progress. Those who need to secure multi-cloud, on-premises, and hybrid infrastructure can begin by considering the following component-level considerations:

Microsoft Defender for Cloud   Secure your hybrid workloads in the cloud and on-premises with a unified infrastructure security management method that supports the security posture of your data centers and delivers advanced threat protection.

Azure AD App Proxy   With Azure Active Directory (Azure AD), users, apps, and data are protected on-premises and in the cloud. IT professionals can implement Azure AD Application Proxy if they want to publish on-premises web applications externally. Users who need internal apps can access them securely from remote locations.

Azure Arc   The Azure Arc allows you to extend the Azure platform to run applications and services across data centers, at the edge, and in multi-cloud environments. Consistently develop, operate, and secure cloud-native applications. It runs on new and existing hardware, virtualization, and Kubernetes platforms, IoT devices, and integrated systems.

Azure Stack   Azure Stack extends Azure services and capabilities from the data center to edge locations and remote offices. With flexibility for diverse workloads, you can build, deploy, and run hybrid and edge computing apps consistently across your IT ecosystem.

Azure Firewall   With Azure Firewall, you can protect your cloud workloads running in Azure with best-of-breed threat protection. With unrestricted cloud scalability and built-in high availability, it is a fully stateful firewall as a service. In addition to inspecting east-west traffic, it also inspects north-south traffic.

Azure Web Application Firewall (WAF)   Azure Application Gateway's Web Application Firewall provides centralized protection from common exploits and vulnerabilities. Malicious attacks exploiting commonly known vulnerabilities are increasingly targeting web applications. The most common attacks are SQL injection and cross-site scripting.

Azure DDOS   Combining Azure DDoS Protection Standard with application design best practices, enhanced DDoS mitigation features are available to defend against DDoS attacks. As you add Azure resources to a virtual network, it will automatically adapt to protect them. Adding protection to new or existing virtual networks is easy and requires no changes to applications or resources.

Azure Key Vault   Azure Key Vault allows you to store and access secrets on the cloud securely. API keys, passwords, certificates, and cryptographic keys are examples of secrets, as are API keys. The Key Vault service supports two types of containers: vaults and managed hardware security modules (HSMs). A vault can store secrets, certificates, and software keys that an HSM backs up, and managed HSM pools only support HSM-backed keys.

Azure Bastion   Azure Bastion lets you connect to a virtual machine using your browser and the Azure Portal using your Azure subscription. It is an Azure PaaS service that you provision inside your virtual network that is fully platform-managed.

Azure Lighthouse   With Azure Lighthouse, multi-tenant management can be scaled and automated, enhancing resource governance. Service providers can deliver managed services utilizing Azure Lighthouse's comprehensive and robust tooling. The Azure Lighthouse management tool streamlines the management of resources for enterprise organizations operating resources across multiple tenants. Customers control who has access to their tenant, what resources can be accessed, and what actions can be taken.

Azure Backup   Data backup and recovery from the Microsoft Azure cloud is simple, secure, and cost-effective with Azure Backup.

Azure ExpressRoute   ExpressRoute establishes a connection between your network and Azure via an ExpressRoute partner. It is a private connection. Traffic does not go over the Internet.

Azure Private Link   Azure Private Link lets you connect to Azure PaaS services (Azure Storage and SQL Database) and Azure-hosted, customer-owned, and partner services over a private network connection.

FIGURE 1.5   High-level Microsoft Cybersecurity Reference Architecture Hybrid Infrastructure building block

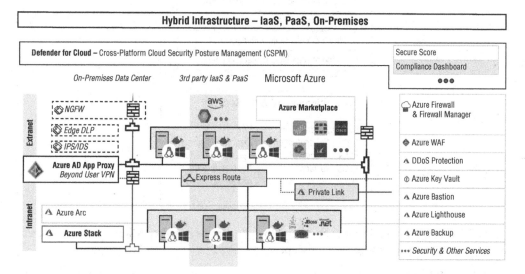

Endpoints and Devices

Endpoints that access enterprise data are highly diverse in today's world. Because of this, endpoints can quickly become the weakest link in your Zero Trust security strategy.

Organizations want visibility into the endpoints accessing our network, whether they are BYOD or corporate-owned and managed devices, to ensure we allow only healthy, compliant devices accessing corporate resources. Microsoft is also concerned about mobile and desktop apps' health and trustworthiness on those endpoints. In addition to ensuring those apps are healthy and compliant, Microsoft wants to ensure that corporate data doesn't leak to consumer apps or services accidentally or maliciously.

Figure 1.6 depicts the MCRA Endpoints and Devices building block.

FIGURE 1.6   High-level Microsoft Cybersecurity Reference Architecture Endpoints and Devices building block

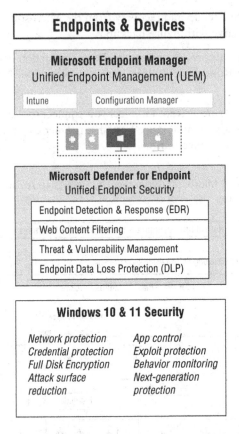

MCRA's Endpoint and Devices building block illustrates how key Microsoft technologies fit into the organization's security landscape.

Microsoft Defender for Endpoint   Endpoint devices across your multiplatform enterprise can be discovered and secured using Microsoft Defender for Endpoint.

Microsoft Endpoint Manager   By integrating Microsoft Intune and Configuration Manager, Microsoft Endpoint Manager provides endpoint device management and security as part of a unified management platform.

Information Protection

Information is an asset, and information security must be understood in the context of the value of information and the consequences of its compromise. In the past, laptops and desktops were the only items thieves would steal. Cybercrime is a growing problem today as thieves steal critical data and information from insurable hardware, including mobile phones. Hackers are now thieves.

Figure 1.7 depicts the MCRA Information Protection building block.

FIGURE 1.7   High-level Microsoft Cybersecurity Reference Architecture Information Protection building block

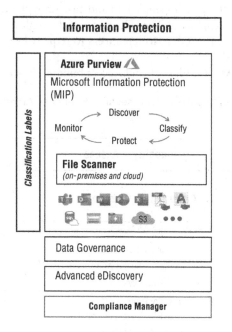

Azure Purview   Microsoft Purview's governance portal provides unified data governance solutions that help you manage on-premises, multi-cloud, and SaaS data. Microsoft Purview's governance portal offers the following features:

- Quickly discover, classify, and trace your data from beginning to end with an end-to-end data lineage and automated data discovery.

- Your data estate can be managed and secured by data curators.

- Data that is valuable and reliable should be made available to consumers.

Azure Compliance Manager   Compliance Manager is a workflow-established risk assessment tool in the Microsoft Purview compliance portal for addressing regulatory compliance actions connected to Microsoft cloud services.

Identity and Access

The Microsoft online services were designed to enable Microsoft engineers to operate the services without gaining access to any of the customer's content. Microsoft engineers do not have privileged access to the production environment or zero-standing access to customer content. Whenever temporary access to production environments is required to support Microsoft online services, the Just-In-Time (JIT) and Just-Enough-Access (JEA) models are utilized by service team engineers. The JIT access model replaces standard, continued administrative access with a procedure for engineers to request interim elevation into privileged roles on demand.

Figure 1.8 depicts the MCRA Identity and Access building block.

FIGURE 1.8   High-level Microsoft Cybersecurity Reference Architecture Identity and Access building block

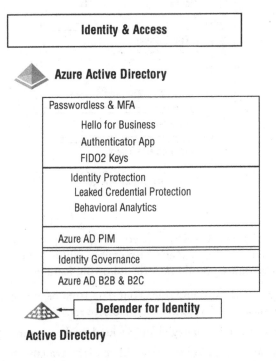

Azure Active Directory   Identities and access are managed using Azure Active Directory (Azure AD). Thousands of SaaS applications are accessible via this service, including Microsoft 365, the Azure Portal, and thousands more. Azure Active Directory also allows them to access internal resources like apps on your corporate intranet and any cloud apps developed for your organization.

Azure Identity Protection   To protect your users, Microsoft has learned from its positions in organizations with Azure Active Directory, the consumer space with Microsoft Accounts, and gaming with Xbox. Microsoft protects customers from threats by analyzing trillions of signals daily.

Azure Identity Governance   Identity Governance in Azure Active Directory (Azure AD) helps you balance security and employee productivity while maintaining visibility. Access to the right resources can be managed with its capabilities. Through Azure AD and Enterprise Mobility + Security features, you can protect, monitor, and audit access to critical assets to mitigate access risk.

Defender for Identity   Microsoft Defender for Identity (aka Azure Advanced Threat Protection) is a cloud-based security solution that identifies, detects, and investigates advanced threats, compromised identities, and malicious insider actions directed at your organization by leveraging your Active Directory signals.

People Security

A comprehensive people security program protects an organization from inadvertent human errors and malicious insider attacks. Figure 1.9 depicts the Microsoft MCRA People Security building block.

FIGURE 1.9   High-level Microsoft Cybersecurity Reference Architecture People Security building block

👤 **People Security**		
Attack Simulator	Insider Risk Management	Communication Compliance

Attack Simulator   Suppose your organization has Microsoft 365 E5 or Microsoft Defender for Office 365 Plan 2. To run realistic attack scenarios in your organization, you can use attack simulation training in the Microsoft 365 Defender portal. Before an attack impacts your bottom line, these simulations can help you identify and locate vulnerable users.

Insider Risk Management   Microsoft Purview Insider Risk Management reduces internal risks by detecting, investigating, and responding to malicious and negligent organizational activities. Defining insider risk policies lets you identify and see risks in your organization and escalating cases to Microsoft eDiscovery (Premium). Ensure that your organization's compliance standards are adhered to by risk analysts in your organization.

Communication Compliance   Microsoft Purview Communication Compliance helps you minimize insider risk by detecting, capturing, and responding to inappropriate organizational messages. You can scan internal and external communications for policy matches with predefined or custom policies so that designated reviewers can examine them. Message standards can be enforced by reviewing scanned email, Microsoft Teams, Yammer, or third-party communications in your organization.

IOT and Operational Technology

A common misconception about the Internet of Things and operational technology (OT) devices has been disproven in the past. Traditional endpoints (workstations, servers, and mobile devices) were assumed to be segmented from IoT and OT devices or deployed within separate air-gapped networks. Visibility is the top challenge in securing IoT and OT devices. Organizational thinking needs to be shifted away from these dated assumptions to implement proper mitigations. Hence, Microsoft defined building block for IOT and OT.

Figure 1.10 depicts the MCRA IOT and OT building block.

FIGURE 1.10   High-level Microsoft Cybersecurity Reference Architecture IOT and Operational Technology building block

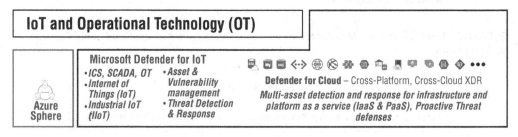

Azure Sphere   With Azure Sphere, you can build high-level applications with built-in communication and security features. Secured, connected, crossover microcontroller units (MCUs), custom Linux-based operating systems (Oss), and a cloud-based security service provide continuous, renewable security.

Microsoft Defender for Cloud   Secure your hybrid workloads in the cloud and on-premises with a unified infrastructure security management method that supports the security posture of your data centers and delivers advanced threat protection.

Defender for IoT   Integrate IoT/OT security across your entire infrastructure to accelerate digital transformation. In addition to being rapidly deployed, Microsoft Defender for IoT supports agentless network detection and response (NDR); works with IoT, OT, and industrial control system (ICS) devices; and is compatible with Microsoft

365 Defender, Microsoft Sentinel, and external SOCs. Using the Cloud or on-premises Defender for IoT offers lightweight agents for more robust device-layer security for IoT device builders.

Design Security Needs to Be Based on Business Goals

Transformation journeys that are most successful start with business goals. It can be time-consuming and costly to adopt the cloud, and a successful project requires the support of IT and other business areas. To help customers identify business outcomes that are concise and defined and drive measurable results, Microsoft has developed a Cloud Adoption Framework.

Microsoft employees, partners, and customers share best practices for cloud adoption in the Cloud Adoption Framework. In addition to tools and documentation, it also consists of proven techniques. You can use the tools included in it to shape your technology, business, and people strategies to achieve the best business outcomes.

Microsoft Azure Cloud Adoption Framework is a complete life cycle framework that helps cloud architects, IT professionals, and business decision-makers adopt cloud services. Cloud computing best practices, documentation, and tools are provided to assist you in creating and implementing cloud computing strategies.

Figure 1.11 depicts Microsoft Cloud Adoption Framework (MCAF).

FIGURE 1.11 Microsoft Cloud Adoption Framework

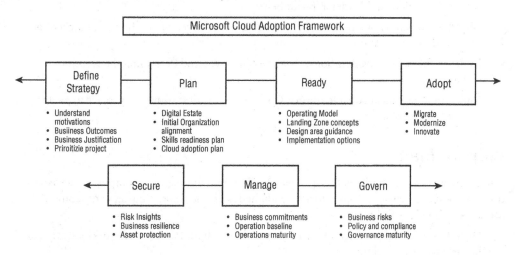

Nine methodologies make up the Microsoft Cloud Adoption Framework. A cloud adoption life cycle includes each of the methodologies listed in Figure 1.11. Throughout the cloud adoption process, the methodologies of the Cloud Adoption Framework are integrated into a life cycle.

- **Strategy:** Establish the business case for adoption and the expected benefits.
- **Plan:** Identify business outcomes and align adoption plans.
- **Ready:** Make sure your cloud environment is prepared for planned changes.
- **Migrate:** Move existing workloads to the cloud and modernize them.
- **Innovate:** Create cloud-native and hybrid solutions.
- **Secure:** Make security better over time.
- **Manage:** Manage hybrid cloud and on-premises solutions.
- **Govern:** Take control of your environment and workload.
- **Organize:** Coordinate the roles and teams supporting cloud adoption in your organization.

Define Strategy

The purpose of cloud migration and what you want to achieve from it are discussed here. Are you looking to expand your market or meet demand? Are costs going to be reduced, or will business agility increase? When defining your cloud business strategy, you should consider the business impact, turnaround time, global reach, performance, and more. Defining your cloud strategy involves the following steps:

- **Define and document motivations:** Discussing your reasons for moving to the cloud with stakeholders and leadership can help.
- **Document business outcomes:** Discuss your goals with leaders in finance, marketing, sales, and human resources.
- **Evaluate financial considerations:** Analyze objectives and determine the return on investment.
- **Understand technical considerations:** Complete your first technical project to evaluate technical concerns.

Prepare Plan

You create a plan that outlines the specific actions you will take to accomplish your aspirations. A good plan ensures your efforts are aligned with the desired business outcomes. Here are steps to build a solid plan:

- **Digital estate:** Make an inventory of your existing digital assets and workloads that will be migrated to the cloud.

- **Initial organizational alignment:** Include the right people in migration efforts from a technical and governance perspective.
- **Skills readiness plan:** Create a plan to help individuals develop cloud-based skills.
- **Cloud adoption plan:** Coordinate development, operations, and business teams toward a shared goal of cloud adoption.

Get Ready

You create a landing zone or environment to host your workloads in the cloud. You can prepare your organization by following these steps:

- **Azure setup guide:** Learn how to create a landing zone by reviewing the Azure setup guide.
- **Azure landing zone:** Build out each of your major business areas' Azure subscriptions in an Azure landing zone. There are several components to a landing zone, including infrastructure, governance, accounting, and security.
- **Expand the landing zone:** Make sure your landing zone meets your operations, governance, and security requirements.
- **Best practices:** Start with best practices and recommendations to help ensure your cloud migration efforts are scalable and maintainable.

Adopt

Adopt cloud security to improve your cyber defenses against businesses or organizations. The adoption methodology is where you start using the cloud and experiencing its benefits.

Migrating, modernizing, and innovating are three approaches to adopting security in the cloud. Each process provides unique benefits and solutions.

- **Migrate:** You migrate your workloads to the cloud with the migrate security approach. The process of rehosting is one of several forms of migration, and rehosting is also known as *lift-and-shift*. Rehosting involves moving a workload to a cloud IaaS solution without altering it.
- **Modernize:** Modernizing security refers to enhancing existing applications to improve operations, increase efficiency, and maximize developer velocity. The modernization of your business uses PaaS solutions.
- **Innovate:** By adopting cloud-native technologies, you can create customer-focused, cloud-native security solutions that rapidly transform business outcomes.

Secure

A Cybersecurity Architect will be interested in the Secure methodology of the Cloud Adoption Framework. Secure provides a comprehensive view of your security program's end state to guide its improvement over time. In Figure 1.12, security is visually mapped with the larger organization and its disciplines.

FIGURE 1.12   Cybersecurity business alignment and disciplines

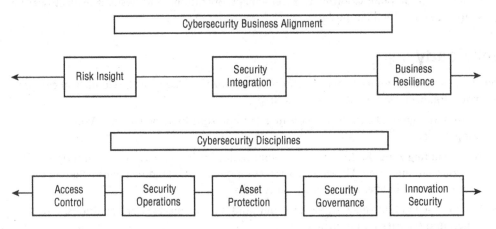

As part of your cybersecurity program, you should incorporate three ways to integrate security into the larger organization and five security disciplines.

Cybersecurity Business Alignment and Integrated Approaches

Listed below are the areas to focus on when aligning business demands with cybersecurity security measures.

- **Risk insights:** The security team learns about an organization's operations to identify business goals and asset risks. In turn, security recommends which risks are acceptable to decision-makers. It is essential to understand that the asset or process owner is responsible for making these decisions.

- **Security integration:** Everyone should be responsible for security, just as they should be responsible for business requirements, performance, and reliability. It is essential for security professionals to understand your organization's overall business priorities, IT initiatives, and risk appetite. A thread of security should connect every aspect of your business, and a business's security should feel like a natural part of security.

- **Business resilience:** While security attacks can never be completely thwarted, an organization can become more resilient to them. In the same way that we are never totally protected from all health and safety risks in the physical world, we are also never 100 percent secure from all attacks on our data and information systems. Increase business operations' resilience to security incidents by focusing your security efforts. As a result of these efforts, risk can be reduced, and your ability to respond to incidents and improve security posture can be continuously improved.

Cybersecurity Disciplines

Listed below are the areas to focus on cybersecurity security disciplines.

- **Access control:** People are most likely to experience access control as part of security. They see it whenever they sign into computers or mobile phones, share a file or access an application, or use an ID card key to enter a building or room. Access control isn't everything in security, but it's critical and needs to be handled properly to ensure both the user experience and security assurances.

- **Security operations (SecOps):** Managing security operations reduces risk by limiting the damage caused by attackers gaining access to your organization's resources.
  - An organization that combines internal security practices with IT operations practices to improve collaboration and reduce risks is known as SecOps. Security and IT operations have traditionally been handled by separate organizations using different approaches and methodologies by independent organizations.
  - SecOps team members are responsible for various activities, including proactive monitoring, incident response and recovery, remediation activities, compliance, and coordination and context.

- **Asset protection:** Physical and virtual assets include laptops, databases, files, and virtual storage accounts. Critical business assets are often protected by the security of underlying systems, such as storage, data, endpoints, and applications. Generally, data and applications, such as business websites, production lines, and communications, are the most valuable technology assets.

- **Security governance:** It is the bridge between your business priorities and technical implementations such as architecture, standards, and policies that form the basis of security governance. As security posture improves, governance teams provide oversight and monitoring. As required by regulators, these teams report compliance as well.

- **Innovation security:** An organization's innovation process and data must be protected against cyberattacks in the digital age, and innovation security protects them against cyberattacks. With DevOps and DevSecOps, applications are developed rapidly without waiting for traditional waterfall release schedules that can take months or years.

Manage

Cloud strategies require solid planning, readiness, and adoption. Digital assets provide tangible business outcomes when they are operated continuously, and cloud solutions will be of little value without a reliable, well-managed operational plan.

Govern

When a business is hosted in the cloud, new paradigms emerge for the technology supporting it. These new paradigms are transforming technology adoption, management, and governance. You can delete and rebuild an entire virtual data center with a line of code that's executed by an unattended process. Especially in the case of governance, this reasoning is valid.

Iterative processes are involved in cloud governance. An organization's on-premises IT policies should be complemented by cloud governance. Depending on cloud governance maturity and the nature of the digital estate in the cloud, corporate policies between on-premises and the cloud are integrated to varying degrees. Cloud governance processes and procedures evolve with the cloud estate.

Decode Security Requirements to Technical Abilities

Many organizations are undergoing several simultaneous transformations. Nearly all external markets are changing in response to new customer preferences for mobile and cloud technologies, driving these internal transformations. Startup disruption and the digital transformation of traditional competitors are common threats to organizations.

Organizational transformations typically involve the following:

- Capturing new opportunities and competing with digital native startups requires business transformation.
- As the threat environment becomes more sophisticated, IT organizations must implement cloud computing services, modernize development practices, and make other changes to support the initiative and security.

Implementing a Zero Trust architecture requires enforcing security design principles based on the organization's security transformation. Secure architecture principles describe a system that is hosted on the cloud or on-premises (or a combination of both). Your security architecture will be more likely to be confidential, intact, and available if you apply these principles.

The following critical design principles are used as lenses to evaluate the security of an Azure application. Using these lenses provides a framework for assessing applications.

Resource Planning and Hardening

The following are Microsoft's recommendations for Cybersecurity Architects concerning resource planning and hardening:

- Planning workload resources should take security into account.
- Become familiar with the types of protection offered by cloud services.
- Evaluate service enablement using a framework.

Reduce Privileges and Automate

Microsoft's recommendations for Cybersecurity Architects concerning automating and applying the least privilege are the following:

- Data exfiltration and malicious actor scenarios can be prevented by implementing the least privilege at every level of the application and control plane.

- Utilize DevSecOps to automate and minimize human interaction.

Protect Data by Classifying and Encrypting It

Microsoft's recommendations for Cybersecurity Architects concerning data protection, classification, and encryption are the following:

- Data should be classified according to its risk level.

- Securely store and manage keys and certificates using industry-standard encryption at rest and in transit.

Monitor System Security and Plan Incident Response

Microsoft's recommendations for Cybersecurity Architects concerning system security and implementing incident response are the following:

- Assess application health by correlating audit and security events.

- Identify active threats by correlating audit and security events.

- Automate and manually respond to incidents by establishing procedures.

- Track security events using security information and event management (SIEM) tools.

Identify and Protect Endpoints

Microsoft's recommendations for Cybersecurity Architects concerning identifying and protecting endpoints are the following:

- Monitoring and protecting the network integrity of internal and external endpoints with security appliances and Azure services.

- DoS attacks like SlowLoris are common attack vectors, so use industry-standard approaches to protect against them.

Protect Against Code-Level Vulnerabilities

Cybersecurity Architects should follow Microsoft's recommendations for protecting against code-level vulnerabilities:

- Cross-site scripting vulnerabilities and SQL injection vulnerabilities should be identified and mitigated.

- Regularly incorporate the following into the operational life cycle:

  - Fixes for security problems
  - Patching codebases and dependencies

Model and Test Against Potential Threats

Cybersecurity Architects should follow Microsoft's recommendations to model and test against potential threats:

- Establish procedures for identifying and mitigating known threats.
- Penetration testing can be used to verify that threats have been mitigated.
- Static code analysis is a valuable tool for preventing future vulnerabilities.
- To prevent future vulnerabilities, use code scanning.

Design Security for a Resiliency Approach

A resilient security strategy protects the integrity of each aspect of your business from unforeseen threats or changes. We live in an era of uncertainty. As change accelerates, businesses invest heavily across the enterprise to strengthen resilience. Companies can benefit from these initiatives as they adjust to change, from financial resilience to operations resilience to organizational resilience to supply chain resilience. Security is integral to all of these initiatives, so if businesses fail to invest in security resilience, their investments will fall short.

As the world becomes more interconnected, security resilience must change as well. Corporations, customers, suppliers, and partners operate as integrated ecosystems where boundaries blur between them. In addition, the number of touchpoints between people, devices, and data is constantly expanding. Hybrid work is here to stay as businesses adapt to constantly shifting work patterns.

The goal of security resilience is to support the resilience of your business and has two main objectives:

- Improve your business's ability to innovate and adapt to a rapidly changing environment.
- Limit the impact and likelihood of disruptions on business operations before, during, and after active attacks.

According to Figure 1.13, security resilience is achieved by managing risk throughout the entire life cycle.

Before an Incident

Continually improve security posture and response capability. A continuous improvement in security posture reduces the likelihood and impact of a security incident on your business operations and assets. Security disciplines cover many techniques, but all aim to raise the attack cost. By stopping their old methods, you force the attackers to come up with new ones. They are slowed down and limited in success by these techniques, which raise prices and friction.

FIGURE 1.13   Security resiliency managing risk

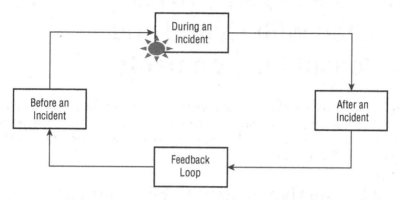

During an Incident

During an incident, business operations must continue, no matter how degraded, slower, or limited. During an attack, a hospital cannot stop caring for patients, ships cannot stop moving cargo, and planes can't stop flying. When an incident occurs, the following two priorities are essential:

- All efforts should be directed toward protecting and sustaining critical business operations if threatened.

- Detecting and quickly evicting attackers from an environment is the default priority for security operations. This eviction prevents retaliation by the attackers.

After an Incident

After an attack damages business operations, repairs must be started immediately to restore entire operations. Repairs are necessary, even if that means restoring operations without data that was lost in an attack, as in a ransomware incident or a destructive attack like NotPetya.

Feedback Loop

Attackers have found repeated attacks or copies of other attacks to be effective. It would be best if you continuously learned from attacks on your organization, since attackers learn from attacks on your organization. Consider taking proven and available techniques that have been tried in the past. Next, make sure you can block them, detect them, respond rapidly, and recover from them. Deterring or slowing down future attacks through your efforts increases the cost of an attack on your organization.

Identify the Security Risks Associated with Hybrid and Multi-Tenant Environments

Organizations can extend their existing on-premises environment to the cloud with a hybrid deployment. A hybrid deployment enables an organization to move seamlessly between an on-premises and a cloud environment. It is also possible to move entirely to a cloud environment using a hybrid deployment.

Deploy a Secure Hybrid Identity Environment

Managing users on-premises and in the cloud poses a challenge as businesses and corporations increasingly combine on-premises and cloud applications.

Microsoft's identity solutions spread across on-premises and cloud-based capabilities. These solutions create a standard user identity for authentication and authorization of all resources, regardless of location, and Microsoft defines it as a hybrid identity.

Figure 1.14 depicts a design reference for a hybrid identity solution facilitating IT admins to incorporate the present Windows Server Active Directory solution on-premises with Microsoft Azure Active Directory to allow users to use single sign-on (SSO) around applications located in the Azure and on-premises.

FIGURE 1.14   Hybrid security identity environment

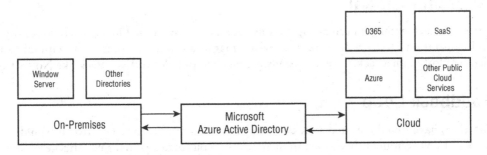

Deploy a Secure Hybrid Network

The reference architecture shown in Figure 1.15 depicts a secure hybrid network that extends an on-premises network to Azure. An Azure virtual network is connected to an on-premises network through a DMZ (also known as a *perimeter network* or *screened network*). All inbound and outbound traffic passes go throw via the Azure Firewall.

FIGURE 1.15   Deploying a secure hybrid network

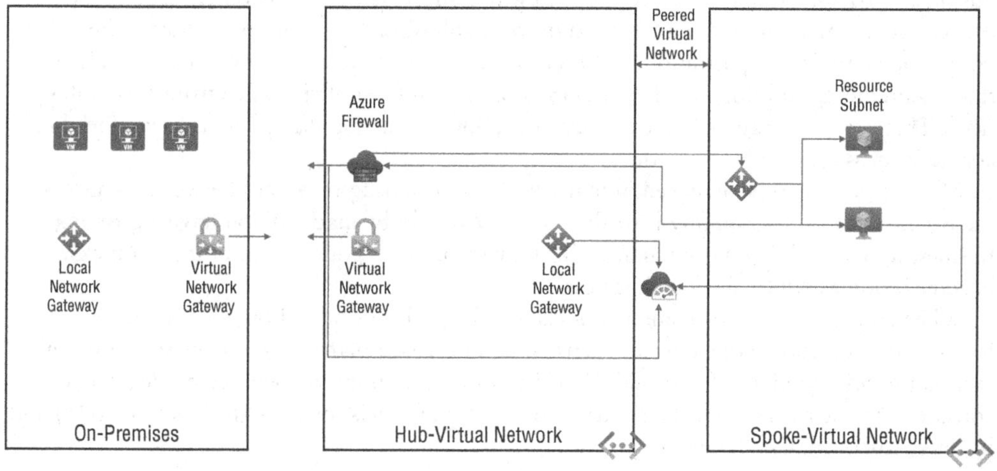

Design a Multi-Tenancy Environment

Multi-tenant architectures share some or all their resources between tenants. As a result, a multi-tenant architecture can save you money and improve operational efficiency. Multi-tenancy, however, poses a number of challenges, including the following:

- For your specific solution, how do you define a tenant? Do tenants refer to customers, users, or teams?

- How will you deploy your infrastructure to support multi-tenancy, and how will tenants be isolated from one another?

- Does your tenant require a certain level of service? Think about performance, resilience, security, and compliance requirements.

- What is your plan for growing your business or solution, and can it accommodate a large number of tenants?

- Is there anything unusual or unique your tenants need? Do your biggest customers require stronger guarantees or higher performance?

- How will you monitor, automate, manage, scale, and govern your Azure domain, and how will multi-tenancy impact this?

You must understand your customers' or tenants' requirements regardless of the architecture you use. You need to know your customers' requirements when you design your solution and if you have made sales commitments to them or have contractual obligations. You may also have implicit expectations about how multi-tenant solutions should work or behave, which may affect how you design them.

Suppose you're a software developer who sells multi-tenant solutions to financial service businesses. To add your solution to their firewall's allow list, your customers require a comprehensive list of all domain names used by your solution. As a result, you must ensure that your tenants are isolated from one another and that the Azure services you use comply with this requirement. Additionally, they require a minimum level of resilience from their solutions. There may be many similar expectations, both explicit and implicit, that you need to consider across your whole solution.

Multi-tenancy can be achieved in many ways, and sharing resources between tenants is the primary factor determining how this decision should be made. If you have a growing business and are adding more tenants, this may seem like a good idea, but it can quickly become costly as you scale your business.

When considering multi-tenancy models, it is helpful to look at how you define tenants for your organization, your business drivers, and how you plan to scale your solution. This section provides guidance for technical decision-makers about the tenancy models you can consider and their trade-offs. There are two standard models: business-to-business (B2B) and business-to-consumer (B2C).

Business-to-Business

If your customers are other organizations, you will likely consider your tenants to be those customers. However, think about whether your customers might have divisions such as teams or departments or whether they have a presence in multiple countries. Consider having a single customer map to multiple tenants if there are different requirements for these subgroups.

In the same way, a customer might want to keep their development and production environments separate by maintaining two instances of your service. You will generally find that a single tenant will have multiple users; for example, all your customer's employees will be users.

Business-to-Consumer

The relationship between customers, tenants, and users is often more complicated if your customers are consumers, and a consumer could be a tenant of their own in some scenarios. Families, friends, clubs, associations, or any group that needs to access and manage their data together might use your solution. For example, a music-streaming service might support both individual users and families, and it might treat each of these account types differently when separating them into tenants.

Multi-tenant architectures must consider the degree of isolation that each tenant needs. The following are the design considerations that need to be made for isolation:

- On a single shared infrastructure, each tenant has their own instance of your application and their own database.

- It is possible to share some resources with other tenants while keeping other resources separate.

- Separating data from physical infrastructure. Deployed dedicated hosts or separate Azure resources for each tenant in the cloud may even be necessary.

Rather than thinking of isolation as a discrete property, it would help if you thought about isolation as a change; it progresses into the future. Depending on your business requirements, you can deploy components of your architecture that are more or less isolated from other components in the same architecture.

Your architecture of isolation is affected by the level of isolation in many ways, including the following:

- **Security:** Sharing infrastructure between multiple tenants requires caution when returning responses to one tenant from another. It would help if you had a solid identity strategy and an authorization process that considers tenants' and users' identities.

- **Cost:** Shared infrastructure is cheaper because multiple tenants can use it.

- **Performance:** The system's performance may suffer if you're sharing infrastructure, since the resources may be consumed faster as more customers use it.

- **Reliability:** An outage can affect everyone using a single set of shared infrastructures.

Responsiveness to Individual Tenants' Needs

It may be possible to tune the configuration of dedicated infrastructure for a specific tenant if it is dedicated to a particular tenant. Your pricing model may even support allowing customers to pay more for isolated deployments.

The architecture of your solution can affect the isolation options available to you. Let's consider an example of a three-tier solution architecture:

- All tenants may access the same hostname through your multi-tenant web application.

- Your middle tier could be a shared application layer with shared message queues.

- Data tiers can be isolated databases, tables, or blob containers.

The levels of isolation can be mixed and matched at each tier. Choosing what should be shared and what should be isolated will depend on many factors, such as cost, complexity, customer requirements, and the number of resources you can deploy before you reach Azure quotas.

Azure Arc Enables Hybrid Environments to Be Run at Scale

In today's world, organizations struggle to control and govern increasingly complex environments spanning multiple data centers, multiple clouds, and network boundaries. New DevOps and ITOps operational models can be challenging to implement across resources because each domain and cloud has its management tools.

Microsoft Azure Arc simplifies governance and management by delivering a consistent management platform for multi-cloud and on-premises environments. Microsoft Azure Arc platform offers a centralized, unified way to do the following:

- Manage an entire environment by projecting existing non-Azure and on-premises resources into Azure Resource Manager.

- Practice Azure-like management of virtual machines, Kubernetes clusters, and databases.

- Access and manage Azure services regardless of where they are located.

- Support cloud-native patterns in an environment, continuing to use traditional IT operations practices while introducing DevOps practices.
- Configure Kubernetes clusters and extensions with custom locations as an abstraction layer.

Azure Policy Enables Hybrid Environments to Be Run at Scale

Organizational standards can be enforced and compliance can be assessed at scale with Azure Policy. Through its compliance dashboard, users can see an aggregated view of the environment and drill down to the level of per-resource, per-policy granularity. Additionally, it allows bulk remediation of existing resources and automatic remediation of new ones to bring them into compliance.

The most common use cases for Azure Policy include implementing governance for resource consistency, regulatory compliance, security, and cost control. Azure environments already offer built-in policy definitions for these everyday use cases to assist architects.

The logic used to determine whether a resource is compliant is expressed in Java-Script Object Notation (JSON). A policy rule and metadata are included in the definition. Functions, parameters, logical operators, conditions, and property aliases can be used to define a rule. In an assignment, the policy rule determines what resources are evaluated.

Throughout the resource and policy assignment life cycles and for regular ongoing compliance evaluations, resources are evaluated at specific times. Resources are evaluated at the following times or events:

- A policy assignment creates or updates a resource in a scope.
- Scopes are newly assigned to policies or initiatives.
- The scope of a procedure or initiative is updated.
- Every 24 hours, the standard compliance evaluation cycle takes place.

Plan Traffic Filtering and Segmentation Technical and Governance Strategies

The perimeter of a network assumes that all systems within it are trustworthy. However, today's employees can access their organization's resources from anywhere via various devices and apps, rendering perimeter security controls irrelevant. To master the balance between safety and productivity, security admins need to consider how resources are accessed and who can access them. More than focusing on who has access to resources is required regarding access control policies.

One endpoint within a trusted boundary can be compromised and can quickly spread its reach across the entire system if network security is compromised, as opposed to traditional defenses. The location of the network within the perimeter is not a factor in determining trust in Zero Trust networks. For new initiatives, adopt Zero Trust approaches that validate trust during access using devices and user trust claims. Zero Trust architectures use devices, and user trust claims to access organizational data and resources.

Logically Segmented Subnets

An organization's virtual machine, physical server, network, and security devices are isolated from each other through segmentation. This is an effective way of detecting and containing adversary movements. Segmentation can be achieved by isolating networks. Because different technical teams may not be aligned with business use cases and application workloads, this approach is not recommended. It can lead to reduced velocity or, worse cases, to wide network firewall exceptions due to this mismatch, especially regarding on-premises networking. A unified segmentation strategy should incorporate network control as part of a segmentation strategy.

Enterprise security has traditionally relied heavily on network security. As a result of cloud computing, network perimeters are increasingly porous, and attackers can bypass network controls when they attack identity system elements. Because of these factors, focusing primarily on identity-based access controls rather than network-based access controls has become increasingly essential to protect resources.

All technical teams (IT, security, applications) should use segmentation strategies to isolate access through networking, applications, identity, and other controls. For the strategy to be successful, it should do the following:

- Align your operational practices with your business applications to minimize operational friction.

- By adding cost to attackers, you can reduce risk. As a result, you are doing the following:

  - Protecting sensitive workloads from other assets' compromise

  - Protecting high-exposure systems from being used as pivots

- Monitor operations that might threaten segment integrity (account usage, unexpected traffic).

A virtual network in Azure, for example, is similar to a local area network (LAN) on an on-premises network. All Azure virtual machines can be located on a single IP address. Class A (10.0.0.0/8), Class B (172.16.0.0/12), and Class C (192.168.0.0/16) are the three private IP address spaces that are currently known.

Deploy Perimeter Networks for Security Zones

A perimeter network, also called a DMZ, serves as an additional layer of security between assets and the Internet. As part of a virtual network, specialized access control devices allow only desired traffic to enter a perimeter network. A perimeter network in Azure helps manage, monitor, log, and report on virtual network edge devices. Perimeter networks are used for the prevention of distributed denial of service (DDoS), intrusion detection and prevention systems (IDS/IPS), firewall rules, web filtering, and network antimalware. A network security device sits between an Azure virtual network and the Internet and has an interface on both networks.

Azure or a third-party solution can provide a perimeter network based on the Zero Trust concept to provide the next level of security between assets and the Internet.

Avoid Exposure to the Internet with Dedicated WAN Links

The hybrid IT approach has been adopted by many organizations. Hybrid cloud deployment model uses Azure to store some information assets, while on-premises storage is used for others. Many services run some components in Azure and others on-premises. It is common for hybrid IT scenarios to include cross-premises connectivity, and Azure virtual networks can be connected to the organization's on-premises networks

Use Virtual Network Appliances

A certain degree of network security can be provided by network security groups and user-defined routing at the network and transport layers. But in some situations, security must be enabled at high stack levels. Microsoft recommends deploying virtual network security appliances that Azure partners provide in such cases. Network-level controls cannot provide as much security as Azure network security appliances.

Summary

This chapter explored several topics related to the basics of cloud networking and presented a brief overview of cloud computing and cybersecurity in cloud.

As your organization moves to Microsoft Azure, you must design and deploy a secured cloud environment. End users must obtain the cloud resources they need seamlessly and safely in a secure manner.

The Microsoft Cybersecurity Reference Architecture (MCRA) overviews Microsoft's cybersecurity capabilities. Throughout this chapter, you have read about how Microsoft security capabilities integrate with Microsoft platforms such as Microsoft 365, Microsoft Azure, and other third-party platforms.

In this chapter, you learned how to adopt Microsoft Cybersecurity Reference Architecture, convert business goals into security requirements, convert security requirements into technical capabilities, define security resiliency strategy, and develop governance strategy for Microsoft Azure.

Exam Essentials

Understand cloud computing and cybersecurity.   You should have a conceptual knowledge of cloud computing, Microsoft Azure, security policies, requirements, Zero Trust architecture, and management of hybrid environments. Developing security requirements based on business goals, applying Zero Trust strategies, and applying security policies are essential for the SC-100 exam.

Develop integration points in an architecture.   The Microsoft Cybersecurity Reference Architecture describes Microsoft's cybersecurity abilities. The reference architectures define how Microsoft's security abilities integrate with Microsoft cloud services such as Azure and Microsoft 365, third-party apps such as ServiceNow and Salesforce, and third-party platforms such as Amazon Web Services (AWS) and Google Cloud Platform (GCP). The reference architectures are comprised of detailed technical, logical building blocks on Microsoft cybersecurity abilities, Zero Trust user access, security operations, operational technology (OT), multi-cloud and cross-platform abilities, attack chain coverage, Azure native security controls, and security organizational functions. A Microsoft Cybersecurity Architect must understand end-to-end MCRA.

Develop security requirements based on business goals.   Cloud adoption can be time-consuming and costly, and a breach of your cloud solutions will be even more expensive. Successful transformation begins with the business goals. You can overcome this barrier using the Microsoft Cloud Adoption Framework; Microsoft has created a framework for helping customers identify business outcomes that drive observable results or changes in business performance.

Translate security requirements into technical capabilities.   Several organizational transformations are occurring in many organizations at once. These internal transformations typically begin as nearly all external markets transform to meet customer preferences for mobile and cloud technology. It is common for organizations to be subject to the competitive threat of new startups and the digital transformation of traditional competitors who have the potential to disrupt the market. To overcome these challenges, translate the security requirements into Microsoft Azure capabilities. Understanding of each modernizing capability is essential.

Design security for a resiliency strategy.   Security resiliency is focused on supporting the resiliency of your business. It has two main goals. Number one is to enable your business to innovate and adapt to the ever-changing business environment rapidly. Number two limits the impact and likelihood of disruptions before, during, and after active attacks on business operations.

Design security strategy for hybrid and multi-tenant environments.   By deploying hybrid solutions, organizations can take advantage of the features and administrative control they already have on-premises. An organization can use a hybrid deployment to create a seamless transition between an on-premises and cloud environment. Hybrid deployments can also be an intermediate step before moving entirely to the cloud.

Design technical and governance strategies for traffic filtering and segmentation.   To protect networks against breaches, networks need to evolve from traditional defenses. A single endpoint within a trusted boundary can be compromised by an attacker and then rapidly spread throughout the entire network. Instead of relying on network location within a perimeter to establish trust, Zero Trust architectures use user trust claims to access organizational resources and data. Zero Trust approaches should be adopted for new initiatives that validate trust at the point of access.

Review Questions

1. Which of the following are types of cloud computing service models provided by Microsoft Azure? (Choose three.)

    A. Infrastructure as a service

    B. Platform as a service

    C. Personal computer as a service

    D. Software as a service

2. Which of the following cloud deployment models is provisioned for exclusive use by a single organization comprising multiple consumers?

    A. Private cloud

    B. Public cloud

    C. Community cloud

    D. Hybrid cloud

3. Which cloud deployment models are provisioned for exclusive use by a specific community of clients from organizations with shared concerns (for example, objective, task, security, and compliance concerns)?

    A. Private cloud

    B. Public cloud

    C. Community cloud

    D. Hybrid cloud

4. Which cloud computing model allows customers to use some public cloud computing resources for free, while other resources can be purchased through subscription or pay-per-usage pricing models?

    A. Private cloud

    B. Public cloud

    C. Community cloud

    D. Hybrid cloud

5. Which of the following protects your Azure virtual network resources by providing managed cloud-based network security?

    A. Azure Firewall

    B. Azure Virtual WAN

    C. Azure Virtual WAF

    D. None of above

6. Which of the following evolving set of cybersecurity paradigms says that before granting or maintaining access to applications and data, users must be authenticated and authorized, whether inside or outside the organization's network?

    A. Zero Trust

    B. Azure Virtual WAN

    C. Azure Virtual WAF

    D. Azure Firewall

7. Microsoft defines Zero Trust using which of following three fundamental principles?

    A. Verify explicitly, apply least privilege access, assume breach

    B. Verify explicitly, apply least privilege access, assume risk

    C. Verify none, apply least privilege access, assume breach

    D. Verify none, apply no privilege access, assume breach

8. Which of the following allows you to extend the Azure platform to run applications and services across data centers, at the edge, and in multi-cloud environments?

    A. Defender for Endpoint

    B. Azure Arc

    C. Defender for Cloud

    D. Azure Firewall

9. Which of the following is a cloud-based security solution that identifies, witnesses, and analyzes advanced threats, hacked identities, and malicious insider activities executed at your organization?

    A. Defender for Endpoint

    B. Defender for Identity

    C. Defender for Cloud

    D. Azure Firewall

10. Which of the following is a network service that lets you connect to Azure PaaS services (Azure Storage and SQL Database) and Azure-hosted, customer-owned, and partner services over a private network connection?

    A. Azure ExpressRoute

    B. Azure S2S VPN

    C. Azure P2S VPN

    D. Azure Private Link

11. Among the following reference architectures, which provides a high-level technical diagram of Azure's cybersecurity capabilities, including Zero Trust access to users, SecOps, OT, hybrid cloud and cross-platform capabilities, attack chain scope, native Azure security management, and security organizational procedures?

    A. Microsoft Cybersecurity Reference Architecture

    B. The Open Group Cybersecurity Reference Architecture

    C. Zachman Cybersecurity Reference Architecture

    D. None of the above

12. Which of the following enhances the availability and performance of your applications and services by enabling you to collect, analyze, and act on telemetry from the cloud and on-premises?

    A. Azure SOAR

    B. Azure SIEM

    C. Azure Monitor

    D. None of the above

13. Which of the following lets you connect to a virtual machine using your browser and the Azure Portal using your Azure subscription? It is an Azure PaaS service that you provision inside your virtual network that is fully platform-managed.

    A. Azure VM

    B. Azure Jump Server

    C. Azure Bastion

    D. None of the above

14. Which of the following enable you run hybrid environments to be run at scale securely? (Choose two.)

    A. Azure Arc

    B. Azure Policy

    C. Azure Bastion

    D. None of the above

15. Which of the following are Microsoft's recommendations for Cybersecurity Architects concerning resource planning and hardening? (Choose three.)

    A. Plan workload resources to take security into account.

    B. Become familiar with the types of protection offered by cloud services.

    C. Evaluate service enablement using a framework.

    D. None of the above.

16. Which of the following are Microsoft's recommendations for Cybersecurity Architects concerning automating and applying the least privilege? (Choose two.)

    A. Implement the least privilege at every level of the application and control plane to prevent data exfiltration and malicious actor scenarios.

    B. Utilize DevSecOps to automate and minimize human interaction.

    C. Evaluate service enablement using a framework.

    D. None of the above.

17. Cybersecurity Architects should follow which of the following Microsoft recommendations for protecting against code-level vulnerabilities? (Choose three.)

    A. Identified and mitigated cross-site scripting vulnerabilities and SQL injection vulnerabilities

    B. Fixes for security problems

    C. Patching codebases and dependencies

    D. None of the above

18. Microsoft's recommendations for Cybersecurity Architects include which of the following concerning data protection, classification, and encryption? (Choose two.)

    A. Classify data according to its risk level.

    B. Securely store and manage keys and certificates using industry-standard encryption at rest and in transit.

    C. Patch codebases and dependencies.

    D. None of the above.

19. Which of the following let you store and access secrets on the cloud securely? (API keys, passwords, certificates, and cryptographic keys are examples of secrets.)

    A. Azure Key Vault

    B. Azure SIEM

    C. Azure Monitor

    D. None of the above

20. Microsoft multi-tenancy has two standard models; which of the following are they? (Choose two.)

    A. Enterprise deployment

    B. Business-to-business (B2B)

    C. Business-to-consumer (B2C)

    D. None of the above

Chapter

2

Define a Security Operations Strategy

**THE MICROSOFT SC-100 EXAM
OBJECTIVES COVERED IN THIS CHAPTER
INCLUDE:**

✓ Design a logging and auditing strategy to support security
operations

✓ Develop security operations to support a hybrid or multi-
cloud environment

✓ Design a strategy for SIEM and SOAR

✓ Evaluate security workflows

✓ Evaluate a security operations strategy for incident
management life cycle

✓ Evaluate a security operations strategy for sharing technical
threat intelligence

In this chapter, we will focus on designing a security operations strategy. The prerequisites for designing a security operations strategy include understanding and developing security policies and requirements based on business goals, applying Zero Trust strategies to building a Zero Trust architecture, applying security policies, and managing a hybrid environment.

In security operations centers (SOCs), cyberthreats are monitored, prevented, detected, investigated, and responded to around the clock. Organizational assets, such as intellectual property, personnel data, business systems, and brand integrity, are monitored and protected by SOC teams. To monitor, assess, and defend against cyberattacks, the SOC team implements the organization's overall cybersecurity strategy.

In this chapter, you will learn about these components of security strategy development:

- Designing a logging and auditing security strategy
- Developing security operations for hybrid and multi-cloud environments
- Designing a strategy for security information and event management (SIEM) and security orchestration, automation, and response (SOAR)
- Evaluating security workflows
- Reviewing security strategies for incident management
- Evaluating security operations for technical threat intelligence
- Monitoring sources for insights on threats and mitigations
- Developing integration points in an architecture

Foundation of Security Operations and Strategy

Let's get started with the basics of a security operation strategy. A security operations center aims to address organizational and technological security challenges. A SOC can be a team within your organization or can be outsourced to a third party specializing in managed detection and response. Although "SOC" is used interchangeably to describe both in-house and outsourced teams, the correct name for outsourced teams is *SOC as a service* (SOCaaS).

Whether an organization employs or outsources a team of IT security professionals, cybersecurity events are detected in real time and responded to efficiently and effectively by a group of professionals. Often called an *information security operations center* (ISOC), a security operations center operates around the clock.

Additionally, SOCs select, operate, and maintain cyber technology for an organization and constantly analyze threat data to maintain and improve the organization's security posture.

Organizations can synchronize their security tools, practices, and responses to security incidents whether a SOC is operated or outsourced. By improving preventative measures and security policies, detecting security threats more quickly, and responding more effectively and efficiently to them, security threats can usually be reduced. Furthermore, SOCs can simplify and strengthen compliance with industry, national, and international privacy laws.

Traditionally, you had to keep track of each level. The good news about cloud providers is that they are responsible for intrusion detection and response in their areas of responsibility, just as they are for other controls. A provider breach could affect you, in which case you will be notified and may have to perform response and recovery activities specific to the services you use. However, in the extended bulk of cases, all your detection, response, and recovery activities will be in the areas marked by consumer responsibility.

By the service and deployment models, cloud providers will have security operations centers overseeing the various cloud data centers and underlying infrastructure, along with platforms and applications. However, cloud customers may be responsible for monitoring their own users and accounts and their security operations.

Let's do a deep dive into the SOC operating model.

SOC Operating Model

A SOC is a group of highly qualified and experienced Cybersecurity Analysts and engineers committed to ensuring high IT security standards. These individuals use specialized security processes and computer programs to identify weaknesses in the company's virtual infrastructure and prevent them from being exploited.

The SOC monitors, detects, and responds to incidents on the computers, servers, and networks it supervises to prevent cybersecurity threats. Because employees work in shifts, rotating and logging activity around the clock, a SOC has a unique ability to monitor all systems on an ongoing basis.

Data can be monitored across multiple platforms using firewalls, probes, security information, and event management systems employed by SOCs.

The SOC operating model consists of three building blocks: SOC framework, functions, and operations. Figure 2.1 depicts the SOC operating model.

SOC Framework

A SOC is a facility where the information security team constantly monitors and analyzes an organization's security. The SOC team detects, analyzes, and responds to cybersecurity incidents using technology, people, and processes. SOC analysts manage and improve security across the three pillars of an organization: people, processes, and technology. An effective SOC requires close coordination between people, processes, and technologies. We'll discuss who, what, and how to build a SOC.

FIGURE 2.1 SOC operating model

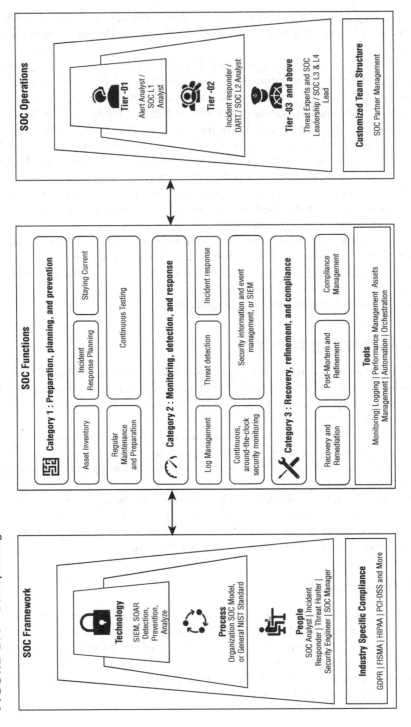

People

Cybersecurity organizations must have highly trained personnel and be familiar with security alerts and attack scenarios. As attack types constantly change, we need teammates willing to research and adapt quickly to new attacks.

Processes

SOC team processes vary according to the organization's size and the industry, but most share similar roles and responsibilities. Typically, a SOC is a centralized function within an organization that monitors and improves an organization's cybersecurity posture by preventing, detecting, analyzing, and responding to cybersecurity incidents.

Technology

It is necessary to have various tools for many facets of cybersecurity, including penetration testing, detection, prevention, and analysis. The best solution for you depends on following the market and technology closely. Occasionally the best product on the market may not be the best for you, which may be due to your low budget.

In most small or midsize data centers, a centralized facility will monitor network performance and security controls continuously. Network operations centers (or groups known by similar terms) are also known as *security operations centers*. Security personnel and administrators typically have access to live and historical feeds from security devices and agents placed throughout the IT environment. Security operations centers will receive logs and reports from data loss prevention (DLP), antimalware, SIEM/security event management (SEM)/security information management (SIM), firewalls, and intrusion detection systems/intrusion prevention systems (IDSs/IPSs) for analysis and real-time response.

Industry-Specific Compliance

Cybersecurity pain points differ across all industry sectors, but they also overlap. Phishing is particularly problematic across all sectors because it taps into our behavior and has a lot of success as an attack vector. Each industry has regulations and compliance measures to deal with cyberthreats against our nation's enterprises, including security and privacy requirements.

- **General Data Protection Regulation (GDPR):** As the world's strictest privacy and security law, GDPR imposes obligations on organizations anywhere European citizens' data is collected or targeted.

- **Health Insurance Portability and Accountability Act (HIPAA):** All health information, whether in paper form, electronic form, or oral form, is protected under HIPAA.

- **Title III of FISMA (Federal Information Security Management Act):** U.S. federal executive branch agencies' information and information systems are protected comprehensively.

- **Cybersecurity Framework (National Institute of Standards and Technology Cybersecurity Framework):** NIST CSF provides guidelines, standards, and best practices for managing cybersecurity risks.
- **Other:** Regulations and compliance standards specific to specific industries abound.

SOC Operations

As far as cybersecurity is concerned, prevention always outweighs reaction. A SOC monitors the network around the clock rather than responding to threats as they occur. Detecting malicious activities and preventing them before they cause damage is the responsibility of the SOC team.

When SOC analysts witness something suspicious, they assemble as many details as possible for a deeper analysis. An analyst performs a threat analysis at the investigation stage to determine whether and to what extent a threat has penetrated the system. By viewing the network and operations of the organization from an attacker's perspective, the security analyst searches for crucial indicators and vulnerabilities before they can be exploited.

By identifying and triaging various types of security incidents, the analyst understands how attacks unfold and how to respond before things get out of hand. The SOC analyst incorporates information about the organization's network with the latest global threat intelligence that includes specifics on attacker tools, methods, and movements to perform a useful triage.

The SOC team coordinates a response following the investigation. Immediately after an incident's confirmation, the SOC isolates endpoints, terminates harmful processes, prevents them from executing, deletes files, and so on.

The SOC team works to restore systems and recover data after an incident. To counter ransomware attacks, you may need to wipe and restart endpoints, reconfigure systems, or deploy viable backups to circumvent the ransomware.

The typical IT environment does not have durable security controls that a SOC environment would possess. For a control to be considered complete (and the associated risk to be permanently mitigated), it cannot be purchased, implemented, and then regarded as complete. You must monitor IT resources continuously to ensure that controls are adequate, operating as intended, and addressing the risks or vulnerabilities they are supposed to mitigate. Furthermore, new or emerging threats or hazards must be monitored continuously to ensure they are dealt with appropriately.

An IT environment might be considered protected for a particular period if the study was successful or did not show significant results under older security paradigms. It is recommended that continuous monitoring be used in accordance with current industry guidance and best practices. It is a central principle of protecting an IT environment that NIST (in the Risk Management Framework), ISO (in the 27000 series of IT security standards), and the CIS (formerly SANS Top 20 security controls guidance) emphasize.

The SOC operations team consists of the following roles:

- **SOC analyst:** According to the SOC structure, this role can be divided into levels 1, 2, and 3. A security analyst classifies alerts, determines the cause, and recommends remedial measures.

- **SOC level 1/analyst:** At this level, analysts review and categorize new alerts into those that can be handled at their level or require escalation to level 2. They also identify recent events and alerts from security tools within the organization.

- **SOC level 2/incident responder:** Initial assessments of security breaches are conducted by incident response officers. They conduct investigations of affected systems, review logs focused on containment, and initiate remediation actions to handle higher-complexity incidents posed by tier 1. Additionally, analysts at this level can conduct root-cause analyses, restore systems, and develop security reports.

- **SOC level 3/threat hunter:** This person searches for anomalous behavior test security controls and protects assets using internal and external threat intelligence. By performing penetration tests and vulnerability assessments and reviewing security controls regularly, tier 3 analysts find weaknesses proactively. It is this team member's responsibility to find vulnerabilities before an attacker can exploit them.

- **Security engineer:** The job of a security engineer is to maintain the security infrastructure of SIEM solutions and SOC products, as well as to prepare the connection between SIEM and SOAR solutions.

- **SOC manager:** The SOC manager deals with operational matters rather than technical issues, such as budgeting, strategizing, managing personnel, and coordinating operations.

- **Forensic investigator:** The forensic investigator must collect evidence to support his findings to identify the root cause and locate all attacks' sources.

- **The compliance auditor:** As a quality control department, compliance auditors ensure that the processes within the SOC are standard.

Microsoft SOC Strategy for Azure Cloud

Hacktivists disrupt systems to make political statements and grab headlines. Organized crime syndicates use sophisticated financial ruses to make money. Nation-state actors take advantage of extensive resources to advance their agendas. Global threats are everywhere, and no person or organization is safe. Our adversaries continue to use sophisticated tactics to engage us in new ways. Although the threats we face today aren't new, they continue to gain sophistication.

Moving away from trust-by-default toward trust-by-exception is a hallmark of a Zero Trust security framework. Once trust is needed, it still requires a reliable method of establishing it. To prove a proposal's point-in-time trustworthiness, you must select a form to attest to the proposal's reliability since you no longer assume requests are trustworthy. Getting visibility into the activities on and around the request is essential for this attestation.

Investing in all these things increases your visibility, allowing you to make better trust decisions based on better data. When applying Zero Trust to other areas such as identities, endpoints, infrastructure, and networks, SOCs must mitigate more incidents.

To better defend against threats and validate trust in transactions, an integrated capability is needed to manage the influx of data generated by each area. Following Microsoft's recommendation, the following capabilities are needed:

- Detect vulnerabilities and threats

- Perform an investigation

- Respond to an incident

- Hunt for threats

- Provide additional context using threat analytics

- Assess vulnerabilities

- Obtain help from experts from around the world

- Ensure that events do not occur across the pillars by preventing them or blocking them

To manage threats, your SOC team needs tools that support reactive and proactive detection.

- **Reactive detection:** Identities, devices, applications, data, infrastructure, and networks can trigger incidents. In addition, a management product such as a SIEM will likely support another layer of analytics to enrich and correlate the data, resulting in identifying harmful incidents. The subsequent action would be to investigate the attack to understand what happened.

- **Proactive detection:** Data mining is performed to prove a hypothesis about the compromise based on the available information. Hunting for evidence that confirms a breach begins with the assumption that one has occurred.

Attackers can conduct attacks and access sensitive or valuable systems every minute they remain in the environment. The control of the environment ensures compliance with industry and organizational security standards.

The following functions should be considered by Microsoft Cybersecurity Architects as they apply the Microsoft security operations strategy:

- Multiple engineering teams working in your organization environment in Microsoft Azure.

- Multiple subscriptions to manage and secure by an Azure administrator for your organization.

- Regulatory requirements must be enforced in your organization's Azure environment, and compliance standards must be followed for all cloud resources.

- Designing and deploying, logging & auditing security processes should be considered.

Detecting, prioritizing, and triaging potential attacks are the responsibilities of the security operations team (also called the *security operations center* or *SecOps*). By eliminating false positives and focusing on actual attacks, these operations reduce the mean time it takes to resolve actual incidents.

The central SecOps team monitors telemetry data related to security and investigates security breaches. Communicating, investigating, and hunting activities must be aligned with the application team. Microsoft Cybersecurity Architects must follow the following general best practices when designing SOC operations.

Implement the following NIST cybersecurity framework functions as part of your operations:

- **Identify:** Establish an organizational understanding of cybersecurity risk to systems, people, assets, data, and capabilities.

- **Protect:** Ensure critical services are delivered by developing and implementing appropriate safeguards.

- **Detect:** Analyze the system to detect the presence of adversaries. Neutralizing an adversary quickly is possible if one has been detected. The chances of them conducting attacks and reaching sensitive systems should be reduced.

- **Respond:** By investigating it promptly, identify whether it is a false alarm or an actual attack. Respond quickly to an alert. As defenders triage false positives, detected adversaries should not be ignored.

- **Recover:** Restore confidentiality, integrity, and workload availability during and after an attack.

Based on the NIST framework core, SOC results can be achieved through specific activities and guidance.

For more information, refer to the following link:

nvlpubs.nist.gov/nistpubs/CSWP/NIST.CSWP.04162018.pdf

As your system matures, actively hunt for adversaries. If you make this effort, an adversary with high skill levels will have less time to operate in the environment.

Microsoft SOC Function for Azure Cloud

Microsoft defines that SOC functions need to address three critical objectives: incident management, incident preparation, and threat intelligence. Let's take a high-level view of each one of them.

- **Incident management:** Protect the environment from active attacks, including the following:
  - Responding to detected attacks in a reactive manner as per the agreed service level agreement.
  - Detecting attacks proactively may elude traditional threat detection methods.
  - Security incidents have legal, communication, and other business consequences that need to be managed.

- **Incident preparation:** Organizations need to prepare for future attacks, which involves a broader set of activities to build muscle memory and context across all levels. People will be better prepared for significant attacks due to this strategy, and security processes will be improved.
- **Threat intelligence:** This means delivering collected, processed, and disseminated threat intelligence to security operations, security teams, and business leaders.

It is critical for security operations teams to focus on the essentials to achieve required business outcomes. It is common for SecOps teams to break the outcome into subteams in larger organizations.

Now, let's explore each level; we'll start with tier 0.

Tier 0

Tier 0 is the ultimate efficiency to automate and optimize your security posture through SOC automation. Detection and remediation of threats can be sped up with SOC automation.

Manage threats and vulnerabilities, respond to incidents, and automate security operations. Automating processes, such as scanning for vulnerabilities or searching for logs or resolving well-known attacks, allows them to be handled automatically.

Tier 1

Tier 1 is a security incident's first point of contact. In triage, alerts generated by automation and tools are processed at high volumes. Most of the common incident types are resolved within the team through triage. A tier 1 incident should be escalated if it is more complex or has not been seen before.

Tier 2

The SOC should focus on incidents requiring further investigation, often requiring data points from various sources to be correlated. Tier 2 investigates escalated issues to provide repeatable solutions, so tier 1 can address similar problems in the future. A business-critical system alert will also be handled by tier 2, which will reflect the severity of the risk and the need for immediate action.

Tier 3

To mature security controls, SOCs should proactively hunt for highly sophisticated attack processes and guide broader teams. Tier 3 teams also serve as escalation points for significant incidents, supporting forensic analysis and response.

Microsoft SOC Integration Among SecOps and Business Leadership

SecOps has multiple possible value exchanges with business leadership, including SecOps's business context, joint practice exercises with SecOps, SecOps's major incidents, and SOC business intelligence.

SecOps's Business Context

To apply context to fluid real-time security situations, SecOps must understand what is important to the organization.

- What would be the most detrimental effect on the business?
- Is there a critical system outage?
- Has your reputation been damaged and your customers' trust lost?
- Has sensitive data been disclosed?
- Are adversaries trying to tamper with essential data or systems?

Throughout Microsoft, leaders and SOC employees have learned that understanding this context is critical. Triage incidents; prioritize their time, attention, and effort; and wade through the constant flood of information.

Joint Practice Exercises with SecOps

In response to significant incidents, business leaders should join SecOps regularly. A training program like this builds the muscle memory and relationships necessary for quick and adequate decision-making during actual incidents, which helps reduce the risk to the organization. Additionally, this practice reduces risk by exposing gaps and assumptions before an incident happens.

SecOps's Major Incidents

Businesses should be informed by SecOps as soon as significant incidents occur. Business leaders can use this information to understand their risk and take proactive and reactive steps to manage it.

SOC Business Intelligence

Occasionally, SecOps finds adversaries targeting unexpected systems or data sets. Business leaders should be informed of these discoveries as soon as they are made, as they might trigger insights. For instance, someone outside the business might become aware of a secret project, or an attacker could target a data set that would otherwise be overlooked.

Microsoft SOC People and Process

In addition to being highly technical, security operations are also highly human. The people make security operations effective, and their experience, skill, insight, creativity, and resourcefulness are the most valuable assets.

People such as criminals, spies, and hacktivists can also plan and conduct attacks on your organization. While some entity attacks are fully automated, the most dangerous ones are often done by live human attack operators.

Focus on Empowering People

Automating should not be your goal. Tools that simplify your employees' daily tasks will empower them. These tools can keep up with or even get ahead of human adversaries.

Investing in both humans and automation is necessary to rapidly sort out the signals from the noise (false positives). Technology and automation can reduce human work, but attackers are human, and human judgment is crucial to their defeat.

Diversify Your Design and Deployment Thinking Portfolio

Security operations are another version of forensic investigation in many career fields, like criminal justice. Employ people with a strong competency in the investigation or deductive or inductive reasoning and train them in technology.

Make sure your culture is healthy and you measure the right outcomes. These practices can improve productivity and employee pleasure in their jobs.

Microsoft SOC Metrics

Measuring success is an essential element of driving behavior. By defining clear, measurable goals, metrics translate culture into results.

Microsoft recommends focusing on and enforcing the organization-specific metrics. Managing security operations requires dealing with variables beyond their control, such as attacks and attackers. Any deviations from the aim should be viewed mainly as a learning opportunity for process or tool progress rather than assumed to be a defeat by the SOC to fulfill a goal.

The following metrics directly influence organizational risk:

- **Mean time to acknowledge (MTTA):** Among the few things SecOps has direct control over, responsiveness is one. Measure the time between when an alert occurs, such as when a light blinks, and when an analyst discovers the alert and begins the investigation. By avoiding false positives, analysts can improve their responsiveness. Keeping alert feeds that require analyst responses as accurately as possible can be achieved through ruthless prioritization.

- **Mean time to remediate (MTTR):** Next time, reduce risk measures more effectively. Analysts begin investigating and resolving incidents during that period. In SecOps, MTTR refers to the time it takes to remove an attacker's access from an environment. Analysts can use this information to determine where to invest in processes and tools to reduce risk.

- **Incidents remediated (manually or via automation):** Another crucial step is informing staffing and tool decisions by measuring how many incidents are manual and automated.

- **Escalations among each tier:** Keep track of how many incidents are escalated from one level to another. In addition to staffing decisions, accurate workload tracking is used to make other decisions. For example, work on escalated incidents isn't attributed to the wrong team.

Microsoft SOC Modernization

Similarly, to other security disciplines, security operations are subject to the transformative effects of continuously evolving business models, attackers, and technology platforms.

Security operations are transforming as a result of the following trends:

- **Cloud platform coverage:** Cloud resources must be included in security operations' attack detection and response. For SecOps professionals, cloud resources are a new and rapidly evolving platform.

- **Shift to identity-centric security:** In addition to network-based tools, SecOps now must integrate endpoint, application, and identity tools. The reasons for this integration are as follows:

  - Identity attacks, including phishing, credential theft, password spray, and other attacks, are incorporated into attackers' arsenals, evading network-based detections reliably.

  - The utility of network detections is limited when assets of value, such as bring-your-own devices, spend some or all of their life cycle outside the network perimeter.

- **Internet of Things (IoT) and operational technology (OT) scope:** As part of their attack chain, adversaries actively target IoT and OT devices. A target might be a means to access or traverse an environment or the ultimate purpose of an attack.

- **Cloud processing of telemetry:** As cloud-based telemetry increases, security operations must be modernized. With classic methods and on-premises resources, this telemetry is difficult or impossible to process. Thus, SecOps embraces cloud services that provide massive-scale analytics, machine learning, and behavior analytics. By using these technologies, security operations can extract value quickly.

SOC MITRE ATT&CK

MITRE ATT&CK is a global knowledge base based on real-world adversary tactics and techniques observations. In the private sector, in the government, and in the cybersecurity product and service community, the ATT&CK knowledge base is used to develop specific threat models and methodologies.

By joining communities to develop more effective cybersecurity, MITRE fulfills its mission of creating a safer world. All individuals and organizations are welcome to use ATT&CK without charge.

Cyberattacks typically progress through several steps in the MITRE ATT&CK framework.

The following is MITRE's ATT&CK matrix for the enterprise to protect cloud-based resources, which includes tactics and techniques.

Reconnaissance

To plan future operations, the adversary gathers information.

An adversary may conduct reconnaissance by actively or passively gathering information to support targeting. Organizations, infrastructure, and staff/personnel of the victim may be included in this information. Adversaries can use this information to plan and execute initial access, scope and prioritize post-compromise objectives, or lead and execute reconnaissance in other stages of their life cycle.

Resource Development

The adversary is making attempts to establish resources supporting operations.

An adversary can create, purchase, compromise, or steal a resource. For example, it can be an infrastructure piece, an account, or a capability. In addition to initial access, these resources are also helpful in stealing code-signing certificates or buying domain names to evade defenses.

Initial Access

Attempts are being made to gain access to your network by the adversary.

The initial access method uses a variety of entry vectors to gain a foothold in a network. Attackers use spear phishing and exploit vulnerabilities in public-facing web servers to gain a foothold. As a result of initial access, you may retain access to external remote services, valid accounts, or limited access due to password changes.

Execution

The adversary is running malicious code.

A remote or local system can run adversary-controlled code through techniques used in the execution process. Malicious code often combines with other tactics to accomplish broader goals, such as exploring a network or stealing data. An adversary might run a PowerShell script using a remote access tool in remote system discovery.

Persistence

Maintaining a foothold is the adversary's goal.

Persistence refers to techniques adversaries use to maintain access to systems even after restarts, credential changes, and other interruptions. Persistent attacks can maintain a foothold on systems by replacing or hijacking legitimate code or adding startup code.

Privilege Escalation

The adversary is seeking higher-level permission.

An adversary can escalate privileges on a system or network using privilege escalation techniques. Adversaries can often use unprivileged access to explore a network but require elevated permissions to carry out their activities. System weaknesses, misconfigurations, and vulnerabilities are commonly exploited.

Defense Evasion

To avoid detection, the adversary is trying to hide.

In defense evasion, adversaries use techniques to avoid detection throughout the compromise process. In defense evasion, the software is uninstalled/disabled, or data is obfuscated/encrypted. Furthermore, adversaries abuse trusted methods, hiding and masquerading their malware. Techniques of other tactics are listed here when they also subvert defenses.

Credential Access

An adversary is trying to steal passwords and account names.

Passwords and account names are stolen through credential access techniques, and a keylogger or credential dump can be used to obtain credentials. By using legit credentials, adversaries can gain access to systems, be harder to detect, and create more accounts to achieve their goals.

Discovery

Your adversary is trying to figure out your environment.

A discovery technique involves gaining knowledge about the system and internal network from an adversary. Before deciding how to act, adversaries use these techniques to observe and orient themselves to the environment. Moreover, they enable adversaries to explore what they control and what is around their entry point to discover how it can benefit them. This post-compromise information gathering is often accomplished with native operating system tools.

Lateral Movement

Your adversary is trying to move through your environment.

In lateral movement, adversaries gain access to remote systems on a network and control them. Finding their target and gaining access to it is often the first step toward achieving their primary objective. To reach their goal, they often pivot through multiple systems and accounts. To accomplish lateral movement, adversaries might install their own remote access tools or utilize legitimate credentials with native network and operating system tools, which may be stealthier.

Collection

The adversary is gathering data of interest to the adversary.

Collections include techniques that adversaries may use to gather information and sources relevant to achieving the adversary's objectives. Once data has been collected, it is frequently stolen (exfiltrated). The most common sources of target data are drives, browsers, audio, video, and email; input from the keyboard and screen shots are two common ways of collecting data.

Command and Control

The adversary controls compromised systems through communication.

Adversaries may communicate with their controlled systems within a victim network using command-and-control techniques. To avoid detection, adversaries often try to mimic regular, expected traffic. Based on a victim's network structure and defenses, an adversary may establish command and control using varying stealth levels.

Exfiltration

Attempts are being made to steal data from the adversary.

Exfiltration refers to the theft of data from your network by adversaries. Data collected by adversaries is often packaged and removed to avoid detection. Encryption and compression can be used in this process. A target network typically transfers data over its command-and-control channel or an alternate channel to get data out. Furthermore, size limits may be imposed on transmissions.

Impact

The adversary manipulates, interrupts, or destroys your systems and data.

An adversary's impact is when they manipulate business and operational processes to disrupt availability or compromise integrity. Data can be destroyed or tampered with as a way of causing impact. The adversaries may alter business processes to benefit their goals even if they look fine. Adversaries could use these techniques to achieve their end goal or to cover up a breach of confidentiality.

Microsoft recommends adopting the following critical best practices to monitor system security and plan your incident response:

- Model application health by correlating security and audit events.
- Assess active threats by analyzing audit and security events.
- Respond to incidents using automated and manual procedures.
- Use a SIEM tool to track information security events.

Design a Logging and Auditing Strategy to Support Security Operations

With the advent of cloud computing, the role of the operations team has changed dramatically. Applications are no longer hosted on hardware and infrastructure managed by them. An application's operations are still crucial to its success. The operations team performs the following functions:

- Deploy
- Monitor

- Escalate
- Respond to an incident
- Audit

In cloud applications, robust logging and tracing are essential. Provide the operations team with the needed data and insight by involving them in the application's design and planning.

Microsoft recommends the following design considerations for logging and auditing alignment to enterprise cloud security strategy:

Make everything observable.   A solution's logs and traces provide instant insight into the system once deployed and running. A trace traces a system's path and helps pinpoint bottlenecks, performance issues, and failure points. Event logging records events such as changes in application state, errors, and exceptions. The secret to getting insight is to log about production environment. Otherwise, you will lose it just when you need it the most.

Tool for monitoring.   Application monitoring provides insight into an application's availability, performance, and system health, for example, monitoring whether SLAs are met continuously. The monitoring process should be conducted in real time during the system's normal operation so that the operations staff can react quickly to any problems. The goal of monitoring is to prevent problems from becoming critical before they occur.

Tool for root-cause analysis.   Root-cause analysis is the process of identifying underlying causes of failures that have already occurred.

Use distributed tracing.   Scalability, concurrency, and asynchrony are all addressed by distributed tracing systems. Cross-service correlation IDs should be included in traces. A single operation may involve calls to multiple application services, and the correlation ID helps identify the failure's cause.

Standardize logs and metrics.   Various services in your solution require log aggregation by your operations team. In this case, getting valuable information from each service is impossible or difficult if each uses its own logging format. Create a standard schema that includes fields such as correlation IDs, event names, IP addresses of senders, and so on. Individual services can create custom schemas incorporating additional fields into the base schema.

Automate management tasks.   Monitoring, provisioning, and deployment are included. Repeatability and error reduction can be achieved by automating a task.

Treat configuration as code.   You should check configuration files into a version control system so that you can track and roll back changes.

A cyber kill chain should be aligned with logging and auditing.   The Cyber Kill Chain, developed by Lockheed Martin (2022), describes how attackers find and exploit vulnerabilities online. An attacker uses Cyber Kill Chain steps to attack a target in cyberspace. Microsoft Cybersecurity Architects are responsible for defending a network. It can help you understand the stages of a cyberattack and how you can prevent or intercept it.

The Cyber Kill Chain consists of seven stages: reconnaissance, weaponization, delivery, exploitation, installation, command and control (C2C2), and action on objectives.

Overview of Azure Logging Capabilities

Security auditing and logging in Microsoft Azure can be configured to identify security gaps in policies and mechanisms. A cloud application has many moving parts, which makes it complex. Insights can be gained from logging data about your applications, and you can prevent future problems by troubleshooting past ones, ensuring maintainability or performance of an application, and making manual tasks more efficient by automating them.

The following types of logs are available in Microsoft Azure:

- **Control/management logs:** Describe how Azure Resource Manager performs CREATE, UPDATE, and DELETE operations.

- **Data plane logs:** The events that are raised as part of using Azure resources are provided. Among these types of logs are the Windows event system, the security and application logs in a VM, and the diagnostics logs configured through Azure Monitor.

- **Processed events:** Describe the events/alerts that have been analyzed. Examples of this type are Microsoft Defender for Cloud alerts, where subscriptions have been processed and analyzed and security alerts have been provided.

Table 2.1 lists the most important types of logs available in Microsoft Azure.

TABLE 2.1   Azure Logs

Log Category	Log Type	Integration	Usage
Azure resource logs	Azure Resource Manager resource usage data for the subscription	Azure Monitor	A resource's operations can be viewed in this report.
Activity logs	Events occurring in the control plane of Azure Resource Manager resources	REST API, Azure Monitor	Information about the operations performed on your subscription's resources.

Log Category	Log Type	Integration	Usage
Virtual machines and cloud services	Linux Syslog and Windows Event Log	Windows (using Microsoft Azure Diagnostics WAD storage) and Linux in Azure Monitor	Logging and system data are captured on virtual machines and transferred to a storage account of your choice.
Azure Active Directory reporting	A log and a report	Graph API	Provides information about users and group management activity, including sign-ins and system activity.
Network security group (NSG) flow logs	Outbound and inbound flows are displayed in JSON format per the rule	Azure Network Watcher	Network Security Groups display ingress and egress IP traffic information.
Azure Storage analytics	Statistical information about a storage account is provided by storage logging.	REST API or the client library	Analysis of usage trends, insight into trace requests, and diagnosis of storage account issues.
Application insight	Diagnostics, logs, and exceptions	REST API, Power BI	This service provides monitoring of web applications (Application Performance Monitoring) across multiple platforms.
Process data/ security alerts	Alerts generated by Microsoft Defender for Cloud, and alerts generated by Azure Monitor	REST APIs, JSON	Information and alerts related to security.

You can configure Azure's security auditing and logging options to identify security policies and mechanisms' gaps. In Table 2.2, you can learn how to collect, analyze, and generate security logs for various Azure services.

TABLE 2.2   Security Logs

Component	Services Overview
Dynamics CRM	Implement change auditing for your solution's sensitive entities.
Web Application	It is essential to enforce application auditing and logging.
	Make sure that logs are rotated and separated.
	Don't log sensitive user information in the application.
	Log files and audit logs should be restricted.
	Make sure user management events are logged.
	Protect the system from misuse with built-in defenses.
	Enable diagnostic logging for Azure App Service web apps.
Database	On SQL Server, ensure that login auditing is enabled.
	Detect threats in Azure SQL.
Azure Storage	Analyze Azure Storage access with Azure Storage Analytics.
Windows Communication Foundation	Ensure that adequate logs are maintained.
	Make sure sufficient measures are in place to handle audit failures.
Web API	On web APIs, ensure that auditing and logging are enforced.
IoT Field Gateway	Field gateway auditing and logging should be implemented appropriately.
IoT Cloud Gateway	Logging and auditing should be enforced on cloud gateways.

Develop Security Operations to Support a Hybrid or Multi-Cloud Environment

Microsoft Azure is a cloud-based platform that offers everything you need to build and operate your technology solutions and multiple private and public clouds if your business requires them.

Private clouds (on-premises infrastructure) and public clouds (computing services offered by third parties over the Internet) form hybrid clouds. A hybrid cloud allows data and applications to move seamlessly between two cloud environments. Businesses often choose hybrid cloud strategies to address various business needs, including regulatory requirements, maximization of on-premises technology investments, and latency reduction.

As hybrid cloud workloads become increasingly important, public cloud edge computing devices deliver computing power to the private cloud, closer to IoT devices, connected devices, and mobile consumer services. Devices can operate reliably, even offline, for extended periods by reducing latency by moving workloads to the edge.

As part of a heterogeneous computing environment, multi-cloud computing uses multiple cloud computing services from multiple cloud providers (including private and public clouds). Using various clouds allows for greater flexibility and risk mitigation. With this strategy, you can choose from cloud providers that best suit your needs or take advantage of the services offered by a specific provider in a particular location.

A hybrid or multi-cloud environment scenario illustrates how you can be successful during your organization's cloud adoption effort by following a standard hybrid and multi-cloud narrative. The scope of this general narrative is not limited to a single cloud adoption methodology but encompasses the entire adoption process.

There are many advantages to using a hybrid cloud platform for your organization: greater flexibility, control, scalability, more deployment options, global scale, integrated cross-platform security, unified compliance, and improved workload, operational, and cost efficiency across the enterprise. Hybrid cloud computing enables you to scale up your on-premises infrastructure seamlessly to the public cloud to handle any overflow without exposing your entire data library to a third-party data center. Using the public cloud for specific workloads provides flexibility and innovation while keeping highly sensitive data in your own data center for compliance.

As a result, mission-critical applications and data can be modernized and protected while scaling computing resources. Make fewer capital investments or free up local resources to handle more sensitive data by eliminating short-term spikes in demand. Instead of purchasing, programming, and maintaining additional resources and equipment that might be idle for long periods, cloud billing models allow your organization to pay only for resources it temporarily uses as it uses them.

Investments in off-site backup and disaster recovery infrastructure can also be eliminated. Using the public cloud is a compelling option when on-premises workloads and associated data aren't restricted from residing in a public cloud. The public cloud offers customers significant benefits, such as privacy and security, scalability on demand, ease of use, and speed of recovery.

The edge, multiple clouds, and on-premises infrastructure are all being utilized by organizations. Microsoft often hears from customers that they have four everyday needs.

- Customers want a single pane of glass that provides visibility into all existing and future infrastructure and applications.

- Organizations understand the need for a governance standard because cloud infrastructure and on-premises policies need to integrate better. Organizations understand the need for a governance standard.

- Different application development teams often operate in the organization, so there is a wide range of skills across on-premises and cloud. To unify development practices, customers want consistent interoperability between the two.

- Customers want to manage a security posture without modifying current operations heavily. Multi-clouds and cloud computing compound this challenge, decreasing trust and increasing apprehension.

You should consider cloud-native services if you are deploying hybrid and multi-cloud services. Cloud services include moving data and applications to the public cloud. Hybrid strategies can support customer operations by prohibiting public clouds in highly regulated industries, such as government infrastructure, healthcare, and financial services. Protecting internal and customer data on-premises may be necessary, depending on geography and data sovereignty regulations. On-premises data centers must be close to the source data because data latency is so sensitive, and Internet connectivity disruptions may be severe. Hybrid solutions can be deployed in on-premises data centers to provide cloud services, reduce management overhead, and offer pay-as-you-go cloud billing.

Integrated Operations for Hybrid and Multi-Cloud Environments

Use a single dashboard for hybrids, multi-cloud, and edge clouds.

Operating costs often increase when hybrid, multi-cloud, and edge deployments are used. In this case, the unexpected cost increase is caused by duplicated or disparate operations, where each cloud provider has its own working practices. Through standard governance and operations management practices, Microsoft Unified Operations maintain one set of tools and processes for managing each cloud provider. Through formal governance and operations management practices, Microsoft Unified Operations maintain one set of tools and techniques for managing each cloud provider.

Duplication of cloud platform utilities such as identity, governance, security, and operations tooling may cause the first increase in overhead costs in hybrid and multi-cloud strategies. Business challenges, such as staffing core functions or teams with diverse skills, could emerge in the longer term.

Because of hybrid and multi-cloud strategies, cloud costs are incorrectly perceived to be higher than on-premises costs. In a recent Forrester Consulting study commissioned by Microsoft, it was found that hybrid and multi-cloud strategies are significantly less expensive than on-premises infrastructure and staff. According to an Accenture and WSP study on energy and environment, cloud solutions increase energy efficiency for large deployments. Organizations save more than 30 percent on energy and carbon emissions by comparing cloud solutions with on-premises business applications. In small deployments, cloud solutions can reduce costs by more than 90 percent.

Organizations can use a simple approach to reduce risks, increase and decrease overhead costs, and efficiently staff core functions. Unified operations can minimize short-term duplication and long-term strain on your technology staff using hybrid, multi-cloud, and edge-cloud strategies.

Microsoft Azure–specific unified operations focus on inventorying, organizing, and governing IT assets on any infrastructure, anywhere. This centralized enterprise control plane can manage on-premises, multi-cloud, and edge environments.

Your organization will be able to innovate more, be more agile, and grow its business as a result of this implementation by integrating hybrid and multi-cloud strategies. Organizations can achieve consistent management and governance by extending cloud controls to on-premises, multi-cloud, and the edge. With a hybrid and multi-cloud strategy, your organization can grow, innovate, and become more agile. Hybrid, multi-cloud, and edge deployments can be controlled with an extension (or gateway).

Figure 2.2 illustrates how the various components of unified operations are interconnected.

For more information, refer to the following:

learn.microsoft.com/en-us/azure/cloud-adoption-framework/scenarios/hybrid/unified-operations

Customer Processes

One of the primary objectives for unified operations primary objectives is ensuring consistency across deployments. Cloud providers can achieve 100 percent feature parity only across hybrid clouds, multi-cloud, or edge deployments. But the provider should be able to offer baseline feature sets shared among all implementations so that your governance and operations management processes stay uniform.

The most common requirement of customers is the ability to deliver consistency within their defined governance and operations management processes. Your unified operations solution must scale to fulfill these standard processes to meet long-term requirements.

The following is the list of tasks performed in common governance processes:

- **Cost management:** Identify and mitigate cloud-based IT risks and analyze, manage, and optimize costs.

- **Security baseline:** Incorporate authentication and authorization across user identities and guide identifying and mitigating potential identity-related business risks.

- **Resource consistency:** Organize, configure, and identify potential business risks and provide mitigation guidance for them.

- **Identity baseline:** Provide identification and mitigation guidance for potential identity-related business risks and enforce authentication and authorization across user identities.

- **Deployment acceleration:** Implement templates, automation, and pipelines to ensure compliant, consistent, and repeatable resource deployments and configurations (for deployments, configuration alignments, and reusable assets).

FIGURE 2.2 Microsoft unified operations

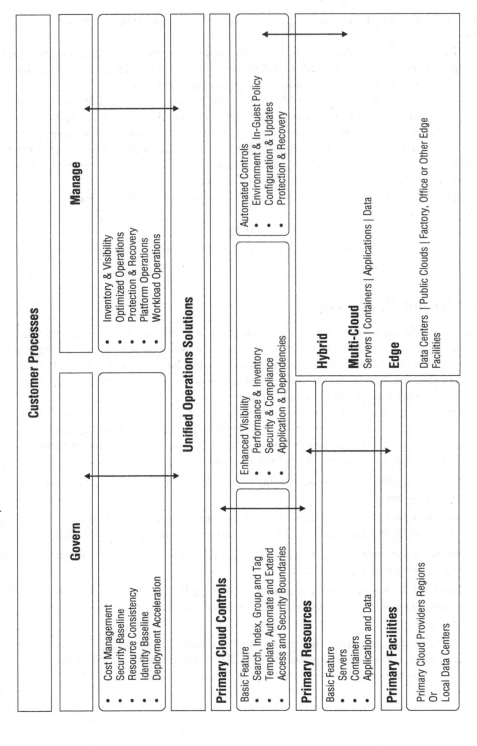

The following is the list of tasks performed in common operations management processes:

- **Inventory and visibility:** Track and report on all assets in enterprise-grade environments.
- **Optimized operations:** Inconsistencies in patching or configuration drift can cause business interruptions if not monitored, patched, and optimized.
- **Protection and recovery:** Backing up, ensuring business continuity, and planning for disaster recovery can reduce the duration and impact of unavoidable outages.
- **Platform operations:** Managing standard technologies like SQL databases, Azure virtual desktops, and SAP (for medium- to high-critical workloads).
- **Workload operations:** Operational excellence (for mission-critical workloads) for specialized operations.

Throughout platform and workload operations, iterative processes are used to improve system design, automate remediation, scale changes, and continuously improve systems' design, automation, and scale.

A unified operations solution should support hybrid, multi-cloud, and edge deployments and the required technical capabilities and management tools.

Primary Cloud Controls

To facilitate or automate customer processes typically required in the cloud, your primary cloud platform should include the essential features.

Delivering cloud adoption at scale requires all these essential features:

- Expand visibility and management by searching, indexing, grouping, and tagging all deployed assets.
- Make consistent deployments easier by automating, templating, and extending tooling.
- Establish security and access boundaries to protect deployed assets.

The following enhanced features are likely to be required to operate a hybrid and multi-cloud environment at scale:

- Reports on inventory and performance
- Automated security and compliance audits
- Application and dependency tracking and reporting

Modernize and optimize your operations by automating your environment.

- Policy and environment for guests
- Updating and configuring
- Providing protection and recovery

These features are likely already included in your primary cloud provider's control set. Many other features and automated processes will probably be included in that set of controls. Those features should be available in your unified operations solution across hybrid, multi-cloud, and edge.

Hybrid, Multi-Cloud Gateway, and Enterprise Control Plane

An extension or gateway can be configured to extend the control of your primary cloud. Developing your rules to external resources ensures visibility across disparate, heterogeneous environments and creates one control plane.

The Azure Arc extension is part of Microsoft's cloud platforms. As you govern your Azure cloud, Azure Arc extends those controls and processes to other public and private clouds and the edge. In heterogeneous on-premises, multi-cloud, and edge environments, these cloud controls enable a unified operations approach to consistent governance and operations management processes.

With Azure Resource Manager (ARM), Azure's operating system, you can extend its reach through unified operations. In ARM, scattered resources are brought into Azure and represented. With unified functions, Azure's reach and capabilities can be extended to any infrastructure, enabling hybrid and multi-cloud solutions.

Using a unified operations approach, any environment can be managed, governed, and secured anywhere while ensuring compliance, visibility, and operations are all centralized. Azure Arc–enabled services allow you to deploy Azure services anywhere, faster, and more consistently. From deployment to monitoring, you can build cloud applications from anywhere, at scale.

With hybrid and multi-cloud scenarios, you can support traditional applications, cloud-native applications, and distributed edge applications. With hybrid and multi-cloud scenarios, you can support the following:

- Streamlined management
- A faster development process for applications
- Consistent Azure experiences

Across your entire IT estate, these scenarios can apply to any infrastructure.

Hybrid and multi-cloud infrastructures benefit from a central Azure control plane that is standardized, interoperable, and compliant.

- Ensures consistent visibility and management of operations and governance
- Enhances productivity
- Achieves risk reduction
- Allows organizations to adopt and migrate to cloud technologies and practices more quickly

Azure Security Operation Services

Data, applications, and other assets in Microsoft Azure can be protected using the services, controls, and features of Azure security operations. Through its unique capabilities, Microsoft has gained knowledge incorporated into the framework. A few of these capabilities include the Microsoft Security Development Lifecycle (SDL), Microsoft Security Response Center, and a deep understanding of cybersecurity threats.

IT operations teams manage hybrid and multi-cloud environments, including data center infrastructure, applications, and data, as well as their security and stability. As IT environments become increasingly complex, organizations must often integrate data from multiple security and management systems to gain security insights.

Managing and protecting your on-premises and cloud infrastructure is accessible with Microsoft Azure Monitor logs. The Azure services listed next provide its core functionality. On-premises and cloud infrastructure can be managed and protected with Azure's multiple benefits. Each service offers a specific management function, and different management scenarios can be achieved by combining services.

In the Microsoft Azure cloud platform, Microsoft operational security covers the following services, and unified operations architectures also require the following management services:

- **Azure Monitor:** Azure Monitor collects managed data sources, and centralized data stores are used to store them. Events, performance data, or custom data provided through APIs can be included. Data can be analyzed, alerted, and exported after it is collected.

- **Azure Automation:** Azure Automation automates manual, long-running, error-prone, and frequently repeated tasks in a cloud and enterprise environment. In addition to saving time, it improves the reliability of administrative tasks.

- **Azure Backup:** You can back up (or protect) and restore your Azure data using Azure Backup. A cloud-based backup solution that's reliable, secure, and cost-effective replaces existing on-premises or off-site backup solutions.

- **Azure Site Recovery:** In Azure Site Recovery, virtual and physical machines on-premises are replicated to Azure or a secondary site if the primary site cannot be reached so that users can keep working.

- **Azure Active Directory:** The Azure Active Directory (Azure AD) is a comprehensive identity service that offers the following features:

  - Manages cloud and hybrid environments' identity and access.

  - Manages access and provides single sign-on (SSO) and reports. It works with a broad ecosystem of security solutions to detect threats that would otherwise go undetected.

  - Provides integrated access management for thousands of Azure Marketplace applications, including Salesforce, Google Apps, Box, and Concur.

- **Microsoft Defender for Cloud:** You can see (and control) the security of Azure resources with Microsoft Defender for Cloud to prevent, detect, and respond to threats. With it, you can manage your subscriptions' security policies and monitor your security. It helps detect threats that might otherwise go unnoticed and works with a broad ecosystem of security solutions.

Using Microsoft Sentinel and Defender for Cloud to Monitor Hybrid Security

Monitoring is one of the most important aspects of hybrid security. An architecture built on good hybrid monitoring practices should be resilient in hybrid and multi-cloud environments to provide log insights about attacks and confidentiality, integrity, and availability.

Azure Monitor resources, Azure VMs, and even VMs hosted by other cloud providers can be monitored by Microsoft Defender for Cloud.

Data collection can be simplified with Microsoft Sentinel across different sources, including Azure, on-premises solutions, and clouds with built-in connectors. Data is collected at cloud scale by Microsoft Sentinel—across all users, devices, applications, and infrastructure, including on-premises and in multiple clouds.

Figure 2.3 illustrates architecture hybrid security using Microsoft Defender for Cloud and Microsoft Sentinel to monitor on-premises and Azure operating system workloads' security configurations and telemetry.

FIGURE 2.3 References architecture for Microsoft Sentinel and Defender for Cloud used to monitor hybrid security

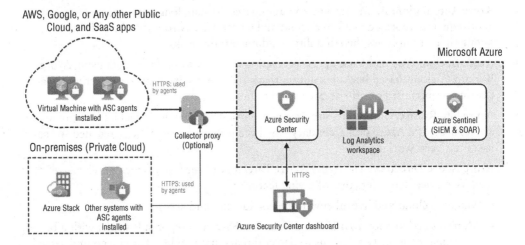

This architecture is applicable to the following use cases:

- Getting the most out of your Azure workloads by integrating on-premises security and telemetry monitoring

- Integrating Microsoft Defender for Cloud with Azure Stack

- Microsoft Sentinel and Microsoft Defender for Cloud integration

In this architecture, the workflow is as follows:

- **Microsoft Defender for Cloud:** Azure subscribers can access this advanced, unified security-management platform. With Defender for Cloud, you can protect cloud workloads and manage cloud security postures. A workload-centric security protection solution is typically an agent-based solution. Including Windows and Linux virtual machines, containers, databases, and the Internet of Things (IoT), Microsoft Defender for Cloud provides threat protection for Azure workloads, both on-premises workloads and workloads in other clouds. Azure Virtual Machine automatically deploys the Log Analytics agent when activated. Windows and Linux servers and virtual machines can be deployed by script, or your organization's deployment tool, such as Microsoft Endpoint Protection Manager, can be used. Once Defender for Cloud is installed, it assesses the security state of all your virtual machines, networks, applications, and data.

- **Microsoft Sentinel:** A cloud-native SIEM solution based on cloud-native technology detects, hunts, and prevents threats across your enterprise with advanced AI, security analytics, and threat hunting.

- **Azure Stack:** Azure Stack allows you to extend Azure services and capabilities to any area of your choice, from data centers to edge locations. Azure Stack is usually integrated with four to sixteen racks of server hardware, delivered directly to your data center by trusted hardware vendors.

- **Azure Monitor:** Monitoring telemetry can be gathered from various on-premises and Azure monitoring sources, including Microsoft Defender for Cloud and Azure Automation.

- **Log Analytics workspace:** Azure Monitor stores log data, whereas Log Analytics workspaces contain data and configuration information.

- **Log Analytics agent:** This scenario uses the Microsoft Operations Management Suite (OMS) Gateway to collect monitoring data from Azure guest operating systems and VM workloads.

- **On-premises network:** An HTTPS egress firewall is configured for defined systems.

- **On-premises Windows and Linux systems:** Install the Log Analytics Agent on a system.

- **Azure Windows and Linux VMs:** Microsoft Defender for Cloud monitoring agents is installed on systems.

When you design, consider scalability, manageability, security, and cost optimization following Azure's Well-Architected Framework.

The following are the requirements for integrating Microsoft Sentinel with Microsoft Defender for Cloud:

- It is necessary to have a Microsoft Azure subscription.
- Microsoft Defender for Cloud is a requirement.
- Microsoft Sentinel is a paid service, and your workspace should be part of a resource group where you have contributor or reader permissions.

The following is the key consideration:

- Activating Microsoft Defender for Cloud does not create a Log Analytics workspace by default, because custom workspaces retain data according to their pricing.

Design a Strategy for SIEM and SOAR

With proactive and reactive detection tactics, a SOC administrator can detect, investigate, remediate, and hunt threats; use threat intelligence; understand known vulnerabilities; consult experts; and block threats across all six pillars. By integrating these tools into a single workflow, SOC analysts can provide a seamless experience that enhances their effectiveness.

Microsoft Sentinel from Azure is a scalable, cloud-native solution that provides the following:

- Security information and event management
- Security orchestration, automation, and response

Using Microsoft Sentinel, you can detect attacks, gain insight into threats, take proactive steps to counter them, and monitor them intelligently across the enterprise.

Azure services, such as Log Analytics and Logic Apps, are natively incorporated into Microsoft Sentinel. Microsoft Sentinel enhances intelligence-driven investigations and detection, and it delivers Microsoft's threat intelligence stream and enables an organization to bring its own threat intelligence.

Security operation centers often use SIEM and SOAR technologies to collect, detect, investigate, and respond to threats. Microsoft's SIEM-as-a-service offering, Microsoft Sentinel, collects data from Microsoft Defender for Identity and third-party sources.

Providing context-aware protection, detection, and response across all Microsoft 365 components, Microsoft 365 Defender is an essential element of Microsoft Sentinel. To protect endpoints, collaboration tools, identities, and applications, Microsoft 365 customers must be context-aware and coordinated.

Microsoft customers can maximize their focus by utilizing this hierarchy. With its context awareness and automated remediation, Microsoft 365 Defender can detect and stop a wide range of threats without increasing alert fatigue for SOC personnel already overloaded. In Microsoft 365 Defender, advanced hunting focuses on several key attack points by considering the context of the hunt. Microsoft Sentinel also provides the ability to gain visibility across the entire ecosystem while minimizing operator cognitive load in a heterogeneous environment.

Microsoft recommends focusing on the following deployment objectives when implementing an end-to-end Zero Trust framework:

- Ensure visibility using Microsoft Defender.
- Automate the process.
- Set up additional protection and detection controls.

To provide a centralized incident investigation and response platform, it is essential to connect Microsoft 365 Defender, other data connectors, and relevant third-party products to Microsoft Sentinel to gain visibility into incidents resulting from deploying a Zero Trust model. The data connection process, analytics, and incident activation can be integrated to create workbooks that visualize data over time.

It is possible to enrich Microsoft Sentinel by ingesting threat intelligence data in addition to machine learning and fusion analytics, which are provided out of the box.

You can enhance your visibility and ability to orchestrate responses by adding additional controls to Microsoft 365 Defender and Sentinel.

Attack surfaces are all the places your organization is vulnerable to cyberthreats and attacks. You can reduce your attack surfaces by using Defender for Endpoint.

Attack surface reduction controls designate one such opportunity. By blocking certain malware-related activities, these protective controls can minimize adversaries' likelihood of leveraging these techniques earlier in the attack cycle.

Security Operations Center Best Practices for SIEM and SOAR

Based on current Azure platform capabilities and feature settings, the following are operational best practices for protecting data, applications, and other Azure assets.

Receive Microsoft Incident Notifications

In the event that Azure resources are compromised, security operations teams should receive Microsoft Azure incident notifications. This allows them to respond quickly and remediate potential security risks.

The admin contact information for the Azure enrollment portal, which includes an email address and phone number, is used to notify security operations.

Keep an Eye Out for Unexpected Behavior Changes in Storage Services

Cloud environments are more complex than traditional environments for diagnosing and troubleshooting distributed applications. You can deploy applications on-premises, in a PaaS or IaaS environment, on a mobile device, or in a combination of these environments. An application's network traffic can traverse public and private networks using multiple storage technologies.

Watch for any unexpected changes in the behavior of application storage services (such as slower response times). You can analyze a problem in depth by logging more detailed data. An application's root cause can be determined by monitoring and logging diagnostics information. Troubleshoot the problem and choose the proper action plan once it has been identified.

Microsoft recommends using Azure Storage Analytics to analyze issues with storage accounts, track demand, and examine usage trends.

Prevent, Detect, and Respond to Threats

The following are best practices for preventing, detecting, and responding to threats:

- Increase your SIEM's speed and scalability by using a cloud-based SIEM. Compare Microsoft Sentinel's features and capabilities with your existing on-premises SIEM tool. If your organization's SIEM requirements are met, Microsoft Sentinel may be a good choice for you.

- Check the Azure Secure score to see recommendations from Azure policies and initiatives built into Microsoft Defender for Cloud to prioritize investigating the most severe security vulnerabilities. These recommendations include security updates, endpoint protection, encryption, configurations, missing WAF, Internet-connected virtual machines, and many others.

- Discover and prioritize potential security issues, and monitor machines, networks, storage, data services, and applications.

- Simplify the SIEM by integrating Defender for Cloud alerts. An organization with a SIEM tool typically uses it to clear security alerts that require analyst attention. Defender for Cloud publishes processed events to the Azure Activity Log, one of the logs available through Azure Monitor.

- You can collect and export Azure logs with your SIEM tool using Azure Monitor. Online log retention is limited, and this practice is essential for security incident investigation.

- Integrating Microsoft Defender for Endpoint through a Defender for Cloud security policy will speed up investigation and hunting processes and reduce false positives.

Monitor End-to-End Scenario-Based Network Monitoring

A network can be built in Azure by combining network resources such as virtual networks, ExpressRoute, Application Gateway, and load balancers. All network resources can be monitored.

Regional Azure Network Watcher services are available. Its diagnostic and visualization tools monitor and diagnose network conditions within and from Azure.

Monitoring a network can be done using the following tools and best practices:

- Network Watcher automates remote network monitoring with packet capture. Diagnose networking issues without logging into your VMs. Get access to real-time performance information at the packet level by setting alerts. It is possible to make a more accurate diagnosis when issues are observed by investigating them in detail.

- Use network security group flow logs to gain insight into network traffic patterns. A network security profile can be monitored, audited, and confirmed using the information inflow logs.

- Network Watcher is capable of diagnosing VPN connectivity issues. You can recognize the problem and use detailed logs to investigate further.

Monitor Azure AD Risk Reports

Most security breaches occur due to attackers stealing user identities, and it is not easy to discover compromised identities. Machine learning algorithms and heuristics are used by Azure AD to detect suspicious user actions. A record called *risk detection* is kept for each suspicious activity that is detected, and security reports for Azure AD record risk detections.

- Monitor for suspicious actions related to your user accounts.

- Monitor for users at risk and risky sign-ins using Azure AD security reports.

 Security operations teams can address threats more effectively and efficiently with Microsoft 365 Defender's automated investigation and response (AIR) capabilities. It works across your email, devices, content, and identities.

Evaluate Security Workflows

The incident response process is part of every security program. In addition to notifying relevant stakeholders, a change management process may be launched, and specific remediation steps may be applied. You should automate as many steps as possible of those procedures. By automating, overhead is reduced. Also, it ensures that the process steps are done quickly, consistently, and under your predefined requirements, thereby improving your security.

Microsoft Best Practices for Incident Response

According to Microsoft's recommendations, technical and operations perspectives can be effectively addressed when responding to incidents.

Technically, the incident response should aim to achieve the following goals:

- Find out how many persistence mechanisms the adversary uses. Most adversaries use multiple persistence mechanisms.

- Determine the purpose of the attack. Persistent attackers frequently return for their purpose (data/systems) in a future attack.

The following are some goals for security operations (SecOps) aspects of incident response:

- Remain focused. Keep your attention on critical business data, customer impact, and remediation preparation.

- Coordinate operations and clarify roles. Assure that the technical, legal, and communications teams communicate.

- Keep your business perspective. You should always consider the impact of adversary actions and your response actions on your business operations.

Microsoft Best Practices for Recovery

Using these recommendations, you can effectively recover from incidents from both a technical and operational standpoint. Here are some technical goals to consider when recovering from an incident:

- Response scope should be limited so that recovery can be executed within 24 hours or less. Prepare for contingencies and corrective actions over the weekend.

- Refrain from making large and complex security system investments or replacing anti-malware solutions until the recovery operation is complete. Distractions are anything that does not directly affect the current recovery operation.

During recovery from an incident, the following goals should be considered:

- **Create a clear plan with a limited scope:** Work closely with your technical teams to develop a clear plan. Limiting scope expansion and taking on additional tasks when planning based on adversary activity is essential.

- **Establish clear ownership of the recovery plans:** Recovery operations involve many people doing multiple tasks at once, so designate a project lead to ensure that all the crisis team members are on the same page and know what to do.

- **Communicate with stakeholders:** Provide timely updates and manage expectations for organizational stakeholders with the help of communications teams.

Azure Workflow Automation Uses a Few Key Technologies

Azure workflow automation can be achieved using a few key technologies.

- Azure Logic Apps can automate workflows that integrate your apps, data, services, and systems. This platform can develop business-to-business (B2B) integration solutions quickly. Azure Logic Apps simplify the process of connecting legacy, modern, and cutting-edge systems across cloud, on-premises, and hybrid environments.

- Logic Apps can be triggered by Microsoft Defender for Cloud's workflow automation feature when security alerts, recommendations, and regulatory compliance changes are made.

- Azure Logic Apps and the Microsoft Graph Security connector let you automate integrating Microsoft security products, services, and partners into your app to detect, protect, and respond to threats. You can create playbooks in Microsoft Defender for Cloud that monitor and manage Microsoft Graph Security entities.

- Microsoft Sentinel provides both playbooks and automation rules. Automation rules can be used to help triage incidents by changing incident attributes or running playbooks. Microsoft Sentinel can run a playbook responding to an alert or an incident.

Microsoft 365 Defender, if your organization uses it, enables automated investigation and response (AIR). Your security operations team may take remediation actions automatically or after approval, depending on how AIR capabilities are configured. Actions are listed in the Action Center, whether pending or completed. Security operations teams can benefit from AIR features by doing the following:

- Analyzing threats and determining whether they need to be addressed
- Taking any remedial action that needs to be taken (or is recommended)
- Identifying whether and what other investigations should be conducted
- Repeating the process for other alerts as needed

Create automated workflows to integrate Microsoft security products and services and partner with Azure Logic Apps and the Microsoft Graph Security connector.

You can use actions in your logic app's workflow to get responses from Microsoft Graph Security and make that output available to other workflow actions once they are deployed. In addition, you can use the output from the Microsoft Graph Security connector actions in other workflows.

Evaluate a Security Operations Strategy for the Incident Management Life Cycle

NIST describes the incident response as "the mitigation of violations of security policies and recommended practices."

SOCs kick into high gear during the incident response (IR) to contain, eradicate, and recover from attacks—before data is lost or a business is irreparably harmed. A multistep process requires synchronized teamwork to restore the business to normal operations after an incident. To address security incidents, security response teams and service teams should work together.

Customer data or personal data are impacted by a security incident when they are accidentally or unlawfully destroyed, lost, altered, disclosed, or accessed. A security incident, for instance, would occur if unauthorized access to infrastructure or exfiltration of customer data were to occur; compliance events, on the other hand, would not constitute a security incident.

An organization's services and customer data should be protected quickly and efficiently whenever a security incident occurs. There should be an effective strategy for efficiently investigating, containing, and removing security threats.

Employees should receive annual training on recognizing and reporting potential security incidents, as well as automated security monitoring and alerting. The service-specific security response teams should be contacted if any suspicious activity is detected by employees, customers, or security monitoring tools. Service operations teams, including security teams, should maintain a deep on-call rotation so that resources are available 24/7/365 for incident response. Many companies are now outsourcing managed service-specific response capabilities.

An investigation, containment, eradication, and recovery process should be initiated when a suspicious activity has been detected. As part of their investigation, these teams should determine the scope of the potential incident, including any impact on customers or customer data. A security response team should be able to work with impacted service teams to create a plan to contain the threat and minimize its impact, eradicate the threat from the environment, and ultimately restore systems to a known secure state based on this analysis.

Service teams should implement lessons learned after an incident has been resolved so that future incidents can be prevented, detected, and responded to better. A complete postmortem inquiry should be carried out after a security incident, mainly if it affects customers or results in a data breach. Post-mortems should be designed to identify technical lapses, procedural failures, manual errors, and other process flaws that might have contributed to the incident.

Improvements identified during the post-mortem should be implemented with coordination from security response teams to prevent future incidents and improve detection and response capabilities.

- **Preparation:** This refers to the organizational practices necessary to respond, such as tools, processes, competencies, and readiness.

- **Detection and analysis:** In a production environment, this activity involves detecting a security incident and analyzing all events to verify its authenticity.

- **Containment, eradication, and recovery:** Based on the analysis done in the previous phase, this refers to the actions needed to contain the security incident. Recovery from a security incident may also require additional analysis during this phase.

- **Post-incident activity:** The process of analyzing security incidents post-mortem after they have been recovered. The preparation or detection and analysis phases are reviewed to determine if any changes need to be made.

Preparation

A prepared response facilitates rapid response to incidents and may even prevent them from occurring. To prepare for security incidents, Azure dedicates a significant number of resources.

Security incidents and response procedures appropriate to each employee's role should be taught to employees using Azure services. Training should be provided to every employee upon joining and annually after that. For all employees to understand the organization's approach to security upon completion of training, the following should be covered:

- An overview of security incidents

- Employees being responsible for reporting security incidents

- What to do if you suspect a security breach

- Identifying security incidents and responding to them

- Concerns regarding privacy, particularly the privacy of customers

- What to do if you have questions about security or privacy, as well as who to contact for escalation

- Other relevant security areas (if necessary)

Security refresher training should be provided annually to the appropriate employees. Refresher training consists of the following topics:

- Standard operating procedures that have been modified in the past year

- Security incidents that should be reported by everyone and how they should be reported

- What you need to know about security and privacy and how to get in touch with escalation

Every year, you may need to focus on other new security topics.

Detection and Analysis

Organizations should centralize audit logging and analysis to detect anomalous or suspicious activity. Creating a central, consolidated database for Azure log files would be beneficial. Security response teams can monitor the environment comprehensively and correlate log entries from different services through centralized log analysis.

In addition to antivirus and antimalware suites, network-based and host-based intrusion detection systems, and manual detection methods, there should be centrally managed detection tools.

The security response team is the orchestrator of the security incident response process when a potential incident is detected with a preliminary severity rating. A security incident should be detected and the severity level adjusted, if necessary, by the security response team based on the detection indicators. Security response should initiate a security notification process if the team discovers any disclosure, modification, or destruction of data.

As part of the investigation, the security response team should record all information relevant to the incident. Information pertinent to a specific case may include the following:

- The incident, in a nutshell

- Impact and severity of the incident based on its potential

- A list of all the indicators that led to the discovery of the incident

- A list of any related incidents

- A record of the security response team's actions, as well as those of any associated service teams

- Any evidence gathered as part of the incident response process

- Actions and next steps recommended

Containment, Eradication, and Recovery

For security incidents to be minimized and threats removed from the environment, an appropriate containment and recovery plan should be developed based on the analysis performed by the security response team. Security response should support relevant service teams in implementing the program to ensure the threat is successfully eliminated and the impacted services are fully recovered.

Containment

Data, systems, and applications must be protected from harm through containment. This phase involves determining the impact of the security incident and preventing further damage to affected service teams. An automated response solution within Azure should assist the group in containing the incident.

As part of the eradication and recovery plan, all impacted services and tenants should be included in the data collection and analysis throughout the containment phase. Eradication and recovery are possible only after tracing all affected services successfully.

Eradication

To achieve high levels of confidence, a security incident's root cause must be eliminated. Eradication involves two goals: evicting the adversary from the environment and mitigating any vulnerabilities that allowed the adversary to enter.

To evict the adversary and mitigate vulnerabilities, eradication steps are applied based on the analysis from the previous incident response phase. To ensure that the threat is successfully removed from the environment, the security response team should coordinate with the affected service teams. Prior to recovery, the underlying causes must be addressed and the threat removed.

Recovery

As soon as the security response team is confident that the adversary has been expelled and all known vulnerabilities have been fixed, the security response team should work with affected service teams to initiate recovery. When recovered, affected services are restored to a known secure configuration. The following are the steps in the recovery process:

1. The last known good state of the service should be identified.

2. This state can be restored from backups.

3. As soon as the restored state is confirmed, the vulnerabilities that contributed to the incident are mitigated.

The recovery process includes enhanced detection controls to ensure that the recovery plan has been executed successfully and that no signs of breach remain. Additional detection controls include network-level monitoring, targeted alerting, and increased security team vigilance for critical resources. By monitoring the environment, the organization can ensure the adversary cannot re-enter, and eradication will be successful.

Post-Incident Activity

A full incident post-mortem should be conducted after a security incident is resolved, especially if it has affected customers or resulted in a data breach; the post-mortem process should be designed to identify technical lapses, procedural failures, manual errors, and other process flaws that might have contributed to or been identified during the incident response process. As part of the process, the following should be included:

- Identify opportunities for improving the security incident response process or system security by investigation and analyzing the root cause.

- Identify process, training, or technology improvement opportunities with product group subject-matter experts and security and privacy experts.

- New automated monitoring and detection mechanisms will be implemented to discover future issues.

Continuous Improvement

The security response team should implement lessons learned from the security incident to prevent future security incidents and improve detection and response capabilities. The efficiencies and effectiveness of incident response depend on continuous improvement. To defend organizations and their customers from evolving threats, post-incident activities ensure that lessons learned are successfully implemented across the enterprise.

Following Microsoft's standard SDL, any findings are recorded as work items or bugs for product teams to address, and these items are assigned to the appropriate owner teams. In senior management's monthly security incident review meetings, the results of the post-mortem are discussed.

Evaluate a Security Operations Strategy for Sharing Technical Threat Intelligence

An organization's threat intelligence team provides context and insights using a threat intelligence platform (TIP). Many different facets could be included in these insights, such as the following:

- How to respond to active incidents with technical research during the incident

- The study of attacker groups, attack trends, high-profile attacks, and emerging techniques in a proactive manner

- Analyses, research, and insights to guide priorities and processes in the business and security technical teams

A large, diverse set of threat intelligence data needs to be applied to your processes and tools to succeed, and Microsoft does both.

You must ensure that the data Microsoft collects from various sources is used only in ways agreed upon by our customers by passing it through a strict privacy/compliance boundary. It is a responsibility that Microsoft takes seriously.

The following are the sources of data:

- Specialized Microsoft security products

- Black market insights (criminal forums)

- Insights from Microsoft's incident response engagements

Disinformation, nation-states, ransomware, IoT, and operational technology (OT) security are some critical topics that Microsoft researches and helps solve. The Microsoft Digital Defense Report (MDDR) posts learnings and actionable recommendations.

The following are some notable parts of this process:

- In the data collection and analysis phase, the data is normalized, various analytics are applied (listed) to identify relevant security insights and findings, and APIs are published.

- In the data integration phase, Microsoft's security capabilities access the data to provide findings, context, and insights related to that capability. These findings are then automatically fed into other Microsoft products to enrich them.

- In addition to AI, human teams constantly use this intelligence to hunt for adversaries in Azure, Office 365, Microsoft IT, and Microsoft 365 Defender. Also, these teams are developing, tuning, and validating new analytics to improve detection.

Cybersecurity attacks are characterized by multiple complex malicious events, attributes, and contexts. Making the distinction between suspicious and nonsuspicious activities is a challenging task. When determining whether an observed behavior is suspicious, knowing known attributes and abnormal activities specific to your industry is crucial.

The Microsoft network provides organizations with access to various signals that can be used to collect cyberthreat intelligence. Cyberthreat intelligence can be obtained from many sources. An organization's security investigations may collect local intelligence through its open-source data feeds, threat intelligence-sharing communities, commercial intelligence feeds, and commercial intelligence feeds. Every second, Microsoft Intelligent Security Graph adds hundreds of gigabytes of data.

The following are the sources of this anonymized data:

- The Microsoft data center network spans the globe with more than 100 data centers.

- Threats faced by over 1 billion PCs updated by Windows Update each month.

- Microsoft conducts extensive research through Microsoft's Digital Crime Unit and Cybersecurity Defense Operations Center and partner with industry and law enforcement to collect external data points.

Threat intelligence in Azure provides monitoring insight from the various sources, helping to mitigate the threats with the help of the following:

- It utilizes billions of signals across the Microsoft network (signals mean information traffic).

- Machine learning and artificial intelligence are used.
- It integrates multiple data across different security products to address different attack scenarios.

Using the Intelligent Security Graph and other third-party feeds, Microsoft uses Windows, Azure, and Microsoft 365 to obtain signals. Microsoft integrates these signals for security services on one platform to communicate with security services on another. Any threat that is seen in Windows is automatically and quickly added to Azure's view of threats as a result. This design provides deep insight into the evolving cyberthreat landscape.

Microsoft Sentinel's Threat Intelligence

A SIEM solution such as Microsoft Sentinel uses threat indicators, otherwise known as *indicators of compromise* (IoCs), as the most common form of cyberthreat intelligence (CTI). A threat indicator identifies observed artifacts, such as URLs, file hashes, or IP addresses, with known threats, such as phishing, botnets, or malware. To assist security investigators in determining how to respond to malicious activity observed in your environment, Microsoft Sentinel provides threat indicators to assess.

The following activities are used to integrate threat intelligence (TI) into Microsoft Sentinel:

- By enabling data connectors to various TI platforms and feeds, threat intelligence can be imported into Microsoft Sentinel.
- The Microsoft Sentinel threat intelligence page and logs allow you to view and manage the imported threat intelligence.
- Detect threats and generate security alerts and incidents based on threat intelligence imported into built-in Analytics rule templates.
- The threat intelligence workbook in Microsoft Sentinel allows you to visualize essential information about your imported threat intelligence.

Defender for Endpoint's Threat Intelligence

You can track possible attack activities in your organization using Microsoft 365 Defender by creating custom threat alerts. You can flag suspicious events to gather clues and stop an attack chain by flagging suspicious events. Unlike generic threat alerts, these alerts will appear only within your organization and will flag only the events you have set up to track.

Knowing the concepts behind alert definitions and IoCs is essential before creating custom threat alerts.

Alert Definitions

Alert definitions are contextual attributes that can collectively identify early clues on a possible cybersecurity attack. These indicators are typically a combination of activities and characteristics, that an attacker took actions to achieve the objective of an attack successfully.

Monitoring these combinations of attributes is critical in gaining a vantage point against attacks. Monitoring based on these indicators can help interfere with the chain of events before an attacker's objective is reached.

Indicators of Compromise

IoC refers to known malicious events that indicate a network or device has already been compromised. IoCs are often visible after an attack has been carried out and the objective, such as exfiltration, has been achieved. In contrast to alert definitions, these indicators are considered evidence of a breach, and forensic investigations require them to be tracked. While it cannot intervene in the attack chain, the collection of these indicators can aid in the creation of better defenses for future attacks.

Relationship Between Alert Definitions and IoCs

In Microsoft 365 Defender and Microsoft Defender for Endpoint, alert definitions are containers for IoCs and define the alert, including the metadata raised for a specific IoC match. In addition to identifying signals, alert definitions include a description, name, severity, and attack description.

Microsoft 365 Defender defines the concrete detection logic based on an IoC's type, value, and action and how it's displayed in an alert.

Defender for IoT's Threat Intelligence

IoT and operations technology (OT) devices, vulnerabilities, and threats are identified and managed through a central interface with Microsoft Defender for IoT.

Microsoft Defender for IoT comes with native threat intelligence capabilities using threat intelligence packages, and it can be deployed in Azure-connected environments, hybrid environments, or on-premises. Defender for IoT and Microsoft Sentinel provide threat intelligence from Defender for IoT and enriched threat intelligence from Sentinel.

Defend for IoT offers both agent-based and agentless monitoring:

- Microsoft Defender for IoT offers agentless, network-layer monitoring for end-user organizations. You can deploy Microsoft Defender for IoT on-premises or in an Azure-connected hybrid environment.

- In addition, Microsoft Defender for IoT offers a lightweight micro-agent for IoT device builders that supports Linux and real-time operating system (RTOS) operating systems. With the Microsoft Defender device builder agent, you can ensure that IoT/OT projects are secure from the cloud.

Defender for Cloud's Threat Intelligence

Defend for Cloud detects threats by collecting and analyzing information about your Azure resources. A security alert containing detailed information regarding the event, including suggestions for remediation, is triggered when Defender for Cloud detects a threat.

To assist incident response teams in investigating and remediating threats, Defender for Cloud provides threat intelligence reports. The threat intelligence report includes the following information:

- An attacker's identity or affiliations (if any)
- Objectives of attackers
- Information about current and historical attack campaigns (if available)
- Tools, techniques, and tactics used by attackers
- URLs and file hashes associated with indicators of compromise
- Identifying the risks to your Azure resources by taking a look at the victimology of your industry and geographical location
- Information on mitigation and remediation

Microsoft 365 Defender's Threat Intelligence

In the Microsoft 365 Defender, threat investigation and response capabilities allow your organization's security team to protect its users from email- or file-based attacks. These insights can help your security team protect users. With these capabilities, you can monitor signals and gather data from multiple sources, including user activity, authentication, email, compromised PCs, and security incidents. Business decision-makers and your security operations team can use this information to understand and respond to threats against your organization and protect your intellectual property.

Microsoft 365 Defender includes a set of tools and response workflows for investigating threats.

- Explorer
- Incidents
- Attack simulation training
- Automated investigation and response

A workflow that integrates apps, data, services, and systems can be analyzed and run using Azure Monitor.

You can use Microsoft Sentinel to evaluate threat indicators in an Azure environment to detect malicious activity and inform security investigators about what to do.

To monitor security incidents, you can use other Azure services, such as Activity Logs, Azure AD Reporting, and Network Security Group flow logs.

Summary

This chapter explored several topics related to the foundation of security operation centers and various strategies required to be adopted in your organization's security operation center.

As your organization moves to Microsoft Azure, you must define and deploy a SOC team that is enabled with the appropriate SOC strategy, resources, tools, and processes to manage and respond to cybersecurity incidents.

In this chapter, you learned about developing security operations for hybrid and multi-cloud environments, designing logging and auditing security strategies, and developing security operations for hybrid and multi-cloud environments. Develop an approach to security information and event management and security orchestration, automation, and response to evaluate security workflows, review security strategies to manage incidents, evaluate security operations for technical threat intelligence, and monitor sources to identify threats and mitigations.

Exam Essentials

Understand the security operations strategy. Zero Trust security frameworks are characterized by a significant shift from trust-by-default to trust-by-exception as one of their considerable changes in perspectives. It is, however, still necessary to establish trust once it is required. To prove the trustworthiness of a request at a point in time, you must select a means of attesting to its reliability. It is necessary to gain visibility into the activities associated with the request to perform this attestation.

Understand the method to develop a logging and auditing security strategy. Security operations teams are responsible for identifying, prioritizing, and triaging potential threats. It reduces the time it takes to resolve real incidents by reducing false positives and concentrating on real attacks. Adopt the MITRE ATT&CK framework.

Understand the method to develop security operations for hybrid and multi-cloud environments. Managing the hardware and infrastructure hosting the application is no longer the responsibility of the operations team due to the cloud. Operating a successful cloud application is still dependent on operations. The operations team is responsible for deploying, monitoring, escalating, responding to incidents, and performing security audits.

To ensure the application gives the operations team the data and insight they need, incorporate robust logging and tracing into its design and planning.

Understand the method to develop SIEM and the SOAR method. Through standard governance and operations management practices, unified operations consistently maintain one set of tools and processes to manage each cloud provider.

To use proactive and reactive detection tactics to manage threats, you should have a central console that allows SOC administrators to detect, investigate, remediate, and hunt threats; use threat intelligence; understand known vulnerabilities; rely on threat experts; and block threats across any of the six pillars. A seamless experience that increases the effectiveness of the SOC analyst is achieved when the tools required to support these phases are converted into a single workflow.

Know the method to evaluate security workflows.   Microsoft recommends that security practitioners automate as many steps of those procedures as possible. These processes can include notifying relevant stakeholders, launching a change management process, and applying specific remediation steps. By automating the processes, you reduce overhead and improve your security by ensuring the steps are done in a timely, consistent manner and according to your predefined requirements.

Review security strategies for incident management.   An incident of security occurs when customer data or personal information is destroyed, lost, altered, or accessed unauthorized due to a security breach. Security incidents include, for example, unauthorized access to infrastructure and exfiltration of customer data. Compliance events that do not affect confidentiality, integrity, or availability of customer data aren't considered security incidents.

A security incident should be investigated, and lessons learned implemented in conjunction with the security response team to prevent future incidents. Continuous improvement is essential for effective and efficient incident response programs.

Know the method to evaluate security operations for technical threat intelligence.   Threat intelligence teams support all other functions such as security analysts in large organizations (for example, through threat intelligence platforms).

It takes a large, diverse set of data and the ability to apply it to your processes and tools to succeed at threat intelligence, and Microsoft does both. Microsoft collects data from various sources to ensure that our customers' data is used only in ways they have agreed to. It passes through a strict privacy/compliance boundary.

Know to monitor sources for insights on threats and mitigations.   As a result of accessing various signals across the Microsoft network, organizations use cyberthreat intelligence to gather information. It can be gathered from many different sources. It includes open-source data feeds, threat intelligence–sharing communities, commercial intelligence feeds, and local intelligence from security investigations. The Microsoft Intelligent Security Graph receives hundreds of gigabytes of data every second.

Review Questions

1. Which of the following allows you to select, operate, maintain, and continually analyze threat data to find ways to improve the organization's security posture?

   A. Security operations center

   B. Incident management

   C. Problem management

   D. Forensic team

2. In general, traditional environments categorize applicable SOC activities and choose those relevant to the cloud environment for which of the following choices?

   A. Preparation, planning, and prevention

   B. Monitoring, detection, and response

   C. Recovery, refinement, and compliance

   D. All of the above

3. Microsoft recommends the SOC team be enabled with tools that support which type of detection?

   A. Reactive and proactive

   B. Reactive-only tools

   C. Proactive-only tools

   D. None of the above

4. As a Microsoft Cybersecurity Architect, you will need to consider a Microsoft security operations strategy with which of the following requirements?

   A. Multiple engineering teams working in Microsoft Azure.

   B. Multiple subscriptions to manage and secure.

   C. Regulatory requirements must be enforced.

   D. All of the above.

5. As a Microsoft Cybersecurity Architect, you will need to consider SOC functions in line with Microsoft definitions; which of the following will you consider in your SOC strategy?

   A. Incident management, incident preparation, and threat intelligence

   B. Change management, change preparation, and threat management

   C. Incident management, change preparation, and threat intelligence

   D. None of above

6. As a Microsoft Cybersecurity Architect, you will need to consider which of the following metrics that directly influences organizational risk?

   A. MTTA

   B. MTTR

   C. Incidents remediated and escalation among each tier

   D. All of the above

7. In which of the following phase in the MITRE ATT&CK framework is malicious code being run by the adversary?

   A. Reconnaissance

   B. Resource development

   C. Initial access

   D. Execution

8. In which of the following phases in the MITRE ATT&CK framework does the adversary gather information to plan future operations?

   A. Resource development

   B. Initial access

   C. Reconnaissance

   D. Execution

9. As a Microsoft Cybersecurity Architect, you will need to consider which of the following logging and auditing strategies for aligning to the enterprise cloud security strategy?

   A. Tool for monitoring

   B. Tool for root-cause analysis

   C. Using distributed tracing and much more

   D. All of the above

10. Which of the following types of logs are available in Microsoft Azure?

    A. Control/management logs

    B. Data plane logs

    C. Processed events

    D. All of the above

11. As a Microsoft Cybersecurity Architect, you have been asked to review a resource's operations in Microsoft Azure Cloud; which report will you ask for from the SOC?

    A. Azure resource logs

    B. Activity logs

    C. Virtual machines and cloud services

    D. Azure Active Directory reporting

12. As a Microsoft Cybersecurity Architect, you have been asked to review information about users and group management activity, including sign-ins and system activity in Microsoft Azure Cloud; which report will you ask for from the SOC?

    A. Azure resource logs

    B. Activity logs

    C. Virtual machines and cloud services

    D. Azure Active Directory reporting

13. As a Microsoft Cybersecurity Architect, you have been asked to review information about the analysis of usage trends, insight into trace requests, and diagnosis of storage account issues in Microsoft Azure Cloud; which report will you ask for from the SOC?

    A. Azure resource logs

    B. Azure storage analytics

    C. Azure Active Directory reporting

    D. Activity logs

14. As a Microsoft Cybersecurity Architect, you have been asked to review information about web applications (APM) across multiple platforms in Microsoft Azure Cloud; which report will you ask for from the SOC?

    A. Azure resource logs

    B. Application insight

    C. Azure storage analytics

    D. Activity logs

15. As a Microsoft Cybersecurity Architect, you have to use which of the following Azure services to collect the data, events, performance data, and alerts?

    A. Azure Automation

    B. Azure Monitor

    C. Azure Backup

    D. None of the above

16. As a Microsoft Cybersecurity Architect, you have to use which of the following Azure services to avoid repeated work, human error, and ultimately security misconfiguration?

    A. Azure Automation

    B. Azure Monitor

    C. Azure Backup

    D. None of the above

17. As a Microsoft Cybersecurity Architect, you have to use which of the following Azure services to restore and protect data in your resiliency requirements?

    A. Azure Automation

    B. Azure Monitor

    C. Azure Backup

    D. None of the above

18. Which of the following in Microsoft Sentinel allows you to visualize essential information about your imported threat intelligence?

    A. Azure Log Analytics

    B. Azure Monitor

    C. Threat intelligence workbook

    D. None of the above

19. Which of the following comes with native threat intelligence capabilities using threat intelligence packages and can be deployed in Azure-connected environments, hybrid environments, or on-premises?

    A. Microsoft Defender for IoT

    B. Defender for Cloud

    C. Threat intelligence workbook

    D. None of the above

20. Which of the following comes with threat detection capabilities, as well as correlates alerts and contextual signals into incidents about your Azure resource?

    A. Microsoft Defender for IoT

    B. Defender for Cloud

    C. Threat intelligence workbook

    D. None of the above

Chapter

3

Define an Identity Security Strategy

THE MICROSOFT SC-100 EXAM OBJECTIVES COVERED IN THIS CHAPTER INCLUDE:

✓ Design a strategy for access to cloud resources

✓ Recommend an identity store (tenants, B2B, B2C, hybrid)

✓ Recommend an authentication strategy and authorization strategy

✓ Design a strategy for conditional access

✓ Design a strategy for role assignment and delegation

✓ Design security strategy for privileged role access to infrastructure including identity-based firewall rules and Azure PIM

✓ Design security strategy for privileged activities including PAM, entitlement management, and cloud tenant administration

In this chapter, we will focus on designing an identity security strategy. To design an identity security strategy, you need to understand how to secure access to Azure resources and be able to recommend and apply best practices around authentication and authorization.

Microsoft assists with your identity and access challenges by protecting your organization's users, smart devices, and services from threats. Using strong authentication and risk-based adaptive access policies, Microsoft's identity and access management strategy helps protect access to resources and data. It also helps to keep your users productive, reduce time managing passwords, and increase end-user productivity by providing an accessible, fast sign-in process. Using Microsoft's identity and access management strategy, you can manage all your identities and access all your apps in a central location, in the cloud or on-premises, to improve visibility. By automating identity governance, Microsoft's identity and access management strategy helps control access to apps and data for all users and admins.

By the end of this chapter, you will know how to design a strategy for access to cloud resources, recommend an identity store (tenants, B2B, B2C, hybrid), recommend an authentication strategy, and recommend an authorization strategy You'll also know how to design a strategy for conditional access, for role assignment and delegation, for privileged role access to infrastructure including identity-based firewall rules and Azure PIM, and for privileged activities including PAM, entitlement management, and cloud tenant administration.

Design a Strategy for Access to Cloud Resources

Let's first understand identification and authentication differences before diving deep into the Microsoft method to secure access against Azure resources. A subject must provide an identity to a system to initiate authentication, authorization, and accountability. Identity is the process of claiming or professing an identity. A person may provide their identity by typing a username, swiping a smartcard, waving a token device, speaking a phrase, or positioning a camera or scanner in front of their face, hand, or finger. A core principle of authentication is that all subjects must have unique identities.

Authentication verifies the subject's identity by comparing one or more factors to a database of valid identities, such as user accounts. It is essential to protect the authentication information used to verify identity. Passwords are rarely stored in clear text within databases. Instead, authentication systems store hashes of passwords. The knowledge of the subject and system to keep the secrecy of the authentication information for identities instantly reflects the level of security of that system.

Identification and authentication consistently occur jointly as a single two-step process. Delivering an identity is the first step, and providing the authentication information is the second step. Without both, a subject cannot gain access to a system.

Let's now move into the Microsoft method to secure access against Azure resources. With cloud applications and the mobile workforce, security perimeters have been redefined. Employees bring their own devices and work remotely, and data is shared with external partners and vendors outside the corporate network. As corporate applications and data move into hybrid and cloud environments, traditional network security controls are no longer sufficient. Controls must move to where data is: on devices, apps, and partners.

Today's networks, endpoints, and applications are interconnected by identities representing people, services, and IoT devices. Identity functions as a powerful, flexible, and granular security control in the Zero Trust model. An organization must take the following steps before allowing an identity access to a resource:

- Use strong authentication to verify the identity.

- Maintain compliance with the identity and ensure access is appropriate.

- Follow the principle of least privilege access.

Identity needs to be verified, and then Microsoft can maintain that identity's access to cloud resources based on organization policies, ongoing risk analysis, and other mechanisms.

To develop a successful access control strategy, you must consider more than one tactic or technology and take a pragmatic approach that embraces the right technology and tactics for the particular situation at hand.

Modern access control must complete the productivity requirements of the organization and also be all of the following:

- **Secure:** During access requests, verify the trustworthiness of users and devices using all available data and telemetry. This configuration prevents attackers from impersonating legitimate users without being detected. Implementing an access control strategy that eliminates unauthorized privilege escalation is also essential. For example, granting a privilege can be used to gain higher privileges. The section on securing privileged access contains more information about protecting privileged access.

- **Consistent:** The environment should be consistently and seamlessly secured. By implementing this standard, attackers cannot sneak in through weaknesses in a disjointed or complex access control implementation, improving the user experience. To avoid configuration inconsistencies and drift, you should use a single access control strategy that uses the fewest number of policy engines.

- **Comprehensive:** Enforcing access policies close to resources and access paths improves security coverage and allows security to fit seamlessly into the scenarios and expectations of users. Drive policy enforcement closer to the business assets of value with security controls for data, applications, identity, networks, and databases.

- **Identity-centric:** Utilize identity and related controls whenever possible. Identity controls provide rich information about access requests and application context that raw network traffic does not. Even though networking controls are necessary and sometimes the only available option (such as in operational technology environments), identity should always be the first option. It will be easier for the user to resolve a problem without contacting a help desk if a failure dialog is displayed during application access from the identity layer.

This building block in Figure 3.1 shows an enterprise access solution based on Zero Trust, which is applicable to all types of internal and external users, services, applications, and privileged accounts with administrative access.

Deployment Objectives for Identity Zero Trust

Organizations are often troubled by their approach to identity before they begin their Zero Trust journey. Identity providers on-premises are used, SSO between cloud and on-premises apps is not present, and visibility into identity risk is limited.

As a first step in deploying an end-to-end Zero Trust identity framework, Microsoft recommends focusing on the following goals:

1. Ensure integration between cloud identity and on-premises identity.

2. Provide remediation activities through conditional access policies.

3. Enhance visibility with analytics.

4. Manage identities and access privileges through identity governance.

5. Perform real-time analysis of user, device, location, and behavior to determine risks and provide ongoing protection.

6. Detect, protect, and respond to threats using other security solutions.

For example, today many organizations start with limited (or zero) segmentation of internal traffic at their network ingress/egress points (along with other supporting security elements such as intrusion detection and prevention, proxies, and so on).

Using this standard configuration, any device connected to another device on the network could directly communicate with any other device (regardless of trust level or asset sensitivity). Even though this creates no productivity barriers, it creates a significant risk where a single compromised device can quickly attack any other resource (often with privileged internal credentials stolen from the compromised device, for example, from a successful phishing attack).

In many organizations, seemingly low-impact initial attack vectors (phishing attacks, user device compromises, and so on) quickly become significant incidents due to the lateral traversal allowed by this de facto architecture.

It is common for organizations (including Microsoft) to implement dedicated security controls for privileged access. These controls include separate accounts, privileged access workstations (PAWs, aka.ms/PAW), and just-in-time (JIT) solutions utilizing privileged identity/access management (PIM/PAM).

A Zero Trust approach focuses on reducing risk by explicitly validating the trust of users and devices before allowing access to resources. To enable remote work and contain the damage from attacks, users and devices must prove safe (without impacting the user experience and productivity).

FIGURE 3.1 Enterprise access solution based on Zero Trust

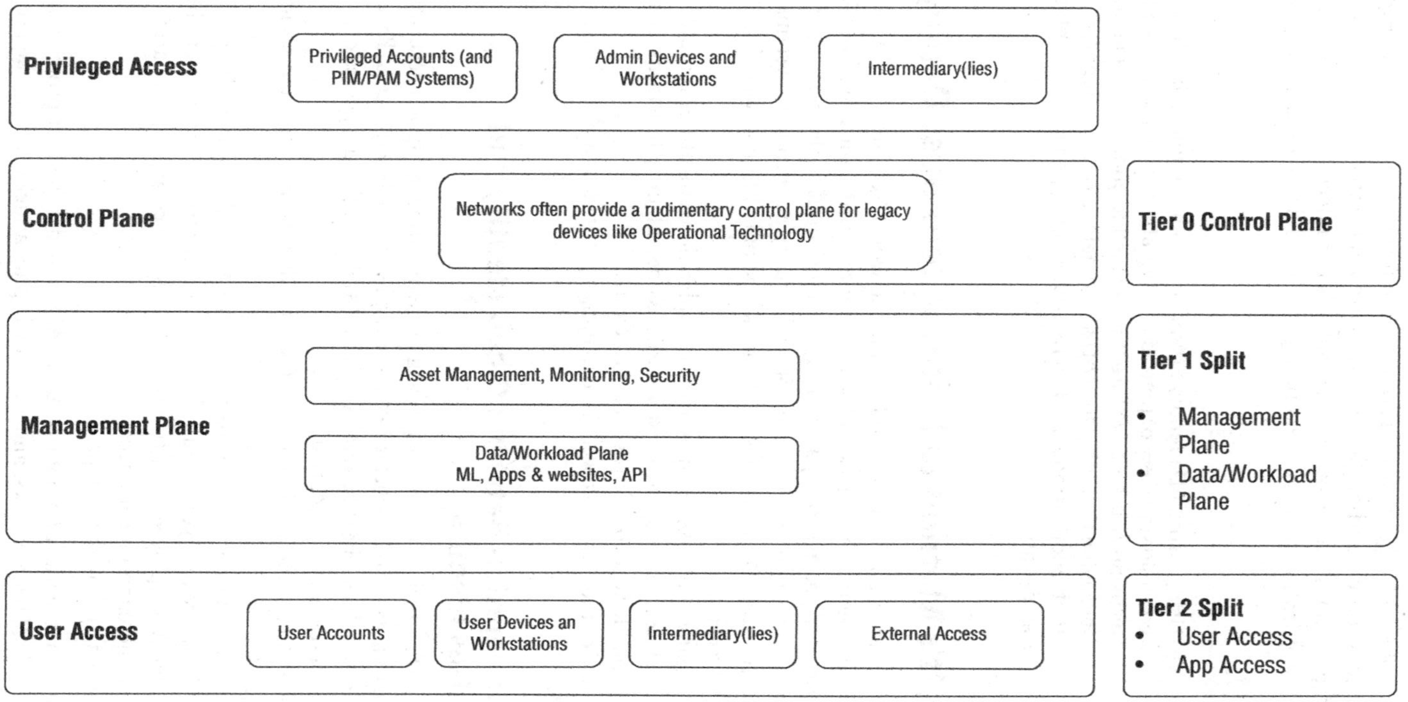

Privileged Access

Privileged Accounts (and PIM/PAM Systems)

Admin Devices and Workstations

Intermediary(Ies)

Tier 0 Control Plane

Control Plane

Networks often provide a rudimentary control plane for legacy devices like Operational Technology

Tier 1 Split
- Management Plane
- Data/Workload Plane

Management Plane

Asset Management, Monitoring, Security

Data/Workload Plane
ML, Apps & websites, API

User Access

User Accounts

User Devices an Workstations

Intermediary(Ies)

External Access

Tier 2 Split
- User Access
- App Access

As a result of the changes to access control architecture, managed devices are allowed access to cloud resources and on-premises resources only after they have been explicitly validated (configuration is compliant, the computer is not infected, and so on). As part of the Azure AD authentication process, conditional access validates a user against the organization's policy.

Using Azure AD Identity Protection, your organization will receive a consolidated view of potential vulnerabilities and risk detections. As well as using Azure Active Directory's existing anomaly detection capabilities (available through Azure AD's Anomalous Activity Reports), Identity Protection introduces new risk detection types that can detect anomalies in real-time.

Microsoft's Method to Identity Zero Trust Deployment

Security perimeters are redefined in today's mobile workforce and cloud-based applications. Employees bring their own devices and work remotely. Data is accessed outside the corporate network and shared with partners and vendors outside the network. Organizations cannot rely on traditional network controls for security as corporate systems are constantly in use from anywhere. Devices, apps, and partners should be empowered with controls wherever the data resides.

In today's many networks, endpoints, and applications, identities represent people, services, or IoT devices. In the Zero Trust security model, identity functions as a decisive, adaptable, and acceptable way to control access to data.

An overview of the steps involved in managing identities in a Zero Trust security framework follows.

Step 1: Integration Between Cloud Identity and On-Premises Identity

Azure Active Directory (AD) enables strong authentication, endpoint security integration, and the core of user-centric policies to ensure the least privileged access. Based on user identity, environment, device health, and risk, Azure AD's conditional access capabilities determine how resources can be accessed.

Microsoft's integration method between cloud identity and on-premises identity consists of four stages.

In stage 1 ("Connect all of your users to Azure AD and federate with on-premises identity systems"), ensure that your cloud identities and controls are consistent by maintaining a healthy pipeline of employee identities as well as the necessary security artifacts (groups for authorization and endpoints for access policy controls).

To get started, follow these steps:

1. Choose an authentication option. Azure AD provides the best protection against brute-force attacks, DDoS attacks, and password spray attacks. Create the proper determination for your organization and compliance requirements.

2. Take advantage of going to the cloud to leave behind accounts that make sense on-premises only. Leave behind privileged roles from on-premises.

3. If your company has more than 100,000 users, groups, and devices combined, build a high-performance sync box that will keep organization lifecycle stay current.

In stage 2 ("Establish identity foundation with Azure AD"), in a Zero Trust strategy, you must verify explicitly, use least privileged access principles, and assume breaches. Azure AD can act as your policy decision point for enforcing your access policies based on insights about your users, endpoints, and target resources.

Microsoft recommends taking this step:

1. Every access request should be sent to Azure AD. Azure AD receives the signal from this identity control plane to determine the best authentication/authorization risk for each user and each app or resource. The use of a single sign-on and a consistent policy guard-rail improves the user experience and increases productivity.

In stage 3 ("Integrate all your applications with Azure AD"), by using single sign-on, users are prevented from leaving copies of their credentials in various apps and from surrendering their credentials to excessive prompting.

You should also make sure your environment does not have more than one identity access management (IAM) engine. With two or more IAM engines, Azure AD does not see as much signal, allowing bad actors to live between the IAM engines. It can also result in poor user experiences and your business partners questioning your Zero Trust strategy for the first time.

Microsoft recommends following these steps:

1. Implement OAuth2.0 or SAML-enabled enterprise applications.

2. Use Azure AD Application Proxy to integrate Kerberos and form-based authentication applications.

3. Integrate Azure AD with most major application delivery networks/controllers (such as Citrix, Akamai, and F5) if you publish legacy applications.

4. Understand you should migrate your applications from existing/older IAM engines using Azure resources and tools.

5. Provide a tighter integration of identity life cycles between your various cloud applications.

In stage 4 ("Verify explicitly with strong authentication"), Microsoft recommends taking the following steps:

1. As a foundational component of reducing user session risk, roll out Azure AD MFA (Premium 1). The ability for users to respond to a multifactor authentication (MFA) challenge as they move around the world is one of the most direct ways they can convince us that these are familiar devices and locations (without having administrators parse individual signals) as they appear on new devices and from unknown locations.

2. Malicious actors frequently exploit legacy authentication mechanisms, such as SMTP, that can't handle modern security challenges, such as stolen or replayed credentials.

Step 2: Provide Remediation Activities Through Conditional Access Policies

Azure AD conditional access (CA) automates decisions and enforces organizational access policies by analyzing user, device, and location signals. You can implement security controls such as MFA using CA policies. CA policies allow users to be prompted for MFA when necessary and remain out of their way when not.

Microsoft offers standard conditional policies called *security defaults* as a basic security measure. In contrast, your organization may require more flexibility than security defaults can provide. With conditional access, you can configure new policies that meet your requirements and customize security defaults with more granularity.

In a Zero Trust deployment, planning your CA policies and having an active and fallback policy are essential to enforcing your access policy. You should configure your trusted IP locations in your environment. Even if these IPs aren't used in conditional access policies, configuring them informs you about Identity Protection risks.

Microsoft recommends registering devices with Azure AD to restrict access from compromised and vulnerable devices. If you manage the user's laptop/computer, use that information to help you make better decisions by enabling Azure AD Hybrid Join or Azure AD Join. If you know a user is coming from a machine your organization controls and manages, you may allow them access to data (clients with offline copies on the computer). Without this, your users may try to work around your security or use shadow IT if you block access from rich clients.

To manage and enroll mobile devices for your users, enable the Intune service in Microsoft EMS.

Using mobile devices is similar to using laptops: the more you know about the device's function, the more you can rely on or disbelieve them and deliver a justification for why you block/allow access.

Step 3: Enhance Visibility with Analytics

Having solid operational insights into what is happening in your directory is crucial as you build your Azure AD estate with authentication, authorization, and provisioning. Configure your logging and reporting using your SIEM system or Azure AD reporting and monitoring to improve visibility.

Step 4: Identity Governance Manages Identities and Access Privileges

Once the initial three steps are completed, the next step concentrates on further objectives, such as more robust identity governance. Figure 3.2 depicts Microsoft's identity governance method to manage identities and access privileges.

In stage 1 ("Secure privileged access with Privileged Identity Management"), control users' endpoints, conditions, and credentials to access select operations/roles.

FIGURE 3.2   Microsoft identity governance method to manage identities and access privileges

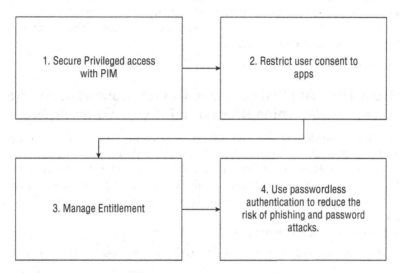

Microsoft recommends following this step:

1. Secure privileged identities with Privileged Identity Management. The power of privileged identities cannot be underestimated in a digitally transformed organization. Privileges go beyond admin access.

In stage 2 ("Restrict user consent to applications"), modern applications often require user consent to access organizational resources.

Microsoft recommends following these steps:

1. Ensure your organization's data isn't exposed to apps without consent by limiting user consent and managing consent requests.

2. If there is any excessive or malicious consent in your organization, review prior/existing consent in your organization.

In stage 3 ("Manage entitlement"), now that Azure AD is used to authenticate applications, you can streamline the process of requesting, approving, and recertifying access so that the right people have the proper access and you have a trail as to why users have the access they do.

Microsoft recommends following these steps.

1. Implement entitlement management to allow users to create access packages that provide access to the resources associated with their teams/projects (such as applications, SharePoint sites, group memberships).

2. Self-service group management and self-service application access can be enabled in your organization if entitlement management cannot be implemented at this time.

In stage 4 ("Use passwordless authentication to reduce the risk of phishing and password attacks"), Azure AD supports FIDO 2.0 and passwordless phone sign-in so you can reduce the number of credentials your users (susceptible/privileged users) use daily. In addition to serving as significant authentication factors, these credentials can mitigate risk well.

Microsoft recommends following this step.

1. Begin adopting passwordless credentials in your organization.

Step 5: Real-Time Analysis of User, Device, Location, and Behavior Is Performed to Determine Risks and Provide Ongoing Protection

Microsoft classified real-time analysis critical for determining risk and delivering ongoing protection for the user, device, location, and behavior into four stages.

In stage 1 ("Deploy Azure AD password protection"), it is essential not to ignore weak passwords, password spray, or breach replay attacks, even though they can be prevented with other methods. Classic complex password policies can control only some of the password attacks.

Microsoft recommends following this step:

1. Enable password protection for Azure AD users on-premises and in the cloud.

In stage 2 ("Enable Identity Protection"), by using Identity Protection, you can get a more granular session/user risk signal. This will help the engine better understand what risk looks like in your environment so that you can confirm or dismiss the signal.

Take this step:

1. Make sure Identity Protection is enabled.

In stage 3 ("Enable Microsoft Defender for Cloud Apps integration with Identity Protection"), by monitoring the behavior of users inside SaaS and modern applications, Microsoft Defender for Cloud Apps gets information about what happened after they authenticated and received a token in Azure AD. When a user's behavior looks suspicious (for example, downloading gigabytes of data from OneDrive or sending spam emails in Exchange Online), Azure AD can be notified that a user seems compromised or high risk. In the future, Azure AD can verify or block the user on their subsequent access request.

Microsoft recommends following this step.

1. The Identity Protection signal can be enhanced by enabling Defender for Cloud Apps monitoring.

In stage 4 ("Enable conditional access integration with Microsoft Defender for Cloud Apps"), you can monitor sessions going to SaaS applications and enforce restrictions by using signals emitted after authentication and Defender for Cloud Apps proxying requests.

Microsoft recommends following these steps:

1. Integration of conditional access should be enabled.

2. On-premises applications can be added to conditional access.

Enable restricted session for use in access decisions; when a user's risk is low but signs in from an unknown endpoint, you may want to give them access to critical resources, but do not let them do things that leave your organization noncompliant. In Exchange Online and SharePoint Online, you can now configure the user's session so they can only read emails or view files but not download them or save them to untrusted devices.

Microsoft recommends following these steps:

1. Limit SharePoint Online and Exchange Online access.

Step 6: Detect, Protect, and Respond to Threats Using Other Security Solutions

The integration of other security solutions can also enhance effectiveness. Integrating with Microsoft Defender for Identity allows Azure AD to detect risky behavior by users accessing on-premises, nonmodern resources (like file shares). It can then be considered general user risk, and high user risk might block further access in the cloud.

Microsoft recommends following these steps:

1. Microsoft Defender for Identity can be integrated with Microsoft Defender for Cloud Apps to integrate on-premises risk signals.

2. For a holistic view of which users are most at risk, combine Investigation Priority scores for each user.

By assessing the health of Windows machines and determining whether they have been compromised, Microsoft Defender for Endpoint helps you mitigate risk at runtime. Domain Join gives you a sense of control. Defender for Endpoint can detect patterns where multiple user devices are hitting untrustworthy sites and raise their device/user risk at runtime when faced with a malware attack near real-time.

Microsoft recommends following this step:

1. Microsoft Defender for Endpoints can be configured to allow conditional access.

As a point of integration for endpoint security, Azure AD ensures least-privileged access and enables strong authentication. With Azure AD's conditional access capability, access to resources is decided based on identity, environment, device health, and risk, verified explicitly at the point of entry.

Recommend an Identity Store (Tenants, B2B, B2C, Hybrid)

Azure Active Directory is Microsoft's cloud-based identity and access management service. Enterprises can protect and automate identity processes at scale with single sign-on authentication, conditional access, passwordless and multifactor authentication, automated user provisioning, and many other features.

You can integrate your solution with Azure Active Directory in various ways. Using Azure Active Directory's built-in security features, foundational integrations protect your customers, and advanced integrations enhance the security capabilities of your solution.

Let's get started with the foundational points.

Integrating the foundations   A foundational integration protects your customers with Azure Active Directory's built-in security features.

Enabling SSO and publisher verification   Publish your app in the Azure Active Directory app gallery to enable single sign-on. This will increase customer trust because they know your application is compatible with Azure Active Directory. It's possible to become a verified publisher so customers know you're the publisher of the app they're adding.

> Incorporating the app gallery into your tenant with automated app registration will make it easy for IT admins to integrate the solution. Adding your app to the gallery will prevent these issues with your app, as manual registrations are a common cause of support issues.

Integrating the ability to provision users   Organizations with thousands of users face challenges managing identities and access. You can keep user access consistent when changes occur by synchronizing information about users and access between your application and Azure Active Directory when large organizations use your solution.

> Users and groups can be automatically provisioned between your application and Azure Active Directory by using the System for Cross-Domain Identity Management (SCIM) user management API.

Azure Active Directory B2C   Customer identity and access management (CIAM) in Azure Active Directory B2C supports millions of users and billions of daily authentications. This solution enables branded web and mobile applications to blend seamlessly with white-label authentication experiences.

> With Azure Active Directory B2C, partners can integrate using Microsoft Graph and key security APIs such as conditional access, confirm compromise, and risky user APIs.

Integrating with RESTful endpoints   Multifactor authentication (MFA) and role-based access control (RBAC) can be enabled by independent software vendors using RESTful endpoints and identity verification. Proofing can also be enabled, security can be improved with bot detection and fraud prevention, and Secure Customer Authentication (SCA) requirements can be met.

The RESTful APIs from Microsoft come with detailed guidance and sample integration walkthroughs from partners:

- Customer identity verification and proofing, allowing them to verify their end users' identities
- Providing end users with granular access control via role-based access control

- Hybrid access to the on-premises application, enabling end users to access both on-premises and legacy applications securely

- Providing customers with fraud protection against bot attacks and fraudulent login attempts

Azure AD External Identities refers to how you can securely interact with users outside your organization.

If you allow external users to log in to your Microsoft applications or other enterprise applications (SaaS applications, custom-developed apps, and so on) using their preferred identity, you can collaborate with them. In your directory, B2B collaboration users appear as guest users.

With B2B Direct Connect, you can establish a mutually beneficial, two-way trust with another Azure AD organization. With B2B Direct Connect, external users can access your resources from within their Teams instance using shared channels. In Teams admin center reports, users who use B2B Direct Connect aren't shown in your directory but can be viewed in the Teams shared channel.

You can manage identity and access for modern SaaS and custom-developed apps (excluding Microsoft apps) using Azure AD B2C.

Recommend an Authentication and Authorization Strategy

Microsoft Cybersecurity Architects design IAM solutions to implement authentication and authorization for all users, applications, and devices. Strong identity and access management solutions should provide unified identity management, secure, adaptive access, simplified identity governance, and seamless user experiences.

Think about these characteristics of a robust IAM solution as you consider your authentication and authorization options:

- Improve visibility and control by managing all identities and access to all your applications in one place, whether in the cloud or on the premises.

- Keep your users productive and reduce password management time by providing an easy, fast sign-in experience.

- Strong authentication and risk-based adaptive access policies ensure secure access to resources and data without compromising user experience.

- Control access to applications and data for all users and admins: automated identity governance ensures only authorized users can access applications and data.

Organizations require an identity control plane that amplifies their security and keeps their cloud application secure from intruders. A user signs into a device, application, or service using credentials verified or authenticated by an identity control plane. It is essential for organizations wanting to move their apps to the cloud to choose the correct authentication method.

- An organization moving to the cloud must make this decision first.
- An organization's presence in the cloud is dependent on its authentication method. It controls access to all cloud data and resources.
- As a result, Azure AD provides advanced security and user experience features.

Organizations access the cloud application through authentication, which acts as a new control plane of IT security.

Azure AD authentication involves more than just verifying the username and password. The following are some components that contribute to improved security and reduced help-desk support:

- Password reset by self-service
- Authentication using multiple factors in Azure AD
- Integration with on-premises environment to write password changes back
- Hybrid integration for on-premises password protection
- Passwordless authentication

Authentication is the foundation of cloud access when Azure AD hybrid identity is your new control plane. To implement an Azure AD hybrid identity solution, it is crucial to select the right authentication method. By using Azure AD Connect as a login method, users can also be provisioned in the cloud.

Organizations should choose authentication methods based on the time, existing infrastructure, complexity, and cost involved in implementing them. These factors vary from organization to organization and might change over time.

In hybrid identity solutions scenario, Azure AD supports the following authentication methods:

- Cloud authentication
- Federated authentication

Cloud Authentication

Azure AD handles users' sign-in processes when you choose the authentication method. Cloud authentication contains single sign-on (SSO), so users can sign into cloud apps without re-entering their credentials. The following are two options for cloud authentication:

- Azure AD password hash synchronization
- Azure AD pass-through authentication

Azure AD Password Hash Synchronization

On-premises directory objects can be authenticated in Azure AD using the same username and password. No additional infrastructure is required. Azure AD's premium features, such as Identity Protection and Azure AD Domain Services, require password hash synchronization regardless of the authentication method used.

Figure 3.3 depicts the reference architecture for Azure AD password hash synchronization.

FIGURE 3.3   Microsoft Azure AD password hash synchronization reference architecture

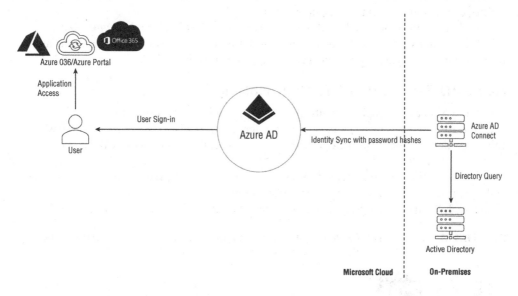

While you design Azure AD password hash synchronization, consider the following:

- **From an effort's perspective:** Organizations that sign in only to Microsoft 365, SaaS apps, and Azure AD resources require password hash synchronization for minor deployment, maintenance, and infrastructure effort. Password hash synchronization occurs every two minutes during Azure AD Connect sync when enabled.

- **From a user experience perspective:** A seamless SSO solution with password hash synchronization will improve the users' sign-in experience. Seamless SSO removes unnecessary prompts during sign-in.

- **From an advanced use case perspective:** With Azure AD Premium P2, organizations can use insights from identities in Azure AD Identity Protection reports. Windows Hello for Business has specific requirements when using password hash synchronization. An example is the leaked credentials report. To provision users with their corporate credentials in the managed domain, Azure AD Domain Services requires password hash synchronization.

Azure AD Multifactor Authentication or conditional access custom controls must be used by organizations that require multifactor authentication with password hash synchronization. The organizations cannot use federated multifactor authentication methods on-premises or from third parties.

- **From a disaster recovery and business continuity perspective:** As a cloud service that scales to all Microsoft data centers, password hash synchronization with cloud authentication is highly available. If password hash synchronization goes down for extended periods, deploy an Azure AD Connect server as a standby server in staging mode.

At the time of writing this book, password hash synchronization doesn't immediately enforce changes in on-premises account states.

Cloud apps can be accessed until the user account state is synchronized with Azure AD. After administrator's bulk update on-premises user account states, organizations may want to run a new synchronization cycle to overcome this limitation.

Azure AD Pass-Through Authentication

The Azure AD pass-through authentication service validates passwords for Azure AD authentication services by utilizing a software agent on-premises. To ensure that password validation does not occur in the cloud, the servers validate users directly with your on-premises Active Directory.

An organization that requires immediate enforcement of on-premises password policies and sign-in hours may use this authentication method.

Figure 3.4 depicts the reference architecture for pass-through authentication.

FIGURE 3.4 Microsoft Azure AD pass-through authentication reference architecture

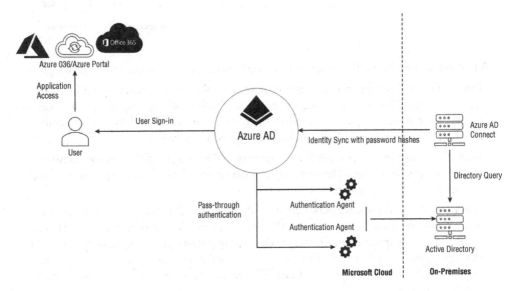

While you design Azure AD pass-through authentication, consider the key elements for Azure AD pass-through synchronization.

- **From an effort's perspective:** To use pass-through authentication, you must install one or more lightweight agents on existing servers (Microsoft recommend three). You must provide the agents access to Active Directory Domain Services, including your AD domain controllers on-premises. For this reason, deploying the agents in a perimeter network is not recommended, and they require outbound Internet access and access to your domain controllers.

  In pass-through authentication, domain controllers must have unrestricted network access, and all network traffic must be encrypted and limited to authentication requests.

- **From a user experience perspective:** Pass-through authentication improves users' sign-in experience by removing the unnecessary prompts. Seamless SSO avoids needless prompts after a user's login.

- **From an advanced use case perspective:** At the time of sign-in, pass-through authentication enforces the on-premises account policy. An on-premises user's login attempt may be denied access if their account is disabled or locked out, if their password expires, or if the login attempt falls outside the sign-in hours.

Azure AD MFA or CA custom controls are required for organizations that require multi-factor authentication with pass-through authentication. These organizations can't use multi-factor authentication that relies on federation. Password hash synchronization is needed for advanced features, whether you choose pass-through authentication or not.

For disaster recovery and business continuity, Microsoft recommends deploying two more pass-through authentication agents. In addition to the Azure AD Connect server agent, these additional agents ensure high availability for authentication requests. Even with three agents deployed, one agent can still fail if another agent is down for maintenance.

Combining password hash synchronization with pass-through authentication also makes sense since it serves as a backup authentication method in the case of a failed primary authentication attempt. Suppose a significant on-premises failure prevents the agents from validating a user's credentials. In that case, password hash synchronization can work as a backup authentication mechanism for pass-through authentication. It would help if you used Azure AD Connect to manually switch to password hash synchronization.

Federated Authentication

When you use this authentication method, Azure AD passes the authentication process to an external authentication system, such as AD FS. Smartcard-based or multifactor authentication by third parties can be provided as additional advanced authentication requirements.

Figure 3.5 depicts the reference architecture for federated authentication.

FIGURE 3.5   Microsoft federated authentication reference architecture

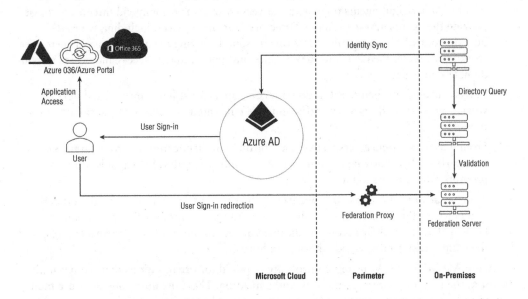

While you design federated authentication, consider the following.

- **From an effort's perspective:** Authentication is handled by an external trusted system in a federated authentication system. A hybrid identity solution based on Azure AD allows some companies to reuse existing investments in federated systems. Azure AD is not responsible for maintaining and managing the federated system; the organization's responsibility is to use the federated system securely and handle the authentication load.

- **From a user experience perspective:** The user experience of federated authentication depends on how the federation farm's topology, configuration, and features are implemented. Some organizations must be flexible enough to adapt and configure federation farm access based on their security requirements. For example, internally connected users and devices can be configured to sign in automatically without prompting for credentials since they have already logged in. Advanced security features sometimes make the sign-in process more difficult for users.

- **From an advanced use case perspective:** Customers with authentication requirements that Azure AD does not support natively should consider using federated authentication. Here are some common scenarios to consider:
  - Require smartcards or certificates for authentication.
  - Require federated identity providers for on-premises or third-party multifactor authentication servers.
  - Provision an authentication solution provided by a third party.

- Install a sign-in protocol that, rather than using a User Principal Name (UPN) (for instance, user@domain.com), requires a SAMaccountName (for example, DOMAIN/username).

- **From a disaster recovery and business continuity perspective:** The federated authentication system typically requires a load-balanced array of servers, called a *farm*, configured in a topology that ensures high availability for authentication requests.

For example, deploy password hash synchronization and federated authentication as backup methods when on-premises servers are unavailable. Providing low-latency authentication requests at multiple Internet ingress points configured with geo-DNS is a requirement for some large enterprise organizations requiring a federation solution.

Most organizations use this choice if they currently have an on-premises federation infrastructure investment and if using only one identity provider is a vital business requirement. By default, federated systems require a higher investment in infrastructure, and the federation is more challenging to operate and troubleshoot than cloud authentication solutions.

Figure 3.6 depicts the decision tree; using it you can decide which authentication method is best for you as a Microsoft Cybersecurity Architect. Using it, you can decide whether to use federated or cloud authentication to manage your Azure AD hybrid identity.

Comparison of Authentication Methods

Table 3.1 compares various authentication methods, which will help Microsoft Cybersecurity Architects define the identity control plane.

The following are the high-level guidelines provided by Microsoft to design an identity layer:

- It protects your organization's sensitive data by controlling access to the cloud and line-of-business apps that you migrate and make available in the cloud.

Regardless of the authentication method you choose, Microsoft recommends it would be best if you used or enabled password hash synchronization for the following reasons:

High Availability and Disaster Recovery Consideration   On-premises infrastructure is required for pass-through authentication and federation. Pass-through authentication includes the server hardware and networking that the agents need. When you use federation, your on-premises footprint is even more critical. It would help if you had proxy servers in the perimeter network to proxy authentication requests and had internal federation servers to handle federation.

By deploying redundant servers, you can prevent single points of failure. In both pass-through authentication and federation, authentication requests are handled if any of the components fail, and domain controllers can also fail to respond to authentication requests. Maintenance is essential to keep these components healthy; when care isn't planned and implemented correctly, outages are more likely. Microsoft Azure AD cloud authentication service scales globally and is always available, so password hash synchronization can be used to avoid outages.

FIGURE 3.6 Microsoft authentication method decision tree

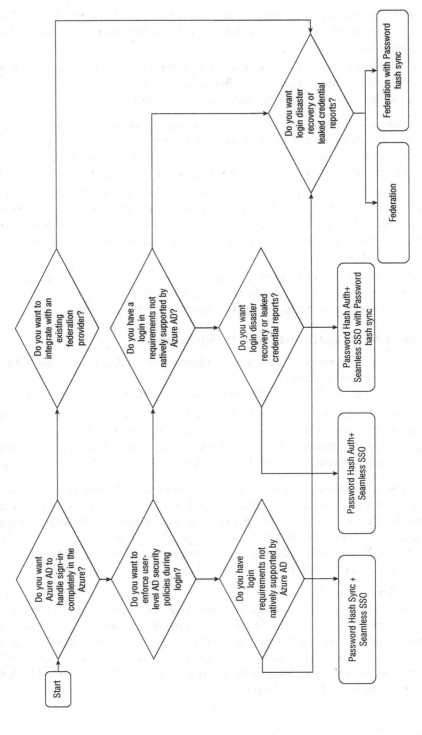

Surviving an Outage On-Premises   During an on-premises outage caused by a cyberattack or disaster, the consequences can be substantial, ranging from reputational damage to paralysis for an organization. Recently, many organizations have been victims of malware attacks, such as ransomware, which caused organizations' on-premises systems to shut down. In its experience dealing with such attacks, Microsoft identifies two types of organizations based on their cybersecurity profiles and how they fared in cyberattacks.

- The primary authentication method for organizations that previously used federated or pass-through authentication and password hash synchronization has been changed to password hash synchronization. Using access to email through Microsoft 365, they quickly resolved issues and accessed other cloud-based workloads. They were back online in hours. Through access to Microsoft 365 email, they were able to resolve issues and access other cloud-based workloads.

- Previously, organizations without password hash synchronization relied on untrusted external consumer email systems to resolve issues. When this happened, it took weeks for the organization's on-premises identity solution to be restored before end users could log in to cloud-based apps.

Identity Protection   Azure AD Identity Protection with Azure AD Premium P2 is one of the best ways to protect users in the cloud. Bad actors sell and make user and password lists available on the dark web, and Microsoft continually scans the Internet for them. In Azure AD, you can use this information to find out whether any of your organization's usernames and passwords are compromised. No matter which authentication method you use, password hash synchronization is critical, whether through federated or pass-through authentication. Using this information, you can block or force users to change their passwords when they try to sign in with leaked credentials.

TABLE 3.1   Authentication Methods

Design and Deployment Consideration	Pass-Through Authentication and Seamless SSO	Password Hash Synchronization and Seamless SSO	Federation with AD FS
What is the process of authentication?	A secure password verification exchange is conducted with the authentication agent on-premises in the cloud.	In the cloud	On-premises.
Are TLS/SSL certificates required?	No.	No	Yes.
How does the provisioning system interact with on-premises Internet and networking requirements?	Authentication agent-based outbound Internet access.	None	A perimeter WAP server can be accessed via the Internet. WAP servers in the perimeter can access AD FS servers through inbound network access. Network load balancing.

TABLE 3.1   Authentication Methods *(continued)*

Design and Deployment Consideration	Pass-Through Authentication and Seamless SSO	Password Hash Synchronization and Seamless SSO	Federation with AD FS
Does Azure AD Connect require any additional on-premises servers?	For every additional authentication agent, there should be one server.	None	Two or more AD FS servers. Two or more WAP servers in the perimeter/DMZ network.
What are the health monitoring solutions available?	Admin center for Azure Active Directory provides agent status.	Not required	Azure AD Connect Health.
Can domain-joined devices within the company network access cloud resources with a single sign-on?	Yes with Seamless SSO.	Yes with Seamless SSO	Yes.
Which sign-in types are supported?	UserPrincipalName + password. Windows-Integrated Authentication by using Seamless SSO. Alternate login ID.	UserPrincipalName + password Windows-Integrated Authentication by using Seamless SSO Alternate login ID	UserPrincipalName + password. SAMaccountName + password. Windows-Integrated Authentication. Certificate and smart card authentication. Alternate login ID.
Does Windows Hello for Business support it?	Key trust model. Hybrid Cloud Trust. Both require Windows Server 2016 Domain functional level.	Key trust model Hybrid Cloud Trust	Key trust model. Hybrid Cloud Trust. Certificate trust model.
Which multifactor authentications are supported?	Azure AD MFA. Custom Controls with conditional access.	Azure AD MFA Custom Controls with conditional access	Azure AD MFA. Azure MFA server. Third-party MFA. Custom Controls with conditional access.
What are the supported states for user accounts?	Disabled accounts. Account locked out. Account expired. Password expired. Sign-in hours.	Disabled accounts (up to 30-minute delay)	Disabled accounts. Account locked out. Account expired. Password expired. Sign-in hours.

Design and Deployment Consideration	Pass-Through Authentication and Seamless SSO	Password Hash Synchronization and Seamless SSO	Federation with AD FS
In what ways can conditional access be used?	Azure AD conditional access, with Azure AD Premium.	Azure AD conditional access, with Azure AD Premium	Azure AD conditional access, with Azure AD Premium. AD FS claim rules.
Can legacy protocols be blocked?	Yes.	Yes	Yes.
Do you have the option of customizing the logo, image, and description on the sign-in pages?	Yes, with Azure AD Premium.	Yes, with Azure AD Premium	Yes.
How are advanced scenarios handled?	Smart password lockout.	Smart password lockout. Leaked credentials reports, with Azure AD Premium P2	Multisite low-latency authentication system. AD FS extranet lockout. Integration with third-party identity systems.

Source: adapted from https://learn.microsoft.com/en-us/azure/active-directory/hybrid/choose-ad-authn#comparing-methods

Secure Authorization

Having successfully authenticated your users to your cloud resources, it's now time to ensure they are limited to only performing the actions they are supposed to. End-user applications often handle authorization themselves. For example, a database row or document containing the access level of each user may be available. It makes sense because each application has its authorizing functions, but you need to check all applications to see what a user can access.

Separation of duties and least privilege are the most critical concepts for authorization. By definition, least privilege means that only the information your users, systems, and tools need to do their jobs should be accessible. This means you usually have a "deny by default" policy, which means identities can't do anything unless you explicitly authorize it.

Regarding financial controls, where two signatures may be required for checks over a certain amount, separation of duties is a common practice. It usually means ensuring that no individual can completely undermine the security of an entire environment in the cloud. An individual who can change systems should not also be able to alter or review the logs from those systems.

As cloud services and internal applications become more popular, centralized authorization is becoming more critical. Authorization verifies the identity attempting to connect has the necessary permissions to access a service, feature, function, object, or method. In the absence of authentication, a connection fails before any authorization check is performed, and authorization always occurs after successful authentication. Authenticating a connection successfully may not allow a specific action if the user or group does not possess the necessary authorization.

To enforce Zero Trust, administrators should understand the following authorization methods:

- Security group membership
- Role-based access control
- Access levels
- Feature flags
- Security namespaces and permissions

 From the SC-100 exam perspective, keep the following in mind: pass-through authentication, password hash synchronization, and federation are the three types of password synchronization. Azure AD does not store passwords in clear text or encrypt them with a reversible algorithm, and custom controls do not yet support device registration in Azure AD conditional access. The Azure AD hybrid identity solution must be deployed using one of Azure AD Connect's supported topologies.

Design a Strategy for Conditional Access

Identity-driven signals can be used as part of an organization's access control decisions to extend its security perimeter beyond its network. As part of the new identity-driven control plane, Microsoft Azure Active Directory conditional access integrates signals to make decisions and enforce policies.

If-then statements are the primary form of conditional access policies. Users must perform a specific action if they want access to a resource.

Administrators are faced with two primary goals.

- Enhance user productivity wherever they are.
- Ensure the assets of the organization are protected.

To keep your organization secure, use conditional access policies. Zero Trust relies heavily on conditional access, because it ensures the right user has access to the right resources based on computed risk and preconfigured policies. Azure Active Directory can make access decisions based on calculated risk. When appropriate, independent software vendors can surface the option of applying conditional access policies to their products.

After first-factor authentication, conditional access policies are enforced. However, conditional access isn't meant to be an organization's first line of defense against scenarios like denial-of-service attacks.

Each company has its security policies and requirements. Using this framework for conditional access, you can create an architecture that meets the company's needs. The guidance includes principles related to Zero Trust that can be used as input when creating architecture. Based on company requirements and policies, adjust the architecture accordingly.

A company might have these requirements, for example:

- A minimum of two factors must be used to protect all access.

- Unmanaged devices cannot contain data.

- Guests are not permitted.

- An authentication method that does not require a password must be used to access cloud services.

Based on conditional access, Microsoft recommends creating a Zero Trust access model that aligns with these three principles: verify explicitly, use least privilege access, and assume breach.

Verify Explicitly

The following are the key considerations for verifying explicitly:

- Integrate apps with Azure AD, and use conditional access to protect them.

- Assume that all clients are external.

Use Least-Privileged Access

The following are the key considerations for using least-privileged access:

- When evaluating access, risks associated with users, sign-ins, and devices should be considered.

- Using conditional access for protection, access the resource directly.

  - The resource can be accessed using Azure AD Application Proxy. The resource can be protected using conditional access.

  - Use conditional access–based VPN to access the resource. Restrict access to the level of the app or DNS name.

Assume Breach

The following are the key considerations for adopting an assumed breach scenario:

- Network infrastructure needs to be segmented.
- Ensure that enterprise public key infrastructure (PKI) is used as little as possible.
- Password hash synchronization (PHS) should replace single sign-on (SSO) from AD FS.
- Use Kerberos Key Distribution Centers (KDCs) in Azure AD to minimize DC dependency.
- Using Microsoft EMS, move the management plane to the cloud.

The following is a list of Microsoft-recommended conditional access principles and best practices to be followed in your design:

- Conditional Access should be based on Zero Trust principles.
- Before putting a policy into production, use report-only mode.
- Both positive and negative scenarios should be tested.
- Conditional Access policies should be subject to change and revision control.
- Use tools such as Azure DevOps/GitHub and Azure Logic Apps to automate conditional access policy management.
- Don't use block mode for general access unless you have to.
- It is essential to ensure that all applications and your platform are protected. conditional access does not have an implied "deny all" function.
- All Microsoft 365 role-based access control (RBAC) systems must protect privileged users.
- High-risk users and sign-ins (enforced by the frequency of sign-ins) require password changes and multifactor authentication.
- Utilize a conditional access policy with an Intune compliance check to restrict access to high-risk devices.
- Access to Office 365, Azure, AWS, and Google Cloud administrator portals should be protected.
- Users with untrusted devices and admins should not be able to persist browser sessions.
- Authenticate with legacy credentials.
- Devices that are not supported or unknown should not be allowed access.
- To access resources, compliant devices should be required.
- Registration with strong credentials should be restricted.
- If the appropriate conditions are met before the outage, consider using a default session policy that allows sessions to continue if there is an outage.

While creating conditional access policies, consider the following list of Microsoft-recommendations.

- **Name conventions:** After defining a naming convention for your policies, you and your colleagues will be able to understand what the policies are for, making policy management and troubleshooting easier.

- **Numbering scheme:** Make sure the numbering scheme is predictable and standard.
- **Policy types:** Microsoft recommends considering five main kinds: base protection, identity protection, data protection, app protection, and attack surface reduction.
- **Standard policy components:** Apps, platform types, grant control types, and names are all components that need to be defined in advance so that all policies are consistent.

Conditional Access Zero Trust Architecture

In terms of conditional access architecture, Microsoft recommends adopting either targeted or Zero Trust in your enterprise design.

This architecture is a good fit for Zero Trust principles. In a conditional access policy, if you select the All Cloud Apps option, all endpoints will be protected by the provided grant controls, such as known users and compliant devices. The policy applies to all endpoints with which the user interacts, not just those supported by conditional access.

Various new PowerShell and Microsoft Graph tools use a device-login flow endpoint. Device-login flow enables signing in from devices that do not have a sign-in screen, such as IoT devices.

The user is shown a code after executing a device-based sign-in command on their device. To use the same code on the next device, the user has to go to aka.ms/devicelogin and enter their username and password. The sign-in on the IoT device in the same user context will succeed after the sign-in from the other device.

This sign-in does not support device-based conditional access, which presents a challenge. If you apply a baseline policy requiring a known user and a known device for all cloud applications, nobody can use the tools and commands. The same problem occurs with device-based conditional access for other applications.

Another architecture is the targeted model, in which you target only the apps you wish to protect in conditional access policies. As a result, conditional access policies do not protect device login for endpoints already covered by all cloud applications (for example, graph calls to Azure Active Directory).

To distinguish the two architectures, you can authenticate with a device login. Suppose each application is targetable and can be excluded from a conditional access policy that requires device-based login. In that case, device login could be allowed for one or a few individual applications.

In a targeted architecture, you may forget to protect all of your cloud applications. Nevertheless, you would select all the selectable applications in conditional access policies, leaving unprotected access to applications not selectable. Several very sensitive portals are accessible to users, such as the Office portal, Azure Enterprise Agreement (EA) portal, and security information portal.

Microsoft and its partners are releasing new features, and your IT admins are integrating various applications with Azure Active Directory (Azure AD) over time, so the number of Office 365 and Azure Active Directory (Azure AD) applications keeps growing. Conditional Access can be protected only by a script that detects new apps and applies a policy automatically, and developing and managing such a script may be super complex.

Conditional Access policies can contain a maximum of 250 apps. You can add as many as 600 before receiving an error saying the payload has been surpassed, but that number isn't supported.

Implementing conditional access policies to protect various types of users from accessing sensitive resources can take time and effort. A policy can be structured according to the resource's sensitivity.

The other approach involves defining access policies based on where the user is within the organization. This approach may result in an unmanageable number of conditional access policies.

To meet the exact needs of a group of users, it is better to structure policies relating to common access needs and bundle them into personas. Enterprise personas share common attributes, responsibilities, experiences, objectives, and access, as well as common enterprise attributes, responsibilities, experiences, and goals. A comprehensive Zero Trust strategy requires understanding how various personas access enterprise assets and resources.

A separate persona should also be defined for identities not part of any persona group. This is called the *global persona*, which is meant to enforce policy for identities that aren't part of any persona group.

Summary of Personas

Microsoft recommends considering the personas listed in Table 3.2 in your enterprise design.

TABLE 3.2   Personas

Role	Persona Description
Global	Global generally represents policies that apply to all personas or do not apply to any specific persona. Use it to define policies that aren't covered by other personas. The persona would help protect all relevant scenarios.
Admin	Administrators are nonguest identities, whether cloud or synchronized, who have an administrator role in Azure AD or Microsoft 365 (for example, in Microsoft Defender for Cloud Apps, Exchange, Defender for Endpoints, or Compliance Manager). This persona excludes guests with these roles because a different persona covers them.
Developers	Users in the developers personas have unique needs. They are based on Active Directory accounts synced to Azure AD but have special access to Azure DevOps, continuous integration/continuous delivery pipelines, device code flow, and GitHub. There can be internal and external users in the developers persona, but a person should be included in only one.
Internals	Microsoft recommends adding developers' internal users to the developer's persona if their Active Directory account is synced with Azure AD.
Externals	External consultants with Active Directory accounts synced to Azure AD. External developers should be added to the developers persona.

Role	Persona Description
Guest	Guests include all users invited to the customer's Azure AD tenant as guest.
Guest Admins	Users with Azure AD guest accounts assigned any of the previous admin roles can be found in the guest admins persona.
Microsoft 365 Service Accounts	Users of this persona access Microsoft 365 services using Azure AD accounts when other solutions, like managed service identities, do not meet their needs.
Azure Service Accounts	A service account for Azure (IaaS/PaaS) is a user-based account created for accessing Azure (IaaS/PaaS) services without using a managed service identity.
Corp Service Accounts	These service accounts are user-based and have the following characteristics: They are authenticated with on-premises Active Directory. IaaS-based virtual machines in another (cloud) data center, such as Azure, are used to access them. They are synced to an Azure AD instance that accesses any Azure or Microsoft 365 service. While this is possible, it is highly recommended not to use this approach.
Workload Identities	Conditional Access now supports protecting access to resources from machine identities, such as Azure AD service principals and managed identities.

Source: adapted from `https://learn.microsoft.com/en-us/azure/`
`architecture/guide/security/conditional-access-architecture#`
`conditional-access-personas`

 Zero Trust architecture relies on conditional access to define and enforce policies. Depending on various signals or conditions, conditional access may block or grant limited access to resources. Microsoft recommends moving control and management into cloud services by using conditional access as a central control plane and policy engine.

Design a Strategy for Role Assignment and Delegation

By assigning roles to Azure AD groups, your Global Administrators and Privileged Role Administrators can simplify the management of role assignments in Azure AD.

For instance, Company XYZ hired people worldwide to manage and reset passwords for its Azure AD clients. Global Administrators and Privileged Role Administrators can create a group called CompanyXYZHelpdeskAdministrators and assign the role to the group instead of assigning the role individually to all employees. People who join a group are assigned roles indirectly.

To ensure only legitimate users are members of the group, help-desk individual users are assigned the Helpdesk Administrator role. Your existing governance workflow can perform the approval process and audit the group's membership.

Using Azure AD Privileged Identity Management (PIM), you can assign roles to groups. Each group member can activate the role assignment for a fixed time frame. Here are the best practices for using Azure Active Directory role-based access control (Azure AD RBAC):

Least privilege management. As a best practice, managing your access control strategy to the least privilege possible is best. The least privilege means giving administrators the permissions they need to do their jobs. When assigning administrators a role, you need to consider three aspects: a specific set of permissions, a specified scope, and a specified period. Initially it seems easier to assign broader roles at broader scopes. It would be best if you avoided them. Azure AD RBAC supports more than 65 built-in roles. In the event of a breach of a security principle, you limit the resources at risk by limiting roles and scopes. A few of Azure AD's roles include the management of directory objects, groups, and applications, as well as the management of Microsoft 365 services such as Exchange, SharePoint, and Intune.

Access can be granted just in time using privileged identity management. There should be a limited period of time for which access should be granted under the principle of least privilege. Microsoft recommends enabling Azure AD Privileged Identity Management (PIM) to grant administrators just-in-time access. In Azure AD, PIM allows an individual to become an eligible member for a limited-time role and activate the role as needed. Privileged access is automatically removed when the timeframe expires. Activating highly privileged roles can also require approval or be notified via email via PIM settings. Notifications alert you when new users have been added.

For all administrator accounts, enable MFA. Based on Microsoft studies available in the below link, there is a 99.9 percent reduction in the likelihood of your account being compromised if you use MFA.

The chance of your account being compromised is 99.9 percent lower if you use multifactor authentication (MFA).

Two methods are available for enabling MFA on Azure AD roles:

- Setting up roles in PIM
- Conditional Access

Restrict access over time by configuring recurring access reviews. Access reviews should ensure that only the system engineers or administrators can access your organization's systems or services. Regular audits are essential for several reasons.

- A malicious actor can compromise an account.
- Without auditing, people can accrue unnecessary access over time as they move between teams.

Ensure that there are no more than five Global Administrators. You should limit the number of Global Administrators in your organization to fewer than five. These accounts should be protected with multifactor authentication, as previously stated. Keeping the attack surface small is in your best interest, as Global Administrators hold the keys to the kingdom.

To ensure that these accounts do not require multifactor authentication, Microsoft recommends keeping two break-glass accounts permanently assigned to the Global Administrator role.

Role assignments in Azure AD can be delegated to groups. If your external governance system uses groups, you should consider assigning roles to Azure AD groups rather than individuals. PIM can also manage role-assignable groups to prevent standing owners and members.

Owners of role-assignable groups can delegate role management on a per-role basis by using groups. Privileged Role or Global Administrators decide who gets added to or removed from the group.

By using privileged access groups, you can activate multiple roles simultaneously. An individual may have five or six Azure AD roles eligible for assignment through PIM. Activating each role individually can reduce productivity, and the problem is further compounded by the fact that they might have tens or hundreds of Azure resources assigned to them.

In this case, the user should be an eligible member or owner of a privileged access group. Create a privileged access group and assign it permanent access to multiple roles (Azure AD and Azure). It takes only one activation for them to access all the linked resources.

Azure AD roles should be assigned to cloud native accounts. In the event an on-premises account is compromised, in turn your Azure AD resources can also be compromised. Do not use on-premises synced accounts for Azure AD role assignment.

Enforce delegation. Let's look at an example to understand how to access governance is delegated in entitlement management.

Jon is the IT administrator, and Ahmed, in Finance, and Tim, in Legal, are responsible for their departments' resources and critical business content.

Access governance can be delegated to these non-administrators through entitlement management since they know what users need access to, when, and for how long. By delegating access to nonadministrators, departments are managed by the right people.

To avoid confusion leading to security risks, clearly define lines of responsibility and separate duties for a company's workload and supporting infrastructure.

Microsoft recommends the following:

- Communicate, investigate, and hunt with the application team in an aligned manner.
- For security teams that need access to the cloud environment resources to assess and report on organizational risk, establish access control for all cloud environment resources by the principle of least privilege.

Design a Security Strategy for Privileged Role Access to Infrastructure Including Identity-Based Firewall Rules and Azure PIM

To gain access to sensitive data, cyberattackers target administrator accounts and other accounts with privileged access in credential theft attacks. Cloud service providers and their customers are jointly responsible for prevention and response.

As a result of SaaS applications and end users' devices connected to the Internet, security perimeters are no longer as effective as they used to be. Azure AD replaces security perimeters with identity layer authentication, with privileged administrative roles assigned to users. It doesn't matter if the environment is on-premises, cloud-based, or hybrid; the user must have access protected.

Microsoft recommends adopting a strategy that helps your organization reduce the risks of high-impact, high-likelihood privileged access attacks. In every organization, privileged access should be a top security priority. Any compromise of these users will have a significant negative impact on the organization.

The security of privileged access is crucial since it is the foundational element of all other security assurances. All other security assurances will fail if an attacker controls your privileged accounts. As a matter of risk, the loss of privileged access is highly likely to occur and is increasing at an alarming rate across industries.

Initial attacks using these techniques resulted in high-profile breaches at familiar brands (and many unreported incidents). More recently, ransomware attackers have adopted these techniques, fueling an explosive growth of highly profitable human-operated ransomware attacks that intentionally disrupt business operations across the industry.

When attackers compromise the accounts of privileged users in an organization, they have access to business-critical assets. Microsoft recommends a three-level security strategy that promotes progressive improvements over time by providing clear guidance and flexibility, as shown in Figure 3.7.

FIGURE 3.7   Microsoft recommends end-to-end security.

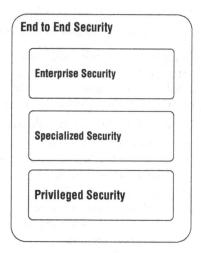

Organizations can deploy these critical protections rapidly using these levels because they provide straightforward technical guidance. The privileged access strategy recognizes that organizations have unique needs and that custom solutions create complexity that causes higher costs and lower security over time.

To balance this requirement, the strategy supplies firm prescriptive direction for each level and flexibility by permitting organizations to determine when each role is mandated to meet the needs of that level.

Even though the underlying technology is complex, it is essential to keep things simple rather than create custom solutions that are difficult to maintain.

The guided privileged access security strategy implements a simple three-level system of guarantees that span areas such as all devices, accounts, intermediaries, and interfaces that are subject to the same security levels.

Enterprise Security   Security for enterprise users and productivity scenarios is suitable for all enterprise users.

In advance of the rapid modernization plan, the enterprise also functions as the starting point for technological and privileged access as they progressively build on the security controls in enterprise security.

Specialized Security   Specialized security controls provide increased protection if an attacker or malicious insider compromises a role with a high business impact.

Identify all roles and accounts meeting your organization's specialized and privileged criteria. Typical specialized roles include the following:

- Business-critical system developers
- Business roles with sensitive business information, including SWIFT terminal users, researchers who have access to sensitive data, payroll administrators, and approvers of sensitive business processes, among others

- Those who regularly handle sensitive information, such as executives and personal assistants/administrative assistants
- High-impact social media accounts, which could damage a company's reputation

  This group includes administrators of individual high-impact workloads with significant privileges that are not enterprise-wide. They typically have significant privileges and impact. (Examples are an administrator of an enterprise resource planning system, a bank administrator, a help-desk administrator, and so on).

  Privileged security is further built upon with specialized account security.

Privileged Security   Security at the highest level is referred to as *privileged security*. It is designed for roles that can cause significant damage and potentially lead to a significant incident in the organization if the attacker or malicious insider gets their hands on them. Technical roles at this level typically have administrative permissions to most or all enterprise systems (sometimes including business-critical ones). Security is the first priority for privileged accounts, while productivity is defined as the ability to quickly and securely complete a fixed set of sensitive job tasks.

Securing Privileged Access

For privileged access to be secured, the following changes are required:

- Knowledge management, administrative practices, and processes
- A host defense, account protection, and identity management component

In the case of on-premises administrator accounts, manage and report your privileged access.

Let's discuss Microsoft Azure AD Privileged Identity Management (PIM) capabilities.

The Azure Active Directory (Azure AD) service Privileged Identity Management provides a way to manage, control, and monitor access to your organization's essential resources. To minimize the risk of compromising secure information or resources, organizations should reduce the number of people who have access to resources.

As a result, there is less chance of the following happening:

- Access by a malicious actor
- An authorized user accidentally impacting a sensitive resource

Organizations can grant privileged users just-in-time privileged access to Azure. Azure AD resources monitor what privileged users do with their privileges. Azure AD, Azure, Microsoft 365, or SaaS apps still need to be used by privileged users to carry out privileged operations. Azure AD Premium P2 licenses are required to use the PIM feature.

In Privileged Identity Management, Azure AD roles can be managed only by users with the Privileged Role Administrator or Global Administrator roles. In Privileged Identity Management, Azure AD roles can be viewed by Global Administrators, Security Administrators, Global Readers, and Security Readers.

Privileged Identity Management allows subscription administrators, resource owners, or resource user access administrators to assign Azure resource roles to other administrators. Users who are Privileged Role Administrators, Security Administrators, or Security Readers cannot view Azure resource role assignments by default in Privileged Identity Management.

Here are some of the critical features of Privileged Identity Management for mitigating the risks of excessive, unnecessary, or misused access permissions on your resources:

- **Just in time:** Azure AD and Azure resources can be accessed just in time.
- **Time-bound:** Using start and end dates, assign resources time-bound access.
- **Approval:** Activating privileged roles requires approval.
- **Multifactor:** Activate any role with multifactor authentication.
- **Justification:** Understanding why users activate can be achieved by using justification.
- **Notifications:** Activate privileged roles and receive notifications.
- **Access reviews:** Ensure users' roles are still needed by conducting access reviews.
- **Audit history:** This includes internal or external audits and downloading the audit history.
- **Last active global administrator and privileged role administrator:** This prevents the last active global administrator and privileged role administrator role assignments from being removed.

Develop a Road Map

Microsoft recommends developing a road map to prevent cyberattackers from accessing privileged resources. As your organization develops its capabilities and requirements, you can continuously adjust your road map to secure privileged access against cyberattackers. Microsoft recommends four stages in its road map to make it more challenging and costlier for adversaries to gain privileged access to your on-premises, cloud, or hybrid assets. Implementations that are most effective and fastest should be scheduled first.

At a very high level, this is the objective of each stage:

- **The first stage (24–48 hours):** Microsoft recommends that you take care of critical items right away.
- **The second stage:** Mitigate the most commonly used attacks (2–4 weeks).
- **The third stage (1–3 months):** Building visibility and controlling administrator activity.
- **The fourth stage (six months and beyond):** Further hardening your security platform.

Stage 1: Critical Items to Do Right Now

Stage 1 of the road map focuses on the fast and easy implementation of critical tasks. To achieve a fundamental class of secure privileged access, Microsoft recommends that you complete these few tasks within 24–48 hours. The following actions are included in this stage of the road map for Secured Privileged Access:

- Enable Privileged Identity Management in Azure AD.
- Recognize and categorize accounts with high privileges.

- Provide emergency access to at least two people.
- Register all highly privileged, nonfederated single-user administrator accounts with multifactor authentication.

Stage 2: Mitigate Frequently Used Attacks

Stage 2 of the Secured Privileged Access road map addresses the most commonly used attack methods of credential stealing and misusage. It can be implemented within 2–4 weeks and includes the following actions:

- A service, owner, and administrator inventory should be conducted.
- Determine which Microsoft accounts need to be switched from administrative roles to work or school accounts.
- Maintain separate user accounts for Global Administrators and forward their email.
- Recent password changes should be made for administrative accounts.
- Enable synchronization of password hashes.
- Ensure that users with privileged roles and those exposed to security risks require multifactor authentication.
- Protect your identity by configuring Identity Protection.
- Prepare an incident/emergency response plan; identify owners.
- Ensure that on-premises privileged administrative accounts are secure.
- Configure conditional access policies.

Stage 3: Take Control of Administrator Activity

As part of this Secured Privileged Access road map stage, the following components will be implemented within approximately 1–3 months.

- Access reviews should be completed for users in administrator roles.
- Continue to roll out stronger authentication to all users.
- Dedicated workstations should be used for Azure AD administration.
- Identify incident handling recommendations from the National Institute of Standards and Technology (NIST).
- Increase the number of administrative roles using Privileged Identity Management for JIT.
- If you use Exchange Online, determine whether you are exposed to password-based login protocols.
- Your virtual machines' privileged accounts should be inventoried.
- Azure AD administrators should implement PIM.
- Monitor activity in connected cloud apps.
- Configure conditional access.

- Assess the roles in Microsoft 365 (if Microsoft 365 is used).

- Integrate information protection.

- User Azure log integration to send relevant logs to your SIEM.

Manage, control, and monitor Azure resource access with PIM. PIM lowers privilege exposure times and increases visibility into use through reports and alerts.

Stage 4: Continue Building Defenses

To protect your privileged access environment from potential attacks known today, stage 4 of the road map should be implemented within six months of completing it. Microsoft recommends viewing security as an ongoing process that increases costs and reduces the success rate for adversaries targeting your environment to protect against tomorrow's security threats. The following components are included in this stage:

- Review Azure AD administrator roles.

- Users who are responsible for managing Azure AD-joined devices should be reviewed.

- Plan for incident response and validate it.

Best Practices for Managing Identity and Access on the Microsoft Platform

Identity forms of cloud-based security assurances. In legacy IT infrastructures, firewalls and network security solutions were often used to protect against outside threats at the Internet egress points. Still, these controls are less effective in cloud architectures, where shared services are accessed through cloud provider networks or the Internet.

With control over the networks hosted by these services, it is easier to write concise firewall rules. As cloud resources spin up and down dynamically, cloud customers may share a common infrastructure, and employees and users expect to be able to access data and services from anywhere, it is challenging or impossible to write concise firewall rules. Protecting data and resources in the cloud requires identity authentication and authorization controls.

As a result of their visibility into a large volume of access requests and threats across many customers, cloud-based identity solutions such as Azure AD offer additional security features that legacy identity services do not.

The following are best practices for managing identity and access on the Microsoft platform:

- Integrate full-time employees' identities with enterprise resources in a single enterprise directory.

- Integrate your existing identity systems with your cloud identity.

- Instead of including vendor, partner, and customer accounts in your on-premises directory, use cloud identity services.

- Eventually, all users should be able to access their accounts without a password or with multifactor authentication (MFA).

- Ensure that Internet-facing services do not use insecure legacy protocols.

- Do not sync highly privileged Active Directory Domain Services accounts (such as Domain, Enterprise, and Schema admins) with Azure Active Directory.

- For accounts that cannot be passwordless, provide modern and adequate protections.

- All platforms (Windows, Linux, and so on) and cloud services should be authenticated using a single identity provider.

- All users should be authenticated to support a Zero Trust strategy, and security attributes should be measured and enforced.

- Educate and empower your users by simulating attacks against them regularly.

There are three related concepts, Privileged Identity Management, Privileged Account Management, and cloud infrastructure entitlements management that all provide just-in-time permission:

- **Privilege Account Management:** A workflow that grants permanent access to an account

- **Privileged Identity Management:** A workflow that grants privileges to authenticated accounts

- **Cloud infrastructure entitlements management:** A workflow for giving access to infrastructure entitlements

Design a Security Strategy for Privileged Activities Including PAM, Entitlement Management, and Cloud Tenant Administration

Microsoft recommends embracing the following privileged-access strategy to rapidly reduce the risks to your organization from high-impact and high-likelihood attacks on privileged access. Because of the potential business impact (and high likelihood) of attackers compromising this level of access, organizations should make securing privileged access the top security priority.

An attack on these users almost always has a significant negative impact on an organization. Privileged users have access to business-critical assets, causing a significant adverse effect on the organization when their accounts are compromised. An IT administrator with privileged access controls large portions of an organization's estate, while other users with privileged access also have access to business-critical assets.

As a result of human-operated ransomware attacks and targeted data theft, attackers frequently exploit weaknesses in privileged access security. A privileged access account or workstation is an attractive target for attackers because it allows them to gain rapid access to the company's assets, often resulting in immediate and significant business losses.

Having privileged access lost can significantly impact business and cause significant damage. The attacker effectively controls all enterprise assets and resources, allowing him to expose confidential data, stop all business processes, or subvert business processes and machines to harm people or damage property.

With the advent of modern credential theft techniques starting with pass-the-hash, privileged access attacks have become increasingly common. With the release of the Pass-the-Hash Toolkit in 2008, these techniques exploded in popularity with criminals and have since evolved into a suite of reliable attack techniques (mainly based on the Mimikatz toolkit). Attacks (and their subsequent impact) increased due to weaponization and automation, limited only by the target organization's vulnerability and the attacker's monetization and incentive models.

Developing a Privileged Access Strategy

As a term used in enterprise environments, *privileged access* describes special abilities or access that extends beyond the capabilities of a standard user. Organizations can maintain privileged access by securing infrastructure and applications, running a business efficiently, and protecting sensitive data and critical infrastructure.

Users with privileged access can be humans and nonhumans, including applications and machines.

As a way of protecting themselves from credential theft and misuse of privileges, organizations implement privileged access management (PAM). PAM is a comprehensive cybersecurity strategy comprising people, processes, and technology that controls, monitors, secures, and audits all privileged identities and activities in an enterprise IT environment.

PAM is also known as Privileged Identity Management (PIM) or privileged access security (PAS), which focuses on giving users only the level of access necessary to accomplish their tasks. As a standard security practice, least privilege is crucial to securing high-value data and assets. An organization can reduce the attack surface and mitigate the risk of malicious insiders or external cyberattacks by enforcing the principle of least privilege.

Quick wins and incremental advancements must characterize the journey of privileged access. You must seal out persistent and flexible attackers from privileged access through every weakness in your privileged access strategy, as they are like water trying to seep into your environment.

Combining multiple technologies with thoughtful, holistic, and prioritized risk mitigations is necessary to reduce the risk from privileged access.

Developing a privileged access strategy involves a combination of accumulative progress and swift wins. As you create your privileged access strategy, you must "close" out persistent and flexible attackers with privileged access.

Attackers prioritize a combination of these paths in practice.

- Techniques that have been established (often automated into attack tools)
- Exploitable new methods

This strategy requires a complete strategy that combines multiple technologies and follows Zero Trust principles due to the variety of technology involved.

- Attackers use any attack that works, regardless of technology.
- Most enterprise systems are integrated with the access control backbone you are defending.

A privileged access solution or network controls alone will not be able to detect or prevent these threats. For privileged access to business-sensitive systems, Microsoft recommends incrementally building a closed loop system for privileged access using trusted clean devices, accounts, and intermediary systems.

It is important to design this strategy with an intentional outcome, to establish and follow standards carefully, and to continue monitoring and auditing the products to eliminate leaks, just as you would when waterproofing something complex in real life, like a boat. A boat wouldn't be waterproof if you just nailed boards together.

Building and waterproofing critical components like the engine and steering mechanism (while leaving ways to get in) would be the priority, followed by comfort items like radios, seats, and the like.

Moreover, you would have to maintain it over time, as even the most perfect system could spring a leak later, so preventative maintenance and monitoring for leaks are essential for keeping it afloat.

There are two simple goals to securing privileged access.

- Ensure privileged actions can be performed through only a few authorized channels.
- Ensure that those pathways are protected and closely monitored.

There are two kinds of pathways to accessing the systems: user access and privileged access.

The user account performs emailing, collaboration, and web browsing tasks. An account logs on to a device or workstation, passes through an intermediary such as a remote access solution, and interacts with enterprise systems as part of this path.

Privileged accounts like IT administrators or other sensitive accounts access business-critical systems and data or perform administrative tasks on enterprise systems. While the technical components may be equal, the harm an opponent can inflict with privileged access is much more significant.

Standard and privileged users are supported by identity systems that host the accounts and administrative groups, synchronize and federate, and provide other identity support functions.

In a PAM/PIM system, authorized elevation paths allow standard users to interact with privileged workflows, such as managers or peers approving administrative access requests to sensitive systems through a JIT process. These components collectively comprise the privileged access attack surface that an adversary may target to attempt to gain elevated access to your enterprise.

Establish privileged identity strategies that work; combining the following methods will be helpful:

- The rapid modernization plan (RAMP) and Zero Trust access control are described throughout this recommendation.

- Asset protection safeguards against direct asset attacks by involving good security hygiene practices to systems.

Plan for Rapid Modernization of Security

At a high level, RAMP incorporates the following steps:

Accounts with privileged access should be separated and managed.

- Organizations should rarely use emergency access accounts due to the potential risk of compromising their Azure Active Directory (Azure AD).

- You can discover and secure privileged accounts with Azure AD PIM. PIM mitigates unnecessary, excessive, or misused access permission risks.

- The process identifies and minimizes the number of people that need separate accounts and privileged access protection (immediately or over time) by identifying and categorizing privileged accounts (Azure AD) with a high business impact.

- Administrators should have mail disabled on their accounts, and personal Microsoft accounts should not be allowed on any administrator accounts (on-premises AD accounts).

- After Microsoft Defender for Identity is deployed, all open alerts should be reviewed and mitigated by the appropriate teams.

Enhance the management of credentials.

- Establish and enforce self-service password reset (SSPR) and combined security information registration in your organization.

- All users who are permanently assigned to one or more Azure AD admin roles require Azure Active Directory MFA at sign-in.

- If legacy authentication protocols are enabled for privileged user accounts, attackers can gain access to their accounts.

- By enforcing the application consent process, a centralized consent process can be established to maintain visibility and control of the applications that have access to data in Azure AD.

- Establish a method for monitoring and managing user and sign-in risks. Clean up accounts and sign-in risks using Azure AD Identity Protection.

Manage privileged activities by executing critical strategic initiatives.   To implement the recommended strategy for privileged activities, several strategic initiatives need to be undertaken. There are four complementary initiatives that need to be implemented, each having a defined outcome and success criterion.

- Session security from end-to-end. Establish explicit Zero Trust validation for privileged, user, and elevated sessions.
  - **Success criteria defined by Microsoft:** Users and devices will be verified for trustworthiness before they are allowed access to the system.
- Maintain identity systems such as directories, identity management, admin accounts, consent grants, and so on.
  - **Success criteria defined by Microsoft:** Each system will be protected to the extent that it is likely to impact the business.
- Protect local account passwords, service account passwords, or other secrets from lateral traversal by mitigating it.
  - **Success criteria defined by Microsoft:** For a single device to succeed, it must not be compromised. As a result, many or all other devices in the environment may be controlled.
- Reduce adversary time and access to the environment by implementing rapid threat response.

  - **Success criteria defined by Microsoft:** MTTR for incidents involving privileged access should be reduced to near zero, and the MTTR for all incidents should be reduced to a few minutes to prevent adversaries from reliably conducting multi-stage attacks in the environment. In this way, adversaries will not have time to target privileged access.

Azure AD Entitlement Management

Through Azure Active Directory entitlement management, organizations can automate access request workflows, assign and review access for users, and expire access at scale. The employees are required to access various groups, applications, and SharePoint Online sites in the course of their jobs. As requirements change, managing this access becomes increasingly challenging, new applications are added, or users require more access rights. If you collaborate with outside organizations, this scenario becomes even more difficult. They may not know what applications, groups, or sites your organization uses, nor do you know who needs access to their resources.

By managing Azure AD entitlements, you can manage internal users' access to groups, applications, and SharePoint Online sites, as well as external users' access. Management of entitlements includes the following capabilities:

- With time-limited assignments and periodic access reviews, you can control who can access apps, groups, Teams, and SharePoint sites.
- Allow users to access those resources based on their departments or cost centers and remove their access when those properties change.
- Defining policies that specify which users can request resources, who must approve those requests, and when access expires for these access packages can be done by delegated access package managers. Users can request resources from these access packages.

- Users who do not yet have access to your directory can request access by selecting connected organizations. Users who request access and are approved are automatically granted access. In your directory, their B2B account can be automatically removed when user access expires without any other access packages assigned.

Access requests, approvals, and re-certifications can be streamlined by leveraging Azure AD to make sure that only the right people have access and that access requests are logged. Here are the steps to follow:

1. When users join different teams/projects, Entitlement Management can create access packages that can be used to assign access to resources (such as applications, SharePoint sites, and group memberships) associated with each team/project.

2. Until Entitlement Management can be deployed in your organization, try enabling self-service paradigms by deploying self-service group management and self-service application access.

 The Azure AD identity and access management solution connects 425 million people monthly to their apps, devices, and data. It verifies and secures each identity across your entire digital estate with solid authentication.

Summary

This chapter has exposed you to different strategies for designing, defining, and recommending a security strategy and architecture for your organization based on Zero Trust.

As part of an identity security strategy, an organization authenticates and authorizes its security principals. Besides controlling information about security principals (identities), it also includes services, applications, users, groups, and so on. Managing identities and access across the company's data center and into the cloud is one of the goals of Microsoft Identity and Access Management solutions.

In this chapter, you learned how to design a strategy for access to cloud resources, recommend an identity store (tenants, B2B, B2C, hybrid), recommend an authentication strategy, recommend an authorization strategy, design a strategy for conditional access, design a strategy for role assignment and delegation, design a security strategy for privileged role access to infrastructure including identity-based firewall rules and Azure PIM, and design a security strategy for privileged activities including PAM, entitlement management, and cloud tenant administration.

Exam Essentials

Understand Identity security.   Azure identity and access management solutions secure your data and applications at the front door. Protect credentials against malicious login attempts and keep them secure with risk-based access controls, identity protection tools, and robust authentication options.

An organization's identity security strategy should describe the process of authenticating and authorizing its security principal. Additionally, it involves controlling information about these principles (identities). Services, applications, users, groups, and other security principal (identities) may be included. Microsoft identity and access management solutions are essential to protect access to applications and resources throughout the corporate data center and into the cloud.

Know the best practices for an identity store for security.   Azure AD allows you to connect to Microsoft cloud services and develop your own cloud services from within the Azure Active Directory service.

Your organization manages identity and access in on-premises environments using Active Directory on Windows Server. Azure AD is Microsoft's cloud-based identity and access management service, and Microsoft ensures that Azure AD is available globally despite your controlling identity accounts. If you're familiar with Active Directory, Azure AD will be expected of you.

Active Directory does not track sign-in attempts when you secure identities on-premises. When Active Directory is connected to Azure AD, Microsoft helps protect you by detecting suspicious sign-in attempts at no extra cost. Azure AD, for instance, detects sign-in attempts from unexpected places or unknown devices.

Know the best practices for secure authentication and security authorization strategies.   Authentication is the method of validating the identity of a person, service, or device. Authentication is like presenting an ID when traveling, requiring a person, service, or device to provide credentials to prove who they are. Several authentication methods are supported by Azure, including standard passwords, single sign-on, multifactor authentication, and passwordless authentication. It doesn't confirm that you're ticketed; it just proves you're who you say you are.

The authentication process ensures that the identity attempting to connect has the correct permissions to access services, features, functions, objects, and methods. Authorization occurs after successful authentication, and a connection not authenticated fails before authorization checks are performed. The user or group may not be authorized to take particular actions even if a connection authentication succeeds.

Know the best practices for secure conditional access.   Zero Trust relies heavily on conditional access because it ensures the right user has access to the right resources. Azure Active Directory can make access decisions based on computed risk and preconfigured policies if conditional access is enabled. By surfacing conditional access policies as a feature when appropriate, independent software vendors can take advantage of conditional access.

A user might not be challenged for a second authentication factor if they are at a known location if conditional access offers a more granular multifactor authentication experience. If, however, their sign-in signals are unusual or they are in an unexpected location, they may have to provide a second authentication factor.

Conditional Access collects sign-in signals, decisions are made based on those signals, and then the decision is enforced by allowing or denying access or requiring multifactor authentication.

Plan for role assignment and delegation.   The concept of least privilege implies that you should give access only to resources in your cloud environment needed to complete a task. When you have multiple IT and engineering teams, how can you control their resource access? It's a good security practice to grant read access to Azure storage only if you need read access, and write access should not be granted to the storage, and read access should not be granted to other storage.

However, that level of permissions would be challenging to manage for an entire team. Through Azure role-based access control, you can control access rather than define detailed access requirements for each individual and update them when new resources are added to the team or new people join the team.

Know the Identity governance for access reviews and entitlement management.   Administrators can easily ensure that users and guests have the appropriate access by default by creating and managing Azure AD entitlement management aspects. The users or decision-makers can take part in an access review and recertify (or attest) their access rights. These users may be aware only of some circumstances in which access packages are needed. After an access review has been completed, you can make changes and remove access from users who do not need it anymore. After the review is complete, reviewers can give their input on each user's need for continued access based on suggestions from Azure AD.

Design a security strategy for privileged role access to infrastructure.   As the name implies, privileged security is intended for roles likely to result in major incidents and material damage if they are in the hands of an attacker or malicious insider. A few business-critical roles at this level usually have administrative permissions to most or all enterprise systems. Privileged accounts are designed to focus on security as a top priority, with productivity characterized as the potential to easily and securely perform a fixed set of sensitive job tasks securely (not general productivity).

The following are key criteria to consider:

- Limit access to secure information and resources by identifying and minimizing the number of people who have access to them.

- Access permissions on sensitive resources may be excessive, unnecessary, or misused.

- Ensure that secure information or resources are not accessible to malicious actors.

- Ensure unauthorized users do not inadvertently access sensitive resources.

Design a security strategy for privileged access.   Zero Trust access control and asset protection should lay the foundations for a successful privileged identity strategy. The rapid modernization plan enables the privileged identity strategy and improves the credential management experience. Try to meet two simple goals for securing privileged access.

- Ensure that privileged actions can be performed only through a few authorized pathways.
- Ensure that those pathways are protected and closely monitored.

Review Questions

1. As a Microsoft Cybersecurity Architect, you are responsible for securing access to on-premises applications outside your private network, such as SharePoint sites, Outlook Web Apps, and IIS-based applications. Which Azure identity capability will you adopt in your enterprise identity and access management solution?

   A. Azure AD Application Proxy

   B. Multifactor authentication

   C. Single sign-on

   D. Device registration

2. As a Microsoft Cybersecurity Architect, you are responsible for securing access to data and applications; Which Azure identity capability will you adopt in your enterprise identity and access management solution?

   A. Azure AD Application Proxy

   B. Multifactor authentication

   C. Single sign-on

   D. Device registration

3. As a Microsoft Cybersecurity Architect, you are responsible for securing that all the applications and resources you need are accessible through a single user account so you have to sign in only once. You do not need to authenticate (for example, type a password) again once you have signed in to all applications. Which Azure identity capability will you adopt in your enterprise identity and access management solution?

   A. Azure AD Application Proxy

   B. Multifactor authentication

   C. Single sign-on

   D. Device registration

4. As a Microsoft Cybersecurity Architect, you are responsible for deploying device-based conditional access policies so your security administrators can block or allow resources. Which Azure identity capability will you adopt in your enterprise identity and access management solution?

   A. Azure AD Application Proxy

   B. Multifactor authentication

   C. Single sign-on

   D. Device registration

5. As a Microsoft Cybersecurity Architect, you are responsible for protecting your organization's identities by providing a consolidated view of risk detections and potential vulnerabilities. Which Azure identity capability will you adopt in your enterprise identity and access management solution?

    A. Azure AD Identity Protection

    B. Multifactor authentication

    C. Single sign-on

    D. Device registration

6. As a Microsoft Cybersecurity Architect, you are responsible for protecting and automating identity processes at scale with single sign-on authentication, conditional access, passwordless and multifactor authentication, and automated and user provisioning. Which Azure identity capability will you adopt in your enterprise identity and access management solution?

    A. Azure Active Directory

    B. Azure S2S VPN

    C. Azure P2S VPN

    D. ExpressRoute

7. As a Microsoft Cybersecurity Architect, you are responsible for designing and deploying hybrid identity solutions. Which Azure identity authentication methods are supported for your enterprise? (Choose two.)

    A. Azure Active Directory

    B. Cloud authentication

    C. Federated authentication

    D. Microsoft Active Directory

8. As a Microsoft Cybersecurity Architect, you are responsible for designing and deploying hybrid identity solutions; you have selected cloud authentication. Which are the two options available in your cloud authentication? (Choose two.)

    A. Azure AD password hash synchronization

    B. Microsoft Active Directory

    C. Azure AD pass-through authentication

    D. None of the above

9. Which of the following features in Azure Active Directory B2C supports millions of users and billions of daily authentications? This solution enables branded web and mobile applications to blend seamlessly with white-label authentication experiences.

    A. Customer identity and access management (CIAM)

    B. Microsoft Active Directory

    C. Azure AD pass-through authentication

    D. Azure AD password hash synchronization

10. Which of the following passes the authentication process to an external authentication system, such as Active Directory Federation Services (AD FS)?

    A. Azure Active Directory (Azure AD)

    B. Microsoft Active Directory

    C. Azure AD pass-through authentication

    D. None of the above

11. What is the process of authentication when you adopt pass-through authentication and seamless SSO in your solution?

    A. A secure password verification exchange is conducted with the authentication agent on-premises in the cloud.

    B. Authentication happens in the cloud.

    C. Authentication happens on-premises.

    D. Authentication happens on another identity service provider.

12. What health monitoring solutions are available when you adopt federation with AD FS in your solution?

    A. Admin Center for Azure Active Directory provides agent status.

    B. Not required.

    C. Azure AD Connect Health.

    D. On-premises.

13. As a Microsoft Cybersecurity Architect, you are responsible for designing and deploying conditional access solutions. Which of the Microsoft recommendations will you adopt in creating a Zero Trust access model?

    A. Verify explicitly.

    B. Use least privilege access.

    C. Assume breach.

    D. All of the above.

14. Which of the following does Windows Hello for Business support when you adopt the pass-through authentication and seamless SSO in your solution? (Choose two.)

    A. Key trust model

    B. Hybrid cloud trust assume breach

    C. Certificate trust model

    D. None of the above

15. As a Microsoft Cybersecurity Architect, you are responsible for designing and deploying role assignment and delegation. Which of the Microsoft recommendations will you adopt in your solution? (Choose two.)

    A. Configure recurring access assessments to withdraw unnecessary permissions over time.

    B. Without auditing, people can accrue unnecessary access over time as they move between teams. Turn off multifactor authentication for all your administrator accounts.

    C. None of the above.

16. As a Microsoft Cybersecurity Architect, you are responsible for designing and deploying enterprise cloud security for your organization. Of the following Microsoft recommendations, which of the following will you adopt?

    A. Enterprise security

    B. Specialized security

    C. Privileged security

    D. All of the above

17. As a Microsoft Cybersecurity Architect, you are responsible for developing a road map to secure privileged access against cyberattackers. Which of the following Microsoft recommendations will you consider? (Choose two.)

    A. In stage 1 (24–48 hours), Microsoft recommends you do these critical items right away, and the second stage is to mitigate the most commonly used attack techniques (2–4 weeks).

    B. The third stage (1–3 months) involves building visibility and controlling administrative activities altogether, and the fourth stage (6 months and beyond) consists of building defenses to further harden your security platform.

    C. The fifth stage (24 months and beyond) is to release new features.

    D. All of the above.

18. Securing privileged access has two simple goals; which of the following are they? (Choose two.)

    A. Monitoring is not essential.

    B. Limit access to privileged actions to a few authorized paths.

    C. Protect and closely monitor those pathways.

    D. None of the above.

19. A successful privileged identity requires a combination of which two of the following key considerations? (Choose two.)

    A. Zero Trust access control

    B. Asset protection

    C. Identity protection

    D. User protection

20. Which of the following helps you manage entitlement and allows your organization to automate access request workflows, assign and review access for users, and expire access at scale?

    A. Azure Active Directory

    B. Microsoft Active Directory

    C. Microsoft LDAP

    D. None of the above

Chapter

4

Identify a Regulatory Compliance Strategy

THE MICROSOFT SC-100 EXAM OBJECTIVES COVERED IN THIS CHAPTER INCLUDE:

✓ Interpret compliance requirements and translate into specific technical capabilities (new or existing)

✓ Evaluate infrastructure compliance by using Microsoft Defender for Cloud

✓ Interpret compliance scores and recommend actions to resolve issues or improve security

✓ Design implementation of Azure Policy

✓ Design for data residency requirements

✓ Translate privacy requirements into requirements for security solutions.

In this chapter, we will focus on designing a regulatory compliance strategy for ensuring governance risk compliance (GRC).

In regulatory compliance, an organization follows laws enforced by governing bodies in their area or industry standards that have been voluntarily adopted. An organization's IT regulatory compliance process involves monitoring its corporate systems to detect and prevent violations of policies and procedures established by these governing laws, regulations, and standards. This, in turn, applies to a wide variety of monitoring and enforcement processes. These processes can be lengthy and complex depending on the industry and geography.

Healthcare and financial services industries are heavily regulated, making compliance challenging for multinational organizations. Standards and regulations abound and occasionally may continually change, making it challenging for businesses to keep up with shifting international electronic data handling laws.

In this chapter, you will read about getting started with a regulatory compliance strategy, assessing the technical capabilities of compliance requirements, assessing infrastructure compliance with Microsoft Defender for Cloud, identifying compliance issues and recommending actions to resolve them, developing and validating Azure policies, designing data residency requirements, and converting privacy requirements into security requirements.

Interpret Compliance Requirements and Translate into Specific Technical Capabilities

Currently, Azure offers hyper-scale cloud services in more than 60 regions worldwide. Azure services allow the organization to choose the region where your end-user data will be stored. Microsoft can provide data resiliency by replicating end-user data to other Azure regions within the same geography. However, Microsoft will not copy customer data beyond that geography.

Several Azure cloud environments are available from Microsoft:

- **Azure:** Azure is a global service available through its commercial, public, and global names.

- **Azure China:** One of the country's largest Internet providers, 21Vianet, partners with Microsoft to offer Azure China.
- **Azure Government:** Microsoft Azure Government is available in five U.S. regions. The U.S. Department of Defense takes advantage of two regions (US DoD Central and US DoD East).
- **Azure Government Secret:** Three Azure Government Secret regions cater exclusively to U.S. government needs, all designed to accommodate classified secret workloads.
- **Azure Government Top Secret:** Azure Government Top Secret processes national security workloads classified as US Top Secret to serve the intelligence community, the Department of Defense, and federal civil service agencies.

Independent third-party audits of Azure services are clearly stated in Azure compliance certificates and audit reports. Different audits may include other online services as part of their audit scope. At the time of writing this book, the Azure audit scope covers the following online services:

- Microsoft Azure
- Azure DevOps
- Dynamics 365
- Intelligent Recommendations
- Microsoft 365 Defender (aka Microsoft Threat Protection)
- Microsoft AppSource
- Microsoft Bing for Commerce
- Microsoft Cloud for Financial Services
- Microsoft Defender for Cloud (aka Azure Security Center)
- Microsoft Defender for Cloud Apps (aka Microsoft Cloud App Security)
- Microsoft Defender for Endpoint (aka Microsoft Defender Advanced Threat Protection)
- Microsoft Defender for Identity (aka Azure Advanced Threat Protection)
- Microsoft Defender for IoT (aka Azure Defender for IoT)
- Microsoft Graph
- Microsoft Intune
- Microsoft Managed Desktop
- Microsoft Sentinel (aka Azure Sentinel)
- Microsoft Stream
- Microsoft Threat Experts
- Nomination Portal
- Power Apps

- Power Automate (aka Microsoft Flow)
- Power BI
- Power BI Embedded
- Power Virtual Agents
- Universal Print
- Update Compliance

Office 365 maintains separate compliance certificates and audit reports for its services. You need an Azure subscription or Azure Government free trial account to download audit documents. On the Service Trust Portal (STP), you can access audit reports associated with Azure. To access audit reports, you must be logged in.

Microsoft Azure has compliance offerings across categories such as global, U.S. government, financial services, health and life science, automotive, education, and media and telecommunications. Azure also has regional compliance offerings for the Americas, EMEA, and Asia–Pacific.

Table 4.1 illustrates Azure-covered compliance.

For more information and the latest updates, visit `learn.microsoft.com/en-us/ azure/compliance`.

TABLE 4.1   Azure Compliance

Classification	Compliance offering
Global	<ul><li>CIS benchmark</li><li>CSA STAR Attestation</li><li>CSA STAR Certification</li><li>CSA STAR self-assessment</li><li>SOC 1 Type 2</li><li>SOC 2 Type 2</li><li>SOC 3</li><li>ISO 20000-1</li><li>ISO 22301</li><li>ISO 27001</li><li>ISO 27017</li><li>ISO 27018</li><li>ISO 27701</li><li>ISO 9001</li><li>WCAG</li></ul>

Classification	Compliance offering
U.S. government	■ CJIS
	■ CMMC
	■ CNSSI 1253
	■ DFARS
	■ DoD IL2
	■ DoD IL4
	■ DoD IL5
	■ DoD IL6
	■ DoE 10 CFR Part 810
	■ EAR
	■ FedRAMP
	■ FIPS 140
	■ ICD 503
	■ IRS 1075
	■ ITAR
	■ JSIG
	■ NDAA
	■ NIST 800-161
	■ NIST 800-171
	■ NIST 800-53
	■ NIST 800-63
	■ NIST CSF
	■ Section 508 VPATs
	■ StateRAMP
Financial services	■ 23 NYCRR Part 500 (US)
	■ AFM and DNB (Netherlands)
	■ AMF and ACPR (France)
	■ APRA (Australia)
	■ CFTC 1.31 (US)
	■ EBA (EU)
	■ FCA and PRA (UK)
	■ FFIEC (US)
	■ FINMA (Switzerland)
	■ FINRA 4511 (US)
	■ FISC (Japan)

TABLE 4.1   Azure Compliance *(continued)*

Classification	Compliance offering
	■ FSA (Denmark) ■ GLBA (US) ■ KNF (Poland) ■ MAS and ABS (Singapore) ■ NBB and FSMA (Belgium) ■ OSFI (Canada) ■ OSPAR (Singapore) ■ PCI 3DS ■ PCI DSS ■ RBI and IRDAI (India) ■ SEC 17a-4 (US) ■ SEC Regulation SCI (US) ■ SOX (US) ■ TruSight
Healthcare and life sciences	■ ASIP HDS (France) ■ EPCS (US) ■ GxP (FDA 21 CFR Part 11) ■ HIPAA (US) ■ HITRUST ■ MARS-E (US) ■ NEN 7510 (Netherlands)
Media	■ CDSA ■ MPA ■ FACT (UK) ■ DPP (UK)
Energy	■ NERC (US)
Education	■ FERPA (US)
Automotive	■ TISAX
Telecommunications	■ GSMA

Classification	Compliance offering
Azure Regional – Americas	<ul><li>Argentina PDPA</li><li>Canada privacy laws</li><li>Canada Protected B</li><li>US CCPA</li></ul>
Azure Regional – Asia Pacific	<ul><li>Australia IRAP</li><li>China GB 18030</li><li>China DJCP (MLPS)</li><li>China TCS</li><li>India MeitY</li><li>Japan CS Gold Mark</li><li>Japan ISMAP</li><li>Japan My Number Act</li><li>Korea K-ISMS</li><li>New Zealand ISPC</li><li>Singapore MTCS</li></ul>
Azure Regional – EMEA	<ul><li>EU Cloud CoC</li><li>EU EN 301 549</li><li>ENISA IAF</li><li>EU GDPR</li><li>EU Model Clauses</li><li>Germany C5</li><li>Germany IT-Grundschutz workbook</li><li>Netherlands BIR 2012</li><li>Qatar NIA</li></ul>
Azure Policy regulatory compliance built-in initiatives	<ul><li>Australian Government ISM PROTECTED</li><li>Canada Federal PBMM</li><li>CIS Azure Foundations Benchmark</li><li>FedRAMP High</li><li>HIPAA HITRUST</li><li>IRS 1075</li><li>ISO 27001</li><li>PCI DSS</li><li>NIST SP 800-171</li><li>UK OFFICIAL and UK NHS</li></ul>

Table 4.1 shows that compliance is fundamental to Azure. Microsoft put a lot of effort into providing Microsoft customers with the most extensive and comprehensive compliance offerings available in the cloud computing industry.

The compliance resources include audit reports, privacy information, compliance implementations, mappings, white papers, and analyst reports. You must log in to your Azure cloud service to access Azure Resources. Country and region privacy and compliance guidelines are also available.

A workload may be subject to regulatory requirements that require operational data, such as application logs and metrics, to remain within a particular geographical region.

In addition to requiring strict security measures, these requirements impact the selection, configuration, and scheduling of specific PaaS and SaaS services. They also have implications for how workloads should be operationalized.

As a true lasting transformation doesn't happen overnight, cloud governance results from an ongoing adoption effort. In some industries, third-party compliance affects initial policy creation, so assessing risk tolerance is critical in creating minimally invasive policies governing cloud adoption and managing risks.

The purpose and scope of these standards and regulations vary. Regulatory organizations frequently publish standards and updates that define good security practices to prevent negligence. However, data protection and retention design, network access, and system security can be influenced by security requirements.

Review the Organization Requirements

To help organizations avoid negligence, regulatory organizations should regularly review and publish standards and updates that define good compliance practices. Nevertheless, compliance requirements can influence the design of data protection and retention, network access, and system security. These standards and regulations' purpose and scope vary according to industry or country.

Today's globalized world demands that you know if your cloud resources comply with country standards mandated by governments or industry organizations.

For example, credit card transactions are governed by Payment Card Industry (PCI) standards, which prohibit Internet access into any system component storing cardholder data.

The following options can be used to deploy a restrictive environment:

- Provide your own virtual network (VNet) for the workload hosted in a different Azure compute option.

- By using private endpoints, you can remove all Internet-facing endpoints.

- Inbound and outbound access rules should be defined using network security groups (NSGs).

There may be more business impacts if you don't comply with a standard. Review the standard thoroughly to learn each requirement's intent and literal wording.

- What are the methods for measuring compliance?

- The workload must meet the requirements, but who approves it?

- Attestations can be obtained through what processes?
- What are the documentation requirements?

Microsoft-Recommended Action

Assess your current compliance score with Microsoft Defender for Cloud and identify the gaps.

With Microsoft Defender for Cloud, you can streamline the process of meeting regulatory compliance requirements using the regulatory compliance dashboard. Defender for Cloud continually assesses your hybrid cloud environment to identify the risk factors based on the controls and best practices applied to your subscriptions. Your compliance status is reflected on the dashboard.

Microsoft cloud security benchmarks are automatically assigned to Azure subscriptions when Defender for Cloud is enabled. Based on CIS, PCI-DSS, and NIST controls, this widely acknowledged benchmark emphasizes cloud-centric security controls.

Your regulatory compliance dashboard summarizes all the assessments for the standards and regulations you have selected in your environment. You will improve your compliance posture as you implement the recommendations and reduce the risk factors in your environment.

This regulatory compliance dashboard displays all the requirements associated with your selected compliance standards and the corresponding security assessments. Compliance with the standard is reflected in the status of these assessments.

You can use the regulatory compliance dashboard to assist you in identifying gaps in compliance with the standards and regulations you have chosen. By focusing on compliance within dynamic cloud and hybrid environments, you will also be able to monitor compliance over time.

The regulatory compliance dashboard can be used to investigate any issues that may be impacting your compliance.

There are both automated and manual assessments within regulatory compliance that may require remediation. Resolve regulatory compliance recommendations directly within the regulatory compliance dashboard using the information provided.

Design a Compliance Strategy

A Microsoft Cybersecurity Architect can develop a regulatory compliance strategy once the business risks are mapped and converted into policy statements. Additionally, this strategy considers the type of transaction an organization performs or the industry to which it belongs. A good compliance strategy needs to ensure that security controls are implemented to map regulatory compliance requirements directly; that's why it's crucial to establish a regulatory compliance strategy with a thorough understanding of the type of business, transactions, and overall business requirements.

Working with your regulators and carefully reviewing the standard to understand the language and intent of each requirement is key to avoiding fines or other business impacts down the road.

The corporate policy creates the working definition of governance in traditional and incremental governance.

Figure 4.1 depicts the value exchange between business risk, policy, compliance, monitoring processes, and enforcement processes to create a governance strategy.

FIGURE 4.1   Microsoft's five cybersecurity disciplines of cloud governance

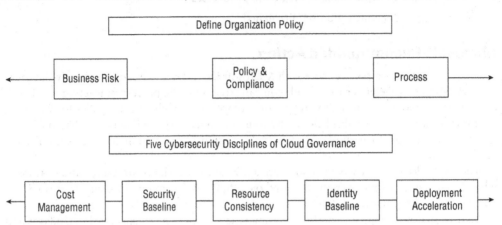

Most IT governance actions strive to deploy technology that monitors, enforces, operates, and automates those organization policies; and cloud governance is built on similar concepts. You can use the five disciplines shown in Figure 4.1 to develop a cloud governance strategy.

Cost Management   Developing cost control policies for all cloud platforms is a primary concern for cloud users.

Security Baseline   A company's security requirements are unique. Once these requirements are established, cloud governance policies and enforcement apply the conditions across networks, data, and assets.

Resource Consistency   Managing onboarding, drift, discoverability, and recovery risks in the cloud requires consistent resource configuration. With governance tooling, resources can be configured consistently.

Identity Baseline   By applying identity requirements consistently across cloud adoption efforts, the Identity Baseline discipline reduces the risk of breach.

Deployment Acceleration   Centralization, standardization, and consistency in deployment and configuration methods improve governance approaches. When delivered through cloud-based governance tooling, they complete a cloud factor that can accelerate deployment actions.

In the organization policy definition phase, you will consult with the organization to coordinate risk tolerance and cost mitigation. You will investigate current cloud adoption plans and data classification in this phase.

To create minimally intrusive policies to govern cloud adoption and manage risks, you must determine the business risks and assess risk tolerance. Remember that third-party compliance can affect some industries' initial policy creation process. As adoption and innovation activities progress, policy violations will naturally occur, and monitoring and enforcing policy compliance will be easier if relevant processes are executed.

To ensure compliance over time, as new workloads are provisioned, you'll need an organization policy strategy that includes regulatory compliance requirements.

Key Compliance Consideration

Organizations may need to follow several industry standards. The compliance process involves various assurances, including formal certifications, attestations, validations, authorizations, and assessments, as well as contractual amendments, self-assessments, and customer guidance documents.

In addition to regulatory risks, there are also operational risks. According to U.S. federal regulators, operational risks are characterized by a lack of internal controls and independent assurance functions. Organizations face threats such as significant fraud, defalcation, and other operating losses.

It is possible to face legal or regulatory sanctions, financial loss, or reputational damage due to noncompliance with laws, regulations, rules, or other regulatory requirements. The planning of a compliance strategy should consider operational compliance that supports regulatory compliance.

The lack of adherence by these external organizations to regulatory compliance may be one of the most significant business risks your organization faces if you use vendors or other trusted business partners. Identify and understand third-party compliance requirements before beginning a policy review. This risk is often unresolvable and may require strict adherence by all parties.

Improving operational compliance decreases the possibility of an outage attributable to configuration implications or systems' vulnerabilities being improperly patched.

Table 4.2 provides examples of operational compliance problems, Azure solutions, and compliance objectives.

TABLE 4.2   Operational compliance problems and solutions

Problem	Azure solution	Compliance objective
Patch management	Azure Automation Update Management	Scheduling and managing updates.
Policy enforcement	Azure Policy	Enforcing policies to ensure compliance with the environment and guests.
Environment configuration	Azure Blueprints	Compliance automation for core services.
Resource configuration	Desired State Configuration	Configuration of guest OS and some environment aspects automated.
Cloud Security Posture Management (CSPM) and Cloud Workload Protection Platform (CWPP)	Microsoft Defender for Cloud	Enforce and automate your organization's governance decisions.

Organizational standards can be enforced, and compliance can be assessed at scale with Azure Policy. In addition to providing an aggregated view of the environment, it offers the ability to drill down to the granularity level per resource and policy through its compliance dashboard. With bulk remediation for existing resources and automatic remediation for new ones, it also assists you in bringing your resources into compliance.

Azure Policy can be used to implement governance for resource consistency, regulatory compliance, security, cost, and management. To help you get started, Azure already includes built-ins for these everyday use cases.

Microsoft Azure Policy compares the properties of resources with business rules. These business rules (also known as *policy definitions*) are described in JSON format. A policy initiative (sometimes called a *policySet*) is a collection of several business rules grouped to simplify management. Once your business rules are formulated, the policy definition or initiative can be assigned to any Azure resource, including management groups, subscriptions, resource groups, and individual resources. It is possible to exclude resources from the assignment that are in the scope of the Resource Manager.

To find out whether an Azure resource is compliant, Azure Policy uses a JSON format to form the evaluation logic. In addition to metadata, there is also a policy rule defined. The defined rule can match any scenario using functions, parameters, logical operators, conditions, and property aliases. A policy rule determines which resources should be evaluated under the assignment.

Azure Blueprints allow cloud architects and IT departments to define repeatable Azure resources that implement and adhere to an organization's standards, patterns, and requirements. By using Azure Blueprints, development teams can rapidly create and start up new environments aligning to organizational compliance requirements with a set of built-in components, such as networking, to speed up development and delivery.

In Azure Resource Manager templates (ARM templates) and resource groups, blueprints serve as a declarative way to orchestrate the deployment of multiple resource templates.

The globally distributed Azure Cosmos DB powers Azure Blueprints. The blueprint objects are replicated across multiple Azure regions. Azure Blueprints deploys your resources in whichever region is most convenient for you, providing low latency, high availability, and consistent access to your blueprint objects.

During deployment and for already existing resources, policies validate that resource properties within a subscription adhere to the requirements and standards of cloud governance.

Azure Security Benchmark associates each control with an Azure Policy. The built-in initiative definition of Azure Policy Regulatory Compliance maps to compliance domains and controls. You might use these policies to assess compliance with control, but there are often no one-to-one or complete matches between controls and policies.

You are not fully compliant with all control requirements if you are compliant only with the policy definitions in Azure Policy. Furthermore, the compliance standard includes controls that are not addressed in Azure Policy definitions. Therefore, compliance with Azure Policy provides only a partial picture of your overall compliance. There may be changes in the associations between compliance domains, controls, and Azure Policy definitions for this compliance standard in the future.

Included in every subscription is the Azure Security Benchmark, which is a set of Microsoft-authored guidelines for security and compliance best practices.

At the time of writing this book, Microsoft covered the following standards:

- PCI-DSS v3.2.1:2018
- NIST SP 800-53 R4
- NIST SP 800 171 R2
- SOC TSP
- UK OFFICIAL and UK NHS
- Canada Federal PBMM
- Azure CIS 1.1.0
- New Zealand ISM Restricted
- CMMC Level 3
- Azure CIS 1.3.0
- HIPAA/HITRUST
- SWIFT CSP CSCF v2020
- ISO 27001:2013
- NIST SP 800-53 R5
- FedRAMP H
- FedRAMP M

Microsoft Cybersecurity Architects and central IT groups can define reusable Azure resources using Azure Blueprints. Azure Blueprints allow development teams to quickly build and create new environments based on your organization's standards, patterns, and requirements. Your organization's standards, patterns, and conditions can be set up and adhered to with Azure resources. Because of a set of built-in components, like networking, the development team trusts that they are within organizational compliance.

You can create, assign, and manage policies using Azure Policy to ensure your resources follow corporate standards and service levels. Azure Policy scans your resources and identifies those that don't comply.

Your governance strategy depends heavily on Microsoft Defender for Cloud. Using a unified view across your workloads, it collects, searches, and analyzes security data from many sources, including firewalls and other partner solutions, so that you can remain on top of security. Defender provides actionable security recommendations to fix problems before they are exploited and applies security policies across hybrid cloud workloads to maintain compliance with information security standards.

Evaluate Infrastructure Compliance by Using Microsoft Defender for Cloud

Through Cloud Security Posture Management (CSPM) and Cloud Workload Protection Platform (CWPP), Microsoft Defender for Cloud manages Azure, on-premises, and multi-cloud resources. Defender for Cloud meets three crucial needs as you work your resources and workloads in the cloud and on-premises.

- The secure score provides a continuous assessment of your security posture so you can keep track of new security opportunities.

- Report on the progress of your security efforts.

- Following Defender for Cloud recommendations, you can protect your workloads from known security risks.

CWPP and CSPM enable you to manage Azure, on-premises, and multi-cloud resources.

In Microsoft Defender for Cloud, compliance standards and all their requirements are displayed on the regulatory compliance dashboard, where supported conditions correspond to security assessments. These assessments indicate if you comply with the standard.

Microsoft Defender for Cloud protects Azure, on-premises, and other clouds. The solution protects hybrid data, cloud-native services, and systems from ransomware and other threats; and its services interact with existing security workflows such as SIEM solutions.

To streamline threat mitigation, Microsoft uses its vast threat intelligence.

Azure Arc provides protection for on-premises and multi-cloud virtual machines and SQL databases using Microsoft Defender for Cloud.

Using the regulatory compliance dashboard in Microsoft Defender for Cloud, you can streamline the process of complying with regulatory requirements. Defender for Cloud continuously assesses your hybrid cloud environment to analyze risk factors based on the controls and best practices you've applied to your subscriptions. These standards are reflected in the dashboard, as depicted in Figure 4.2.

FIGURE 4.2   Microsoft Defender for Cloud

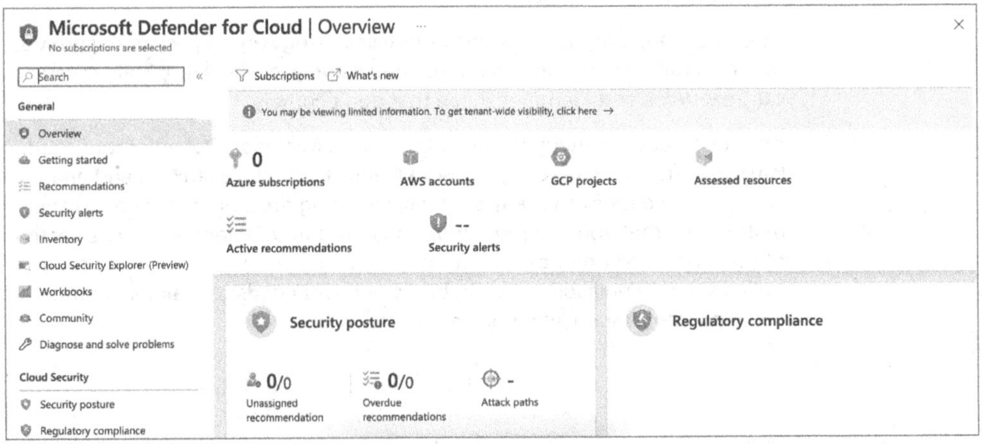

The Microsoft cloud security benchmark is automatically applied to an Azure subscription when Defender for Cloud is enabled. CIS, PCI-DSS, and NIST controls are used to create this widely respected benchmark, which emphasizes cloud-centric security in addition to controls mandated by the Center for Internet Security (CIS), PCI-DSS, and NIST.

Several advanced, intelligent protections for your workloads are included in Defender for Cloud, powered by Microsoft threat intelligence. In addition to workload protections, Microsoft Defender offers subscription plans tailored to the resources you subscribe to.

Protect All of Your IT Resources Under One Roof

Defender for Cloud allows you to monitor and protect Azure services without requiring any deployment like an Azure-native service does. However, you can also add resources located in on-premises or in other public clouds.

Defender for Cloud becomes a single pane of glass for all your cloud security needs with its broad approach. If needed, Defender for Cloud can automatically deploy a Log Analytics agent. Azure Arc is used to extend Microsoft Defender plans to non-Azure machines in hybrid and multi-cloud environments. Multi-cloud machines can access CSPM features without the need for agents.

Protect Your Azure-Native Resources

Detect threats across the following platforms with Defender for Cloud:

- Protect Azure PaaS services, including Azure App Service, Azure SQL, Azure Storage Account, and more. You can detect anomalies in your Azure activity logs by integrating Microsoft Defender for Cloud apps (formerly known as Microsoft Cloud App Security).

- Defender for Cloud offers several features, including the ability to classify your data automatically in Azure SQL. It can also assess vulnerabilities across Azure SQL and Azure Storage and recommend mitigation measures.

- Your network is protected against brute-force attacks with Defender for Cloud. Limiting access to virtual machine ports and using just-in-time VM access can prevent unnecessary access to your network. For selected ports, you can restrict access to authorized users, specific IP addresses, or IP ranges for a limited period.

Protect Your On-Premises Resources

With Defender for Cloud, you can protect your hybrid and Azure environments by protecting your non-Azure servers. To focus on what matters most, you'll receive customized threat intelligence and prioritized alerts based on your environment.

Defender can protect on-premises machines with Defender for Cloud's enhanced security features.

Protect Your Resources Running Other Clouds

Amazon Web Services and Google Compute Engine are two clouds that Defender for Cloud can protect.

You can enable these protections if your AWS account is connected to your Azure subscription.

- In addition to Defender for Cloud's CSPM features, your AWS resources are assessed based on AWS-specific security recommendations, which are included in your secure score. Additionally, AWS built-in security standards (AWS CIS, AWS PCI DSS, and AWS Foundational Security Best Practices) will be evaluated. Asset inventory in Defender for Cloud is a multi-cloud feature that lets you manage your AWS resources alongside your Azure resources.

- Amazon EKS Linux clusters are protected by Microsoft Defender for Kubernetes.

- Windows and Linux EC2 instances can benefit from Microsoft Defender for Servers' threat detection and advanced defenses. Microsoft Defender for Endpoint is included in this plan, along with baseline security assessments, OS-level assessments, vulnerability assessments, adaptive application controls, file integrity monitoring, and more.

You can enable these protections if your GCP account is connected to your Azure subscription.

- The native cloud connector (recommended by Microsoft) provides an agentless connection to your Google Cloud Platform account, which can then be extended with Defender for Cloud's Defender plans to ensure the security of your Google Cloud Platform resources.

- Defender for Cloud uses the classic cloud connector to connect to your GCP environment, which requires configuration in your GCP project.

- A single Azure subscription can be used to connect multiple projects.

- It is possible to connect multiple projects to multiple Azure subscriptions.

Vulnerability assessment solutions are part of Defender for Cloud's enhanced security features for virtual machines, containers, and SQL servers.

Automatic, native integration is available between Microsoft Defender for Servers and Microsoft Defender for Endpoints. You can review these vulnerability scan results within Defender for Cloud and respond to them.

In your governance strategy, Microsoft Defender for Cloud plays a crucial role. Security data is collected, searched, and analyzed from many sources, including firewalls and other partner solutions, to make sure you stay on the cutting edge of security through a unified view across your workloads. Defender ensures compliance with security standards by providing actionable security recommendations to fix problems before they are exploited and ensures that security policies are applied across hybrid cloud workloads.

Interpret Compliance Scores and Recommend Actions to Resolve Issues or Improve Security

Your compliance posture improves as you act on the recommendations and reduce risk factors in your environment and as you see the results of all the environmental assessments for your chosen standards and regulations.

With the Microsoft Defender for Cloud CSPM module, you are able to assess and remediate security issues through the tools provided. These tools include the following:

- Governance and compliance with security regulations
- Security graph for the cloud
- Analysis of attack paths
- Machine-agentless scanning

In the regulatory compliance dashboard, you can see all the compliance standards you have chosen and the requirements supporting these standards. This dashboard displays the status of those security assessments and shows your compliance with those standards. Implementing your environment's security recommendations will improve your security score. Using filters, you can find the recommendations that have the most significant impact on your score or the ones you are supposed to implement from the list of suggestions.

Go to the Azure Portal, in Search box look for Defender for cloudIn Defender for Cloud's overview, select Security Posture and then choose View Recommendations.

You can use the search box and filters above the list of recommendations to search for specific recommendations. Use the details of each recommendation as a guide to deciding whether it should be remedied, exempted, or disabled. Finding and remediating recommendations with unhealthy resources is essential to increase your security score and improve your security posture.

Your security score can be accessed via API, allowing you to query the data and create your own reporting mechanism. A ready-made report is included in Defender for Cloud's workbooks page for tracking your subscriptions, security controls, and more.

Implementing all of the recommendations in the security control will result in a potential score increase. The percentage points listed for security control are increased when you implement all its recommendations.

Focus on compliance gaps with your chosen standards and regulations using the regulatory compliance dashboard. Using this dashboard, you can continuously monitor your compliance over time within dynamic cloud and hybrid environments. To view the details for any failing assessment, select it from the dashboard. The recommendations include remediation steps to resolve the issue. You can view the details of any failing evaluation you choose from the dashboard. Remediation steps are provided for each recommendation.

Some controls may be grayed out because they do not have any Defender for Cloud assessments. Check your organization's requirements and assess them in your environment. Some of these controls might be process-related and not technical.

When you receive recommendations in the Microsoft Defender for Cloud dashboard, you follow the remediation steps provided in the recommendation to secure your resources more effectively. Microsoft recommends prioritizing the security controls that will increase your security score. After reviewing all the recommendations, decide which one to remediate first. The Fix option is included in many recommendations to simplify remediation and improve your environment's security (and increase your secure score).

The remediation operation applies the configuration to the resource using a template deployment or REST API patch request. It is logged in the Azure activity log.

Design and Validate Implementation of Azure Policy

Azure Policy is a service from Microsoft Azure that allows you to create, assign, and manage policies that maintain or audit your organizational Azure resources. As a result of these policies, your resource configurations remain compliant with corporate standards across different configurations.

Because of its dynamic nature, continuous monitoring is imperative for organizations adopting cloud computing. New workloads are provisioned every day, making it imperative to ensure that these workloads are secure by default. Implementing guardrails at the beginning of the pipeline is essential to prevent users from provisioning insecure workloads.

You will expose your environment to risks if you don't provide continuous monitoring and policy enforcement since workloads won't be secure by default.

Policies must be designed with the organization's infrastructure and compliance needs. Having all your compliance data in one place can help you reduce the time required to audit your environment by developing a tailored policy. Table 4.3 defines critical terminology used in Azure Policy.

TABLE 4.3   Azure Policy Glossary

Terms	Description
Alias	Fields used in policy definitions that map to resource properties.
Applicability	An assessment of resources against a policy is based on their relevance. When a resource is within the scope of the policy assignment, it is not excluded or exempt from the policy assignment, and it meets the conditions specified in the policy rule's if it is blocked, it is considered applicable to the policy.
Assignment	A JSON-defined object determines the resources to which a policy definition is applied.
Azure Policy	A service that enforces organizational standards and assesses compliance with Azure resources.
Built-in	This is an alternative to custom policy definitions that are available by default and generated by Azure Resource Providers.
Category	Metadata property in the policy definition classifies the definition based on its area of focus. The category often indicates the target resource provider (compute, storage, monitoring).
Compliance state	It can be compliant, noncompliant, exempt, conflicting, not started, or protected in terms of its adherence to applicable policies.
Compliant	According to the policy definition, a resource complies if it adheres to a policy rule.
Control	A regulatory compliance group is another term used for a group.
Custom	The alternative to a built-in policy definition that the policy user authors.
Definition	The purpose of policy objects is to describe resource compliance requirements and the consequences of violating them.
Definition location	A management group or subscription can be assigned to an initiative or policy definition, and assignments can be made above or below that scope.
Effects	When a policy's rule is met, action is taken on a resource.
Enforcement	Policy effects can have preventative effects.
Enforcement mode	Policies can be configured so that certain policy effects can be enabled or disabled, while still evaluating compliance and providing logs.
Evaluation	Describes the process of scanning resources in the cloud environment to determine the applicability and compliance of assigned policies.
Event	Event Grid can be used to integrate an incident or outcome when something changes in Azure Policy.

TABLE 4.3 Azure Policy Glossary *(continued)*

Terms	Description
Exclusion	It is also known as NotScopes. Excluded scopes do not appear on the Azure Portal compliance blade because they don't include child resource containers or child resources.
Exempt	A compliance state indicates an exemption.
Exemption	The JSON-defined object eliminates a hierarchy of resources or an individual resource from evaluation. The resource still counts toward overall compliance, but it is not evaluated.
Group	In an initiative definition, a subset of IDs corresponds to policy definitions.
Identity	In Azure Policy, a managed identity is assigned by the system or by a user.
Initiative	The set of policy definitions is a type of policy definition consisting of a collection of policy definitions. It allows the management of a group of policy definitions with a single assignment, sharing parameters and identities.
JSON	It is used by Azure Policy to define policy objects using JavaScript Object Notation (JSON).
Noncompliant	Resource resources that do not comply with policy rules are categorized as noncompliant.
Policy rule	A rule provides an aggregated compliance status for a policy assignment.
Mode	An Azure Resource Manager (ARM) property or a Resource Provider (RP) property determines which resource types are evaluated for a policy definition.
Policy State	A state describes how a policy assignment is doing in terms of compliance.
Regulatory compliance	This describes a specific type of initiative that allows grouping policies into controls and categorizing policies into compliance domains based on responsibility (customer, Microsoft, shared). Custom Regulatory compliance built-ins are available, and customers can create their own.
Remediation	JSON-defined objects correct resources that violate policies with deployIfNotExists or modify effects. Remediation is automatic for resources created or updated but must be triggered for existing resources.
Scope	ARM describes the set of resources an assignment applies to, including subscriptions, management groups, resource groups, and individual resources.
Template info	In Azure Policy for Kubernetes clusters, the constraint template is defined as part of the policy definition.

Key Inputs You Need to Be Aware of About Azure Policy

The following are inputs that Microsoft Cybersecurity Architects need to be aware of:

- The policies and initiatives in Azure Policy can be defined as individual policies or as groups of related policies called *initiatives*. Several policy and initiative definitions are built into Azure Policy.

- Azure policies are inherited. A resource's assignment is inherited by all of its children.

- Azure policies can be scoped and enforced at different organizational levels.

- Azure Policy highlights resource compliance with current policies.

- Automate the remediation of noncompliant resources using Azure Policy.

- Azure Policy applies pre-deployment and post-deployment policies in conjunction with Azure DevOps.

By setting guardrails throughout your resources, Azure Policy can help you ensure cloud compliance, avoid misconfigurations, and practice consistent resource governance throughout your organization. In addition to increasing developer productivity and optimizing your cloud spending, Azure Policy can be used to reduce the number of external approval processes by implementing policies at the heart of the Azure platform.

By establishing resource conventions, Azure Policy makes it easy to govern Azure resources, enforce policies, audit compliance, and monitor compliance constantly. Policy definitions describe resource compliance conditions and the effects if these conditions are met.

An alias is used to access resource property fields. Conditions compare a resource property field to a required value. A unique array alias can select values from all array members and apply a condition to each value when the resource property field is an array.

Azure Policy evaluates your resources and highlights resources that aren't compliant with the policies you've created. Azure Policy can also prevent noncompliant resources from being created.

Storage, Networking, Computing, Security Center, and Monitoring have built-in policy and initiative definitions in Azure Policy. For example, suppose you define a policy that allows only a specific stock-keeping unit (SKU) size to be used for virtual machines (VMs) in your environment. Azure Policy is invoked when you create a new VM or resize an existing one. All VMs in your environment are evaluated and monitored by Azure Policy.

A noncompliant resource or configuration can be remedied automatically by Azure Policy in some cases to ensure resource integrity. If Azure Policy does not apply a tag to all resources in a certain resource group with the AppName tag and the SpecialOrders value, it will automatically apply that tag.

In addition, Azure Policy can be integrated with Azure DevOps to apply continuous integration pipeline policies for pre- and post-deployment phases for your applications.

Using Azure Policy at the beginning of the pipeline allows policies to be enforced after the resources have been created, as shown in Figure 4.3.

FIGURE 4.3   Azure policy logical view

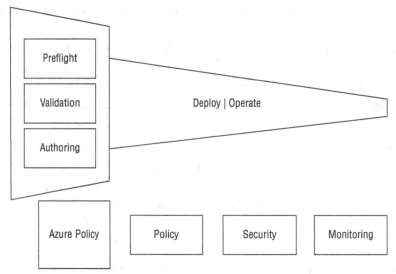

Costs can be controlled, and resources can be managed more efficiently when conventions are defined. For example, a particular type of virtual machine can be allowed only if the resource has a specific tag and the policy assignments are passed down to child resources. If an Azure policy assignment is applied to a resource group, it spreads to all the resources in that resource group.

Azure Policy and Azure Resources

Your Azure Policy must address business standards and compliance requirements when designing your Azure resources.

A request for creating or updating a resource by a person, process, or pipeline is reviewed by Azure Policy.

A policy definition effect, such as Modify, Append, or DeployIfNotExists, changes or adds to a request. An activity log entry is created for new and updated resources when the policy definition effect is Audit or AuditIfNotExists. When the policy depiction effect is Deny, the request cannot be created or altered.

Validate New Policy

Following these steps is a Microsoft-recommended approach to validating a new policy definition:

1. Define your policy carefully.

2. Perform a resource audit.

3. Audit resource requests that are new or updated.

4. Implement your policy on resources.

5. Monitor continuously.

. Let us get started with each stage one by one.

Defining your policy carefully   Understanding how Azure resources are connected to other Azure services and how business policies are implemented because policy definitions are crucial. Identifying the requirements and determining the resource properties allow you to see beyond the narrow purpose of your business policy.

- Do your policies state, for instance, "All virtual machines must be compliant as per your organization standards."
- Is HDInsight or AKS another Azure service that uses VMs?

It is essential to consider how your policy will affect other services' resources. As a result, you should define your policies as tightly as possible to focus on what resources and properties you need to assess for compliance.

At a high level, policy definition in Azure Policy involves three steps: defining the policy, assigning it to resources, and reviewing the evaluation.

VMs can be prevented from being deployed in specific Azure regions through a policy definition. Storage accounts can also be audited to ensure that only allowed networks are connected.

These are some examples of policy definitions and the conditions under which they are enforced. Policy definitions also have accompanying effects when the conditions are met.

- **Allowed VM SKUs:** You can specify which VM SKUs your organization can deploy with this policy.
- **Allowed locations:** When your organization deploys resources, this policy restricts the locations it can specify, and it enforces your geographical compliance requirements.
- **MFA should be enabled on accounts with write permissions on your subscription:** To prevent account or resource breaches, accounts with write privileges must enable multifactor authentication (MFA).
- **CORS should not allow every resource to access your web apps:** For security reasons, cross-origin resource sharing (CORS) enables web applications to access resources outside their domain. To ensure security, modern browsers restrict cross-site scripting by default. Only required domains can interact with your web app under this policy.
- **System updates should be installed on your VM:** The Azure Security Center recommends security system updates to your servers when missing.

Assigning it to resources   Assigning definitions to resources is how policy definitions are implemented. Policy definitions can be assigned to a management group (a cluster of subscriptions), a resource group, or a single subscription.

Resources members of a resource group inherit policy assignments within that group. When a policy is applied to a resource group, it applies to all resources within that group.

When there are specific child resources you need to be excluded from a subscope, you can exclude them from the policy assignment.

Reviewing the evaluation The compliance results for your existing resources are marked as compliant or noncompliant when conditions are evaluated against the existing resources.

Policy evaluation occurs about one-time per hour. If you modify your policy definition and make a policy assignment, that policy is evaluated over your Azure resources within the hour.

Performing a resource audit Before managing new or updated resources, you should check how the new policy definition evaluates a small subset of existing resources, such as a test resource group. To prevent the effect from triggering or creating activity log entries, set your policy assignment to Disabled (DoNotEnforce).

The new policy will be able to be evaluated without impacting workflow as a result of this step. Ensure no resources you expect to be noncompliant are marked as noncompliant (false positive). Expand the evaluation of all existing resources gradually after the initial subset is validated.

In addition, evaluating existing resources allows for remediating noncompliant resources before fully implementing the new policy.

Auditing new or updated resources To determine whether your new policy definition will affect resources created or updated, you need to validate that it reports correctly on existing resources. Using an audit is recommended if the policy definition affects parameterization. To determine whether the new policy definition triggers noncompliant resource entries in the Azure Activity log without affecting existing work or requests, use this configuration to monitor resource creation and updates.

To ensure that the Audit effect is correctly triggered when expected, you should update and create new resources that match your policy definition. When the new policy definition triggers the Audit effect, watch out for resource requests that shouldn't be affected. As another example of false positives, these affected resources must be corrected in the policy definition before being fully implemented.

If the policy definition is changed at this testing stage, Microsoft recommends that existing auditing resources begin the validation process. New or updated resources will likely be affected by a change to the policy definition for false positives.

The validation process needs to ensure that only noncompliant resources are identified and that compliant resources are not included in the results incorrectly (known as a *false positive*).

Implementing your policy on resources You can begin implementing your new policy definition with existing and new resources as soon you have validated it. Before implementation, it is advisable to assign the new policy definition to a subset of all resources, such as a resource group. The policy scope should be expanded to new levels, such as subscriptions and management groups after the initial deployment has been validated. Create a new assignment at the target scope until your new policy definition covers all resources intended to be covered by your new policy definition. Remove the assignment once your new definition covers all resources intended to be covered by your new policy definition.

The following steps should be taken if resources are located that are exempt from your new policy definition during the rollout:

- To reduce unintended impacts, update the policy definition.

- By removing and creating a new policy assignment, the scope of the policy assignment can be changed.

- Add the exclusion list to the policy assignment.

Your security and compliance organizations should be notified of any changes to scope (level or exclusions) to ensure no gaps exist.

Monitoring Continuously   You need to continuously monitor the compliance level of your resources with your new policy definition and set up Azure Monitor alerts and notifications when noncompliant devices are detected. Implementing and assigning your policy definition isn't the end of the process. As part of the evaluation process, the policy definition and its assigned tasks should be reviewed regularly to ensure that they meet business policy and compliance requirements. If policies are no longer needed, they should be removed. Policies also need updating from time to time as the underlying Azure resources evolve and add new properties and capabilities.

Key Design Consideration You Need to Be Aware of About Azure Policy

The following are things a Microsoft Cybersecurity Architect needs to be aware of from design and deployment perspectives.

- You can analyze the overall state of your environment using the Azure Policy compliance dashboard. The dashboard offers an aggregated view in which you can drill down to see your organization's policies for each resource and level. To resolve issues rapidly and effectively, the tool offers bulk remediation for existing resources and automatic remediation for new resources.

- Think about how Azure Policy evaluates resources. Plan how Azure Policy evaluates your organization resources at specific times. Understand when and how evaluations are triggered. Noncompliant resources may be detected later. Evaluations are triggered by the following events or times:

  - An assignment of a policy creates, deletes, or updates a resource in scope.
  - There is a new scope assigned to a policy or initiative.
  - Scopes are updated with assigned policies or initiatives.
  - Every 24 hours, a compliance evaluation is conducted.

- Decide how to handle a noncompliant resource. An organization can address noncompliance differently depending on the resource. Here are some examples:

  - Refuse to accept changes.
  - Make a note of any changes to the resource.
  - Before or after a change, alter the resource.
  - Compliant resources should be deployed.

- Consider when to automatically remediate noncompliant resources. Determine if Azure Policy should perform automatic remediation for noncompliant resources. Remediation is especially useful in resource tagging. Azure Policy can apply resource tags, and removed tags can be reapplied. With Azure Policy, you can ensure that all resources in a particular resource group are tagged with a specific tag, such as location so that the region can be identified.

- It would be best if you used Azure RBAC and Azure Policy to achieve complete scope control. It would be best to use Azure RBAC and Azure Policy to gain complete scope control.

  - The Azure Policy evaluates the state of a resource and acts to ensure it remains compliant with the organization's business rules. Compliance does not depend on who made the change or had permission to make it. The Azure Policy ensures a resource stays compliant by evaluating its state.

  - Azure RBAC controls who can access Azure resources, what they can do with them, and what areas they can access by focusing on user actions at different scopes. If actions need to be controlled, use Azure RBAC. Even if a user is given access to complete an action, Azure Policy still blocks it, resulting in noncompliant resources.

- Table 4.4 illustrates the Azure Policy's configuration maximum.

TABLE 4.4   Azure Policy's configuration maximum

Applies to	Applicable	Max counts
Scope	Policy definitions	500
Scope	Initiative definitions	200
Tenant	Initiative definitions	2,500
Scope	Policy or initiative assignments	200
Scope	Exemptions	1000
Policy definition	Parameters	20
Initiative definition	Policies	1000
Initiative definition	Parameters	300
Policy or initiative assignments	Exclusions (notScopes)	400
Policy rule	Nested conditionals	512
Remediation task	Resources	50,000
Policy definition, initiative, or assignment request body	Bytes	1,048,576

You can also integrate Azure Policy with Azure DevOps to apply continuous integration or delivery pipeline policies related to your applications' pre-deployment and post-deployment phases.

With Azure Policy, regulatory compliance can be accessed through built-in initiative definitions, allowing users to determine which controls and compliance domains pertain to which organization (customer, Microsoft, shared).

Regulatory compliance enables customers to create their own regulatory compliance initiatives.

Currently, regulatory compliance is a preview feature.

Design for Data Residency Requirements

Microsoft uses multilayered security and encryption protocols to secure your data. Data that persists on physical media is always encrypted using FIPS 140-2 compliant encryption protocols by default with Microsoft Managed Keys. Further data protection can be provided by customer-managed keys (CMKs), double encryption, and hardware security modules (HSMs).

The traffic between data centers is protected by IEEE 802.1AE MAC Security Standards, preventing physical man-in-the-middle attacks. Microsoft maintains resiliency by using variable network paths that sometimes cross geographical borders, but customers' data is always replicated via encrypted connections between regions.

As part of Microsoft's global cloud service (including running and improving services, billing, and fraud prevention), Azure generates pseudonymous identifiers to minimize privacy risk. According to Microsoft, a pseudonymous identifier can never be used to identify an individual directly, and access to customer data that identifies individuals is always protected.

Different organizations may have different data residency and sovereignty requirements based on regional and industry-specific regulations.

In addition to implying data residency, data sovereignty also introduces rules and requirements governing who controls and has access to customer data. In many cases, data sovereignty mandates that customer data be subject to the laws and legal jurisdiction of the country or region in which data resides. Even platform maintenance and customer support requests can be affected by these laws.

Depending on the jurisdiction in which the data resides, data residency regulations govern where and how it can be stored, processed, and accessed internationally.

A compliance consideration may support or even mandate the data storage location and how and when it can be transferred internationally due to data residency considerations. As a result, Azure's regions and services provide customers with various options for selecting and limiting data residency and access based on the jurisdiction. Regulations can differ significantly depending on the jurisdiction. As a result of this flexibility, customers in regulated industries can run mission-critical workloads in the cloud and utilize all the benefits of Microsoft hyper-scale cloud computing.

Storage of Data for Regional Services

Virtual machines, storage, and SQL databases are some of the Azure services that can be deployed regionally and assigned to a specific region.

Your customer data will not be stored or processed outside the geographic region (Geo) you specify without your authorization.

Microsoft may copy customer data between regions within a given geographic area to ensure data redundancy or for other operational purposes. For enhanced data reliability in the case of a significant data center disaster, georedundant storage replicates blobs, files, queues, and tables between two regions within the same geographical area. The remote data processing systems in the Geo may be controlled by Microsoft personnel outside the Geo, but customer data will not be accessed without your permission.

Some data may be stored or processed outside of the specified geographic area by the following services:

- Backup is provided by Azure Cloud Services for web and worker-role software deployment packages, regardless of deployment region.

- A European-based cluster stores partial usage data and service traces for a limited period of time in Azure Data Explorer (ADX).

- Depending on which authoring region the customer uses, Language Understanding may store live learning data in the United States, Europe, or Australia.

- Azure Machine Learning may store freeform text of asset names provided by the customer (such as workspace names, resource group names, experiment names, file names, and image names) as well as experiment execution parameters or experiment metadata, for debugging purposes.

- Databricks in Azure may store identity information, table names, and object paths.

- When Azure Serial Console is used in conjunction with the Azure Portal, console commands and responses are processed outside of the Geo selected by the customer to deliver the console experience to that portal.

Storage of Data for Nonregional Services

Some Azure services do not allow the customer to specify the region in which the service will be deployed. The customer data may be stored and processed anywhere in one of the Microsoft data centers within the Azure public regions unless otherwise specified.

Some data may be stored or processed by the following services for nonregional services:

- Customer data is cached at edge locations worldwide by the Azure Content Delivery Network.

- It is possible to store Azure AD data globally, except for deployments in the United States (where Azure AD data is stored exclusively within the United States) or Europe (where Azure AD data is stored in either the United States or Europe).

- Authentication data is stored in the United States by Azure Multi-Factor Authentication.

- Data taken from or associated with customer resources (like virtual machines or Azure AD tenants) may be stored in Microsoft Defender for Cloud.

- The data will be stored in the same geocode as the resource, except in geocodes where Microsoft has yet to deploy Microsoft Defender for Cloud, in which case it will be stored in the United States.

  - Geocoding means your API requests can include search terms such as an address or place name and will return the results as latitude and longitude coordinates.

- The data may also be stored according to the geolocation rules of another Microsoft Online Service that processes such data.

- Microsoft Defender for IoT may use other Microsoft Online Services to process security-related customer data depending on the geolocation rules of the other online service.

- Global routing services that don't process or store customer data, such as Azure Traffic Manager.

Data Sovereignty

A data residency solution design will need to consider data sovereignty requirements. Data sovereignty implies data residency, but it also introduces rules and requirements that define who can access and control cloud-based data. As a result of data sovereignty, much customer data is subject to the laws and legal jurisdiction of the country or region where it resides. When platform maintenance or customer support requests are initiated, these laws can directly affect data access.

You can combine Azure's public multi-tenant cloud with Azure Stack products for on-premises and edge solutions to meet your data sovereignty requirements. It is possible to deploy these other products to put you solely in control of your data, including storage, processing, transmission, and remote access.

Personal Data

All rights, titles, and interests remain with you when you store and host customer data using Azure services, such as personal information and other content. Microsoft does not store or process customer data outside your geographic area except for certain services and scenarios. You can also move, copy, and access customer data worldwide. Most Azure services are deployed regionally, allowing you to determine where the customer data will be stored and processed. Examples of regional services include virtual machines, storage, and SQL databases. Microsoft maintains resiliency by using variable network paths that cross geographical boundaries; however, data replication between regions is always encrypted.

Azure Policy Consideration

It is essential to consider Azure Policy when designing your data resident solution. With Azure Policy, you can manage cloud infrastructure and data. Governance entails defining where resources can be deployed, what services can be deployed, and how resources must be monitored. Customers can use the Allowed Locations policy to restrict data and resources to certain Azure regions, such as for data residency. To ensure ongoing compliance, newly deployed resources will be checked against policies, and older resources will be periodically scanned.

Azure Blueprints Consideration

Azure Blueprints is a free service that provides templates for creating, deploying, and updating fully governed cloud environments, which helps customers comply with regulatory requirements.

Consider using Azure Blueprints to manage data residency for specific compliance needs by specifying both permitted and allowed locations for resource groups. Azure Blueprints can be helpful when you need templates for creating, deploying, and updating entirely governed cloud environments.

Several common standards, including HIPAA, FedRAMP, and PCI DSS, are mapped into Azure Blueprints. It maps a core set of policies for ISO 27001 and PCI DSS to any Azure environment, for example.

Using Blueprints, you can deploy multiple Azure subscriptions and manage them from a central location, and they are scalable for large-scale migrations and production implementations. In Azure Blueprints, ARM templates, resource groups, policy assignments, and role assignments are all packaged together in one container, which differs from Azure Resource Manager (ARM) and Azure Policy.

Blueprints simplifies large-scale Azure deployments by packaging policies in a single blueprint definition. Packaging policies in a single blueprint definition allows you to quickly and easily deploy all these components.

To ensure that your data is stored only in the region of your choice, you should select the following options:

- Azure services are deployed regionally, so you can specify where the service should be deployed. Microsoft won't store your data outside the specified region except for a few regional and preview services described on the Azure data location page. In this way, your data will remain in the region where it was stored when you provided it.

- Certain Azure services can be deployed in specific regions, but your services can't. The data location page describes how to specify the regions.

Data is replicated for durability and maximum availability whenever your data is stored in an Azure Storage account. Azure Storage copies your data in case of transient hardware failures, network outages, or even massive natural disasters. The same data center, availability zone within a region, or geographically separated region can replicate your data.

One example of a nonregional service is Azure Active Directory (Azure AD). In other words, Azure AD may store identity data globally, except for Azure AD deployments in the United States, Europe, Australia, and New Zealand.

When a disaster occurs, Azure Backup keeps your data safe and recoverable. Using the Microsoft Azure Recovery Services (MARS) agent, you can back up files, folders, and desired system state and backups of entire Windows/Linux VMs (using backup extensions). Azure Files shares, SQL Server VMs running on Azure VMs, and SAP HANA databases running on Azure VMs can also be backed up.

Azure Backup, Azure Data Factory, Azure Site Recovery, Azure Stream Analytics, and locally redundant storage (LRS) are among the Azure services, tiers, and plans that can store customer data only in one region.

Protecting Organizational Data

A Microsoft Cybersecurity Architect can protect organizational data from unauthorized access. A key component of ensuring the confidentiality of cloud workloads is encryption. Multiple encryption methods, protocols, and algorithms are used across Microsoft's products and services to deliver a secure path for data to travel via the Azure infrastructure and to ensure the confidentiality of data stored within it. To protect its customers' data, Microsoft uses some of the strongest encryption protocols in the industry.

As part of Azure, customers can also manage and control the security of their data, including encrypting data at rest, in transit, and during processing. Managing encryption keys properly is essential to best encryption practices, and Azure Key Vault helps secure encryption keys. Azure, the customer in Key Vault, or the customer on-premises can manage and store encryption keys.

A key management strategy can include server-side keys managed by Azure services or client-side encryption where Azure does not have access to encryption keys.

Encryption of Data at Rest

Whenever customer data is written to Azure Storage, including azure managed disks, azure blobs, queues, and table storage, it is automatically encrypted. As well as being compliant with FIPS 140-2, Azure storage data is encrypted with 256-bit AES encryption.

Azure offers several options for encrypting OS and data disks for Windows Server and Linux instances (VMSSs).

For infrastructure as a service (IaaS) virtual machine disks, Azure Disk Encryption provides full-volume encryption based on BitLocker on Windows and DM-Crypt on Linux. An Azure Key Vault is required to manage and control disk encryption keys and secrets.

As part of BitLocker, Windows Server 2016 Shielded VMs are encrypted to prevent restricted administrators from accessing information inside the virtual machine. The key vault and VMs must be located in the same region and subscription. As part of the Shielded VMs solution, the Host Guardian Service certifies virtualization hosts and releases encryption keys.

Encryption Technologies for Specific Storage Types

For specific storage types, additional encryption technologies are available, including the following:

- Data stored in Azure Synapse Analytics is encrypted at rest by Transparent Data Encryption (TDE).

- With Always Encrypted95, data can be encrypted within client applications before being stored in Azure SQL Database. By enabling in-place encryption and richer confidential queries, Always Encrypted with secure enclaves extends the confidential computing capabilities of Always Encrypted.

- As with Azure SQL Database, Azure Data Lake Storage (ADLS) is protected by transparent encryption at rest. By default, ADLS performs key management, but it is possible to manage the keys independently if desired. Storage Service Encryption (SSE), similar to blob storage, automatically encrypts data at rest with Microsoft-managed keys or customer-provided encryption keys in ADLS Gen 2.

- Azure Cosmos DB is by default encrypted using secure key storage systems, encrypted networks, and cryptographic APIs. Microsoft manages the encryption keys, rotating them according to Microsoft internal policy.

Key Management

Azure can manage keys for customers or perform encryption on their behalf.

With server-side encryption, you can choose between three server-side encryption models depending on your organization's needs.

- Service-managed keys combine control and convenience with low overhead through Azure Key Vault. Azure resource providers perform encryption and decryption operations, and Microsoft manages keys.

- Customer-managed keys offer complete control over keys, including bring-your-own-key (BYOK) support or the ability to generate new ones. Azure resource providers handle encryption and decryption operations. Customers control keys via Azure Key Vault.

- By using customer-provided keys (CPK), you can manage keys in key stores other than Azure Key Vault on-premises.

With client-side encryption, the encryption keys are unavailable to Microsoft, and the data can't be decrypted. In this model, the customer encrypts data, uploads it as an encrypted blob, and maintains full control over the keys. The keys are not available to Azure services.

Encryption of Data in Transit

Ensure that data is encrypted in transit in any data protection strategy. Companies that do not protect their data in transit are more likely to experience man-in-the-middle attacks, eavesdropping, and session hijacking. The general recommendation is that customers always exchange data across different locations using Secure Sockets Layer/Transport Layer Security (SSL/TLS) protocols because data is moving back and forth from many locations.

To encrypt communications over the network, Microsoft offers customers the option of using TLS (TLS handshake) and symmetric cryptography (shared secrets) to encrypt customer data while in transit to Azure data centers.

Authentication, integrity, and confidentiality of data as the data is transferred across a network are also protected by Microsoft's Internet Protocol Security (IPsec), an industry-standard protocol set.

Each Azure server is equipped with Azure SmartNICs, which use Field Programmable Gate Array (FPGA) technology. FPGAs are programmable hardware modules that greatly speed up data processing, including encryption of data during transit. The hardware design is published under an open-source license by Microsoft, so the community and customers can benefit from it. The following are the benefits:

- Hardware design is open-source, so licensing is not required.

- Customers can use the encryption if they choose without additional costs.

A virtual private network (VPN) can isolate the communications channel between on-premises and cloud infrastructures and protect data in transit. The following are some ways to protect data in transit:

- Use appropriate safeguards such as HTTPS or VPN when moving data between on-premises infrastructure and Azure.

- Azure Site-to-Site VPN is the best solution for organizations that need to secure access to Azure from multiple on-premises workstations.

- Using a Point-to-Site VPN is the best option for organizations that require secure access from one workstation on-premises to Azure.

- ExpressRoute allows you to move large data sets over a dedicated high-speed WAN link and encrypt them at the application level with SSL/TLS.

- When interacting with Azure Storage through the Azure Portal, you can also access Storage REST API, Azure Storage, and Azure SQL Database over HTTPS.

Encryption During Data Processing

Cloud-based Intel SGX and virtualization-based security protect customer data while processing with Azure confidential computing. When data needs to be in the clear (unencrypted) for efficient processing, confidential computing protects it in a Trusted Execution Environment (TEE).

It is essential to keep data and operations inside TEEs protected from outside views, even with a debugger. The TEE enforces these protections while data is processed, including access by Microsoft employees. Also, if the code is altered or tampered with, the environment is disabled, and operations are denied. Furthermore, this ensures that data can be accessed only by authorized code.

SGX-enabled Intel XEON E-2288G processors are the perfect choice for customers using confidential computing.

For more information, refer to `https://azure.microsoft.com/en-us/updates/intel-sgx-based-confidential-computing-vms-now-available-on-azure-dedicated-hosts`.

Azure Customer Lockbox

As part of Microsoft's efforts to safeguard customer data, Azure customers now have the Customer Lockbox, which lets Microsoft engineers access customer data if they require it in response to a support ticket initiated by a customer or a problem identified by Microsoft, except in cases of an emergency or external legal demand. Customers can control Microsoft requests for customer data by reviewing, approving, or refusing them.

Customers can access the logs related to this service via the Azure Portal and integrate them into their SIEM systems. Integrate this service's logs into your SIEM system via the Azure Portal.

Microsoft provides a variety of assurances as part of its compliance offerings, including certifications, attestations, validations, authorizations, and assessments, as well as contractual amendments, self-assessments, and customer guidance.

Microsoft adheres to all laws and regulations applicable to its online services, including those governing security breaches. No matter which laws or regulations apply to customers or their industries, Microsoft is not liable for complying with them. Microsoft cannot determine whether customer data is subject to specific laws or regulations.

To determine whether Azure services comply with the specific laws and regulations that apply to your business, Microsoft can provide audit reports and certificates regarding Microsoft compliance programs.

Translate Privacy Requirements into Requirements for Security Solutions

With Azure, you can protect your data in the cloud with industry-leading security controls, compliance tools, and privacy policies, including data categories governed by specific security or privacy regulations. As well as complying with these standards, you are also in compliance with European Union-U.S. Privacy Shield, European Union Model Clauses, HIPAA/HITECH, and the HITRUST Act.

The following tools are available in Azure to assist you in achieving your privacy goals:

- For the GDPR portal, azure data subject requests provide step-by-step guidance on finding and acting on personal data stored in Azure by GDPR requirements. In addition to the Microsoft Azure Portal on public and sovereign clouds, Microsoft offers pre-existing APIs and UIs across Microsoft online services that allow users to execute data subject requests.

- As a deep integration of Azure Resource Manager, Azure Policy makes it easier for your organization to enforce policies across resources. Using Azure Policy, you can manage resources at an organizational level and prevent developers from allocating resources that violate those policies by accident. Using Azure Policy, GDPR compliance can be ensured by encrypting or storing data in a specific location.

- Your regulatory compliance can be managed within the shared responsibility model of the cloud with Compliance Manager, a workflow-based risk assessment tool. In addition to Microsoft control implementation details, test results, and customer-managed controls, it provides a dashboard view of standards, regulations, and assessments. You can track, assign, and verify regulatory compliance activities within your organization.

- Microsoft Purview Information Protection identifies sensitive data on on-premises servers; labels, classifies, and protects it; enabling better data governance.

- With Azure Security Center, you can manage and protect your hybrid cloud workloads with unified security policies. Integrating Azure Policy with hybrid cloud workloads enables encryption, limiting organizational exposure to threats and responding to attacks.

- You can build and launch GDPR-compliant cloud applications using Azure Security and Compliance GDPR Blueprint. By leveraging Microsoft common reference architectures, deployment guidance, implementation mappings of GDPR articles, customer responsibility matrixes, and threat models, you will be able to simplify the adoption of Azure in support of your GDPR compliance efforts.

Leverage Azure Policy

Azure Policy, deeply integrated into Azure Resource Manager, allows your organization to enforce privacy policies across all resources. Azure Policy allows you to manage resources at the organizational level and prevent developers from allocating resources that violate those policies. With Azure Policy, you can encrypt your data or keep it in a specific region to comply with specific security regulations.

Azure's Secure Foundation

By enabling privacy-sensitive cloud scenarios, such as financial and health services, you can accelerate your move to the cloud by achieving compliance more efficiently, allowing you to enable the cloud confidently. A company's privacy requirements will vary depending on its industry and compliance standards. In addition to providing robust data security on its own infrastructure, Azure provides customers with customer-enabled services.

State of the Data

You should consider the state of the data at a particular point when designing your solution to meet privacy requirements. You may need to protect your data while in transit in some scenarios, not just when it is at rest. For example, PCI DSS requirement 4 encrypts card-holder data while it is in transit, and your solution must encrypt data in transit to fulfill this requirement. The following are some examples of protection based on the data stage:

- **At-rest data protection:** Physical access to the data's storage hardware may allow an attacker to compromise the data. During maintenance, an attacker could have removed the hard drive from a server, resulting in the attack. Once the hard drive was removed, a computer controlled by the attacker could attempt to access it. Attackers attempt to compromise data at rest when they gain physical access to the hardware on which it is stored. An attacker may have removed the hard drive during maintenance on a server, resulting in the attack. Once the hard drive was removed, the attacker would use a computer they controlled to gain access to the data. Customers can encrypt all of their data in Azure Storage Service Encryption.

- **In-transit data protection:** As part of any data protection strategy, the protection of data in transit is vital. Because data is moving back and forth between many locations at the same time, Microsoft recommends using SSL/TLS protocols to exchange data across multiple locations. You may need a VPN to isolate your on-premises and cloud communication channels. For securing data in transit, Microsoft offers several options to customers both inside the Azure network and across the Internet to end users. Azure virtual machines communicate with a variety of protocols (such as Windows IPsec or SMB) using TSL 1.2 or later (via Azure components such as Azure Front Door or Application Gateway).

One or more of the encryption models at rest are supported by Microsoft Azure Services. However, some services may not support one or more encryption models, and Azure Key Vault may support only a subset of critical encryption keys that customers manage. Moreover, services may release these scenarios and key types on varying schedules.

As of this writing, the following Azure data storage services support encryption at rest:

- **Azure Disk Encryption:** Customers can encrypt their IaaS VMs and disks at rest through Azure Disk Encryption.

- **Azure Storage:** There is server-side encryption at rest available for all Azure Storage services (Blob storage, Queue storage, Table storage, and Azure Files); customer-managed keys and client-side encryption are also available for some services.

- **Azure SQL Database:** Azure SQL Database supports Microsoft-managed service-side and client-side encryption scenarios for encryption at rest. Azure SQL Database customers can also use Transparent Data Encryption and server encryption. TDE keys can be enabled automatically, and both database and server encryption at rest can be enabled. TDE has been enabled by default. The Azure Key Vault supports RSA 2048-bit customer-managed keys for Azure SQL Database, Data Warehouse, and Bring Your Own Key. Client-side encryption is available for Azure SQL Database, Data Warehouse, and Bring Your Own Key. The SQL Server Management Studio allows SQL users to select which key to encrypt each column of the Azure SQL Database. The client creates and stores the encryption key in Windows, in Azure Key Vault, or on the local hardware security module.

Data Classification

To prioritize the data essential to security, you will need to classify it to ensure you are prioritizing secure data. Security controls will also vary depending on the privacy level required by the data. The concept of data classification entails assigning logical labels or classes to data assets based on the context of the business. A passport number, a driver's license number, a credit card number, a SWIFT code, or the name of a person can be used to classify assets.

You can manage and govern your on-premises, multi-cloud, and software-as-a-service (SaaS) data in Azure using Microsoft Purview, a unified data governance service. Automate data discovery, classify sensitive data, and trace your data lineage from end to end to create a comprehensive, up-to-date picture of your data landscape. Manage and secure your data estate with data curators. Make data consumers able to find valuable, reliable information. A common data management platform such as Microsoft Purview provides access to common data management functions such as a catalog, insights, and maps for data producers and consumers. In addition to integrating with on-premises, cloud, and SaaS applications, it can also integrate with Azure Synapse Analytics, SQL Server, Power BI, Azure SQL, and Microsoft 365 cloud data services.

Identity Protection

A compromised user's identity could compromise data and affect your privacy requirements. One of the essential aspects of privacy is ensuring that you have a system to protect the user's identity. If you want to meet privacy requirements, consider enhancing your identity protection strategy with Azure AD Identity Protection.

To identify and protect customers from threats, Microsoft analyzes 6.5 trillion signals a day. A security information and event management tool can also be used to investigate signals generated by Identity Protection and fed to conditional access to make access decisions.

Microsoft provides a variety of solutions to fit your privacy requirements.

- Sensitive data can be discovered, classified, and controlled with Azure Information Protection.
- Cloud App Security identifies cloud apps, infrastructure (IaaS), and platform (PaaS) services to help discover and control shadow IT.
- Authentication for cloud and on-premises services can be managed and deployed through Azure Active Directory.
- Telemetry data from Azure and on-premises environments can be collected, analyzed, and acted upon using Azure Monitor.
- You can encrypt data at rest or in transit with the Azure platform.
- HSMs that never leave the HSM boundary can be imported or generated with Azure Key Vault.
- Multiple options are available for deploying multifactor authentication in Azure Active Directory.
- Discover, classify, and control sensitive data with Azure Information Protection.

Summary

This chapter has exposed you to different strategies for designing, defining, and recommending regulatory compliance strategies.

Data protection and privacy in Azure are grounded in a commitment to giving organizations control and ownership over customer data. In Azure, all your data is owned by you, and Microsoft uses it only for its agreed-upon services, not for marketing or advertising.

It's up to you to control where, who, and how your customers' data is stored and used. You can access customer data at any time and for any reason. Microsoft closely regulates government and law enforcement requests for customer data, and if you discontinue service, your data is deleted according to strict standards.

Hence, consider all of them in your design and deployment of regulation strategy.

Exam Essentials

Understand the Microsoft GRC capabilities. Regulatory environments are becoming increasingly complex and dynamic, necessitating a more structured approach to managing governance, risk, and compliance (GRC).

By implementing a framework for compliance and risk management, the GRC competency assists organizations in reducing risk and improving compliance effectiveness.

The following are the capabilities that can help you with GRC for your enterprise cybersecurity solution:

- A centralized hub and specialized workspace are provided by the Microsoft 365 Defender portal for identity and access management, threat protection, information protection, and security management professionals to manage and maximize Microsoft 365 intelligent security solutions.

- Your organization's compliance needs can be easily managed with Microsoft Purview's compliance portal.

- In addition to strengthening your data center's security posture and providing advanced threat protection across hybrid workloads in the cloud, whether in Azure or not, Microsoft Defender for Cloud is a unified infrastructure security management system.

- With Azure Policy, you can create, assign, and manage policies over your Azure resources to ensure compliance with corporate standards.

- An organization's standards, patterns, and requirements can be implemented and adhered to with Azure Blueprints.

  Understand compliance requirements and align with Microsoft's best practices. Design, deploy, and manage compliance projects faster with built-in controls, configuration management tools, implementation and guidance resources, and third-party audit reports from Azure.

- With Azure Security and Compliance Blueprints, you can easily create, deploy, and update compliance environments, including those for ISO:27001, PCI DSS, and UK OFFICIAL certifications.
- Integrate security management across hybrid cloud workloads with Azure Security Center (aka Microsoft Defender for Cloud).
- Define and enforce policies that help your cloud environment become compliant with internal and external regulations.

Assess infrastructure compliance by using Microsoft Defender for Cloud. Microsoft Defender for Cloud plays an integral part in your governance strategy and helps you stay on top of security. The regulatory compliance dashboard in Microsoft Defender for Cloud reflects your compliance with the standard. Data from various sources is collected, searched, and analyzed, including firewalls and other partner solutions, allowing you to see all your workloads in one place.

Analyze compliance scores and recommend actions to resolve issues or improve security. With Microsoft Defender for Cloud, you can view the status of all your compliance assessments for your chosen standards and regulations on the regulatory compliance dashboard. You improve your compliance posture by acting on the recommendations and reducing risk factors in your environment.

Design, deploy, and validate the implementation of Azure Policy. In addition to helping you ensure cloud compliance and avoid misconfigurations, Azure Policy can help you practice consistent resource governance and set guardrails for your resources. In addition to reducing the number of external approval processes, Azure Policy can also be used to increase developer productivity and optimize your cloud spending by implementing policies at the core of the Azure platform. Once your new policy definition has been validated with existing resources and new or updated resource requests, you can begin implementing it.

Understand data residency and retention requirements. For data to be stored within a particular geographic boundary, such as within a national boundary, it needs to be resident within that boundary. There are many kinds of data residency requirements: local, national, or regional laws or regulations; nongovernmental requirements such as industry standards and certifications of compliance; or contractual requirements. Regulations require data residency if adequate protective measures are taken when addressing data transfer. All customer data is usually to meet data residency requirements. Still, specific types of data may be required only to comply in some cases, such as financial information, personal information, or health information. There are more than 35 countries where Microsoft offers data residency for many of its services, and more are being added. As a result, Microsoft Cloud customers have an ever-increasing number of options for storing and processing their data locally.

- Data storage and processing regions can be specified for most Azure services.

- Customers' data is typically stored in the geography associated with their first Dynamics 365 and Power Platform subscription. Microsoft replicates Dynamics 365 and Power Platform customer data within the borders of the selected geography to ensure data durability.

- Core customer data is stored in a Geo based on the billing address when a customer signs up for Microsoft 365.

Decode privacy requirements into needs for security solutions.   Using Microsoft Azure's security controls, compliance tools, and privacy policies, your data is safeguarded in the cloud, including any categories of personal data identified by specific security or privacy regulations.

Review Questions

1. Which of the following Azure compliance services delivers protection for all resources directly within the Azure experience and extends protection to on-premises and multi-cloud?

   A. Microsoft Defender for Cloud

   B. Azure Policy

   C. Azure Desired state configuration

   D. Azure Automation Updated Management

2. As a Microsoft Cybersecurity Architect, you are responsible for managing and scheduling updates for your Windows and Linux VMs in Azure, as well as physical or VMs in on-premises and other cloud environments. Which Azure compliance capabilities will you adopt in your enterprise solution?

   A. Azure Policy

   B. Azure Blueprint

   C. Azure Desired State Configuration

   D. Azure Automation Updated Management

3. As a Microsoft Cybersecurity Architect, you are responsible for policy enforcement to ensure environment and guest compliance. Which Azure compliance capabilities will you adopt in your enterprise solution?

   A. Azure Policy

   B. Azure Blueprint

   C. Azure Desired State Configuration

   D. Azure Automation Updated Management

4. As a Microsoft Cybersecurity Architect, you are responsible for automated compliance for core services. Which Azure compliance capabilities will you adopt in your enterprise solution?

   A. Azure Policy

   B. Azure Blueprint

   C. Azure Desired State Configuration

   D. Microsoft Defender for Cloud

5. As a Microsoft Cybersecurity Architect, you are responsible for automated updates on a guest OS. Which Azure compliance capabilities will you adopt in your enterprise solution?

   A. Azure Policy

   B. Microsoft Defender for Cloud

   C. Azure Desired State Configuration

   D. Azure Automation Updated Management

6. As a Microsoft Cybersecurity Architect, you are responsible for enforcing and automating your organization's governance decisions. Which Azure compliance capabilities will you adopt in your enterprise solution?

   A. Azure Policy

   B. Microsoft Defender for Cloud

   C. Azure Desired State Configuration

   D. Azure Automation Updated Management

7. Which of the following Azure compliance services delivers threat protection for all resources directly within the Azure experience and extends protection to on-premises and multi-cloud, as well as integrates with your SIEM solution?

   A. Microsoft Defender for Cloud

   B. Azure Policy

   C. Azure Desired State Configuration

   D. Azure Automation Updated Management

8. You can protect Azure PaaS services, including Azure App Service, Azure SQL, Azure Storage Account, and more, by integrating with which of the following services?

   A. Microsoft Defender for Cloud Apps

   B. Microsoft Defender for Cloud

   C. Azure Policy

   D. Azure Blueprint

9. Which feature of Microsoft Defender for Cloud helps you to extend your other public cloud resources like AWS into Microsoft Defender for Cloud?

   A. Microsoft Defender for Cloud's CSPM

   B. Microsoft Defender for Cloud's Apps

   C. Microsoft Defender for Cloud's CWPP

   D. None of the above.

10. Which of the following actions will help you to increase your security control score?

    A. Deploy compliance as per industry standard one time.

    B. Remediate all of the recommendations.

    C. Rebuild the environment.

    D. None of the above.

11. Which of the Azure policy terminologies is applicable for following statement? Azure policy terminologies often indicate the target resource's resource provider (for example, compute, storage, monitoring).

    A. Metadata property

    B. Category

    C. Alias

    D. Definition

12. Which policy assignment properties allow users to enable or disable some policy effects, such as denying, while maintaining compliance and providing logs?

    A. Change mode

    B. Enforcement mode

    C. Execute mode

    D. None of the above

13. Which of the Azure policy terminologies creates an incident or outcome when a policy state, such as create, change, or delete, changes in Azure Policy?

    A. Event Grid

    B. Event Hub

    C. Event Spoke

    D. None of the above

14. As a Microsoft Cybersecurity Architect, you are responsible for setting guardrails throughout your resources. Which Azure compliance service can help you ensure cloud compliance, avoid misconfigurations, and practice consistent resource governance throughout your organization?

    A. Microsoft Defender for Cloud Apps

    B. Microsoft Defender for Cloud

    C. Azure Policy

    D. Azure Blueprint

15. Data that persists on physical media is always encrypted using which of the following protocols, and who is managing the keys?

    A. AES and Microsoft Managed

    B. FIPS 140-2 and Microsoft Managed

    C. FIPS 140-2 and Customer Managed

    D. TupleHash and Customer Managed

16. The traffic between data centers is protected by which of the security standards that is also preventing physical man-in-the-middle attacks?

    A. IEEE 802.1 AE MAC

    B. Encrypted using Microsoft standard

    C. IEEE 801.2 AE MAC

    D. Encrypted using customer standard

17. When customer data is written to Azure Storage, including Azure Managed Disks, Azure Blobs, Queues, and Table Storage, it is automatically encrypted. Which standard is all Azure Storage data compliant with, and which encryption method is used?

    A. FIPS 140-2 compliant and 256-bit AES Encrypted

    B. FIPS 140-2 compliant and 128-bit AES Encrypted

    C. TDEA compliant and 128-bit AES Encrypted

    D. HMAC compliant and 256-bit AES Encrypted

18. As a Microsoft Cybersecurity Architect, you are responsible for securing IaaS workloads, especially OS and data disks. Which of the following will you adopt to provide encryption for Windows and Linux VMs?

A. BitLocker on Windows VM and DM-Crypt on Linux VM

B. BitLocker on Linux VM and DM-Crypt on Window VM

C. Microsoft managed unified endpoint protection for Windows and Linux

D. None of the above

19. As a Microsoft Cybersecurity Architect, you are responsible for securing IaaS workloads; which of the following services can be hosted in the specific region?

A. Virtual machines

B. Storage

C. SQL databases

D. All of the above

20. Cloud-based Intel SGX and virtualization-based security protect customer data during which stage of data?

A. Data in rest

B. Data in transit

C. Data in process

D. None of the above

Chapter

5

Identify Security Posture and Recommend Technical Strategies to Manage Risk

---

THE MICROSOFT SC-100 EXAM OBJECTIVES COVERED IN THIS CHAPTER INCLUDE:

✓ Evaluate security posture by using Azure Security Benchmark

✓ Evaluate security posture by using Microsoft Defender for Cloud

✓ Evaluate security posture by using Secure Scores

✓ Evaluate security posture of cloud workloads

✓ Design security for an Azure Landing Zone

✓ Interpret technical threat intelligence and recommend risk mitigations

✓ Recommend security capabilities or controls to mitigate identified risks

In this chapter, we will focus on the approach to identifying security posture and develop a recommendation for technical strategies to manage risk.

In most organizations, the Cloud Security Posture Framework is used when a cloud-first strategy gets adopted and organizations want to deploy security best practices to hybrid clouds.

The framework should aim to identify misconfiguration issues and compliance risks in the cloud and should continuously monitor cloud services for gaps in security policy enforcement.

Even though infrastructure as a service is often associated with technology, the solution has to be used to minimize configuration errors and reduce compliance risks in software-as-a-service and platform-as-a-service offerings.

In this chapter, you will review how to analyze security postures using benchmarks, analyze security postures using Microsoft Defender for Cloud, assess security postures using Secure Scores, evaluate cloud workload security, plan and design security for an Azure landing zone, identify technical threats and recommend mitigation measures, and provide recommendations for reducing identified risks through the use of security controls.

Analyze Security Posture by Using Azure Security Benchmark

Let's get started with what security posture is. NIST defines *security posture* as follows: "The security status of an enterprise's networks, information, and systems based on information security resources (for example, people, hardware, software, policies) and capabilities in place to manage the defense of the enterprise and to react as the situation changes."

Security posture refers to an organization's overall resilience to cyber threats and the strength of its cybersecurity. Digital cyberattacks are complicated and assorted, making it challenging to analyze and improve security postures.

With a constantly evolving threat landscape, organizations are moving away from last-generation security strategies and fragmented solutions. Adopting an automated architecture for managing security posture is vital for the digital era.

The basics of the security posture of your organization can be evaluated in short by the following:

- Obtaining an overview of the assets in your inventory and the attack surface that you have

- Defending your enterprise against cyberattacks with controls and processes

- Detecting and containing attacks
- Reacting to security events and recovering from them
- Determining how automated your security program is

In a nutshell, create an accurate inventory of your IT assets, map the attack surface, and know your cyber risk.

Governance in the digital age must have operational elements that continuously interact with other teams. Security posture management is an evolving function describing a step forward in achieving long-term convergence of security functions. Security compliance reporting and vulnerability management are among the functions that answer the question, how safe and secure is the cloud environment?

Security governance in the on-premises world follows the cadence of data it can obtain about the environment, and it may take time to update this data. Cloud technology provides visibility into on-demand security postures and asset coverage, transforming governance into a more dynamic organization. This organization closely relates with other security teams to provide guidance, monitor security standards, and improve processes. In its ideal state, governance is the heart of continuous improvement. As part of your overall security governance, this improvement engages your organization to improve security posture (a process called *posture management*) continuously, and it fits in the overall security governance, as depicted in Figure 5.1.

FIGURE 5.1   Overall security governance

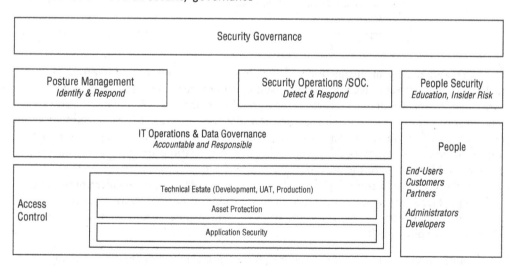

To keep up with the cloud and attackers, governance teams need to continually improve asset security posture by improving standards and enforcing those standards. Information technology (IT) organizations need to react quickly to new threats and adapt as they arise. Further attacks are always emerging, and defenses are constantly improving and may need to be enabled as well. In the initial configuration, you can only sometimes get all the security you need.

Following a rapid modernization plan (RaMP), depicted in Figure 5.2, will allow you to quickly improve your security posture with the smallest number of obstacles.

FIGURE 5.2   Security posture management rapid modernization plan

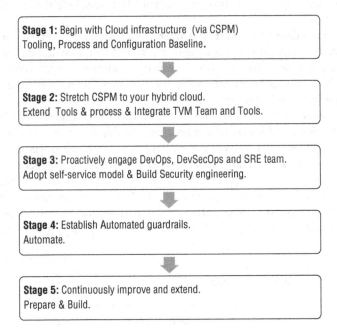

Stage 1: Begin with Cloud infrastructure (via CSPM) Tooling, Process and Configuration Baseline.

Stage 2: Stretch CSPM to your hybrid cloud. Extend Tools & process & Integrate TVM Team and Tools.

Stage 3: Proactively engage DevOps, DevSecOps and SRE team. Adopt self-service model & Build Security engineering.

Stage 4: Establish Automated guardrails. Automate.

Stage 5: Continuously improve and extend. Prepare & Build.

The posture management function will need to grow and continuously improve to tackle the complete set of technical debts resulting from security being a low priority. Posture management will need to secure all the technologies and teams in the organization and meet the organization's needs as it changes (new platforms are adopted, new security tools become available to monitor and reduce risk, and so on). It will be necessary to prepare for any expansions in scope by building leadership support, relationships across technical teams, skillsets, and processes for the posture management team.

Figure 5.3 refers to a company's overall security posture, including its identity security, endpoint protection, user data protection, app security, and infrastructure security.

Figure 5.3 shows the three significant pillars of security posture management. Let us read about all three pillars in detail.

Protect   Security postures for organizations are not static; they change as threats emerge and environmental variables change. Enabling protections for administrators, such as multifactor authentication (MFA), strengthens a company's security posture. Organizations' security posture can be weakened by a lack of awareness and consequent inaction, such as failing to update endpoints or apply available protections. Threat actors are less likely to succeed in compromising your workload when your environment has good security hygiene.

Detect   You must also implement threat detection after implementing all security protection recommendations to quickly identify suspicious activity in your workloads and trigger an alert.

Respond   The last step is to ensure that you have automated processes in place to respond to alerts you receive promptly with measures that can contain and mitigate the attack.

FIGURE 5.3   Security posture management pillars

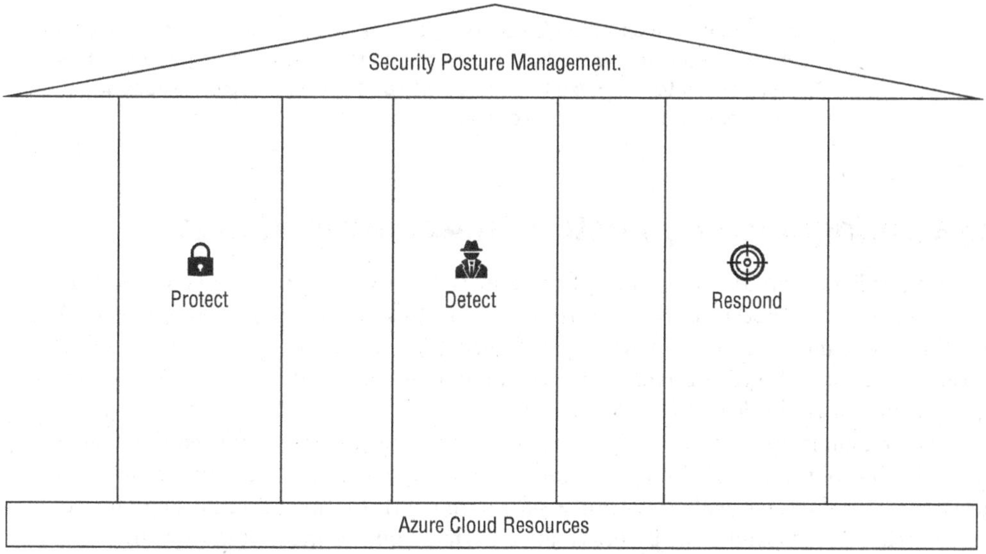

Using benchmarks to evaluate your current environment, understand existing gaps, and provide guidance on improvement is widespread in the IT industry. Benchmarks can provide you with tangible actions to enhance your security posture. They can be derived from industry standards, such as ISO 27001, or from a cloud provider's benchmark, such as Azure Security Benchmark (ASB) for Azure workloads or the Center for Internet Security (CIS) AWS Foundations Benchmark, which is crafted for Amazon Web Services workloads. By providing remediation steps to harden your workloads, benchmarks will also help you identify security gaps faster. By implementing these security recommendations, your workloads will become more secure, and your overall cloud security posture will strengthen. In the role of an architect, you will find that benchmarks serve as guides to improve cloud security postures while following industry standards.

Security hygiene is essential, considering all the options available when evaluating cloud workload. You may need to notify relevant stakeholders, launch a change management process, and implement specific remediation steps as part of these processes. Automation reduces overhead, so consider automating as many steps as possible. In addition to improving security, it ensures that your predefined process steps are followed quickly, consistently, and accurately.

You should also ensure that you use security best practices to harden the cloud workloads and improve their security hygiene. Each workload has a unique set of security best practices to follow.

Conducting a risk assessment before improving your security posture is essential. Once you understand your business's risks, you can optimize your security posture to reduce those risks.

By evaluating a company's security posture, you can determine if the organization is protected and what changes need to be made. Evaluation allows an organization to decrease the probability of a successful cyberattack and limit the extent of damage if one ensues.

Evaluating Security Posture in Azure Workloads

By using ASB, organizations can meet their security control requirements; you can also evaluate your workload's security posture. To meet security and compliance requirements, ASB provides clear and concrete guidance on configuring Azure resources securely. In addition to accelerating initial Azure onboarding and ongoing Azure onboarding/assessment, ASB frequently plays a vital role in Azure onboarding.

When planning and evaluating Azure environments, customers often need to reconcile multiple control frameworks to meet security and compliance requirements. Security teams need to repeat the same evaluation process for each control framework, causing unnecessary overhead, costs, and time. By providing a harmonizing control framework to help you work with established standards in a cloud environment, Microsoft developed CIS Controls v7 and v8, NIST SP800-53 Rev4, and PCI-DSS v3.2.1. Organizations can also use ASB consistently and efficiently to evaluate Azure deployment security postures against industry standards.

Microsoft Defender for Cloud displays ASB in its regulatory compliance dashboard, as depicted in Figure 5.4.

In this benchmark, you can see which security recommendations are open per compliance control. Defender for Cloud runs assessments associated with each compliance control. It does not mean that you are fully compliant with control if they are all green; it indicates that they are currently passing. The Defender for Cloud assessments do not cover all controls for a particular regulation, so this report is only a partial snapshot of your overall compliance.

You may need to use a different benchmark based on your organization's needs, even though this is the preferred benchmark for Azure. Using the tabs assigned to regulatory standards, you can view the compliance controls assessed and the current status of each.

FIGURE 5.4   Microsoft Defender for Cloud regulatory compliance

From the SC-100 exam perspective, keep in mind that the exam may
test how well you can evaluate a system or service's security posture
by examining security benchmarks. Azure security benchmarks are an
example of a system or service's security posture.

Analyze Security Posture by Using Microsoft Defender for Cloud

In your role as a Cybersecurity Architect, you will be responsible for protecting your organization's systems, users, and data. Your users must have easy access to your data, assets, and resources while preventing unauthorized access. Cloud security is a complex area. A unified infrastructure security management system like Microsoft Defender for Cloud helps protect your estate and ensure regulatory compliance.

In addition to providing unified infrastructure security management, Microsoft Defender for Cloud helps you do the following:

- Enhance the security posture of your organization
- Comply with regulatory requirements
- Provide threat protection for both Azure and non-Azure workloads

Get an overview of your company's security posture, compliance, and threats using the workload protection dashboard in the Azure Portal. Microsoft Defender for Cloud looks at your whole environment and provides an aggregate score to show you how secure it is. This is the Secure Score for your domain that you can find in the Policy & Compliance section.

In this section, you can also check if your storage accounts meet compliance requirements and how to resolve them. For example, you'll see if any storage accounts fail to meet a particular compliance control. Microsoft Defender for Cloud recommends remediation steps so that you can act accordingly.

It is also possible with Microsoft Defender for Cloud to set up security policies that protect different parts of your environment. In this way, you are able to identify which parts of your environment aren't adhering to security policies and how you can fix them.

You can always be sure that Microsoft Defender for Cloud is protecting your resources, subscriptions, and organization against security threats. All the findings are then combined into one score so you can see, at a glance, how secure your organization is: the higher the score, the lower the level of risk.

As a security operations center analyst, it is essential for you to identify potential risks and attack vectors in order to prioritize them more effectively. Microsoft Defender for Cloud maps its security recommendations against MITRE ATT&CK, which is based on actual adversary observations, to make prioritization easier. The Microsoft recommendations that are mapped to the MITRE ATT&CK framework can be used by clients to maintain a secure environment.

When you assess your security posture with MITRE ATT&CK, you can develop remediation strategies based on the distinct phases of the MITRE ATT&CK framework. By remediating recommendations that map to the early stages of MITRE ATT&CK's framework, you can prevent a threat actor from gaining access to your workloads in the future. As shown in Figure 5.5, Defender for Cloud has a filter that allows you to visualize this data.

FIGURE 5.5 Microsoft Defender for Cloud Dashboard

Name ↑↓	Max score ↑↓	Current score ↑↓	Potential score increase ↑↓	Status ↑↓	Unhealthy resources	Insights
Secure management ports	8	8.00		Completed	0 of 18 resources	
Restrict unauthorized network access	4	3.00	+ 2%	Unhealthy	3 of 50 resources	
Internet-facing virtual machines should be protected with network security groups				Completed	0 of 19 virtual machines	
All network ports should be restricted on network security groups associated to your virt...				Completed	0 of 19 virtual machines	
Adaptive network hardening recommendations should be applied on internet facing virt...				Completed	0 of 19 virtual machines	
IP forwarding on your virtual machine should be disabled				Completed	0 of 19 virtual machines	
Storage account should use a private link connection				Unhealthy	12 of 12 storage accounts	
Implement security best practices	Not scored	Not scored		Unhealthy	30 of 118 resources	
Enable enhanced security features	Not scored	Not scored		Completed	0 of 5 resources	

Health assessments are provided by Microsoft Defender for Cloud.

Using analytics and monitoring capabilities, Defender for Cloud detects a wide range of potentially malicious activity and displays security alerts in the workload protection dashboard.

Assess the Security Hygiene of Cloud Workloads

Multiple individuals and teams within your organization can use Defender for Cloud for a variety of security-related tasks. Defender for Cloud enables these individuals to complete these various duties.

The SOC analyst must often have a suitable level of privileges in the workload so that recommendations can be remedied more quickly. As shown in Figure 5.6, a user who does not have the right level of privileges will experience the grayed-out Fix button when trying to remediate a recommendation, as shown in Figure 5.6.

FIGURE 5.6   Security hygiene recommendation remediation

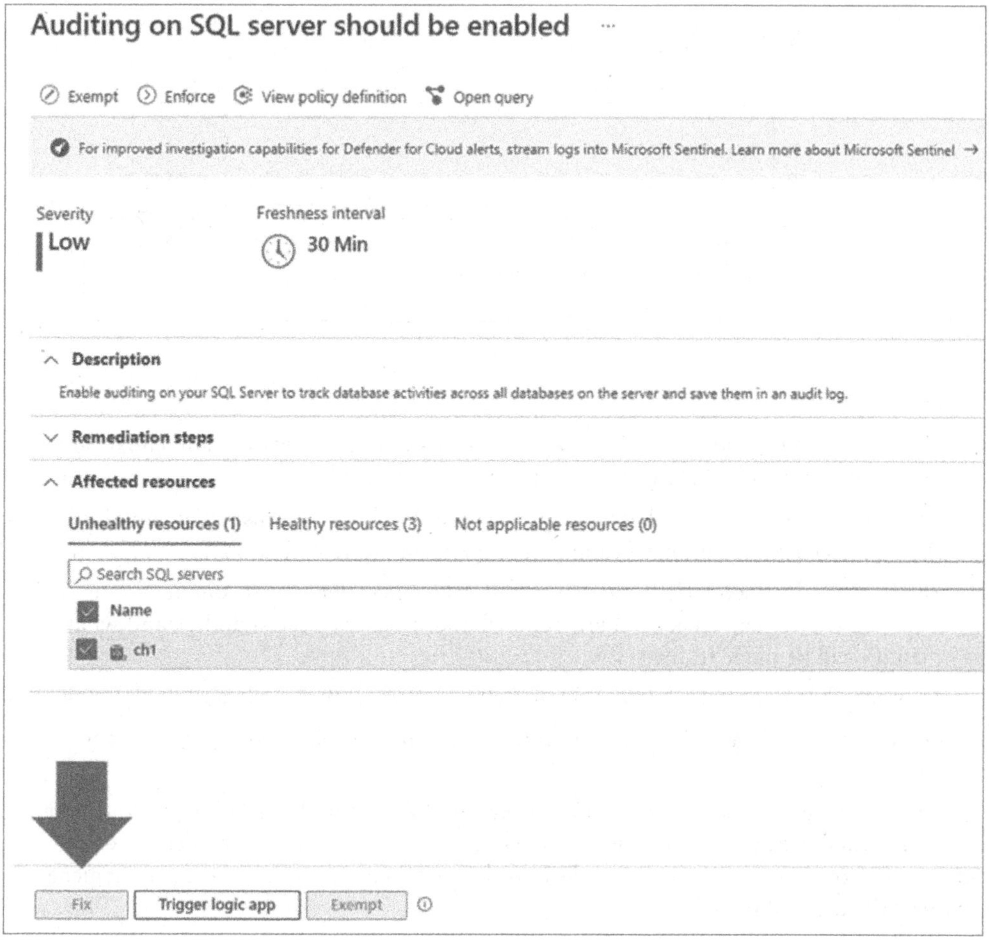

Consequently, workload owners must be notified when security recommendations are open for remediation. The Workflow Automation feature of Defender for Cloud can be used to trigger actions, such as sending an email to the resource owner, whenever a recommendation is triggered. An example of this workflow is depicted in Figure 5.7.

FIGURE 5.7   Security hygiene remediation workflow

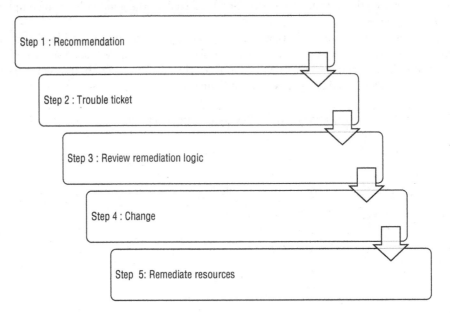

Here are the steps:

1. The Microsoft Defender for Cloud team identifies that a security recommendation needs to be addressed and which resources are affected by it.

2. There is a ticket opened and assigned to the workload owner. This ticket contains details about the security recommendation and suggestions for remediation.

3. The workload owner reviews the ticket and determines that this recommendation has a quick fix. They can click the View Remediation Logic button to understand what changes will be made to the system.

4. They schedule remediation once they feel comfortable with the changes.

5. On the scheduled date, the Azure resource remediation needs to be applied as per the plan.

Alternatively, workload owners can use Defender for Cloud's built-in integration. When a database administrator manages multiple databases, the Microsoft Defender for Cloud option can provide security recommendations that will help improve the security hygiene of their workloads, as shown in Figure 5.8.

FIGURE 5.8   Microsoft Defender for Cloud—security hygiene of workloads

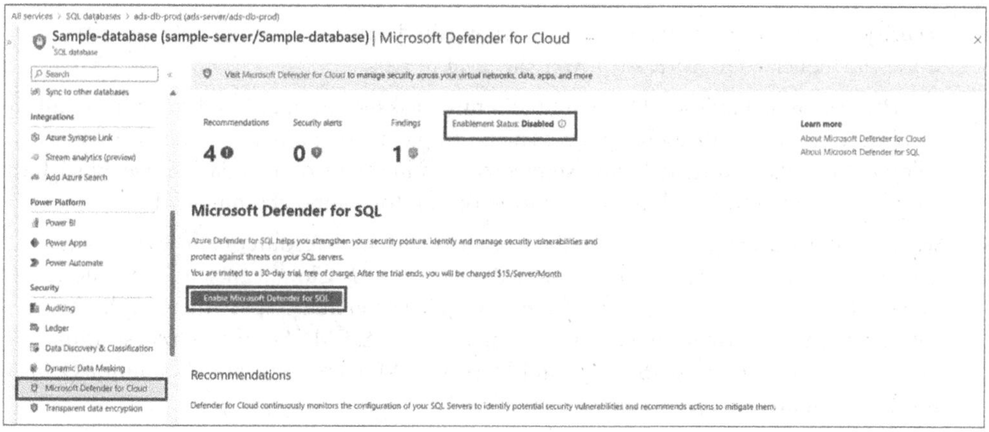

Evaluate the Security Posture of Cloud Workloads

Using Microsoft Threat Intelligence, Defender for Cloud provides security alerts. A range of advanced, intelligent safeguards also protects your workload. Microsoft Defender provides workload protection based on the resources included in your subscription. With Microsoft Defender for Storage, you can receive alerts when suspicious activity is detected on your storage resources.

The Azure-native Defender for Cloud monitors and protects many Azure services without requiring any deployment, although you can also add resources on-premises or in other public clouds.

In addition to hardening your resources, tracking your security posture, and protecting against cyberattacks, Defender for Cloud streamlines the security management process. Its native integration makes deployment easy, allowing you to automatically secure your resources by default thanks to simple autoprovisioning. As you manage the security of your Cloud and on-premises resources and workloads, Defender for Cloud meets three essential needs.

- **Continuously assess:** Maintain a continuous assessment of your security posture.

- **Secure:** Ensure that all resources and services connected to the network are hardened.

- **Defend:** Assist in the detection and resolution of threats posed to those resources and services.

To protect yourself against these challenges, Microsoft Defender for Cloud offers the following tools:

- **Security score:** Your current security situation is indicated by your current security score; the higher your score, the lower the level of risk.

- **Security recommendations:** These are hardening tasks that are tailored to your organization's needs and prioritized for improvement. Implementing a recommendation involves following the detailed remediation steps provided in the recommendation. Defender for Cloud offers an automated implementation option for many recommendations!

- **Security alerts:** Defender for Cloud detects threats to your resources and workloads with its enhanced security features enabled. Defender for Cloud can send these alerts via email to the relevant employees in your organization and display them in the Azure Portal. Security Information and Event Management (SIEM), Security Orchestration, Automation and Response (SOAR), and IT Service Management (ITSM) solutions can also be configured to receive alerts.

Microsoft Defender for Cloud continuously detects all resources across your workload and determines whether they are configured according to best security practices. If they are not identified, they are flagged. A prioritized list of recommendations is provided for what you need to fix to protect your machines.

Microsoft Defender for Cloud groups each recommendation into security controls to make it easier to understand the importance of each recommendation to your overall security posture. Each control is assigned a Secure Score. This scoring is essential to prioritizing your security work.

In addition to protecting Azure-based platforms as a service (PaaS), Defender for Cloud detects and prevents threats at the infrastructure-as-a-service (IaaS) layer.

Microsoft Defender for Cloud comes with Fusion kill-chain analysis. What is Fusion kill-chain analysis? A probabilistic kill chain is applied to the triage alerts by Fusion as a regularizer. A defender prioritizes kill chains that are time bound, as they are based on how real people—Microsoft security experts, vendors, and customers—triage alerts. One enacted within a day will take precedence over one passed over a few days, and one that has all steps completed is even higher in priority. When the probabilistic kill chain is applied to the Fusion machine learning statistical model, Fusion reduces the number of threats from billions to hundreds.

The Fusion kill-chain analysis correlates alerts based on cyber kill-chain analysis in your environment. This analysis enables you to understand better an attack campaign, its origin, and its impact on your resources.

Microsoft Defender for Cloud can deploy a Log Analytics agent automatically when security-related data is needed. Deployment is handled directly on Azure machines. Microsoft Defender plans can be extended to non-Azure machines in hybrid and multi-cloud environments using Azure Arc.

What is Azure Arc? You can use it to build applications and services that are flexible enough to run across data centers, at the edge, and in multi-cloud environments with Azure Arc. This bridge extends the Azure platform. With Azure Arc, you can create cloud-native applications with consistent development, operations, and security models across new and existing hardware, virtualization, Kubernetes platforms, IoT devices, and integrated systems. It allows you to modernize your business with cloud-native solutions to do more with less.

Multi-cloud machines can benefit from Cloud security posture management (CSPM) features without requiring agents. You can detect threats across a wide range of platforms with Defender for Cloud.

- **Azure PaaS services:** The Azure PaaS services can be used to detect threats spreading to Azure services such as Azure App Service, Azure SQL, Azure Storage Account, and more. As part of the native integration with Microsoft Defender for Cloud Apps (formerly known as Microsoft Cloud App Security), you can detect anomalies in your Azure activity logs.

- **Azure data services:** As part of Defender for Cloud, you can automatically classify your Azure SQL data. You can also get assessments of potential vulnerabilities across Azure SQL and storage services and recommendations for mitigation.

- **Networks:** You can minimize the risk of brute-force attacks using networks and Defender for Cloud. By reducing access to virtual machine ports, just-in-time VM access prevents unnecessary access to virtual machine ports. A secure access policy can be set for select ports, for only authorized users, for a limited number of days, and for a limited range of IP addresses.

Microsoft Defender for Cloud's Defender plans provide comprehensive protection for the compute, data, and service layers.

- Microsoft Defender for Servers
- Microsoft Defender for Storage
- Microsoft Defender for SQL
- Microsoft Defender for Containers
- Microsoft Defender for App Service
- Microsoft Defender for Key Vault
- Microsoft Defender for Azure Resource Manager
- Microsoft Defender for DNS
- Microsoft Defender for DevOps

Let's explore each one of them.

- **Microsoft Defender for Cloud:** To monitor for security vulnerabilities and threats, Defender for Cloud collects data from your Azure virtual machines (VMs), virtual machine scale sets, IaaS containers, and non-Azure machines (including on-premises). The data from your workloads is collected by monitoring components in some Defender plans.

- With Microsoft Defender for Cloud, OS posture issues are covered beyond the scope of agent-based assessments. By scanning VMs without agents, network connectivity requirements, or affecting machine performance, you can get frictionless, comprehensive, and instant visibility on actionable posture issues.

- Virtual machines can be scanned agentless with Defender vulnerability management for software inventory and vulnerability assessment in Azure and Amazon AWS environments. It is possible to scan without agents in Defender Cloud Security Posture Management and Defender for Servers P2 through agentless scanning.

- Collecting data for monitoring missing updates, misconfigured OS security settings, endpoint protection status, and health and threat protection is necessary. Data collection is required only for compute resources, such as VMs, VM scale sets, and IaaS containers.

- With Microsoft Defender for Cloud's enhanced security features, there are several plans to select from, including Microsoft Defender for Servers. The Defender for Servers product protects Windows and Linux machines in Azure, AWS, Google Cloud Platform, and on-premises.

- **Microsoft Defender for Containers:** In addition to improving, monitoring, and maintaining the security of your clusters, containers, and their applications, you can secure your containers with Microsoft Defender for Containers, a cloud-native solution.

- **Microsoft Defender for SQL:** Defend your entire Azure database estate with Defender for Cloud database protections that detect and respond to attacks. Depending on the attack surface and security risks of each database engine and data type, Defender for Cloud provides tailored protection.

- **Microsoft Defender for Storage:** Using Azure-native security intelligence, you can detect attempts to access or exploit your storage accounts that are unusual or potentially harmful. Microsoft Threat Intelligence data and advanced threat detection capabilities provide contextual security alerts. Those alerts also contain mitigation and prevention steps for preventing future attacks.

- **Microsoft Defender for App Service:** With Defender for Cloud, you won't have to deploy anything or undergo an onboarding process. The integration is transparent.

  - Suppose you want to use Microsoft Defender for App Service to protect your Azure App Service plan. In that case, you will need a supported App Service plan with dedicated machines and Defender for Cloud's enhanced protections enabled.

- **Microsoft Defender for Key Vault:** Certificates, connection strings, and passwords are safeguarded in Azure Key Vault, a cloud service.

  - For Azure Key Vault, enable Microsoft Defender for Key Vault, which provides advanced threat protection.

- **Microsoft Defender for Azure Resource Manager:** The Azure Resource Manager is a service for managing and deploying Azure resources. Azure account management provides a layer for creating, updating, and deleting resources. After deployment, you can secure and organize your resources using management features such as access control, locks, and tags.

- It is the cloud management layer that connects all of your cloud resources. As a result, attackers may target it as well. We recommend that the security operations team closely monitor the resource management layer.

- **Microsoft Defender for DNS:** As an additional layer of protection, Microsoft Defender for DNS complements Azure DNS' name resolution capabilities.

  - Defender for DNS monitors queries from Azure DNS and detects suspicious activity without requiring additional agents on your resources.

- **Microsoft Defender for DevOps:** You can monitor, manage, and protect your multi-cloud environments across Azure, AWS, Google Cloud Platform, and on-premises resources through Azure Defender for Cloud. Security teams can work DevOps security across multiple pipelines with Defender for DevOps, a service in Defender for Cloud.

  - GitHub and Azure DevOps are just two multipipeline environments Defender for DevOps protects with a centralized console. Comparing Defender for DevOps findings with contextual cloud security insights will allow code remediation to be prioritized based on the results.

Your resources' security is enhanced by increased visibility and control with Microsoft Defender for Cloud, which prevents, detects, and responds to threats. With it, you can monitor security across your subscriptions, detect threats that would otherwise go undetected, and work with a broad ecosystem of security solutions.

Compute, Networking, Storage & Data, and Applications summarize your environment's security posture on the Defender for Cloud Overview page.

Design Security for an Azure Landing Zone

A successful shift to the cloud starts with landing zones, and cloud computing is the basis and backbone of digital transformation in all its forms.

When designing and deploying clouds, architects must consider everyday decisions such as defining a landing zone as a multi-account, well-architected, scalable, and secure cloud environment.

You can launch and deploy workloads and applications in your security and infrastructure environment quickly and confidently using a cloud landing zone. Your organization's future growth and business goals will influence the technical and business decisions made when building a landing zone.

Each cloud landing zone supports a specific requirement and operating model, so they are identical across domains. The cloud environment needs to be reviewed, modified, and iterated for an organization's long-term goals. Cloud landing zones can form the foundation of a customer's digital transformation by enabling cloud consumers to validate, customize, and expand their cloud landing zones together.

An end-to-end cloud landing zone integrates best practices, well-designed architectural patterns, and centralized policies. Monitoring, logging, and cloud consumer management are all integrated. Cloud landing zone, the next-generation governance and security solution, is fully automated, enterprise-scale, and independent of the cloud model.

In Microsoft cloud adoption strategies, landing zones serve as a fundamental component. Besides scalability, security, governance, networking, and identity, it builds an Azure environment that accounts for and underpins those functions. Azure landing zones allow enterprises to migrate applications, modernize, and innovate.

To ensure consistency across cloud consumers' domains and fulfill every dynamic business requirement in an agile manner, cloud landing zones ensure that target environments are well designed, deployed, secured, and governed. The cloud landing zone enables cloud consumers to stay compliant and control costs so they can invest where it matters most.

An Azure landing zone is created by combining scale, security governance, networking, and identity in a multisubscription environment. Enterprises can migrate applications, update their infrastructure, and innovate with Azure landing zones. In these zones, all platform resources necessary to support the customer's application portfolio are considered without distinction between infrastructure as a service and platform as a service.

Several options are available to cloud consumers as they grow their cloud portfolios and have a need for addressing their deployment and operational needs. One solution fits only some technical environments.

Scalable   Landing zones on Azure provide repeatable environments with consistent configurations and controls regardless of what workloads or resources are deployed.

Modular   Based on a standard set of design areas, Azure landing zones allow you to create cloud consumer environments in a modular manner. Each design area can support a variety of different technology platform requirements, including Azure SQL Database, Azure Kubernetes Service, and Azure Virtual Desktop.

For enterprise-scale deployments, a modular architecture is designed. It enables organizations to build and deploy new applications on Azure with a foundational landing zone control plane, regardless of whether they are migrating or developing and deploying new applications. It doesn't matter what scale organizations are at. The architecture scales with them.

Organizations must make various design decisions based on the enterprise-scale architecture to map their Azure journeys as the Azure platform evolves.

Customer-specific Cloud Adoption Frameworks exist for Azure enterprise-scale landing zones, which recognize that not all enterprises adopt Azure similarly. The technical considerations and design recommendations of enterprise-scale architecture may require trade-offs depending on the situation of cloud consumer organizations. Organizations can scale their organizations effectively when they follow the core recommendations.

When migrating to Azure, organizations can use landing zones and Microsoft's Cloud Adoption Framework to make informed decisions about governance, strategy, and security.

Areas for designing landing zones in the Azure environment include the following considerations:

Resource organization   Cloud users will organize their resources in order to grow their business, considering the needs of various teams, management groups, subscriptions, and business areas.

Cloud subscription   A subscription is a way of managing, billing, and scaling Azure services. Designing for Azure adoption on a large scale requires them. Accelerate new application development and migrations by using subscriptions. Business areas and portfolio owners should align subscriptions with their needs and priorities.

Azure billing offers and Active Directory tenants   Azure billing and Azure Active Directory (Azure AD) are the two highest alignment levels across all cloud Azure deployments within this critical area.

Multi-tenancy   Multiple cloud tenants should enforce tagging policies and provide different security profiles for other tenants (dev/staging/prod).

Network connectivity   Cloud consumers can create hybrid systems and multi-cloud adoption models by combining networking patterns with external data centers. Network implementation provides high availability, resilience, and scalability. We should ask the customers questions like the following before designing network connectivity: What will the topology of our network look like? Where will our resources be located?

Identity and access management   An integrated MFA SSO platform is integrated with all hosted production applications and cloud consoles as the foundation of any fully compliant cloud architecture.

Compliance design areas for Azure landing zones include the following considerations:

Security and compliance   Cloud users can implement data residency and compliance policies proactively and deductively through landing zones.

Management   Management of Azure, hybrid, and multi-cloud environments is established here.

Business continuity and disaster recovery (BCDR)   The smooth functioning of applications depends on resilience, and BCDR is a critical element of strength. By using BCDR, cloud consumers can protect cloud consumers' data via backups and recover cloud consumers' applications in the event of an outage.

Governance and operation   How do cloud consumers intend to manage, monitor, and optimize their environment? How will cloud consumers ensure that their environment operates as expected?

Platform automation and DevOps   Organization can increase productivity, scalability, and reliability by using automation. Part of DevOps is that a continuous integration/deployment (CI/CD) pipeline must be followed to deliver a new software version. By automating the software development life cycle, CI/CD pipelines improve software delivery.

Cloud landing zone automates CI/CD pipelines based on Terraform, ARM, or cloud formation templates to deploy multi-account subscription structures and increase productivity, scalability, and reliability.

Multisubscription Azure environments that account for scale, security governance, networking, and identity result in Azure landing zones. With Azure landing zones, enterprise applications can be migrated, modernized, and innovated at scale. There is no differentiation between infrastructure or platform as a service in these zones because they consider all platform resources needed for the customer's application portfolio.

Designing and building an Azure environment requires a good understanding of security, governance, and compliance. These topics help you build solid foundations and maintain solid processes and controls over time.

The tools and processes you implement will help detect and respond to issues as you manage environments. Organizations will refine these compliance design areas iteratively as their cloud environments develop. These tools work in conjunction with controls that help maintain and demonstrate compliance. As a result of new applications introducing specific requirements or a new compliance standard, for example, business requirements may have changed.

Design Security Review

Security should be a core consideration throughout the design and implementation process of an Azure landing zone. Additional guidance is provided on holistic security processes and tools using the Cloud Adoption Framework's (CAF) Secure methodology. Security design focuses on considerations and recommendations for landing zone decisions. The Secure method in Cloud Adoption Framework will help you later enhance this foundation. It creates a solid foundation for security across Azure, hybrid, and multi-cloud environments.

In designing areas, ensure that you establish active roles and functions, what is in scope, and what is out of scope based on the following guidelines:

- **Participating roles or functions:** In this design area, cloud security, specifically the security architects within that team, is in charge. The cloud platform and cloud center of excellence must review networking and identity decisions. Collective roles may be needed to define and implement the technical requirements derived from this exercise. Cloud governance could also provide support for more advanced security guardrails.

- **In scope:** This exercise focuses on understanding and implementing the security requirements for your cloud platform, including Zero Trust and advanced network security.

- **Out of scope:** To streamline the conversation, this exercise must address some CAF Secure disciplines to establish a modern security operations center in the cloud. The discussion of this design area needs to cover security operations, asset protection, and innovation security, which will be based on your Azure landing zone deployment.

Security Design Considerations

The security monitoring and audit logging of Azure platform services are crucial components of a scalable framework. An organization must see what's happening within its technical cloud estate. When designing security operations, follow these guidelines:

- **Security alerts:**
  - What teams need to be notified of security alerts?
  - Is there a group of services for which alerts should be routed to different teams?
  - Monitor and alert in real time to meet business requirements.
  - Integrate Microsoft Defender for Cloud and Microsoft Sentinel for security information and event management.

- **Security logs:**
  - There is a 30-day data retention period for audit data. Azure AD Premium reports have a 30-day data retention period.
  - Logs such as Azure activity logs, VM logs, and PaaS logs can be archived for years.

- **Security controls:**
  - Azure's in-guest VM policy provides basic security configurations.
  - Be sure to align your security controls with governance guidelines.

- **Vulnerability management:**
  - In the event of a critical vulnerability, emergency patches are applied.
  - Extensive offline patching is available for virtual machines.
  - Vulnerability assessment is conducted for virtual machines.

- **Shared responsibility:**
  - Know where the handoffs are for team responsibilities when monitoring or responding to security events.
  - Considering the Secure methodology for security operations is a good idea.

- **Encryption and keys:**
  - In the environment, who needs access to keys?
  - How will the keys be managed?

Security in the Azure Landing Zone Accelerator

The Azure landing zone accelerator puts security at the core of its implementation, deploying various tools and controls to help organizations establish a baseline for security quickly.

The following, for example, are included:

- **Tools:**
  - A free or standard tier of Microsoft Defender for the Cloud
  - Microsoft Sentinel
  - Microsoft Azure DDoS standard protection plan
  - Microsoft Azure Firewall
  - Web Application Firewall
  - Privileged Identity Management
- **Landing zone policies for online and corporate connections:**
  - Deploy secure access, like HTTPS, to storage accounts.
  - Deploy auditing for Azure SQL Database.
  - Deploy encryption for Azure SQL Database.
  - Block IP forwarding.
  - Block inbound RDP from the Internet.
  - Deploy subnets that are associated with the network security group (NSG).

Improve Security in the Azure Landing Zone

Data and assets must be protected when a workload or landing zone hosts sensitive data or critical systems.

Once you leave the Ready state, you must continue maintaining your environment's security. As a cloud security process rather than a static destination, it is essential to envision the end state of security based on objectives and key results. Develop roles and responsibilities for the human domain with concepts, frameworks, and standards in the CAF Secure methodology.

Gain Risk Insights

Using security practices to recognize which risks are appropriate for planning and addressing, the security team should inform and advise decision-makers on how security risks fit into their frameworks.

- **Understand cybersecurity risk:** Determine any potential damage or destruction by human attackers trying to steal the business's currency, confidential information, or technology.

- **Align organization security risk management:** Invest in bridging cybersecurity and organizational leadership to explain security threats using business-friendly terminology, actively listening and communicating with all people across the business.

- **Know the cybersecurity risk:** Recognize human attackers' motives and behavior patterns and identify the potential impacts of different attacks.

Integration of Security Components

Integrate security into everyone's role and minimize friction with business processes by ensuring security is an organizational concern, not a siloed department. Specific guidance includes the following:

- **Normalize relations:** Establish a shared understanding of security goals between operational teams and security teams. Additionally, ensure security controls do not outweigh the business value.

- **Integrate with IT and business operations:** Consider both current business impact and future security risks when implementing security updates.

- **Integrate security teams:** Taking steps to respond to active threats and continuously improving the organization's security posture is the best way to avoid operating in silos.

Business Resilience

Despite that organizations cannot achieve perfect security, business resilience ensures that security risks are addressed throughout their life cycle, before, during, and after incidents.

- **Resilience goals:** Optimize your business's ability to innovate quickly, reduce impact, and adopt technology safely.

- **Security resilience and assume breach:** Practicing pragmatic security behaviors to prevent attacks, limit damage, and recover quickly from attacks is key.

Access Control

Ensure user experience and security are aligned in your access control strategy.

- **Implement a Zero Trust approach to access control:** Establish security assurances in the cloud and use new technology by embracing a Zero Trust approach to access control.

- **Adopt an end-to-end strategy:** Modern access control requires a comprehensive, consistent, and flexible strategy that goes beyond one strategy or one technology per workload, cloud, or business sensitivity level.

- **Known, trusted, allowed:** Use a dynamic three-step process to ensure that applications, services, and data are trusted and that the appropriate rights and privileges are given.

- **Data-driven access decisions:** Determine whether explicit validation requirements are met based on diverse data about users and devices.

- **Segmentation:** Separate to protect. Separate segments of an internal environment so that successful attacks can be contained.
- **Isolation:** Segment people, processes, and technology for business-critical assets.

Security Operations

By mitigating risk, responding rapidly, and recovering quickly, you can establish security operations to protect your organization.

- **People and process:** Empower and train people with solid backgrounds in forensic investigation roles so that they can be your most valuable asset.
- **Security operations model:** Assign responsibility for triaging, investigating, and hunting on high-volume and complex incidents between subteams.
- **SecOps business touchpoints:** Communicate with business leaders about major incidents and determining their impact on critical systems. Enable a continuous practice response to reduce organizational risks.
- **SecOps modernization:** Implement IoT and OT devices, IoT-centric security, and relevant telemetry from the cloud to evolve security operations.

Asset Protection

Integrate security controls uniquely tailored to each asset type to protect business-critical assets. Maintain preventive and detective protection consistent with policies, standards, and architectures.

- **Fetch secure:** Ensure brown- and greenfield assets are configured to the most current security standards and policies.
- **Remain secure:** Regularly assess business and technology requirements and plan to upgrade or retire end-of-life software.
- **Kick-start:** Protect assets by focusing on well-known cloud resources first and utilizing prominent industry and vendor baselines for security configurations.
- **Essential information:** Identify best practices for managing enterprise assets, such as cloud elasticity workload needs and design controls, by using accountable and responsible teams. Calculate the business value of asset security and prefer automated policy to bypass the cost and human repetition.

Security Governance

Maintain and improve security posture over time through oversight and monitoring based on business objectives and risks.

- **Compliance and reporting:** Comply with industry-specific security policies.
- **Architecture and norms:** In most enterprises, both on-premises and cloud resources are used in a hybrid environment.

- **Security posture management:** It can ensure agility through policy-driven governance that monitors security standards, provides guidance, and improves processes. Maintaining agility through policy-driven governance and continuous improvement is key to maintaining a security posture.

- **Governance and protection specializations:** Identify the best solutions through security controls.

- **Governance and security operations:** Combine lessons learned from incidents into operational and governance routines.

Innovation Security

As new applications are developed with innovation security in mind, protect the processes and data of innovation against cyberattacks.

- Integrating security into the DevOps and development processes to reduce innovation risks.

- Ensure security is integrated throughout the DevOps life cycle and that teams are aligned with innovation speed, reliability, and resilience.

- Protecting your organization's IT infrastructure against attackers exploiting weaknesses in the DevOps process protects your customers.

- Incubate ideas using DevOps in two phases, as most organizations do. Identify minimum viable product (MVP) requirements, resolve team conflict using leadership techniques, and integrate security into existing processes and tools.

- Education, time, resourcing, and the overall shift in IT operations will all be common challenges as you transform your security.

DevSecOps Controls

Whenever you make DevSecOps controls, make sure to include security in each stage of CI/CD.

- **Plan and develop:** Implement threat modeling, IDE security plugins, and pre-commit for security in modern development methodologies.

- **Commit the code:** Assess your centralized repository for vulnerabilities and implement vulnerability scanning to uncover and remediate them.

- **Build and test:** Use build and release pipelines for automation and standardization for building and deploying secure code without spending much time redeploying or upgrading existing environments.

- **Go to production and operate:** Ensure the system is secure when it is brought into production. Use tools and techniques for infrastructure scanning and penetration testing to find risks and vulnerabilities that need to be addressed.

With Defender for Cloud, you can manage and protect hybrid and multi-cloud workloads with unified security. You can extend these capabilities to on-premises and other clouds by enabling enhanced security features, while free features offer limited protection for Azure resources. You can try the improved security features of Defender for Cloud without paying a penny. It can find and fix security vulnerabilities, block malicious activity with access and application controls, detect threats and respond faster.

For Defender for Cloud to work, you must have a Microsoft Azure subscription. To allow enhanced security features, you must be assigned a subscription owner, contributor, or security administrator role.

Evaluate Security Postures by Using Secure Scores

To prevent security issues from occurring, we must take a proactive approach and have appropriate solutions in place when problems arise.

The Microsoft Secure Score measures security posture, and a higher number indicates more actions taken to improve security. The Microsoft Secure Score service provides robust visualizations of metrics and trends, integrations with other Microsoft products, and the ability to compare scores with similar companies.

The benefits of Secure Score include the following:

- It provides a report describing the organization's current security posture.
- It provides discoverability, visibility, guidance, and control to improve their security posture.
- It establishes KPIs based on benchmarks.

The Microsoft improvement actions are grouped to make it easier for you to find the information you need.

- Identity (Accounts & Roles in Azure Active Directory)
- Device (formerly Microsoft Secure Score for Devices, now known as Microsoft Defender for Endpoint)
- Microsoft Defender for Cloud Apps and Office 365 (email and cloud apps)

Find out what points are available and how points are split between these groups on the Microsoft Secure Score overview page. Moreover, you can see the overall score, your historical Secure Score trends, benchmark comparisons, and prioritized actions that you can take to improve your score.

If you want to know your Secure Score, go to the Microsoft Secure Score overview page and click Your Secure Score. Your points will be displayed out of the total.

References

See learn.microsoft.com/en-us/microsoft-365/security/defender/ microsoft-secure-score?view=o365-worldwide for more information.

The score tile and point breakdown chart will show a graph with different score views if you click the Include button next to your score.

For a fuller picture of your overall score, you can add the following scores:

- **Planned score:** Displays the projected score when the intended actions are completed

- **Current license score:** Displays the score you can achieve with your current Microsoft license

- **Achievable score:** Determines your achievable score based on Microsoft licenses and risk acceptance

Security recommendations are listed on the Improvement Actions tab, which addresses handling potential attack surfaces. Additionally, the status of each item is included (currently being addressed, planned, risk accepted, eliminated through third parties, eliminated through alternative mitigation, and completed). Security administrators can filter, search, and group all the refinement actions.

You can also sync your Secure Score daily to receive system data about your earned points for each action. Score updates in real time to reflect the information shown in the visualizations and improvement action pages.

Let's explore Microsoft Defender for Cloud Apps in detail.

The Microsoft Defender for Cloud program continuously monitors your organization's subscriptions and resources for security issues. As a result, a single score will be generated, indicating your organization's current security situation. The higher the score, the lower your organization's identified risk level.

You can protect your workloads in the cloud with Microsoft Defender for Cloud by taking proactive steps to protect your assets, including the following:

- Data and storage

- Virtual machines and servers

- Containers

- Internet of Things (IoT) infrastructure

- Azure Key Vault

In the following, let's look at a detailed reference about data and storage.

The workloads you run in your organization are used for various business processes, so you must provide robust, intelligent protection to all of them at any time.

Using Microsoft Defender for Cloud, you can protect your data and storage resources. Detecting threats to your storage and data resources, alerting you, and suggesting remediation steps will help you deal with those threats. To keep your data and storage safe, you don't have to learn multiple security monitoring systems or be an expert. You can be an expert with something other than Microsoft Defender for Cloud. You can protect different data and storage resources and services with Microsoft Defender for Cloud, including the following:

- Azure Storage
- Azure Cosmos DB
- Azure Key Vault
- SQL Database

Each resource or service is protected differently by Microsoft Defender for Cloud. Microsoft Defender protects Azure Storage resources for the cloud with advanced threat protection, including the following:

- Blob containers
- File shares
- Data lakes

You will receive alerts based on events across your Azure Storage accounts. For example, Microsoft Defender for Cloud monitors activity across your Azure Storage accounts.

- **Suspicious activity:** For instance, someone might have accessed one of your storage accounts using an IP address that is an active Tor exit node.

- **Anomalous behavior:** You are alerted when Microsoft Defender for Cloud detects abnormal behavior. Usually, your storage accounts are accessed from the United States, but now access might be attempted from another continent.

Your cloud security posture must be robust to achieve this. You will be able to identify and address any components and systems that don't comply with your security and compliance standards.

Defender for Cloud's Secure Score in Figure 5.9 displays the scores for one or more subscriptions (based on the number of subscriptions selected in the Azure Portal).

You can improve your security by reviewing Defender for Cloud's recommendations page and following the remediation instructions for each recommendation. The recommendations are organized into security controls, and each control represents your vulnerable attack surfaces and groups-related security recommendations logically. A single resource within a control can be remedied only if all recommendations are addressed. Find out how well your organization protects each attack surface by reviewing each security control score.

Figure 5.10 depicts an example of the recommendations dashboard with all security controls arranged in a top-down list, with the controls at the top having the greatest impact on the Secure Score.

As you continuously remediate security recommendations to improve your Secure Score, you can track progress as your key performance indicator (KPI).

The recommended choice is to use the Secure Score to track your progress and remediate security recommendations triggered by Microsoft Defender for Cloud. However, you can still do much more to keep progressing positively toward a better security posture. A company's Secure Score will likely fluctuate up and down if its Azure Governance is not very mature, and a new resource provisioned without security settings can contribute to this problem.

FIGURE 5.9   Microsoft Defender for Cloud Score dashboard

FIGURE 5.10   Microsoft Defender for Cloud recommendation dashboard

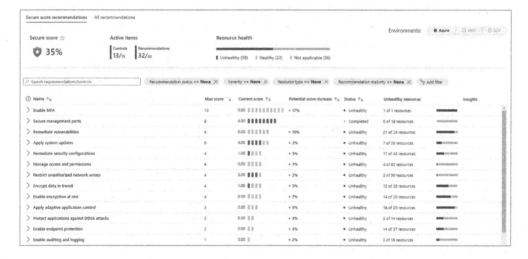

With a solid Azure Governance in place, you can ensure that new resources are deployed by specific standards, patterns, and configurations. To enforce policies and reject resource deployments that do not adhere to particular standards, you can use Azure Policy and Azure Blueprints.

With Defender for Cloud, Azure Policy can enforce secure configuration based on a specific recommendation to help govern those workloads.

A continuous assessment of your cross-cloud resources by Defender for Cloud identifies any security issues. The findings are then compiled into a single score that lets you know your current security situation at a glance: higher scores indicate lower risk levels. You can increase your security by implementing Defender for Cloud's remediation instructions for each issue.

Identify Technical Threats and Recommend Mitigation Measures

Among the threats Microsoft monitors are denial of service, malware, and unauthorized access to data. By leveraging this intelligence, organizations can take targeted actions, such as releasing system updates, enforcing security policies, or implementing other security measures based on the context.

To enable you to learn about threats and mitigate risks, threat intelligence provides context, relevance, and priority. A threat intelligence program provides context, relevance, and priority beyond lists of bad domains and bad hashes. Here are some scenarios where threat intelligence can be used to make faster, better, and more proactive cybersecurity decisions:

- Security analysts use threat intelligence to analyze the highest-priority signals and act.

- Information workers know to watch out for suspicious email links and report them as phishing attempts. If the recipient is made aware of these risks, for example, they may be more vigilant, avoid opening files or clicking questionable links, and report the email as suspicious.

- Organizations use threat intelligence to inform employees that a particular email attachment may contain ransomware.

Cyber threats are not limited to any sector. Organizations must protect themselves against them, integrating them into their strategies and operations. To be prepared, it is crucial to know the type of attack, the target, the frequency, and the source of attacks. Organizations can gain visibility, context, and relevance of security events through threat intelligence. Decision-makers inside and outside security teams need access to and share this knowledge, as it helps them prioritize actions and reduce risk.

Various sources can provide cyber threat intelligence (CTI), including open-source data feeds, threat intelligence sharing communities, paid intelligence feeds, and internal security investigations. An organization can use CTI to gather information on a threat actor, such as its motivations, infrastructure, and techniques, as well as observations of IP addresses, domains, and hashes. Security personnel must act quickly when unusual activity occurs to protect people and assets.

The most utilized CTI in SIEM solutions like Microsoft Sentinel is threat indicator data, sometimes called *indicators of compromise* (IoCs). Threat indicators associate URLs, file hashes, IP addresses, and other data with known threat activity such as phishing, botnets, or malware. This form of threat intelligence is often called *tactical threat intelligence* because security products and automation can use it on a large scale to protect from and detect potential threats. Figure 5.11 depicts the core building block of this solution.

FIGURE 5.11 Building block CTI in SIEM

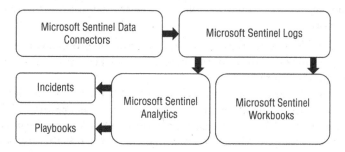

In addition to detecting, responding to, and providing CTI context to malicious cyber activity, Microsoft Sentinel can also be used for the following:

- Structured Threat Information Expression (STIX) and Trusted Automated Exchange of Intelligence Information (TAII) servers or any threat intelligence platform (TIP) can be used to import threat indicators into Microsoft Sentinel.

- Query and view threat indicator data.

- Build analytics rules for generating security alerts, incidents, and automated responses from CTI data.

- Visualize CTI information in workbooks.

In addition to Microsoft Sentinel, another product that uses threat intelligence is Microsoft Defender for Cloud. Defender for Cloud's threat protection monitors information from Azure resources, your network, and your connected partner solutions. This information is analyzed, often correlated from multiple sources, to identify threats. Defender for Cloud triggers a security alert when a threat is detected, which includes detailed information on the event and remediation suggestions. To assist incident response teams in investigating and remediating threats, Defender for Cloud provides threat intelligence reports. The reports include information such as the following:

- Identity or affiliation of the attacker (if available)

- An attacker's objectives

- Historical and current attacks (if available)

- Tools, tactics, and procedures used by attackers
- A URL and a file hash, which can serve as IoCs

To determine whether your Azure resources are at risk, you should review victimology, which is the industry and geographic prevalence.

Defender for Cloud offers three types of threat reports to help mitigate or remediate attacks. The following reports are available:

- **Activity Group report:** A detailed analysis of the attackers' tactics, objectives, and motivations can be found in the Activity Group report.

- **Campaign report:** Details of specific attacks are detailed in the Campaign report.

- **Threat Summary report:** All items in the previous two reports are covered in the Threat Summary report.

Information like this is useful during the incident response process, where an investigation is underway to determine the source of the attack, the attacker's motivations, and how to mitigate the issue in the future.

In other Microsoft Security solutions, such as Azure AD Identity Protection, threat detection is a feature that utilizes threat intelligence. In the Risky Users report, risk detections (both user and sign-in related) contribute to the overall user risk score. Security researchers, law enforcement professionals, Microsoft's security teams, and other trusted sources, including Microsoft's internal and external threat intelligence sources, are used to calculate these risks offline. Figure 5.12 shows risk detection in Azure AD Identity Protection.

FIGURE 5.12 Azure AD Identity Protection risk detection

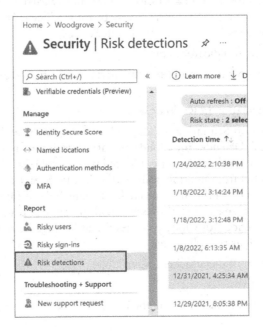

In this model, risks are viewed as potential future events. Each risk describes an event that may occur in the future. This concept is sometimes referred to as the *event-driven risk model*. An analysis of the risk should include some information about its probability of occurrence and how such an event would impact the project. In addition, it may describe methods for reducing the likelihood of occurrence and mitigating the impact.

Risk management has four phases: identification, assessment, response, and monitoring and reporting.

Identification   To manage risk effectively, all potential risks, threats, and vulnerabilities in the environment should be identified, including internal threats and vulnerabilities. Also included in the identification phase are decision logs, active security and compliance exceptions, and mitigation work from previous risk assessments.

Assessment   The impact of each identified risk is measured using three metrics: likelihood, control deficiency, and impact. The likelihood defines the probability of the potential risk being realized, while control deficiency measures the effectiveness of mitigation controls implemented. Impact describes the damage that would occur to the service or business.

Response   Based on the identified risk, you can respond in the following ways:

- **Tolerate:** Allow low-risk areas to be exposed with minimal control.
- **Operate:** Use controls that are deemed adequate for areas with low risk of exposure.
- **Monitor:** Areas where controls deemed adequate for high-risk exposure areas should be monitored for effectiveness.
- **Improve:** Enhance areas of high-risk exposure with a low level of control that are top priorities.

Monitoring and reporting   Several strategies are used to monitor and report risks identified by a risk assessment, including periodic risk reviews, penetration testing, and vulnerability scanning.

A vital component of the security operations center (SOC) analyst's ability to triage and respond to incidents in today's digital era of cyberattacks is cyberthreat intelligence (CTI). The Azure Sentinel SIEM solution allows customers to import threat intelligence data from various sources, such as paid threat feeds, open-source feeds, and ISAC-like threat intelligence sharing communities.

Recommend Security Capabilities or Controls to Mitigate Identified Risks

As employees create, manage, and share data across various platforms and services, they can increasingly access it. Most organizations lack the resources and tools to identify and mitigate organizational risks while maintaining employee privacy and meeting compliance requirements. Departing employees may engage in data theft, and accidental sharing or malicious intent can result in data leaks outside your organization.

The Microsoft Azure Risk Management framework aims to identify, assess, respond to, manage, and report risks to Microsoft Azure services. Microsoft's top priority is proactively identifying and addressing risks that could impact their service infrastructure, customers, data, and trust. In addition, a robust risk management program is necessary to meet cloud contractual obligations and maintain public accreditations that their customers rely on to satisfy their compliance requirements.

A risk management plan identifies, assesses, responds to, monitors, and reports threats to an organization's capital and earnings. Several factors contribute to these risks, including financial uncertainties, legal liabilities, technology issues, strategic management errors, accidents, and natural disasters.

An organization must consider all its risks as part of its risk management program. The cascading effects of risks can also affect an organization's strategic goals.

Figure 5.13 shows Microsoft's recommended risk management framework. Risk management activity is accompanied by an output that feeds the next phase.

FIGURE 5.13   Risk management framework

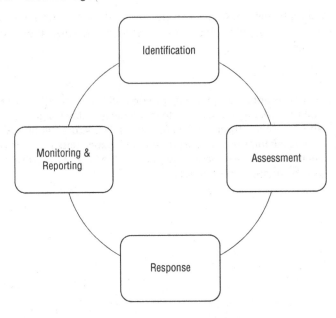

Imagine you are a Cybersecurity Architect responsible for recommending security capabilities and controls to mitigate identified risks.

- As you are identifying the risks, you discovered a production subscription with 10 Azure Storage accounts that were widely accessible over the Internet.

- In the assessment phase, you determined that five of these storage accounts would have a high impact if compromised.

- For the first five, the response is to tolerate the risk, while for the other five, technical controls will need to be added to mitigate it.

In this case, technical controls include the following:

- Add secure access to the storage account (HTTPS).

- Ensure the storage account is locked to prevent accidental or malicious deletions or configuration changes.

- Authorize access to blob data through Azure Active Directory (Azure AD).

- Make containers and blobs inaccessible to anonymous public readers.

- Set the minimum Transport Layer Security (TLS) version required for a storage account.

- Enable firewall rules.

- Make sure Defender for Storage is enabled.

During the monitoring and reporting phase, ensure diagnostic logging is enabled on the storage account and Microsoft Defender for Cloud is enabled on the subscription level to assess storage accounts continuously.

Based on the parameters listed, including the type of threat, risk mitigations should be assessed on a case-by-case basis. It could be compromised if it was determined during the identification that an RDP brute-force attack could compromise Windows VMs with the management port open. As a result, you need to mitigate this risk, and the Defender for Servers Just-in-Time VM access feature is one technical control that can help reduce the attack vector.

Defender for Cloud offers a top-down overview of security controls, so you can prioritize security recommendations using a priority list. In addition to improving your security posture, you'll also see an increase in your overall security score as you remediate all security recommendations that belong to security control. Security control secure management ports have three recommendations that must be addressed in the example depicted in Figure 5.14.

As shown in Figure 5.14 in column "Max score," eight points will be added to your Secure Score once all three issues have been resolved from the secure management ports perspective.

Security controls can also recommend the implementation of a security capability, for example, to protect applications against DDoS attacks, which suggests enabling a Web Application Firewall (WAF) as a mitigation method.

Azure Security Benchmark can also help identify resources at risk and enable security capabilities for mitigating these risks based on remediation steps suggested by the benchmark, as shown in Figure 5.15.

FIGURE 5.14 Security control secure management dashboard

Name ↑↓	Max score ↑↓	Current score ↑↓	Potential score increase ↑↓	Status ↑↓	Unhealthy resources	Insights
› Enable MFA	10	0.00	+ 17%	• Unhealthy	3 of 3 resources	
⌄ Secure management ports	8	5.85	+ 4%	• Unhealthy	6 of 64 resources	
Internet-facing virtual machines should be protected with network security groups				• Unhealthy	1 of 65 virtual machines	ⓘ
Management ports should be closed on your virtual machines				• Unhealthy	7 of 65 virtual machines	ⓘ
Management ports of virtual machines should be protected with just-in-time network a...				• Unhealthy	7 of 65 virtual machines	ⓘ
› Remediate vulnerabilities	6	0.00	+ 10%	• Unhealthy	72 of 85 resources	
› Apply system updates	6	3.97	+ 3%	• Unhealthy	16 of 75 resources	
› Restrict unauthorized network access	4	1.57	+ 4%	• Unhealthy	88 of 270 resources	
› Remediate security configurations	4	1.46	+ 4%	• Unhealthy	52 of 125 resources	
› Manage access and permissions	4	2.90	+ 2%	• Unhealthy	45 of 388 resources	
› Enable encryption at rest	4	0.39	+ 6%	• Unhealthy	80 of 115 resources	
› Encrypt data in transit	4	1.34	+ 5%	• Unhealthy	51 of 103 resources	
› Apply adaptive application control	3	0.71	+ 4%	• Unhealthy	39 of 76 resources	

FIGURE 5.15 Security encrypt data in transit dashboard

⌃ ◉ DP-3. Encrypt sensitive data in transit Control details [MS] [C]		
Customer responsibility	**Resource type**	**Failed resources**
Secure transfer to storage accounts should be enabled [Quick Fix!]	🗄 Storage accounts	**13** of 62
FTPS should be required in function apps	🌐 Web applications	**12** of 12
Windows web servers should be configured to use secure communication protocols	🖥 VMs & servers	**11** of 52
Function App should only be accessible over HTTPS [Quick Fix!]	🌐 Web applications	**9** of 12
Web Application should only be accessible over HTTPS [Quick Fix!]	🌐 Web applications	**6** of 6

Notice that in this scenario, you have a security control called DP-3 that encrypts sensitive data in transit. You have a series of security recommendations for different workloads (storage accounts, web applications, VMs, and servers) within this control. The advantage of this approach is that you're mitigating a specific scenario, which is the encryption of sensitive data in transit, and you're looking at this scenario across different workloads.

As a Cybersecurity Architect, you must select the appropriate security capability for a given risk. For certain scenarios, that may mean the addition of a new service.

Let's consider an example of a company needing to provide customized remote access to employees based on a series of conditions, including limiting access upon an abnormal behavior. Although most users have normal behavior that can be tracked, it could be risky to allow them to sign in when they fall outside of this norm.

To address this risk, you can use Azure AD conditional access and the Sign-in risk-based conditional access policy to block that user or ask them to perform multifactor authentication.

It is also possible to choose the proper security control based on the risk; hardening the current resource might be the best security control in this case. You can reduce the risk of an attacker compromising a database by hardening the database and enabling security controls such as Transparent Data Encryption (TDE). With this technology, you can encrypt data at rest without changing existing applications.

Summary

This chapter has exposed you to different security posture assessment methods, tools, and techniques available in the Microsoft Azure cloud. Business security posture refers to an organization's capability to identify and react to cyberattacks by examining all aspects of its network. Security posture assessments can assist organizations in identifying where they are on their cybersecurity journeys and in developing a strategic roadmap to enhance their cybersecurity.

In this chapter, you learned how to analyze security postures using benchmarks, analyze security postures using Microsoft Defender for Cloud, assess security postures using Secure Scores, evaluate cloud workload security, plan and design security for an Azure landing zone, identify technical threats and recommend mitigation measures, and provide recommendations for reducing identified risks through the use of security controls.

Exam Essentials

Know the method to assess security posture by using Azure Security Benchmark. Governing in the cloud age requires active engagement with other teams. Security posture management is an emerging function, and the convergence of security functions is a step in the right direction.

As part of the Azure Security Benchmark (ASB), prescriptive best practices are provided as recommendations for improving the security of workloads, data, and services on Azure. To enhance their cloud defenses, many organizations use standards such as CISv7.1 and NIST 800-53 R4. With ASB, Azure's security capabilities are consistent with CISv7.1 and NIST 800-53 R4. Providing consistent security standards, compliance, and security baselines is critical for the successful cloud migration and adoption. You can improve your Azure resources' security and compliance posture whether or not you are a new user of Azure.

Know the technique to evaluate security posture by using Microsoft Defender for Cloud. Defender for Cloud monitors your subscriptions, resources, and organization for security issues. All the findings are then compiled into a single score, allowing you to see, at a glance, how secure you are: the higher the score, the lower the risk level.

Know the technique to evaluate security hygiene. Depending on your organization's size and structure, different individuals and teams may use Defender for Cloud for various security-related tasks. Visibility into your Microsoft Defender for Cloud coverage across different resource types, links to configure advanced threat protection capabilities, onboarding, and agent installation status, and threat detection alerts are all features of the workload protection dashboard. Defender for Cloud alerts you when it detects a threat in any area of your environment. There may be an option to trigger a logic app in response to these alerts, which describes details about the affected resources and suggested remediation steps to increase cybersecurity hygiene.

Plan and design security for an Azure landing zone.   A multisubscription Azure environment produces landing zones that account for scale, security governance, networking, and identity. Azure landing zones enable enterprise-scale application migration, modernization, and innovation. An organization must have visibility into what is happening to manage a technical cloud estate effectively. Monitoring and auditing Azure platform services are crucial components of a scalable architecture. Adopt the Azure landing zone accelerator into your enterprise-grade solutions.

Be able to assess the security posture of cloud workloads.   A key feature of Defender for Cloud is using Microsoft Threat Intelligence for security alerts. You can also take advantage of various advanced and intelligent protections for your workloads, and Microsoft Defender plans provide workload protections based on the types of resources in your subscription. If you enable Microsoft Defender for Storage, you will be alerted about suspicious storage activity.

Know the process to determine a security posture by using Secure Scores.   Defender for Cloud displays a dashboard with a Secure Score at the subscription level. Follow Defender for Cloud's remediation instructions to implement each recommendation on its recommendations page to increase your security. There are different security controls for each recommendation.

Interpret technical threat intelligence and recommend risk mitigations.   A threat intelligence program at Microsoft includes internal and external signals related to areas such as denial of service, malware, and unauthorized data access. The proper context can lead to targeted actions, such as system updates, multifactor authentication, and other security measures. Malicious cyber activity can be detected, responded to, and contextualized with Microsoft Sentinel. The threat protection in Defender for Cloud monitors security information from your Azure resources, your network, and your connected partner solutions. Other Microsoft Security solutions also use threat intelligence, such as Azure AD Identity Protection, which has a risk detection feature.

Recommend security capabilities or controls to mitigate identified risks.   In an increasingly connected world, employees have access to a wide range of platforms and services that allow them to manage, share, and create data. In most cases, organizations have limited resources and tools to identify and mitigate organization-wide risks while also meeting compliance requirements and employee privacy standards. It is vital that your organization proactively identifies and addresses risks affecting its data and service infrastructure.

Review Questions

1. In terms of security posture management, what are the three pillars? (Choose three.)

   A. Protect

   B. Detect

   C. Respond

   D. Monitor

2. How can Azure resources be secured so that they meet both security and compliance requirements?

   A. Azure security benchmark

   B. Azure blueprint

   C. Azure Express Route

   D. None of the above

3. In which approach can you improve your security posture quickly and with the least amount of effort?

   A. Rapid Modernization Plan (RaMP)

   B. Continuous improvement plan

   C. Minimal viable plan

   D. None of the above

4. Which of the following continuously monitors your resources, subscriptions, and organization for security concerns?

   A. Defender for Cloud

   B. Azure Active Directory

   C. Azure Sentinel

   D. None of the above

5. Based on the phases of which framework, can you create campaigns to remedy recommendations when evaluating your security posture?

   A. Cloud adoption framework

   B. Open group framework

   C. MITRE ATT&CK framework

   D. None of the above

6. Often, the IT security administrator needs the necessary privileges to expedite the remediation of recommendations. If the administrator does not have the required privileges and attempts to fix a recommendation using the Fix button, they will see that the Fix button is grayed out. What is the next step?

    A. The workload reader has been assigned a ticket. The workload reader reviews the ticket and determines that this recommendation can be resolved quickly. As part of the change management process, the workload reader schedules and deploys the remediation.

    B. The workload modifier has been assigned a ticket. The workload modifier reviews the ticket and determines that this recommendation can be resolved quickly. As part of the change management process, the workload modifier schedules and deploys the remediation.

    C. The workload owner has been assigned a ticket. The workload owner reviews the ticket and determines that this recommendation can be resolved quickly. As part of the change management process, the workload owner schedules and deploys the remediation.

    D. None of the above.

7. Which of the following is a Microsoft cloud security posture management solution that continuously assesses Azure Resources for achieving security hygiene and offers recommendations based on Azure Security Benchmarks?

    A. Azure Security Center

    B. Security Center Score

    C. Azure Defender

    D. None of the above

8. Which Microsoft Azure Services provide advanced protection for hybrid and Azure resources? By doing so, you can access additional policies, regulatory standards, and Azure Security Benchmarks that will enable you to customize your compliance analysis.

    A. Azure Security Center

    B. Security Center Score

    C. Azure Defender

    D. None of the above

9. An Azure landing zone results from a multisubscription Azure environment encompassing scalability, security governance, networking, and identity management. Which of the following features are enabled by Azure landing zones?

    A. Application remediation and rationalization at enterprise-scale in Azure

    B. Application migration, modernization, and innovation at enterprise scale in Azure

    C. Application decommissioning at enterprise scale in Azure

    D. None of the above

10. Regarding security operations design, which of the following Microsoft recommendations and best practices will you follow as a Cybersecurity Architect?

    A. Security alerts and security logs

    B. Security controls and vulnerability management

    C. Shared responsibility and encryption and keys

    D. All of the above

11. No one solution fits all technical environments. Despite this, a few Azure landing zone implementation options can help you meet your growing cloud portfolio's deployment and operational needs. Which two methods help to accomplish this?

    A. Functional

    B. Scalable

    C. Modular

    D. Reliable

12. As a Cybersecurity Architect, which of the following Microsoft recommendations, best practices, and frameworks will you review and adopt in your enterprise-grade security architecture as a foundation?

    A. Azure landing zone

    B. Cloud Adoption Framework

    C. Azure landing zone accelerator

    D. All of the above

13. You are considering using the Azure landing zone accelerator as a Cybersecurity Architect. Your customer is asking for a list of default tools; which of the following default tool sets is included in the Azure landing zone accelerator?

    A. Microsoft Defender for Cloud, standard or free tier, and Microsoft Sentinel

    B. Azure DDoS standard protection plan (optional) and Azure Firewall

    C. Web Application Firewall (WAF) and Privileged Identity Management (PIM)

    D. All of the above

14. Which of the following Azure services helps you to monitor threats and mitigate risks, with the result that context, relevance, and priority are offered to your team?

    A. Security Center Score

    B. Azure Defender

    C. Threat intelligence

    D. None of the above

15. Which Microsoft Azure services can help your team detect and respond to malicious cyber activity and provide context for cyber threat intelligence?

   A.   Security Center Score

   B.   Microsoft Sentinel

   C.   Threat intelligence

   D.   None of the above

16. As per Microsoft, there are four phases to risk management; which of the following are they?

   A.   Identification, assessment, response, monitoring, and reporting

   B.   Identification, estimation, answer, monitoring, and reporting

   C.   Identification, analyze, detect, monitoring, and reporting

   D.   Identification, assessment, response, logging, and documentation

17. Which threat intelligence solution from Microsoft helps to protect works by monitoring security information from your Azure resources, the network, and connected partner solutions?

   A.   Security Center Score

   B.   Microsoft Defender for Cloud

   C.   Threat intelligence

   D.   None of the above

18. As a Cybersecurity Architect, if you want to increase the security score of your organization, which page must you review in Defender for Cloud for remediation issues?

   A.   Secure Score recommendations

   B.   Home page

   C.   Summary

   D.   None of the above

19. Which Azure service can enhance the governance of Azure workloads by enforcing secure configuration using Azure Policy?

   A.   Defender for Cloud

   B.   Threat intelligence

   C.   Microsoft Sentinel

   D.   None of the above

20. As a Cybersecurity Architect, you must select the appropriate security capability for an upcoming risk scenario. You must provide customized remote access to your employees based on several conditions, including limiting access upon evidence of abnormal behavior. What Azure services will you likely adopt in your solution?

   A.   Azure AD conditional access

   B.   Adopt Sign-in risk-based conditional access policy

   C.   Azure WAF

   D.   Both A and B

Chapter

6

Define a Strategy for Securing Infrastructure

THE MICROSOFT SC-100 EXAM OBJECTIVES COVERED IN THIS CHAPTER INCLUDE:

- ✓ Specify security baselines for server and client endpoints

- ✓ Specify security requirements for servers, including multiple platforms and operating systems

- ✓ Specify security requirements for mobile devices and clients, including endpoint protection, hardening, and configuration

- ✓ Specify requirements to secure Active Directory Domain Services

- ✓ Design a strategy to manage secrets, keys, and certificates

- ✓ Design a strategy for secure remote access

- ✓ Design a strategy for securing privileged access.

In this chapter, we will focus on understanding architecture, best practices, and how both are changing with the cloud.

To reduce business risk from attacks, security teams must work to ensure that information systems and data are secured and that confidentiality, integrity, and availability are assured. In this chapter, you'll learn how architecture best practices can help you design a more secure environment and how cloud computing is changing the way architects perform design thinking.

To ensure that servers and client endpoints are protected, to ensure that they are continually assessed to ensure their security postures are updated, and to get enterprise-wide visibility into attack dynamics, a security strategy needs to be established.

In this chapter, you will review how to plan and deploy a security strategy across teams, establish a process for proactive and continuous evolution of a security strategy, and specify security baselines for server and client endpoints. You'll also learn how to specify security baselines for servers, including multiple platforms and operating systems, and specify security requirements for mobile devices and clients, including endpoint protection, hardening, and configuration. Finally, you'll learn how to specify requirements for securing Active Directory Domain Services; design a strategy to manage secrets, keys, and certificates; design a strategy for secure remote access; and design a strategy for securing privileged access.

Plan and Deploy a Security Strategy Across Teams

As with the move from mainframes to desktops, your switch from enterprise servers to the cloud for security is more than a technical change. To navigate the change successfully and increase the effectiveness of your security team, you need to adopt the right mindset and expectations. Although these could be included in any security modernization plan, the rapid change in the cloud makes their adoption urgent.

A partnership between business and IT with common goals is essential, Today, security cannot adopt an arm's-length approach to being able to approve or deny changes to the environment due to fast-paced decisions and constant process evolution. To achieve productivity, reliability, and security, security teams must work closely with business and IT teams.

By integrating security earlier in the process, this partnership represents the ultimate form of shifting left, a method for resolving security issues more effectively and efficiently. To accomplish this, all involved (security, business, and IT) need to learn the cultures and norms of other groups and teach these cultures to each other. The security team must do the following:

- Understand how they are thinking about achieving business and IT objectives as they transform and why each is important.

- Discuss how other teams can achieve security goals and how they should do so based on business goals and risks.

There is always a risk associated with security, but it is not a problem. There is no such thing as a solution to cybersecurity. Security is mainly concerned with human-driven actions rather than natural disasters, since it is a risk-management discipline. It isn't possible to fix security problems with solutions; instead, it's a combination of assessing an adverse event's probability and impact. The activity is similar to preventing corporate espionage and criminal activities in the analog, brick-and-mortar world, where organizations have to defend themselves against human attackers motivated by financial gain.

Organizations must focus on both productivity and security to succeed in today's innovate-or-become-irrelevant environment. If the organization isn't productive and driving innovation, it could lose competitiveness in the marketplace, causing it to become weak financially or eventually fail. The organization could also lose competitiveness in the marketplace if it isn't secure and gives control of assets to attackers, ultimately leading to its demise financially.

Neither Microsoft nor any other organization is flawless in adopting the cloud. Microsoft's IT and security teams face many of the challenges their customers face, including finding the proper structure for programs, maintaining support for legacy software while keeping up with cutting-edge innovation, and even addressing technology gaps in cloud services. The teams are actively sharing lessons learned through documents like this on the IT showcase site or internal landing page of organizations, as they learn how to manage better and secure the cloud while continuously providing feedback to engineering teams and third-party vendors to improve their products and services.

Transformation provides a security opportunity. It is imperative to view digital transformation in this positive light. Although it is easy to recognize the downsides and risks of this change, it is not so easy to overlook the tremendous opportunity to reinvent the security role. This is because you should sit at the table where decisions are made, as security professionals become more connected to the organization's mission and receive increased funding due to partnering with the business. This is because security efforts can be reduced, and the value of security can be increased.

To ensure enterprise systems and data are secure, as a Cybersecurity Architect you need to align all teams around a single strategy.

Security Roles and Responsibilities

Technology and business outcomes are typically driven by a design-deploy-manage framework (which is becoming increasingly agile for digital transformation with rapid iteration throughout all stages). As a result, security outcomes are mapped to a similar governance, prevention, and response framework. In addition, it matches NIST Cybersecurity's identify, protect, detect, respond, and recover functions. As shown in the Figure 6.1, security roles enable business outcomes.

FIGURE 6.1   Microsoft-defined security roles and responsibilities

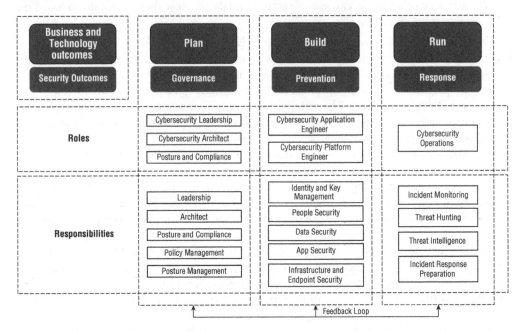

Providing vision, guidance, and coordination across the organization and technical estate are the responsibilities of security leadership roles.

Ensure that top security risks are mitigated by working with subject-matter experts through security posture and compliance roles, which identify and mitigate security risks across the enterprise. Typically, these roles manage security compliance, policies, standards, and posture.

A platform security engineer focuses on enterprise-wide systems like identification and key management, as well as various infrastructures and endpoints, such as network security, server/VM security, and client endpoints/devices.

Usually, application security engineers focus on securing individual workloads and applications at the same time they are developed. In addition to infrastructure and endpoint skills, these responsibilities include application security and DevSecOps, as well as data security on a per-workload basis. As digital transformation increases the adoption of cloud technologies, DevOps/DevSecOps models, and infrastructure-as-code approaches, demand for these skillsets is expected to continue to grow.

People security is an emerging discipline dedicated to educating people, protecting them, and preventing insider threats within organizations.

During the operational phase, a combination of operations teams is responsible for maintaining the production environments (IT and OT operations, DevOps) and security operations.

As part of security operations, reactive incidents and responses are monitored and responded to, and threats are hunted proactively to expose adversaries that have slipped by detection. Security operations often incubate threat intelligence and incident preparation functions, shifting into a broader scope as they mature, and become integrated with technology and organizational practices.

Security effectiveness and the maturation of security processes depend on a healthy feedback loop. As teams continue to automate technical processes and adopt DevOps-style methods focused on rapid, agile iteration, the relationship between prevention and response is expected to grow.

Security Strategy Considerations

Security ensures confidentiality, integrity, and availability for a business. Both internal and external malicious and accidental actions could adversely affect operations, so security efforts have a critical focus. Security should be considered as part of the cloud adoption process at every stage (defining the strategy).

By following these steps, you can integrate security at critical points in the process. Doing so will reduce the possibility of unwarranted disruptions to your business and operations.

An effective cloud security strategy must consider the current threat environment and the nature of the cloud platform hosting enterprise assets. Providing a secure and sustainable enterprise cloud environment requires a straightforward approach that improves the effort of all teams. The security strategy must enable defined business outcomes, reduce risk to an acceptable level, and enable employees to be productive.

As teams prepare for cloud adoption, cloud security strategies guide all teams in addressing technology, processes, and people readiness. A system should not only show the development of cloud architectures and technical capabilities but also influence the development of security architectures and capabilities and influence capabilities.

To develop a secure cloud strategy, it is imperative to include all teams' input and active participation. The format of the process documentation may vary, but it contains the following elements:

Active Input from Teams   The strategy typically works only if people within the organization adopt it. Bring all teams together to co-create the plan. When conducting customer workshops, Microsoft often find organizations operating in de facto silos. Often, these gatherings result in people meeting for the first time. The requirement for inclusiveness is clear to us. The workshop will need to be repeated if some teams do not participate. If they do not participate, the project will not move forward.

Documented and Communicated Clearly   All teams must be aware of the security strategy, which should be documented and communicated clearly. Security strategies should be an integral part of the overall technology strategy, containing reasons to integrate security and what is relevant to security. The security strategy defines what success looks like in the security field. As a result of this strategy, application and development teams will be able to receive clear, organized guidance without having to read through irrelevant information.

Stable, but Flexible   Generally, the strategies are relatively consistent and stable, but architecture and documentation will need to be clarified and accommodate the dynamic nature of cloud computing. Even if you switch from using a third-party next-generation firewall to Azure Firewall and adjust diagrams and guidance on how to filter out malicious external traffic, filtering out malicious external traffic remains a strategic imperative.

Start with Business Alignment   Microsoft recommends aligning your security strategy with your business goals and risk profile. Security teams will address many strategy issues, large and small, but you must start with business alignment. Although starting with concrete questions such as "What would you restore first if all business systems were down?" can be challenging, you can begin to build relationships while establishing quick wins.

Deliverables

To facilitate easy discussion and updating, Microsoft recommends capturing the strategy in a presentation, which can be accompanied by a document depending on your culture and preferences.

An executive audience might receive a summary version of the strategy or a single presentation.

- **Full presentation:** The main presentation or optional reference slides should contain all elements of the security strategy.

- **Executive summaries:** The executive summary for executives and board members includes only the elements relevant to their role, including their risk appetite, top priorities, and accepted risks.

The strategy and plan template allows you to record motivations, outcomes, and business justifications.

Best Practices for Building a Security Strategy

The following elements are incorporated into successful security strategies:

- **Align closely to business strategy:** To maximize internal harmony and align security efforts with business strategy, it's imperative to align security efforts closely with the charter of security, which is to protect business value.

- Create a shared understanding of business, IT, and security requirements.
- Integrate security early in cloud adoption to avoid crises at the last minute.
- Establish minimum security requirements immediately and continuously improve security assurances over time, which requires an agile approach.
- Encourage proactive leadership actions to change security culture.
- **Modernize security strategy:** To maintain adequate security, modern technology environments, threat landscapes, and security community resources must be considered in a security strategy.
  - Adopt a cloud-based model of shared responsibility.
  - Include multi-cloud deployments.
  - Avoid unnecessary friction by using native-cloud controls.
  - Keep up with the evolution of attackers by integrating the security community.

Strategy Approval

Executives and business leaders, such as the board of directors, should approve this strategy with accountability for the outcomes or risks to business lines within the organization.

Deploy a Process for Proactive and Continuous Evolution of a Security Strategy

Security planning defines outcomes, milestones, timelines, and task owners to implement the security strategy. Security planning and cloud adoption planning should be done in collaboration to prevent work stoppage or increased risks caused by security issues discovered too late. Inviting the cloud security team early in the planning cycle is crucial.

Considerations in Security Planning

Being fully integrated into the cloud planning process allows security planning to be enhanced with an understanding of the digital estate and existing IT portfolio.

Deliverables

An organization should include a security plan in the main planning documents for its cloud implementation. It may be a combination of these formats, depending on the organization's size, culture, and standard practices. All of these elements should be included in the security plan:

- Organizational functions plan, so teams are aware of how the move to the cloud will affect current security roles and responsibilities

- A security skills plan aims to support team members as they adapt to significant technological changes, roles, and responsibilities

- A roadmap, provided to technical teams, for technical security architecture and capabilities

Develop a security awareness and education plan for all teams to familiarize themselves with security basics.

A taxonomy aligned with business impact and developed by business stakeholders, security teams, and other parties is developed by business stakeholders, security teams, and other parties interested in identifying sensitive assets.

Changes triggered by the security plan should be reflected in other sections of the cloud adoption plan.

Best Practices for Security Planning

This section will discuss how to increase your security plan's success when using on-premises and cloud-based applications such as software as a service (SaaS) and platform as a service (PaaS).

Identify critical security requirements first and prioritize noncritical items for the next steps. Your plan should not be overly detailed for three to five years. The cloud and threat environments change so rapidly that a plan like that is not applicable. Instead, it would help if you focused on creating the beginning steps and end state.

- The time frame can vary based on organizational culture, standard practices, and other factors, but quick wins will deliver a high impact before longer-term initiatives begin.

- A target-state vision should guide team planning (which might take several years to achieve).

Get stakeholder alignment, feedback, and awareness of the plan. Share the program widely. Align your plan with the security strategy's strategic outcomes and achieve them.

Identify the people who are responsible and accountable for completing each task and what the specific deadline for that task is.

As the security industry transforms and new expectations arise, engage people with the human side by implementing the following strategies:

- Provide coaching and clear communication to team members to support their transformation.

- Tell people the skills they need to acquire (what they need to know and what resources they can use to learn).

- Identify the benefits of learning the skills.

- Encourage people to connect with their roles in keeping the organization safe by making security awareness engaging.

Discover how Microsoft can help your organization plan its transition to the cloud and a modern security strategy by reviewing Microsoft training and guidance. There are recorded training modules, documentation, and best practices and standards recommended for security.

Establish Essential Security Practices

People, processes, and technology elements play a crucial role in cloud security. Additionally, some architectural choices are foundational and are difficult to change later, so they should be carefully considered.

No matter if you are already operating in the cloud or plan to do so in the future, your organization should follow the following 11 essential security practices (in addition to ensuring compliance with any explicit regulatory requirements you may have).

People

- Develop a cloud learning program for teams.
- Provide teams with training on cloud security.

Process

- Assign accountability for decisions about cloud security.
- Update processes for cloud incident response.
- Manage the security posture.

Technology

- Authenticate without a password or with multiple factors.
- Secure your network with a native firewall.
- Detect threats natively.

Foundational Architecture Decisions

- One directory and identity should be standard.
- Access control based on identity.
- Unify security strategies.

Companies' risk posture and tolerance can be affected by a number of factors. For example, a bank might not be able to tolerate even a minor attack on its test system due to its reputational risk. Some organizations could accept the same risk if they accelerated their digital transformation by three to six months.

Security Management Strategy

Cloud services do not change a security organization's ultimate objectives, but how these objectives are achieved will change. To reduce business risks from attacks, security teams must still ensure that information systems and data are secure, reliable, and available.

The organization must modernize strategies, architectures, and technology as it adopts and operates cloud-based services. Security can shed some painful burdens associated with legacy approaches with the modernization of the security program. However, the size and number of changes may seem daunting at first. Despite the pace of change in the cloud and threat environment, an organization can temporarily operate with legacy strategy and tooling.

Continuous Assessment

This system must be continuously assessed and validated to ensure that secure configurations remain intact and previously unknown vulnerabilities are identified. Monitoring your workload's security posture, including virtual machines, networks, storage, and applications, requires continuous assessment. The nature of cloud computing makes it very dynamic, which means new workloads will be provisioned constantly. If your cloud adoption is not mature, you may not have all the safeguards to enforce security by default, so continuous assessment of your workload becomes even more critical.

Defender for Cloud is an IaaS and PaaS solution that can be used to continuously assess the security of your cloud and on-premises resources and workloads. Figure 6.2 depicts the Microsoft approach to continuous assessment to secure and defend against threats.

FIGURE 6.2   Microsoft approach to continuous assessment

Defender for Cloud's Secure Score is the central feature that helps you achieve these goals. Defender for Cloud constantly examines your resources, subscriptions, and organization for security issues. To evaluate your current security situation, the score aggregates all the results into a single score: the higher the score, the lower the risk level.

As new resources are deployed across your workloads, Defender for Cloud continuously checks if they are configured securely. Then they're flagged, and you're given a prioritized list of what needs to be fixed. Microsoft recommendations help you lower the attack surface against each of your resources.

The deployment of Microsoft Defender for Cloud allows your organization to assess its security posture and control measures continuously. In addition to strengthening your cloud resources' security posture, Defender for Cloud includes integrated Microsoft Defender plans that protect workloads running on Azure, hybrid, and other cloud platforms.

You can use Compliance Manager in a Microsoft 365 SaaS environment for continuous assessment. It identifies settings in your Microsoft 365 environment that determine whether specific configurations meet the implementation requirements for improvement actions. In addition to detecting signals from other compliance solutions you may have deployed, Compliance Manager uses Microsoft Secure Score monitoring to detect complementary improvement actions. This includes data life-cycle management, information protection, communication compliance, and insider risk management.

Your action status is updated on your dashboard within 24 hours when a change is made. After following a recommendation to implement a control, the control status is usually updated the next day. When you enable Azure Active Directory multifactor authentication (MFA) in the Azure AD portal, Compliance Manager will detect the setting and display it in the control access solution. If you don't enable Azure Active Directory MFA in the Azure AD portal, Compliance Manager will recommend you enable and configure MFA.

Continuous Strategy Evolution

Setting high-level goals and continuously reviewing progress toward those goals is an essential part of the evolution of your security strategy over time. According to Microsoft, scorecard metrics should focus on these four main areas:

- **Business enablement:** User experience and business processes. How much security friction is there?
- **Security posture:**
  - Is security improving every month?
  - How effective is our security posture at preventing damage?
- **Security response:** Response to and recovery from security breaches. How effective are you at responding and recovering?
- **Security improvement:** What is the plan for continuous improvement programs?

Table 6.1 lists a sample metric from each of these categories. These performance measurements can be used to start a discussion about how to measure a security program's success.

Every organization's business goals, risk appetite, technical portfolio, and other factors will determine the measures and targets/thresholds/weightings.

TABLE 6.1   Sample Metrics

Security Area	Metric
Business enablement	Mean Time for security review
	# days for application security review
	Average boot/logon time for managed devices
	Number of security interruptions in user workflow
	% of IT help desk time spent on low-value security activities

TABLE 6.1   Sample Metrics *(continued)*

Security Area	Metric
Security posture	% of new apps reviewed
	Secure score
	% compliant apps
	# of privileged accounts meeting 100% of requirements
	# of accounts meeting 100% of requirements
Security response	Mean Time to Recover (MTTR)
	Mean Time to Acknowledge (MTTA)
	Time to Restore Critical Systems
	# of high severity incidents
	Incident growth rate (overall)
Security improvement	# of modernization projects open
	# modernization project milestones achieved in last 60 days
	Number of repetitive manual steps removed from workflows
	# of Lessons learned from internal/external incidents

Specify Security Baselines for Server and Client Endpoints

A security configuration still needs to be granular enough for each organization, despite Windows Client and Windows Server being designed to be secure out of the box. Microsoft provides security baselines to guide organizations on how to configure various security features to navigate a large number of controls. Using Microsoft's industry-standard, widely known, and well-tested configurations, you can avoid the need to create baselines yourself.

What Are Security Baselines?

The types of security threats most relevant to one organization can be completely different from those of another organization. As an example, an e-commerce organization may focus on protecting its web apps, whereas a hospital may prioritize safeguarding confidential patient data. There is one thing all organizations have in common, however: they need to protect their apps and devices, and the devices must comply with the organization's security standards (or security baselines).

A security baseline is a preconfigured Windows setting that helps you enforce granular security settings recommended by security teams by creating a security baseline profile using Microsoft Intune.

What Is Microsoft Intune?

The Microsoft Intune endpoint management solution is a cloud-based service. It manages user access to apps and devices across your many devices, including mobile devices, desktops, and virtual machines.

You make a template with multiple device configuration profiles so that only the settings and values you need to enforce can be enforced using Microsoft Intune.

What Are Security Compliance Toolkits?

A feature of the Security Compliance Toolkit (SCT) is the ability to download, analyze, test, edit, and store Microsoft-recommended security configuration baselines for Windows and other Microsoft products.

The SCT simplifies the management of Group Policy Objects (GPOs) within an enterprise. Using the SCT toolkit, organization system administrators can correspond their present GPOs with Microsoft-recommended GPO baselines or different baselines, edit them, keep them in GPO backup file format, and use them broadly via Active Directory or separately via local policy.

Foundation Principles of Baselines

Microsoft recommends a streamlined and efficient approach to baseline definitions based on the following:

- With no administrative rights for standard end users, the baselines are for well-managed, security-conscious organizations.

- A security threat must be mitigated for a baseline to be enforced while preventing operational issues worse than the risks they mitigate.

- When an authorized user would otherwise be able to change a default to an insecure state, a baseline enforces the secure default.

  - Ensure the default state is enforced if a nonadministrator can set an insecure state.

  - If setting an insecure state needs administrative privileges, implement the default only if a misinformed administrator may otherwise choose wrongly.

Selecting the Appropriate Baseline

Understanding the operating system to which the security baseline will be applied is the first step in selecting the appropriate security baseline. In a heterogeneous environment, it may be necessary to have multiple baselines that address the needs of each operating system. When you have a list of operating systems and the versions in use in your organization, you can decide what tool you will use to deploy these baselines.

You may choose to use the SCT as one option. Basically, it is a collection of tools that help enterprise security managers download, analyze, test, edit, and store security configuration baselines for Windows and other Microsoft products. Administrators can manage GPOs effectively with the SCT. Administrators can compare their current GPOs with Microsoft-recommended baselines or other baselines, edit them, create backups in GPO file format, and apply them broadly through Active Directory or on an individual basis through local policies using the toolkit.

The following reference link provides guidance of how to use the toolkit:

```
learn.microsoft.com/en-us/windows/security/
threat-protection/windows-security-configuration-framework/
security-compliance-toolkit-10
```

The Azure Security Benchmark (ASB) also offers security baseline documents for Windows and Linux servers that are based on Azure security baselines.

For example, if your security baseline primarily focuses on installing and configuring endpoints (Windows clients), Intune can be used to automate the process. Using Intune, you can quickly deploy Windows security baselines to protect and secure your users. Intune lets you deploy security baselines for groups of users or devices, and the settings apply to Windows 10/11 devices. In addition to enabling BitLocker on removable drives, the mobile device management (MDM) security baseline requires a password to unlock a device, disables basic authentication, and more. Customize the baseline to apply your settings when the default value does not work for your environment.

It is critical to understand the default values for the baseline types you choose to use and then to modify each baseline to fit your organization's needs.

Intune security baselines are not CIS- or NIST-compliant. Although Microsoft consults with CIS before compiling its recommendations, there is no one-to-one mapping between CIS-compliant baselines and Microsoft baselines.

Microsoft's security team developed these baselines in response to its engagement with enterprise customers and external partners, including the Department of Defense (DOD) and the National Institute of Standards and Technology (NIST). These organizations also have their own recommendations that closely mirror Microsoft's recommendations, and Microsoft shares recommendations and baselines with these organizations. Microsoft developed a similar version of these group policy baselines as MDM continued to grow into the cloud. Microsoft Intune includes these additional baselines, which include compliance reports for users, groups, and devices that adhere to them.

In Azure Policy, organizational standards are enforced, and compliance is assessed at scale. Through its compliance dashboard, it provides a comprehensive view of the environment and the ability to drill down to granular levels for each resource and per policy. You can also bring resources into compliance by performing bulk remediation of existing resources and automating the remediation of new resources.

Azure Policy is commonly applied to implementing governance in resource consistency, regulatory compliance, security, and cost management. Thanks to built-in Azure policy definitions, you can already get started with these simple use cases in your Azure environment.

The following reference link provides security baselines for Windows with Azure Policy:

`learn.microsoft.com/en-us/azure/governance/policy/samples/guest-configuration-baseline-windows`

The following reference link provides security baselines for Linux with Azure Policy:

`learn.microsoft.com/en-us/azure/governance/policy/samples/guest-configuration-baseline-linux`

The following reference link provides security baselines for Docker with Azure Policy:

`learn.microsoft.com/en-us/azure/governance/policy/samples/guest-configuration-baseline-docker`

Security baselines are available on `endpoint.microsoft.com` for Microsoft clients, and it has a list of configurations for Windows 10/11 MDM security baselines in Microsoft Intune.

`learn.microsoft.com/en-us/mem/intune/protect/security-baseline-settings-mdm-all?pivots=mdm-november-2021`

Microsoft provides its customers with secure operating systems with Windows and Windows Server, and Microsoft Edge provides secure apps. You can use Microsoft's various configuration capabilities to have fine-grained control over your environments and the security assurance that comes with its products.

Security baselines can be downloaded from the Microsoft Download Center. The SCT provides admins with tools to manage security baselines and baselines. You can also use the SCT to manage security baselines.

Devices running Windows 10 or Windows 11 can easily be configured with MDM security baselines in Microsoft Intune.

Specify Security Baselines for the Server, Including Multiple Platforms and Operating Systems

Ensuring the servers and client computers of your Windows Server environment are configured securely is an integral part of securing your environment. Hardening the operating system is essential to securing your Windows Server environment. Defining security requirements for servers depends on the server role, since the role will determine what hardening settings are needed.

A server in a unique role may need more configuration, but most servers will have a core foundational security requirement. It is necessary to take additional steps to harden the Active Directory services on your server if it is a domain controller (DC). The Microsoft SCT is a great tool for understanding the server's current state.

Analyze Security Configuration

The Microsoft SCT is a set of tools to download and install security configuration baselines, usually called *security baselines*, for Windows Server and other Microsoft products, including Windows 10, Microsoft 365 Apps for Enterprise, and Microsoft Edge. You implement the security configuration baselines by managing your GPOs.

Additionally, you can use the SCT to compare your current GPOs to the recommended GPO security baselines. Once your existing GPOs are compared to the recommended GPOs, you can edit the recommended GPOs and apply them to your devices.

Additionally, the SCT includes tools for managing GPO settings for Windows Server, including Policy Analyzer and Local Group Policy Object (LGPO) and Set Object Security and GPO to Policy Rules.

Secure Servers (Domain Members)

Following are key areas to secure servers that are part of your domain.

Local Administrator Accounts

Each computer member of a domain keeps a local Administrator account. When you deploy the computer manually or use software deployment tools such as Microsoft Endpoint Configuration Manager, you configure this account automatically. IT staff can sign in to the computer with the local administrator account if they cannot connect to the domain.

For an organization with a larger number of computers, managing the passwords for the local administrator account can be extremely difficult. Each local Administrator account in the organization has a different password, and organizations often assign all local

Administrator accounts the same common password. Using this approach has the drawback of allowing people outside of the IT operations team access to unauthorized computers in your organization by figuring out the password.

In addition to managing local account passwords for domain-joined computers, the Local Administrator Password Solution (LAPS) is available for all currently supported Windows Server and client operating systems.

Local Administrator Password Solution (LAPS) allows domain-joined computers to manage passwords for local administrator accounts. Passwords are created randomly and kept in Active Directory (AD), protected by ACLs, so only qualified users can read or request a reset.

SMB Protocol

The Server Message Block (SMB) protocol, a network protocol that is primarily used for file sharing, is another critical part of server protection. It disables legacy protocols and enforces a more secure communication method. Aside from its use for file sharing, SMB is also frequently used by printers, scanners, and email servers. SMB 1.0 does not support encryption, and version 3.0 introduced SMB encryption.

With SMB encryption, servers can provide secure storage for applications such as Microsoft SQL Server and provide certain data transfers to clients. SMB encryption is generally easier to use than hardware-based encryption, which is usually more complex. Data packet security is provided to users by SMB encryption, which prevents malicious hackers from intercepting or tampering with data packets.

The SMB 3.1.1.c version of SMB included with Windows Server 2019 provides several enhancements to the security of SMB 3.0. This version of SMB includes pre-authentication integrity checks and encryption improvements.

SMB is available on Windows Server systems in several versions. To use SMB 3.1.1, your host server and its communication system must support SMB 3.1.1. This allows them to communicate with servers and clients running other operating systems and Windows versions.

Some wide area network (WAN) accelerators that modify SMB packets won't support pre-authentication with SMB 3.1.1. Therefore, you might have to replace some network equipment.

Azure Security Benchmark

Ensure all servers comply with the ASB OS baseline as an alternative to specifying server requirements. Using Microsoft Defender for Cloud, the ASB OS baseline is available as security recommendations for Windows or Linux, as depicted in Figure 6.3.

Accessing a recommendation will show you a set of rules using the Azure Guest Configuration capability to perform security checks on the operating system to ensure it is configured securely.

As shown in Figure 6.4, clicking each rule will reveal more information about the security check and the affected resources.

FIGURE 6.3   Microsoft Defender for Cloud ASB OSB baseline for Windows and Linux

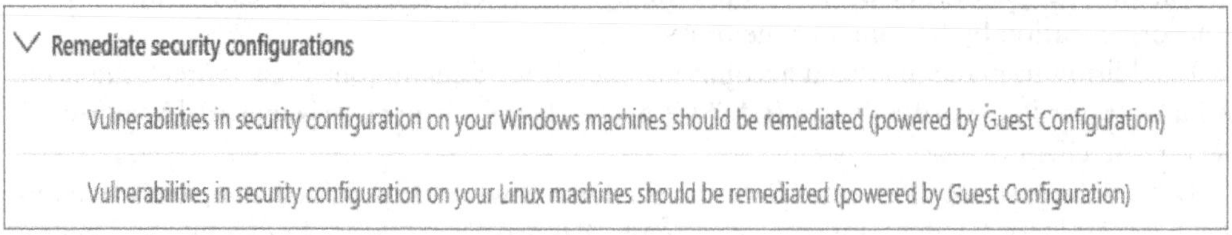

∨ Remediate security configurations

   Vulnerabilities in security configuration on your Windows machines should be remediated (powered by Guest Configuration)

   Vulnerabilities in security configuration on your Linux machines should be remediated (powered by Guest Configuration)

FIGURE 6.4   Detailed view about remediation

Automanage

Automation and best practices are applied to Windows and Linux servers running on Azure or in hybrid environments supported by Azure Arc with Automanage.

Windows and Linux virtual machines can be managed with Automanage, including the following components:

- Boot Diagnostic
- Security Center
- Monitoring
- Update Management
- Automation Account
- Change Tracking and Inventory
- Configuration Management
- Log Analytics
- Backup

With Azure Automanage machine best practices, you do not need to discover, learn how to onboard, and configure certain services in Azure that would benefit your virtual machine. In addition to increasing reliability, security, and management of virtual machines, these services are considered Azure best practices.

Azure Disk Encryption

By protecting and safeguarding your data, you can meet the organizational security and compliance commitments with Azure Disk Encryption (ADE). Using the DM-Crypt or Bit-Locker features in Linux and Windows, ADE encrypts both the OS and data disks of your Azure virtual machines (VMs). ADE is integrated with Azure Key Vault to facilitate the management and control of disk encryption keys and secrets.

Managing encryption keys in your Key Vault requires Azure AD authentication. ADE generates and writes encryption keys to your Key Vault.

The following are the best practices you can adopt in your environment for VM management:

- Making sure only authorized individuals have access to your VMs is the first step in protecting them.
- With Azure AD authentication for Linux VMs, you can centrally control and enforce policies that allow or deny access to the VMs. You can use Azure AD authentication to improve the security of your Linux VMs on Azure.
- Azure Automanage can be used for Windows and Linux virtual machines to keep them up-to-date with updates.
- Use the principle of least privilege approach to enable users to access and set up VMs.
- Azure Disk Encryption helps encrypt your Windows and Linux IaaS virtual machine disks.

- A key encryption key can be created in the Key Vault using the Add-AzKeyVaultKey cmdlet.

- Whenever network security groups allow access from any IP address, Defender for Cloud recommends that you restrict access through Internet-facing endpoints.

Specify Security Requirements for Mobile Devices and Clients, Including Endpoint Protection, Hardening, and Configuration

You can manage apps, devices, and users across your devices using Microsoft Intune, which provides cloud-based endpoint management. You can secure access to data on organization-owned and user-owned devices. Microsoft Intune can help you manage all aspects of device management, from enrollment to configuration to protection to retirement, when a device is no longer needed.

Mobile device security requirements will primarily focus on the configure and protect stages, but you should consider all the following phases:

- **Enroll:** Verify your organization's enrollment options and evaluate available devices.

- **Configure:** In the initial configuration of your device, you can choose from various policies to ensure the device is secure and compliant.

- **Protect:** In addition to what was initially configured, you have additional settings to safeguard your devices against malicious attacks or unauthorized access. Making sure your devices are protected from unauthorized access is one of your most critical tasks.

- **Retire:** In most cases, it is time to retire or wipe a device when it gets lost, stolen, replaced, or when users change jobs. This can be accomplished in various ways, including resetting the device, removing it from management, and wiping corporate data.

App Isolation and Control

Using Microsoft Intune, in a managed app scenario, app protection policies (APPs) ensure an organization's data is protected or contained. When a user attempts to access or move "corporate" data, a policy is enforced, or actions are prohibited or monitored while the user is inside the app. Managed apps can be managed by Intune and have app protection policies applied to them.

Your organization's data can be managed and protected within an application using Mobile Application Management (MAM) policies.

Both personal and work tasks are performed on mobile devices by your employees, and your employees must be able to be productive while preventing intentional or unintentional data loss. The data you store on devices you don't manage will also need to be protected.

Mobile device management (MDM) solutions are not required to use Intune app protection policies. You can protect your company's data regardless of whether your devices are enrolled in a device management solution. By implementing app-level policies, you can limit access to corporation resources and keep your corporate data within your purview.

Using Intune app protection policies with conditional access, an Azure Active Directory capability, your work files can be protected on devices enrolled in Intune.

The example shown in Figure 6.5 shows that the admin has added the Outlook app to an approved list of apps after applying app protection policies.

FIGURE 6.5 Microsoft approach to continuous assessment

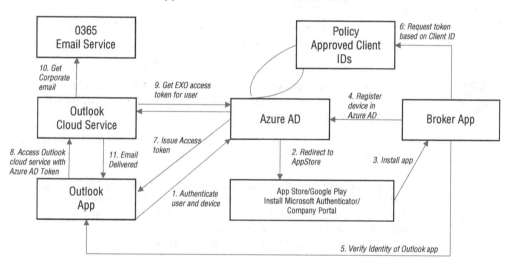

APP protection policies can be set up to enforce rules when a user tries to access or modify corporate data or to prohibit or monitor specific actions inside the application. App protection policies can be applied to managed apps; Intune can manage them.

Choose Between Device Management and Application Management

Microsoft Intune provides MDM for organization-owned devices. Because of the device-centric nature of MDM, features are configured based on who needs them. If the user is signed in with an organization account, you can configure the device to allow access to Wi-Fi.

Intune provides security and protection by configuring features and settings. In addition to the user identities that sign in, the apps that are installed, and the data that's accessed, your organization manages the devices.

Your policies can be deployed during the enrollment process when devices enroll and are ready for use once enrollment is complete.

In BYOD scenarios, you can use Intune for mobile application management (MAM) for personal devices. The app data is protected regardless of which device is being used to access it because MAM is user-centric. The focus is on apps, including protecting data within apps and securely accessing them.

You can do the following with MAM:

- Mobile apps can be published to users.

- You can configure and update apps automatically.

- Reports on app usage and inventory are available.

It is also possible to combine MDM and MAM. You can also use MAM app protection policies if your devices are enrolled and some apps need extra protection.

The management of devices is an important part of any endpoint management solution. An organization has to manage laptops, tablets, mobile phones, wearables, and more.

Intune is a cloud-based service that controls devices with policies, including security policies.

An organization's data is kept safe or contained in a managed app using APP. Using an approach can mean enforcing a rule if the user attempts to access or move corporate data or can mean enforcing a set of actions that the user is forbidden or monitored from within the app. Managed apps can be controlled by Intune and have app protection policies applied to them.

By using Intune MAM, you can control many productivity apps, such as Microsoft Office, and manage and protect your organization's data within them.

In the example in Figure 6.5, if you permit only the Microsoft Outlook application to access Exchange Online, you can block the built-in mail apps on iOS/iPad and Android. Additionally, you can block SharePoint Online access from apps not protected by Intune.

Conditional Access for Exchange Online and other Microsoft 365 services with client app management adds another layer of security by ensuring only client apps that support Intune app protection policies can access these services.

Here's a description of the workflow depicted in Figure 6.5:

1. The user attempts to authenticate via the Outlook app with Azure AD.

2. When authenticating for the first time, the user is directed to the application store to deploy a broker app. Broker apps include Microsoft Authenticator for iOS and Microsoft Company portal for Android.

3. If users try to access a native email app, they'll be redirected to the app store to deploy the Outlook app.

4. Get the broker app installed on your device.

5. The broker app creates the Azure AD registration process, which makes a device record in Azure AD. It differs from the MDM enrollment process, but the conditional access record is necessary to enforce the policies on this device.

6. Azure AD sign-in servers validate access to the requested service based on the Azure AD device ID, user, and application information.

7. The broker app transfers the App Client ID to Azure AD as part of user authentication to verify its approval.

8. Azure AD authenticates and grants access to the app based on the approved apps list. If the app is not on the list, Azure AD denies access.

9. Activating Exchange Online is accomplished through Outlook Cloud Service.

10. Outlook Cloud Service obtains a user's Exchange Online service access token through Azure AD.

11. A user's corporate e-mail is retrieved by Outlook using Exchange Online.

12. Users receive corporate emails in their mailboxes.

Using app protection, you could enforce your mobile device's security requirements, which might include the following:

- Ensure that work files are encrypted.

- Make access to work files require a PIN; after five failed attempts, the PIN must be reset.

- Prevent work files from being backed up into public cloud services such as iTunes, iCloud, or Android backup services.

- Require the saving of work files only to OneDrive or SharePoint.

- Prevent jailbroken or rooted apps from loading work files.

- After 720 minutes of being offline, block access to work files.

- After 90 days of inactivity, work files will be removed.

Device Settings

Along with app isolation and protection, you also need to secure the device's settings. When an end-user mobile device is enrolled to your Microsoft 365 organization, you can manage and connect it using the Mobility and Security feature. Employees can get their work done anywhere, anytime, with mobile devices like smartphones and tablets that can access work email, calendars, contacts, and documents. Therefore, providing security policies and rules for mobile devices and wiping them if they're lost or stolen is critical to protecting your organization's information.

With Basic Mobility and Security, your organization can secure and manage mobile devices like iPhones, iPods, Androids, and Windows Phones. Microsoft 365 email and documents can be accessed using supported mobile devices and apps under MDM policies with settings that can help control access. It is possible to remotely wipe a lost or stolen device to remove sensitive organizational data if it is lost or stolen.

Mobile devices must be hardened following the following requirements:

- Require passwords.
- Ensure that simple passwords are not used.
- Passwords must be alphanumeric.
- Passwords must have a minimum length.
- Before a device is wiped, the number of failed sign-in attempts is counted.
- Set the number of minutes before the device is locked after inactivity.
- Establish the expiration date for password (number of days).
- Prevent reusing passwords by remembering password history.
- Encrypt devices that contain data.
- Do not support rooted or jailbroken devices.
- Block screen captures.
- Require a password for access to the application store.

You should ensure that the security settings you want to manage are available for the type of devices your organization uses when setting up your security requirements.

Client Requirements

Your client workstation should be domain-joined. Many environments use Active Directory (AD) on-premises. A hybrid Azure AD–joined device is an AD domain-joined device that is also part of Azure AD. You can enroll hybrid Azure AD joined devices in Intune using Windows Autopilot. Enrolling would be reasonable if you had a domain join configuration profile.

It is then possible to start planning the security requirements for the operating system configuration once you have determined if the client is domain-joined. Security baselines can also include these requirements applied to devices and groups running Windows 10/11.

Intune can be used to deploy security baselines to groups or devices. The MDM Security Baseline automatically enables BitLocker for removable drives; passwords are automatically required to unlock devices, basic authentication is disabled, and more. Use a customized baseline to apply the settings you need when a default value does not work.

Security policies for clients should manage the following settings:

- Disk encryption

- Antivirus

- Windows firewall

- Attack surface reduction

- Endpoint detection and response

- Account protection

The endpoint security node in Intune provides several settings that can help protect your devices. Security admins can configure device security and manage security tasks when devices are at risk using the endpoint security node in Intune. Using endpoint security policies, you can protect your devices and mitigate risk while focusing on their security.

As recommended by the relevant Microsoft security teams for the product, security baselines in Intune are preconfigured groups of settings. The Microsoft Intune platform allows you to create security baselines for Windows 10/11 device settings, Microsoft Edge, Microsoft Defender for Endpoint Protection, and others.

Establish conditions for devices and users to access network resources and your organization network through a device compliance policy.

Specify Requirements for Securing Active Directory Domain Services

With Active Directory Domain Services (AD DS), organizations can simplify user and resource management; create scalable, secure, and manageable infrastructure; and simplify user and resource management. AD DS can manage branch offices, Microsoft Exchange Server, and multiple autonomous environments, also known as *forests*.

For your AD DS deployment strategy to be successful, you must conduct a high-level assessment and identify your deployment tasks correctly. Depending on your existing network configuration, you may need to adapt your AD DS deployment strategy.

If you want to specify the requirements to secure Active Directory Domain Services, you must first recognize that threat actors often perform credential theft and target some specific accounts. As part of a credential theft attack, an attacker gains access to a computer on a network using the highest level of privilege (root, administrator, or SYSTEM, depending on the operating system) and then extracts credentials from other logged-on accounts using freely available tools. Depending on the system's configuration, these credentials can be removed as hashes, tickets, or plaintext passwords.

Administrators must be aware of activities that increase the likelihood of a credential-theft attack because high-privileged domain accounts and VIP accounts are usually targets of credential theft. Although attackers also target VIP accounts, stealing their credentials requires other attacks, such as social engineering the VIP to provide secret information.

The core vulnerability that allows credential theft attacks to succeed is logging on to computers that are not secure with accounts that are widely and deeply privileged throughout the environment. So you need to minimize the attack surface as part of securing AD DS, which includes the following tasks:

Deploy Least-Privilege Administrative Models   Explores the risks associated with using highly privileged accounts for the day-to-day administration and provides recommendations for reducing those risks.

Deploy Secure Administrative Hosts   Provides examples of approaches to deploying secure administrative hosts and principles for deploying secure administrative systems.

Defending Domain Controllers to Prevent Attack   Describes policies and settings that, although similar to recommendations for implementing secure administrative hosts, provide some domain controller–specific recommendations to help ensure that domain controllers and their management systems are secure.

A trusted system (for example, a domain controller) should never be administered from a less trusted host (a workstation that doesn't have the same level of security as the systems it manages). When performing privileged activities, you should rely on more than one authentication factor; for example, usernames and passwords should not be considered acceptable authentication because they represent only a single factor (what you know). Credentials generated in administrative scenarios should be cached or stored somewhere.

Securing Domain Controllers Against Attack

As well as providing the physical storage for the Active Directory Domain Services (AD DS) database, domain controllers enable enterprises to effectively manage their servers, workstations, users, and applications. Assume that a malicious user obtains access to the domain controller. The AD DS database and, by extension, all the systems and accounts managed by Active Directory can be modified, corrupted, or destroyed in such a scenario.

Because domain controllers can read from and write to anything in the AD DS database, if a domain controller is compromised, your Active Directory forest can be considered trustworthy again only once a known good backup can be recovered. The gaps that led to the compromise are closed.

Irreparable damage can be caused in minutes to hours, not days or weeks, depending on the attacker's preparation, tooling, and skill. When an attacker obtains privileged access to Active Directory, it matters not how long they have had it but how much they have planned for it. Active Directory, member servers, and workstations can be destroyed most easily by compromising a domain controller, and this threat necessitates different and more stringent security measures for domain controllers.

The following are critical essential best practices to be adopted.

Physical domain controllers should be installed in separate secure racks or cages from the rest of the servers in data centers. The domain controller servers should be configured with Trusted Platform Modules (TPM) chips, and BitLocker drive encryption should be used to encrypt all volumes on the domain controller servers. Even if disks are detached from the server, BitLocker protects the directory against compromise.

Virtual domain controllers should be installed on separate physical hosts from other virtual machines in the environment if you have implemented them.

It would be helpful if you ran all domain controllers on the most recent version of Windows Server. Organizations must decommission legacy operating systems from their domain controller population as soon as possible. Maintaining current domain controllers and eliminating legacy domain controllers gives you access to new functionality and security. Domains and forests with legacy operating systems may not be able to use this functionality.

RDP connections should be allowed only from authorized users and systems, such as jump servers, in GPOs associated with all domain controller OUs in a forest. The policy can be applied consistently through a combination of user rights settings and WFAS configuration implemented through GPOs. A refresh of the Group Policy will restore the system to its correct configuration if the policy is bypassed.

Despite what may seem counterintuitive, you should consider patching domain controllers and other critical infrastructure components separately from Windows. All infrastructure components can be compromised or destroyed if all computers are managed by enterprise configuration management software. You can reduce the amount of software installed on domain controllers and tightly control their management by separating patch and systems management from the general population.

You should also take the following steps:

- Active Directory should be continuously monitored for signs of compromise using tools like Microsoft Defender for Identity.

- Ensure audit policies are in place and reviewed.

Microsoft Defender for Identity

Microsoft Defender for Identity (MDI) monitors your domain controllers and analyzes the data for threats and attacks by capturing and parsing network traffic and using Windows events. Defender for Identity learns about your network, detects anomalies, and warns you about suspicious activity using profiling, deterministic detection, machine learning, and behavioral algorithms. Figure 6.6 shows Defender for Identity's core architecture.

FIGURE 6.6   Microsoft Defender for Identity with AD FS

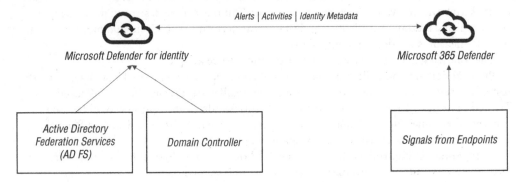

Defender for Identity sensor accesses event logs directly from each server once installed on your domain controller (DC) or AD FS server. Defender for Identity sends only parsed information to the Defender for Identity cloud service after the sensor parses logs and network traffic (only a percentage of the logs are sent).

Security professionals and SecOp analysts struggling to detect advanced attacks in hybrid environments can use Defender for Identity to detect them. Using learning-based analytics, a user, entity, and activity can be monitored via Microsoft Defender for Identity.

Design a Strategy to Manage Secrets, Keys, and Certificates

Using Azure Key Vault, you can store encryption keys, certificates, and server-side tokens centralized in the cloud.

- **Secrets management:** Azure Key Vault can securely store and tightly control API keys, tokens, passwords, and certificates.

- **Key management:** You can use Azure Key Vault to manage encryption keys for encrypting data.

- **Certificate management:** TLS/SSL certificates can be easily provisioned, managed, and deployed using Azure Key Vault.

The Key Vault keeps your application secrets in a central location and provides secure access, permission control, and access logging so you can manage them. Azure Key Vaults use three primary concepts: vaults, keys, and secrets.

Multiple secure containers, called *vaults*, are created using Azure Key Vault. An organization may have various Key Vaults. Storing application secrets centrally reduces the risk of accidental loss of security information. In a Key Vault, you can store cryptographic keys and cryptographically protected data (referred to as *secrets*) that one or more individuals manage within your organization. A Key Vault represents your organization's logical grouping of keys and secrets. They are like file system folders and track and log access to the keys and secrets.

As the central actor in Azure Key Vault, keys play a significant role. Key Vault keys are cryptographic assets destined for specific purposes, for example, the asymmetric master key of Microsoft Azure RMS or the asymmetric keys used for asymmetric data encryption, column-level encryption, and encrypted backups on SQL Server.

With the Key Vault, you can create an HSM-generated key to protect a small (less than 10KB) data blob. Secrets' purpose is to simplify the process of persisting sensitive data such as storage account keys, PFX files, SQL connection strings, encryption keys, and so on.

Key Vault delivers an automatic renewal feature and enables applications and users of Microsoft Azure to store and use certificates.

Include the security best practices shown in Table 6.2. in your Key Vault maintenance strategy.

TABLE 6.2 Best Practices

Best Practice	Solution
Grant access to users, groups, and applications at a specific scope.	RBAC's predefined roles can be used to grant access to users to manage Key Vaults. For example, if you want to give a user access to Key Vaults, assign the user the role Key Vault Contributor at a specific scope. You can define your roles if the predefined roles don't fit your needs. The list of components can be a subscription, a resource group, or a specific Key Vault.
Control what users have access to.	There are two separate interfaces for controlling access to a Key Vault: the management plane interface and the data plane interface. The data plane interface and the management plane are independent of one another. You can manage what users have access to using RBAC. You do not need to grant management plane access for this application if you wish to grant it the right to use keys from a Key Vault, and this application requires only data plane access permissions. If you want a user to have read access to vault properties but no access to keys, secrets, or certificates, you can grant them read access via the management plane without granting them access to the data plane.

TABLE 6.2   Best Practices *(continued)*

Best Practice	Solution
Store certificates in your Key Vault.	You can control who can access your certificates by setting appropriate access policies for the Key Vault. When Azure VMs are deployed, Azure Resource Manager can securely deploy certificates stored in Azure Key Vault. Azure Key Vault also allows you to manage all your certificates in one place.
Ensure that you can recover a deletion of Key Vaults or Key Vault objects.	There are two types of deletion: accidental and malicious. Enable Key Vault's soft delete and purge protection features, mainly when keys are used to encrypt data at rest. Deleting these keys is equivalent to data loss so that you can recover deleted vaults and objects. Practice recovering vaults and vault objects regularly.

Manage Access to Secrets, Certificates, and Keys

The Key Vault's access has two aspects: managing the Key Vault itself and accessing its data. The management and data planes are referred to as the *management* and *data planes*, respectively. Key Vault creation (a management operation) is a distinct role from storing and retrieving secrets stored in Key Vaults, so the two areas are separated. There are two components of a Key Vault: authentication, which identifies the caller, and authorization, which determines the operations the caller is authorized to perform.

Authentication

A vault can be accessed by users and apps using Azure AD. Key Vault access is always authenticated by associating the authenticated identity of the user or app who requests with the Azure AD tenant where the Key Vault is located. Anonymous access to a Key Vault is not supported.

Authorization

An RBAC system is used for management operations (creating a new Azure Key Vault). Key Vault Contributor is a built-in role that can manage Key Vaults but not access the Key Vault data. This is the recommended role to use. Also available is the Contributor role, which comes with full administration rights, including granting access to the data plane.

Access policies for reading and writing data in the Key Vault are separate. A Key Vault access policy assigns users or managed identity access rights to read, write, or delete secrets and keys. You can create an access policy using the CLI, REST API, or Azure Portal.

Restrict Network Access

There are also several things to consider with Azure Key Vault. Typically, endpoints in your network can be exposed to the Internet to access the vault, and a minimum level of network access is required. For example, you can restrict Key Vault endpoints to specific Azure Virtual Network subnets, IP addresses, or trusted Microsoft services such as Azure SQL, Azure App Service, and encryption key-based storage services.

Manage Certificates

The challenge of managing certificates securely is keeping the private key safe and renewing them periodically to ensure your website traffic is secure. It is possible to create self-signed certificates directly in the Azure Portal using the X.509-based certificates supported by Azure Key Vault. In this process, a public/private key pair is generated, and the certificate is signed with its key. Testing and development can be done with these certificates.

Creating a certificate signing request (CSR) for X.509 creates both a public/private key pair in Key Vault and a certificate signing request that can be submitted to your certification authority. Using the key pair held in Key Vault, the signed X.509 certificate can then be merged to finalize the certificate in Key Vault, as Figure 6.7 depicts.

FIGURE 6.7   Microsoft Certified Authority integrated

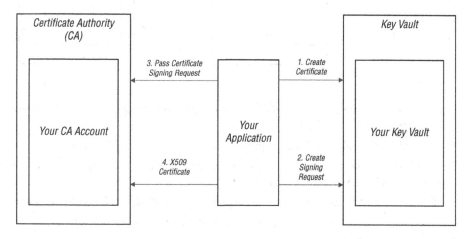

1.   Key Vault sends your application a certificate signing request (CSR) in the first step.
2.   In the second step, a CSR is sent to the CA you select through your application.
3.   In the third step, the A X.509 certificate is issued by the CA you have chosen.
4.   Finally, by merging your CA's X.509 certificate with your application, you create a new certificate.

Because the private key is created and securely stored in Azure Key Vault, it provides better security than handling the CSR directly. Additionally, you can create certificates directly in Azure Key Vault if you connect your Key Vault to a trusted certificate issuer (referred to as an *integrated* CA).

To connect the certificate authority, you need to do a one-time setup. Similarly, to the manual CSR creation process shown earlier, you can request a certificate, and Key Vault will interact directly with the CA to fulfill your request. Figure 6.8 shows a diagram showing the end-to-end details of this process.

FIGURE 6.8   Microsoft Certified Authority and Key Vault integrated

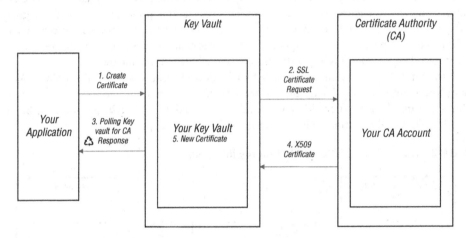

1.   A certificate is created by your application in the previous diagram, which internally makes a key in your Key Vault.

2.   Upon receiving the SSL certificate request from the CA, Key Vault sends it to the CA.

3.   The application polls your Key Vault for certificate completion, which is complete once it receives the CA's x509 certificate response.

4.   The CA issues X.509 SSL certificates in response to Key Vault's SSL certificate request.

5.   Your new certificate will be created once the X.509 certificate for the CA has been merged with the new certificate.

This approach has several distinct advantages, including that the Key Vault can monitor and manage the certificate life cycle since it is connected to the issuing CA. As a result, it can automatically renew your certificate, notify you when it expires, and keep track of certificate revokes.

The Azure Key Vault resource provider supports two resource types: vaults and managed HSMs, enabling users and applications to store and use a wide range of secret/key data types.

There are two tiers of Azure Key Vault services: standard, which uses a software key to encrypt, and premium, which uses a hardware security module (HSM) to protect keys.

You can control the distribution of application secrets by centralizing them in Azure Key Vault, and Key Vault dramatically reduces the likelihood that secrets will be accidentally leaked. By not storing security information in applications, application developers no longer have to write code that contains this information.

Design a Strategy for Secure Remote Access

When designing your remote-access strategy, you must consider all the available options and determine which option is most appropriate. Let's get started with site-to-site (S2S) VPNs. An S2S VPN is established by connecting two gateways at different sites using the Internet, a private network, or an outsourced IPsec network. Any organization can access its IT resources quickly and safely, regardless of whether they are hosted on-premises or in the cloud.

An S2S VPN's primary function is providing secure access to sensitive information and network resources, such as internal customer and sales systems, cloud applications, and local file storage used by end users across many devices.

Cross-premises and hybrid configurations can be supported by S2S connectivity. An S2S VPN gateway is a network connection over an IPsec/IKE (IKEv1 or IKEv2) VPN tunnel. The traffic is encrypted at one end and sent over the public Internet to the other end, which decrypts it and routes it to its destination. A VPN device on-premises that comes with public IP addresses is required for S2S VPN connections. The technology enables the connection of geographically displaced sites or networks using a public Internet connection or a WAN connection. VPN connections require an on-premises VPN device with a public IP address assigned to it.

Figure 6.9 depicts typical deployment topology shows a single-site, S2S VPN to establish a VPN tunnel (IPsec VPN tunnel) between Microsoft Azure and on-premises.

FIGURE 6.9 Site-to-site VPN

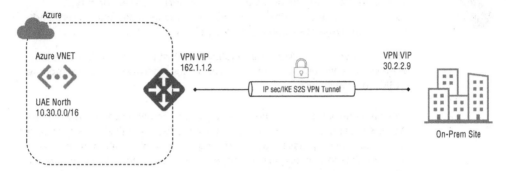

You can create more than one VPN connection from an organization's virtual network gateway, typically connecting to multiple on-premises sites. A multisite type of connection is an extension of an S2S connection. A route-based VPN type (called a *dynamic gateway* when used with classic VNets) is required for multiconnection work. All connections through the gateway share the available bandwidth since each virtual network is restricted to only one VPN gateway.

Figure 6.10 depicts a typical deployment topology and shows a multisite, S2S VPN to establish a VPN tunnel (IPsec VPN tunnel) between Microsoft Azure and on-premises.

FIGURE 6.10 Microsoft Azure multisite S2S VPN

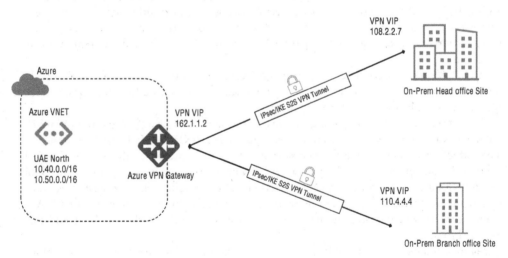

A VPN gateway can be set up in active-standby mode using one public IP address or in active-active mode using two public IP addresses. Setting up a VPN gateway in active-active mode is a Microsoft-recommended method in which both the IPsec tunnels are simultaneously active, with data flowing through both tunnels simultaneously.

Furthermore, cloud consumers benefit from an increase in throughput thanks to active-active. Active standby refers to the operation of having one IPsec tunnel active and another on standby. If the active tunnel experiences any issues, traffic switches over to the standby tunnel.

A point-to-site (P2S) VPN gateway connection lets network engineers build a secure connection to the Azure virtual network from an individual end-user computer.

Connecting to a P2S network is done using the computer of the end user. Connecting to Azure VNets from a remote location, such as from home or during a conference, is an excellent solution for telecommuters. If you have only a few clients connecting to a VNet, a P2S VPN is also appropriate for S2S VPN. A P2S connection requires no public IP address or VPN device on the premises, in contrast to S2S connections. If both links' requirements are compatible, using a P2S link and an S2S link through a single VPN gateway. Figure 6.11 depicts a typical deployment topology and shows a user and P2S VPN to establish a VPN tunnel (P2S SSTP tunnel & P2S IKE Tunnel) between Microsoft Azure and end-user devices.

FIGURE 6.11   Point-to-site VPN

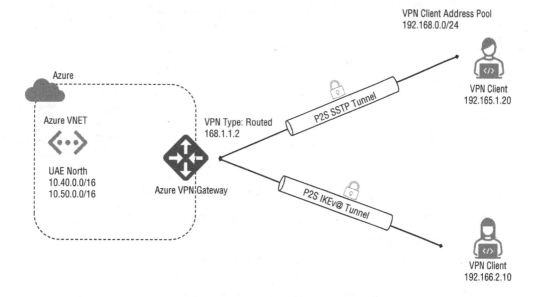

Virtual networks can be joined to each other (VNet-to-VNet) similarly to on-site locations of virtual networks. Both connectivity types provide an IPsec/IKE tunnel via a VPN gateway. You can combine communications between VNets with multisite configurations. Network topologies can be established that combine premise-to-premise and premise-to-virtual connectivity.

Using Azure's P2S solution, users can work from home quickly and easily, as the solution is cloud-based. You can quickly scale up the capacity and turn it off just as easily and quickly when you no longer need it. Using a point-to-site (P2S) VPN gateway, you can securely connect to your (VNet) virtual network from a client's personal computer.

When a P2S connection is started from a client computer, telecommuters can access Azure VNets or on-premises data centers remotely, from home, or at a conference. It can be used if your design requirement is that remote users have access to Azure and on-premises resources, as shown in Figure 6.12.

FIGURE 6.12   Microsoft Azure connectivity

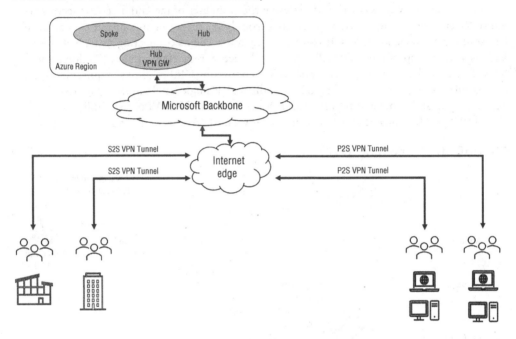

Connecting to Azure resources securely requires the following steps:

1. Create a virtual network gateway (if none already exists).

2. Configure the gateway with a P2S VPN.

3. Configure the Azure virtual network gateway to establish an S2S tunnel using the Internet.

4. Install the Azure virtual network gateway on the on-premises device.

5. The P2S profile can be downloaded from the Azure Portal and distributed to clients after downloading.

If your design requirements state that you need to connect two sites, for example headquarter and branch office, you could use S2S VPN. An S2S (S2S) VPN gateway connection is a connection over an IPsec/IKE (IKEv1 or IKEv2) VPN tunnel. S2S connections can be used for cross-premises and hybrid configurations. An S2S connection requires a VPN device located on-premises that has a public IP address assigned to it.

In some scenarios, the remote worker may just need access to resources deployed in Azure. For this scenario, the remote worker could use an Azure Bastion solution, instead of a VPN connection, to get secure shell access using RDP or Secure Shell Protocol (SSH) without requiring public IP addresses on the VMs being accessed, as shown in Figure 6.13. This solution offers the benefits described in Table 6.3.

TABLE 6.3   Benefits

Benefit	Description
The Azure Portal supports RDP and SSH.	You can connect to your RDP and SSH sessions directly in the Azure Portal with a single click.
Firewall traversal and remote session over TLS for RDP/SSH.	You interact with Azure Bastion using an HTML5 web client version that is automatically streamed to your local device. Your RDP/SSH connection is over TLS port 443 to enhance security.
Azure virtual machines do not require public IP addresses.	You don't need a public IP address on your Azure VM to open an RDP/SSH connection through Azure Bastion.
Management of NSGs is hassle-free.	Azure Bastion does not require any NSGs. You can configure your NSGs to allow only RDP/SSH from Azure Bastion since Azure Bastion connects to your virtual machines over a private IP address. As a result, you no longer have to manage NSGs whenever you need to connect securely to your virtual machines.
Bastion hosts on VMs do not need to be managed separately.	The Azure Bastion PaaS service from Azure is a fully managed platform that provides secure RDP/SSH connectivity through an internal hardening process.
Port scanning protection.	The VMs don't have to be exposed to the Internet, so they are protected from port scanning by rogue and malicious users.
One-sided hardening.	VMs in your virtual network need not be hardened individually since Azure Bastion sits at their perimeter.
Zero-day vulnerability protection.	Azure Bastion keeps you continuously up-to-date and is hardened against zero-day exploits.

Many IT organizations must adjust their capacity, network, security, and governance for work-from-home policies. When employees work from home, they are not protected by layered security policies associated with on-premises services. A scenario such as this might require you to choose a solution that allows you to respond faster to changes in the environment, and that is when Virtual Desktop Infrastructure (VDI) is an appropriate solution. Azure VDI deployments can help organizations respond rapidly to this changing environment. To protect your VDI deployments, you need a way to prevent inbound and outbound Internet traffic. Azure Firewall Destination Network Address Translation (DNAT) rules and its threat intelligence-based filtering capabilities can help you do that.

FIGURE 6.13   Microsoft Azure Remote connectivity

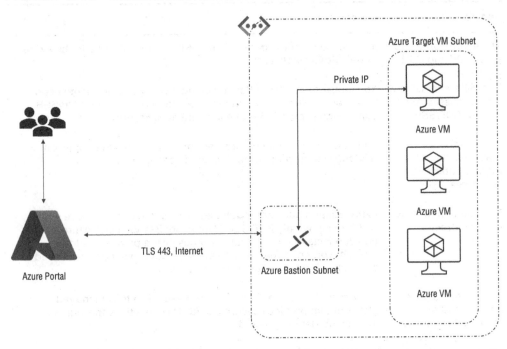

Using Azure Virtual Desktop, you can virtualize your desktop and apps. With it, you can simplify management, run multiple sessions of Windows 10/11, optimize Microsoft 365 apps for enterprise, and use Remote Desktop Services (RDS). With Azure, you can quickly deploy and scale Windows desktops and apps, as well as get built-in security and compliance options. Virtual machines running in your Azure Virtual Desktop network do not need a set of inbound network connections. They do need to allow outbound network connections.

> With Azure Bastion, virtual machines (VMs) can be accessed securely and seamlessly using Remote Desktop Protocol (RDP) and Secure Shell (SSH) without being exposed to public IP addresses. Support all the VMs within your local or peer virtual network by provisioning the service directly.

Secure remote work in minutes with Azure Virtual Desktop. Your end users will be able to use the functionality and compatibility of Windows 11 with the new expandable multisession experience while saving money by using existing Windows licenses. You can manage your Azure Virtual Desktop deployment from end to end from the Azure Portal.

Utilize Azure AD for unlimited single sign-on (SSO) and multifactor authentication (MFA) to enable secure remote work.

To enable remote work, many organizations are using personal devices. Azure AD conditional access and Microsoft Intune app protection policies work together to manage and secure corporate data on approved apps.

Anti-phishing protection can be set up in Microsoft Defender for Office 365 to safeguard your employees from increasingly sophisticated attacks better.

Design a Strategy for Securing Privileged Access

Microsoft's privileged access strategy aims to reduce your organization's risk from high-impact, high-probability, and high-impact attacks. When attackers compromise privileged user accounts, they almost always have a significant impact on business-critical assets in the organization. An attacker controlling your privileged accounts can undermine all other security assurances. The top security priority for every organization should be privileged access.

Data theft attacks using these techniques resulted in many high-profile breaches at familiar brands (and many unreported incidents). Moreover, ransomware attackers have adopted these techniques in recent years, fueling an explosion in highly profitable human-operated ransomware attacks intended to disrupt business operations.

Building the Recommended Design Strategy

A Microsoft-recommended strategy for privileged access is to build a closed-loop system for privileged access incrementally. This assures only trustworthy clean devices, accounts, and intermediaries can be used to provide privileged access.

It is crucial to design a waterproofing strategy for something complex in the real world, such as a boat, to establish and follow standards carefully, and to continually audit and monitor the results to ensure leaks are addressed. You can't nail boards together in the form of a boat and expect the boat to be waterproof. To build waterproof components, such as the hull and engine compartment, and to keep safety and comfort items waterproof, such as radios, seats, and the like, after leaving ways for people to enter, it is crucial to building critical waterproof components first. As even the best systems can leak eventually, you'll have to perform preventive maintenance, watch for leaks, and fix them to keep the boat from sinking.

Securing privileged access has two simple goals.

- Strictly limit the ability to perform privileged actions to a few authorized pathways.

- Protect and closely monitor those pathways.

There are two types of pathways to accessing the systems: user access (to use the capability) and privileged access (to manage the capability or access a sensitive capability).

User Access The lighter path on the bottom of Figure 6.14 depicts a standard user account performing general productivity tasks such as email, collaboration, web browsing, and use of line-of-business applications or websites. This path includes an account logging on to a device or workstations, sometimes passing through an intermediary like a remote access solution, and interacting with enterprise systems.

Privileged Access The darker path on the top of Figure 6.14 depicts privileged access, where privileged accounts like IT administrators or other sensitive accounts access business-critical systems and data or perform administrative tasks on enterprise systems. While the technical components may be similar in nature, the damage an adversary can inflict with privileged access is much higher.

FIGURE 6.14 Microsoft Azure privileged access security strategy guideline

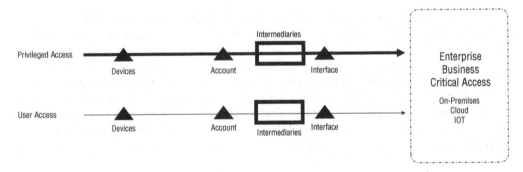

The goal of securing privileged access is twofold.

- A few authorized pathways should be allowed to perform privileged actions.

- Maintain a close eye on those pathways and protect them.

Using a capability gives a user access to it, while managing an ability gives privileged user access.

Identities and authorized elevation paths are also part of the complete access management system.

- **Identity systems:** Users of standard and privileged identities can access identity directories containing accounts, administrative groups, synchronization and federation capabilities, and other identity support functions.

- **Authorized elevation paths:** In a privileged access/privileged identity management system, authorized elevation paths enable standard users to interact with privileged workflows. For example, managers or peers can approve administrative rights requests to sensitive systems as part of a just-in-time (JIT) process.

To gain privileged access to your enterprise, adversaries may target these components simultaneously.

For privileged access strategies to be sustainable and manageable, all unauthorized vectors must be closed off, and a virtual equivalent of a control console physically attached to the system must be created.

Combining the following strategies will be effective:

- **Zero Trust access control:** This guidance discusses Zero Trust access control. (It was discussed in Chapter 1, "Define and Implement an Overall Security Strategy and Architecture" in detail, including rapid modernization plans [RAMPs].)

- **Asset protection:** Using good security hygiene practices, asset protection can prevent direct asset attacks. This guidance does not cover asset protection for resources beyond access control components, but it typically includes rapid deployment of security updates/patches, configuring operating systems to meet manufacturer/industry security baselines, safeguarding data in transit and at rest, and integrating security best practices into development/DevOps processes.

Secure privileged access requires end-to-end Zero Trust authentication of the account being used, and it must be established that the account belongs to the human user and not a hacker impersonating them.

In security alerts, incident investigations, and threat hunting, specialized accounts warrant more attention and priority because of their higher business impact.

The most privileged accounts are the most protected because they are likely to have a significant or material effect on the organization's operations if they are compromised.

Summary

Based on the different options for Microsoft Azure infrastructure services available, selecting the appropriate security baseline depends on understanding which operating system, application, platform, device, and user persona the baseline is intended to be applied to.

In this chapter, you also read about planning your infrastructure, planning and deploying a security strategy across teams, establishing a process for the proactive and continuous evolution of a security strategy, specifying security requirements for mobile devices and clients, and hardening the operating system, as well as application isolation. Furthermore, you learned how to create a strategy for managing secrets, keys, and certificates and specifying requirements for securing Active Directory Domain Services.

Exam Essentials

Know to specify security baselines for server and client endpoints.   You can quickly deploy Windows security baselines with Intune to protect and secure your users.

Although Windows and Windows Server have default security configurations designed to keep you secure, many organizations still prefer to customize their security settings even further. Many organizations seek guidance on configuring different security features because of a large number of controls available, and Microsoft delivers this guidance in the shape of security baselines.

Know to specify security requirements for servers, including multiple platforms and operating systems.   It is crucial to secure your Windows, Linux and any other OS-based Server environment by ensuring that servers and clients are configured as securely as possible, otherwise known as *hardening* the operating system. Because the server's role dictates how hardening settings should be applied, you must first define the security requirements for servers.

Some servers in a unique role may need more configuration than others, but most will have a foundational security requirement. You'll need to take additional steps to harden your directory services if your server is a domain controller. Use the Microsoft SCT to understand the server's current state.

Know to specify security requirements for mobile devices and clients, including endpoint protection, hardening, and configuration.   As you manage your managed devices, Microsoft Intune can help you keep them secure and up-to-date while protecting your organization's data. Both managed and unmanaged devices can be used to protect an organization's data, and it is also possible to protect data by blocking access to it from compromised devices.

You can configure devices to meet your organization's security goals using Intune's device configuration and compliance policies. You can deploy profiles to groups of devices enrolled in policies that support one or more profiles.

Know to specify requirements to secure AD DS.   Microsoft recommends installing physical domain controllers in separate secure racks or cages from the general server population in data centers. A TPM chip should be installed on domain controllers when possible, and BitLocker drive encryption should be enabled for all volumes in domain controller servers.

Although BitLocker typically adds a single-digit percentage of performance overhead, it protects the directory against compromise when disks are removed.

To monitor your domain controllers, Microsoft Defender for Identity captures and parses network traffic and uses Windows events directly from the domain controllers to analyze the data for attacks.

Understand the method to design a strategy to manage secrets, keys, and certificates. With Azure Key Vault, you can store application secrets such as encryption keys, certificates, and tokens in the cloud. Your applications' secrets are safeguarded by Key Vault, where they are kept securely, permissions are controlled, and access is logged. Vaults, keys, and secrets are the three main concepts in an Azure Key Vault.

Key Vaults protect secrets. Security events have a larger blast radius if secrets are grouped in a vault since attacks can access secrets across concerns.

Understand the method to design a strategy for secure remote access. It is imperative to consider the options available when designing your remote access strategy and choose the one that best suits your needs.

The Azure P2S solution is Azure-based and can be deployed quickly in reply to the growing need for users to work from home. When the increased capacity is no longer needed, it can be turned off just as easily and quickly.

The Azure Virtual Desktop service provides a comprehensive virtualization solution for desktops and applications. With it, you get simplified management, multi-session Windows 10 and 11, Microsoft 365 app optimizations for enterprise environments, and RDS support.

Understand the method to design a strategy for securing privileged access. An attacker who controls your privileged accounts can undermine all other security measures because the security of privileged accounts is the foundation of all other security measures. From a risk perspective, loss of security for privileged access is an event with a high impact and a high probability of happening, which is growing at an alarming rate across industries.

Targeted data theft attacks using these techniques have resulted in many high-profile breaches at familiar brands (and many unreported breaches). Recently, ransomware attackers have adopted these techniques, leading to an explosion of highly profitable human-operated ransomware attacks.

Review Questions

1. Which emerging discipline is dedicated to educating employees, protecting them, and preventing insider threats?

   A. Cybersecurity

   B. People security

   C. Apps and data security

   D. AI and ML security

2. As per Microsoft's best practices for building a security strategy, what are the components of a successful security strategy process?

   A. Align closely to business strategy.

   B. Modernize security strategy.

   C. Deploy most valuable plan.

   D. Both A and B.

3. Which of the following Azure security services can continuously assess your organization's security posture and controls?

   A. Microsoft Defender for Endpoints

   B. Microsoft Defender for Cloud

   C. Microsoft Intune

   D. None of the above

4. Which of the following areas does Microsoft recommend scorecard metrics for? (Choose two.)

   A. Business enablement and security improvement

   B. Security posture and security response

   C. Security design and strategy

   D. Monthly improvements in security

5. There are three major elements that contribute to the assurance of security for a business. Which one or the following is not included?

   A. Confidentiality

   B. Redundancy

   C. Availability

   D. Integrity

6. What tool allows enterprise security administrators to download, examine, test, modify, maintain, and manage Microsoft-recommended security configuration baselines for Windows and other Microsoft products?

   A. Microsoft Defender for Cloud

   B. Security Compliance Toolkit

   C. Azure Security Benchmark

   D. None of the above

7. What tool allows enterprise security administrators to download, examine, test, modify, maintain, and manage specific OS hardening for Windows and Linux workloads?

   A. Microsoft Defender for Cloud

   B. Security Compliance Toolkit

   C. Azure Security Benchmark

   D. None of the above

8. It is imperative to ensure that legacy protocols are disabled and that a more secure communication method is enforced. Which protocol do you have to disable as per Microsoft's recommendation because it does not have encryption?

   A. SMB 1.0

   B. Telnet

   C. SMB 3.0

   D. None of the above

9. Which tool is used to manage the password for local accounts on domain-joined computers?

   A. LAPS

   B. MAPS

   C. GPMC

   D. None of the above

10. As a Cybersecurity Architect, you are tasked to protect corporate apps and data isolated from the user's owned apps by the bring-your-own-device program. Which Azure services and Azure policies will you adopt in your solution?

    A. Microsoft Intune and Microsoft Intune app protection policies

    B. Azure AD and conditional policies

    C. Azure AD and app protection policies

    D. None of the above

11. As a Cybersecurity Architect, you are tasked to protect mobile device settings by the bring-your-own-device program. Which Azure services and Azure policies will you adopt in your solution?

    A. Microsoft Intune and Microsoft Intune app protection policies

    B. Mobility and Security to set device security policies and access rules

    C. Azure AD and device protection policies

    D. None of the above

12. As a Cybersecurity Architect, you are tasked with deploying Autopilot solutions for Windows client PCs and to enroll them. What do you need as prerequisite?

    A. To enroll, you need a multi-user subscription.

    B. To enroll, you need a Windows client CAL license.

    C. To enroll, you need a Domain Join configuration profile.

    D. None of the above.

13. Which of the Microsoft Azure services help you to monitor and analyze your domain controllers to identify attacks and threats?

    A. Microsoft 365 Defender

    B. Microsoft Defender for Cloud

    C. Microsoft Defender for Identity

    D. None of the above

14. As a Cybersecurity Architect, you are tasked with adopting the solution to store keys, certificates, and tokens in Microsoft Cloud securely. Which Azure service will you adopt in your organization?

    A. Azure Key Vault

    B. Microsoft Certificate Authority

    C. Microsoft Public Key infrastructure

    D. None of the above

15. Which Azure services does Azure Key Vault use to authenticate users and applications seeking access to a vault?

    A. Organization-owned Microsoft Active Directory running in Azure

    B. Organization-owned Microsoft Active Directory running in a private data center

    C. Microsoft Azure AD

    D. None of the above

16. As a Cybersecurity Architect, you are tasked with adopting a remote-access solution and need to deploy it in a secure manner from Microsoft Azure; which of the Azure solutions will you adopt?

    A. Azure Virtual Desktop

    B. VMware Horizon running in your private data center

    C. Citrix Xenapp and XenDesktop running in your private data center

    D. None of the above

17. As a Cybersecurity Architect, you are tasked with adopting a cost-effective remote-access solution. Which solution from the following will you adopt for your organization?

A. Azure Virtual Desktop

B. Azure Virtual Machine with end to end security

C. Azure Bastion solution

D. None of the above

18. What kind of security solution is required for the Azure Bastion solution?

A. Hardening in one place only

B. Hardening not required

C. Hardening performed by Microsoft

D. None of the above

19. You can connect to your virtual network securely from an individual client computer using which solution?

A. Point-to-site (P2S) VPN gateway

B. Site-to-site (S2S) VPN gateway

C. ExpressRoute

D. None of the above

20. You can connect to your virtual network securely from one site to another site using which solution?

A. Point-to-site (P2S) VPN gateway

B. Site-to-site (S2S) VPN gateway

C. ExpressRoute

D. None of the above

In this chapter, we will focus on understanding a strategy and the requirements for securing PaaS, IaaS, and SaaS services.

You will understand the shared responsibility model of Azure cloud services and which security tasks you and Microsoft handle as you consider and evaluate them. It depends on whether the workload is hosted as a software as a service (SaaS), platform as a service (PaaS), infrastructure as a service (IaaS), or on-premises.

Microsoft is responsible for securing the physical infrastructure and abstraction layer. Security obligations for the rest of the layers, including the business applications, fall on your organization. In IaaS environments, you can deploy a Network Packet Broker (NPB) to visualize cloud network security issues. The NPB sends traffic and data to the Network Performance Management (NPM) system and security tools. In addition, you can ensure network endpoint events are logged.

Microsoft may negotiate specific terms of security responsibility with users of SaaS services. SaaS services provide access to software applications and data through a browser. Security issues in SaaS products can be investigated using logging, auditing, access control, and encryption capabilities offered by Cloud Access Security Brokers (CASBs).

A PaaS platform allows organizations to build applications without managing hardware or back-end software overhead or complexity. Although Microsoft protects most of the environment in a PaaS model, your organization is still responsible for securing its applications. You should ensure that your PaaS application's APIs are protected internally and externally with CASP, logging, and alerting, IP restrictions, and an API gateway.

In this chapter, you will learn about establishing PaaS security baselines, establishing security baselines for IaaS services, establishing SaaS security baselines, establishing security requirements for IoT workloads, establishing data security requirements, defining the security requirements for web workloads, determining the security requirements for storage workloads, defining container security requirements, and providing a security specification for container orchestration.

Establish Security Baselines for SaaS, PaaS, and IaaS Services

Let's get started with shared responsibilities for Microsoft Azure. Organizations must consider and evaluate the privacy, security, and compliance of Azure cloud services before considering and evaluating Azure cloud services. The cloud provider (like Microsoft) must also manage security and compliance, enabling a safe computing solution. Furthermore, many organizations considering the Azure cloud mistakenly believe they no longer have any security or compliance responsibilities after moving to the cloud.

Cloud providers are generally responsible for ensuring the security of certain elements, including physical infrastructure and networks, but organizations should be aware of their obligations. Organizations must also understand their role in protecting the privacy and security of their data, even though Microsoft provides services to help protect data.

Microsoft understands that cloud service providers and organizations share responsibilities that differ depending on the cloud service model. The physical security of cloud computing is wholly the responsibility of Microsoft.

Organizations believe that the principal value of moving services to the cloud is that someone else manages the physical environment. The elements considered part of physical security include buildings or facilities, servers, and networking devices. As part of Microsoft's security policies and processes, the infrastructure is protected from unauthorized physical access, power is maintained in a highly available manner, and the service should failover to a new physical location in case of a disaster.

It is the organization's responsibility to ensure that the data and its classification are done correctly and that the solution complies with regulatory requirements. Cloud service providers and organizations share the remaining responsibilities.

Let's move forward with security baselines for SaaS. Software as a service connects to cloud-based apps via the Internet. The most common examples are email, calendar, and office tools (such as Microsoft Office 365).

Using SaaS, you can purchase a complete software solution on a pay-as-you-go basis. In most cases, your organization rents the use of an app, which users access via the Internet using a web browser. Infrastructure, application, middleware, and data are all stored in the service provider's data center. In addition to managing the hardware and software, your service provider will ensure the availability and security of your app and data with the appropriate service agreement. A SaaS app allows your organization to get up and running quickly with minimal up-front investment.

You may be able to control security options only at the application level when using SaaS solutions because the cloud vendor holds the infrastructure and platform layers. As well as assessing their reputation and track record, it would help if you looked at their security policies. In addition to the application and data security, you should evaluate whether they can provide network security.

With Microsoft Defender for Cloud, you can improve the security posture of Azure workloads by using the Secure Score. With Microsoft 365, you can also use the Microsoft Secure Score to improve your SaaS security posture. A Secure Score recommendation can help your organization protect itself from threats. With a centralized dashboard in the Microsoft 365 Defender portal, organizations can monitor their identities, apps, and devices' security and act. In addition, Microsoft 365 Defender helps organizations to do the following:

- Conduct an assessment of the organization's security posture.

- Provide discoverability, visibility, guidance, and control to improve their security posture.

- Establish key performance indicators by comparing them with benchmarks.

Office cloud policy allows you to enforce policy settings for Microsoft 365 Apps for enterprise on users' devices, even if they are not domain-joined or otherwise managed. Microsoft 365 Apps for enterprise policy settings roam to a device when a user signs in. Windows, macOS, iOS, and Android devices can use policy settings, but not all are available on all operating systems.

When creating policy configurations, you can review and apply policies that Microsoft recommends as a security baseline. If the policy is tagged as a security baseline, you can also filter your view to include only the policies that are tagged as such.

The content is grouped according to the security controls defined by the Azure Security Benchmark and the related guidance for Azure Cloud Services.

Azure Control for SaaS Services (also known as cloud services) focuses on areas such as network security, logging and monitoring, identity and access control, data protection, vulnerability management, inventory and asset management, secure configuration, malware defense, data recovery, incident response, penetration tests, and red team exercises.

What is penetration testing? A *penetration test* is a simulated cyberattack against your system, application, and data to check for exploitable vulnerabilities. In web app security, penetration testing is typically used to expand a web application firewall (WAF).

Penetration testing can concern the attempted breaching of any number of application systems (for example, application protocol interfaces [APIs], front-end/back-end servers) to discover vulnerabilities, such as unsanitized inputs, that are tolerant to code injection attacks.

Understandings by the penetration test can be utilized to fine-tune organization WAF security policies and patch witnessed vulnerabilities.

Table 7.1 provides a complete mapping between Azure Cloud Services and Azure Security Benchmark.

For references and more information, see the following:

```
github.com/MicrosoftDocs/SecurityBenchmarks/raw/master/
Azure%20Offer%20Security%20Baselines/1.1/
azure-cloud-services-security-baseline-v1.1.xlsx
```

TABLE 7.1   Azure Cloud Services and Azure Security Benchmark

Azure Control	Responsibility	Benchmark Recommendation
Network Security	Customer	Protect Azure resources within virtual networks.
Network Security	Customer	Monitor and log the configuration and traffic of virtual networks, subnets, and NICs.
Network Security	Customer	Protect critical web applications.
Network Security	Customer	Deny communications with known malicious IP addresses.
Network Security	Customer	Record network packets.

Azure Control	Responsibility	Benchmark Recommendation
Network Security	Customer	Deploy network-based intrusion detection/intrusion prevention systems (IDS/IPS).
Network Security	Customer	Manage traffic to web applications.
Network Security	Not applicable	Minimize complexity and administrative overhead of network security rules.
Network Security	Customer	Maintain standard security configurations for network devices.
Network Security	Customer	Document traffic configuration rules.
Network Security	Customer	Use automated tools to monitor network resource configurations and detect changes.
Logging and Monitoring	Shared	Use approved time synchronization sources.
Logging and Monitoring	Customer	Configure central security log management.
Logging and Monitoring	Customer	Enable audit logging for Azure resources.
Logging and Monitoring	Not applicable	Collect security logs from operating systems.
Logging and Monitoring	Customer	Configure security log storage retention.
Logging and Monitoring	Customer	Monitor and review logs.
Logging and Monitoring	Customer	Enable alerts for anomalous activities.
Logging and Monitoring	Customer	Centralize antimalware logging.
Logging and Monitoring	Not applicable	Enable DNS query logging.
Logging and Monitoring	Not applicable	Enable command-line audit logging.

TABLE 7.1   Azure Cloud Services and Azure Security Benchmark *(continued)*

Azure Control	Responsibility	Benchmark Recommendation
Identity and Access Control	Customer	Maintain an inventory of administrative accounts.
Identity and Access Control	Not applicable	Change default passwords where applicable.
Identity and Access Control	Customer	Use dedicated administrative accounts.
Identity and Access Control	Customer	Use single sign-on (SSO) with Azure Active Directory.
Identity and Access Control	Not applicable	Use multifactor authentication for all Azure Active Directory–based access.
Identity and Access Control	Customer	Use dedicated machines (privileged access workstations) for all administrative tasks.
Identity and Access Control	Not applicable	Log and alert on suspicious activities from administrative accounts.
Identity and Access Control	Not applicable	Manage Azure resources only from approved locations.
Identity and Access Control	Not applicable	Use Azure Active Directory.
Identity and Access Control	Not applicable	Regularly review and reconcile user access.
Identity and Access Control	Not applicable	Monitor attempts to access deactivated credentials.
Identity and Access Control	Not applicable	Alert on account login behavior deviation.
Identity and Access Control	Not applicable	Provide Microsoft with access to relevant customer data during support scenarios.
Data Protection	Customer	Maintain an inventory of sensitive Information.
Data Protection	Customer	Isolate systems storing or processing sensitive information.

Azure Control	Responsibility	Benchmark Recommendation
Data Protection	Shared	Monitor and block unauthorized transfer of sensitive information.
Data Protection	Shared	Encrypt all sensitive information in transit.
Data Protection	Shared	Use an active discovery tool to identify sensitive data.
Data Protection	Not applicable	Use Azure RBAC to manage access to resources.
Data Protection	Shared	Use host-based data loss prevention to enforce access control.
Data Protection	Customer	Encrypt sensitive information at rest.
Data Protection	Customer	Log and alert on changes to critical Azure resources.
Vulnerability Management	Microsoft	Run automated vulnerability scanning tools.
Vulnerability Management	Shared	Deploy an automated operating system patch management solution.
Vulnerability Management	Customer	Deploy an automated patch management solution for third-party software titles.
Vulnerability Management	Microsoft	Compare back-to-back vulnerability scans.
Vulnerability Management	Customer	Use a risk-rating process to prioritize the remediation of discovered vulnerabilities.
Inventory and Asset Management	Customer	Use automated asset discovery solution.
Inventory and Asset Management	Not applicable	Maintain asset metadata.
Inventory and Asset Management	Customer	Delete unauthorized Azure resources.
Inventory and Asset Management	Customer	Define and maintain an inventory of approved Azure resources.

TABLE 7.1   Azure Cloud Services and Azure Security Benchmark *(continued)*

Azure Control	Responsibility	Benchmark Recommendation
Inventory and Asset Management	Customer	Monitor for unapproved Azure resources.
Inventory and Asset Management	Customer	Monitor for unapproved software applications within compute resources.
Inventory and Asset Management	Customer	Remove unapproved Azure resources and software applications.
Inventory and Asset Management	Customer	Use only approved applications.
Inventory and Asset Management	Not applicable	Use only approved Azure services.
Inventory and Asset Management	Customer	Maintain an inventory of approved software titles.
Inventory and Asset Management	Not applicable	Limit users' ability to interact with Azure Resource Manager.
Inventory and Asset Management	Customer	Limit users' ability to execute scripts in compute resources.
Inventory and Asset Management	Customer	Physically or logically segregate high-risk applications.
Secure Configuration	Customer	Establish secure configurations for all Azure resources.
Secure Configuration	Not applicable	Establish secure operating system configurations.
Secure Configuration	Customer	Maintain secure Azure resource configurations.
Secure Configuration	Not applicable	Maintain secure operating system configurations.
Secure Configuration	Customer	Securely store configuration of Azure resources.
Secure Configuration	Not applicable	Securely store custom operating system images.

Azure Control	Responsibility	Benchmark Recommendation
Secure Configuration	Customer	Deploy configuration management tools for Azure resources.
Secure Configuration	Customer	Deploy configuration management tools for operating systems.
Secure Configuration	Customer	Implement automated configuration monitoring for Azure resources.
Secure Configuration	Customer	Implement automated configuration monitoring for operating systems.
Secure Configuration	Customer	Manage Azure secrets securely.
Secure Configuration	Not applicable	Manage identities securely and automatically.
Secure Configuration	Customer	Eliminate unintended credential exposure.
Malware Defense	Customer	Use centrally managed antimalware software.
Malware Defense	Not applicable	Pre-scan files to be uploaded to non-compute Azure resources.
Malware Defense	Not applicable	Ensure antimalware software and signatures are updated.
Data Recovery	Not applicable	Ensure regular automated backups.
Data Recovery	Not applicable	Perform complete system backups and back up any customer-managed keys.
Data Recovery	Not applicable	Validate all backups including customer-managed keys.
Data Recovery	Not applicable	Ensure protection of backups and customer-managed keys.
Incident Response	Customer	Create an incident response guide.
Incident Response	Customer	Create an incident scoring and prioritization procedure.
Incident Response	Customer	Test security response procedures.

TABLE 7.1 Azure Cloud Services and Azure Security Benchmark *(continued)*

Azure Control	Responsibility	Benchmark Recommendation
Incident Response	Customer	Provide security incident contact details and configure alert notifications for security incidents.
Incident Response	Customer	Incorporate security alerts into your incident response system.
Incident Response	Customer	Automate the response to security alerts.
Penetration Tests and Red Team Exercises	Shared	Conduct regular penetration testing of your Azure resources and ensure remediation of all critical security findings.

PaaS Security Baseline

PaaS is a comprehensive development and deployment atmosphere in the cloud, with resources that allow you to supply everything from straightforward cloud-based apps to refined, cloud-enabled enterprise applications. You buy the resources you need from a cloud service provider on a pay-as-you-go basis and access them over a secure Internet connection.

Comparing Azure PaaS with on-premises deployment, let's examine the advantages in terms of security.

Instead of using a physical computing resource, PaaS cloud platforms use a virtual version. An appealing aspect of PaaS is that it allows you to avoid the costs and complexity of purchasing and managing software licenses while building, testing, deploying, managing, and updating your web applications. Additionally, it offers a ready-to-use development environment for creating highly customized applications.

A key management strategy can be used to mitigate the risk of data governance and rights management, which are at the top of the stack. (Key management is covered in best practices.) Although key management is an additional responsibility, you will have areas in a PaaS deployment that do not need to be managed, so you will have more resources available to manage keys.

Various network-based technologies on the Azure platform provide solid DDoS protection. However, all network-based DDoS protection methods are limited on a link-by-link and data center-by-data center basis. By taking advantage of Azure's core cloud capabilities, you can quickly and automatically scale out to defend against large DDoS attacks to help avoid the impact of large attacks.

With PaaS deployments, you shift your overall approach to security. As a result, you no longer need to control everything yourself but will share responsibility with Microsoft. In addition, PaaS deployments differ significantly from traditional on-premises deployments in that they redefine what defines the primary security perimeter. Your network traditionally defined on-premises security as your primary security perimeter, and most on-premises security designs utilize the network as their primary security pivot. If you are deploying PaaS, you would be better served by considering identity as the primary security perimeter.

All supported PaaS services have security recommendations based on the Azure Security Benchmark. The following list shows services that are supported.

- Azure App Service
- Azure Automation account
- Azure Batch account
- Azure Blob Storage
- Azure Cache for Redis
- Azure Cloud Services
- Azure Cognitive Search
- Azure Container Registry
- Azure Cosmos DB
- Azure Data Lake Analytics
- Azure Data Lake Storage
- Azure Event Hubs namespace
- Azure Functions app
- Azure Key Vault
- Azure Kubernetes Service
- Azure Load Balancer
- Azure Logic Apps
- Azure SQL Database
- Azure SQL Managed Instance
- Azure Service Bus namespace
- Azure Service Fabric account
- Azure Storage accounts
- Azure Stream Analytics
- Azure Subscription
- Azure Virtual Network (including subnets, NICs, and network security groups)

Azure Security Benchmark security recommendations are provided in the recommendation's column as part of Defender for Cloud's free tier. Security alerts represent the alerts generated by each threat detection plan. Vulnerability assessments represent the services that are capable of assessing vulnerabilities.

Azure PaaS security baselines allow you to strengthen your security by providing better tools, tracking, and security features and an improved experience in securing your environment. They focus on cloud-centric control areas when creating security baselines. This baseline guides the control areas listed in the Azure Security Benchmark. It is consistent with well-known security benchmarks, such as those described by the Center for Internet Security (CIS).

The following information is included in each recommendation:

- **Azure ID:** This is the ID associated with the recommendation in Azure Security Benchmark.

- **Recommendation:** The recommendation follows the Azure ID and provides a high-level description of the control.

- **Guidance:** This section guides you on implementing the recommendation and includes links to guidance on how to do so. If Microsoft Defender supports the recommendation for Cloud, that information will also be included.

- **Responsibility:** It is possible for a customer to be responsible for implementing the control, for Microsoft to be responsible, or for responsibility to be shared.

- **Microsoft Defender for Cloud monitoring:** The extent to which the control is monitored by Microsoft Defender for Cloud, together with a link to any references.

All recommendations, including those not relevant to this specific service, are included in the baseline to give you a complete understanding of how the Azure Security Benchmark relates to each service. Controls may occasionally not be applicable for a variety of reasons; for example, IaaS/compute-centric controls (such as those relating to OS configuration management) may not be relevant to PaaS services.

You need to familiarize yourself with the PaaS service you want to protect and then use the appropriate baseline based on your knowledge of the service. The security baseline, for example, establishes security recommendations in the following areas for App Service:

- Network security
- Logging and monitoring
- Identity and access control
- Data protection
- Vulnerability management
- Inventory and asset management
- Secure configuration
- Data recovery
- Incident response

A significant benefit of Defender for Cloud's Inventory dashboard is the ability to identify your PaaS resources and verify open issues. You may create a filter by resource type to identify only the PaaS resources you want to assess.

Now, let's understand the Azure security baseline for App Service. Various security controls make up the Microsoft cloud security benchmark, including security controls that apply to App Services that prescribe how you can secure your cloud solutions on Azure.

Table 7.2 illustrates how the Microsoft App Service maps to the Microsoft cloud security benchmark (also known as the Azure security baseline).

For references and more information, see the following:

```
github.com/MicrosoftDocs/SecurityBenchmarks/tree/master/Azure%20
Offer%20Security%20Baselines/3.0/
app-service-azure-security-benchmark-v3-latest-security-baseline.xlsx
```

TABLE 7.2   App Service Mapping to the Microsoft Cloud Security Benchmark

Azure Control	Responsibility	Benchmark Recommendation
Network Security	Customer	Protect Azure resources within virtual networks.
Network Security	Customer	Monitor and log the configuration and traffic of virtual networks, subnets, and network interfaces.
Network Security	Customer	Protect critical web applications.
Network Security	Customer	Deny communications with known-malicious IP addresses.
Network Security	Customer	Record network packets.
Network Security	Not applicable	Deploy network-based intrusion detection/intrusion prevention systems (IDS/IPSs).
Network Security	Customer	Manage traffic to web applications.
Network Security	Customer	Minimize complexity and administrative overhead of network security rules.
Network Security	Customer	Maintain standard security configurations for network devices.
Network Security	Customer	Document traffic configuration rules.
Network Security	Customer	Use automated tools to monitor network resource configurations and detect changes.
Logging and Monitoring	Microsoft	Use approved time synchronization sources.
Logging and Monitoring	Customer	Configure central security log management.

TABLE 7.2 App Service Mapping to the Microsoft Cloud Security Benchmark *(continued)*

Azure Control	Responsibility	Benchmark Recommendation
Logging and Monitoring	Customer	Enable audit logging for Azure resources.
Logging and Monitoring	Not applicable	Collect security logs from operating systems.
Logging and Monitoring	Customer	Configure security log storage retention.
Logging and Monitoring	Customer	Monitor and review logs.
Logging and Monitoring	Customer	Enable alerts for anomalous activities.
Logging and Monitoring	Not applicable	Centralize antimalware logging.
Logging and Monitoring	Not applicable	Enable DNS query logging.
Logging and Monitoring	Not applicable	Enable command-line audit logging.
Identity and Access Control	Customer	Maintain an inventory of administrative accounts.
Identity and Access Control	Customer	Change default passwords where applicable.
Identity and Access Control	Customer	Use dedicated administrative accounts.
Identity and Access Control	Customer	Use Azure Active Directory SSO.
Identity and Access Control	Customer	Use multifactor authentication for all Azure Active Directory–based access.
Identity and Access Control	Customer	Use secure, Azure-managed workstations for administrative tasks.

Azure Control	Responsibility	Benchmark Recommendation
Identity and Access Control	Customer	Log and alert on suspicious activities from administrative accounts.
Identity and Access Control	Customer	Manage Azure resources from only approved locations.
Identity and Access Control	Customer	Use Azure Active Directory.
Identity and Access Control	Customer	Regularly review and reconcile user access.
Identity and Access Control	Customer	Monitor attempts to access deactivated credentials.
Identity and Access Control	Customer	Alert on account sign-in behavior deviation.
Identity and Access Control	Customer	Provide Microsoft with access to relevant customer data during support scenarios.
Data Protection	Customer	Maintain an inventory of sensitive Information.
Data Protection	Customer	Isolate systems storing or processing sensitive information.
Data Protection	Shared	Monitor and block unauthorized transfer of sensitive information.
Data Protection	Customer	Encrypt all sensitive information in transit.
Data Protection	Shared	Use an active discovery tool to identify sensitive data.
Data Protection	Customer	Use role-based access control to control access to resources.
Data Protection	Not applicable	Use host-based data loss prevention to enforce access control.
Data Protection	Customer	Encrypt sensitive information at rest.
Data Protection	Customer	Log and alert on changes to critical Azure resources.

TABLE 7.2 App Service Mapping to the Microsoft Cloud Security Benchmark *(continued)*

Azure Control	Responsibility	Benchmark Recommendation
Vulnerability Management	Customer	Run automated vulnerability scanning tools.
Vulnerability Management	Not applicable	Deploy an automated operating system patch management solution.
Vulnerability Management	Not applicable	Deploy an automated patch management solution for third-party software titles.
Vulnerability Management	Not applicable	Compare back-to-back vulnerability scans.
Vulnerability Management	Shared	Use a risk-rating process to prioritize the remediation of discovered vulnerabilities.
Inventory and Asset Management	Customer	Use an automated asset discovery solution.
Inventory and Asset Management	Customer	Maintain asset metadata.
Inventory and Asset Management	Customer	Delete unauthorized Azure resources.
Inventory and Asset Management	Customer	Define and maintain an inventory of approved Azure resources.
Inventory and Asset Management	Customer	Monitor for unapproved Azure resources.
Inventory and Asset Management	Customer	Monitor for unapproved software applications within compute resources.
Inventory and Asset Management	Customer	Remove unapproved Azure resources and software applications.
Inventory and Asset Management	Customer	Use only approved applications.
Inventory and Asset Management	Customer	Use only approved Azure services.

Azure Control	Responsibility	Benchmark Recommendation
Inventory and Asset Management	Customer	Maintain an inventory of approved software titles.
Inventory and Asset Management	Customer	Limit users' ability to interact with Azure Resource Manager.
Inventory and Asset Management	Customer	Limit users' ability to execute scripts within compute resources.
Inventory and Asset Management	Customer	Physically or logically segregate high-risk applications.
Secure Configuration	Customer	Establish secure configurations for all Azure resources.
Secure Configuration	Not applicable	Establish secure operating system configurations.
Secure Configuration	Customer	Maintain secure Azure resource configurations.
Secure Configuration	Not applicable	Maintain secure operating system configurations.
Secure Configuration	Customer	Securely store configuration of Azure resources.
Secure Configuration	Not applicable	Securely store custom operating system images.
Secure Configuration	Customer	Deploy configuration management tools for Azure resources.
Secure Configuration	Not applicable	Deploy configuration management tools for operating systems.
Secure Configuration	Customer	Implement automated configuration monitoring for Azure resources.
Secure Configuration	Not applicable	Implement automated configuration monitoring for operating systems.
Secure Configuration	Customer	Manage Azure secrets securely.
Secure Configuration	Customer	Manage identities securely and automatically.
Secure Configuration	Customer	Eliminate unintended credential exposure.

TABLE 7.2   App Service Mapping to the Microsoft Cloud Security Benchmark *(continued)*

Azure Control	Responsibility	Benchmark Recommendation
Malware Defense	Microsoft	Use centrally managed antimalware software.
Malware Defense	Microsoft	Pre-scan files to be uploaded to non-compute Azure resources.
Malware Defense	Microsoft	Ensure antimalware software and signatures are updated.
Data Recovery	Customer	Ensure regular automated backups.
Data Recovery	Customer	Perform complete system backups and back up any customer-managed keys.
Data Recovery	Customer	Validate all backups including customer-managed keys.
Data Recovery	Customer	Ensure protection of backups and customer-managed keys.
Incident Response	Customer	Create an incident response guide.
Incident Response	Customer	Create an incident scoring and prioritization procedure.
Incident Response	Customer	Provide security incident contact details and configure alert notifications for security incidents.
Incident Response	Customer	Incorporate security alerts into your incident response system.
Incident Response	Customer	Automate the response to security alerts.
Penetration Tests and Red Team Exercises	Shared	Conduct regular penetration testing of your Azure resources and ensure remediation of all critical security findings.
Incident Response	Customer	Test security response procedures.

For other PaaS services and Azure Security baselines, refer to the following GitHub page:

```
github.com/MicrosoftDocs/SecurityBenchmarks/tree/master/
Azure%20Offer%20Security%20Baselines/3.0
```

IaaS Security Baseline

Infrastructure as a service (IaaS) is a cloud computing service that provides computing, storage, and networking resources on-demand as a pay-per-use service.

Migrating your organization's infrastructure to an IaaS solution can help you reduce the management and maintenance of on-premises data centers, save cost on hardware, and gain a greater understanding of your business. By utilizing IaaS solutions, you can quickly scale your IT resources up and down, provision new applications rapidly, and increase the reliability of your underlying infrastructure.

Each resource is provided as a separate service component, and you are only charged for the resource as long as you require it. IaaS avoids the expense and complexity of purchasing and managing physical servers and data center infrastructure. Azure is one of the cloud computing service providers that manage the infrastructure.

The primary workload for organizations that use cloud computing is Azure virtual machines (VMs) in IaaS scenarios. Hybrid scenarios in which organizations want to migrate their workloads to the cloud emphasize this fact gradually. In such methods, follow general security considerations for IaaS, and ensure all VMs follow security best practices.

You can improve the security of Linux VMs on Azure by integrating Azure AD authentication with your VMs so that only authorized users can create and access VMs. As a result of Azure AD authentication, you can centrally control and enforce policies that enable or deny access to Linux VMs.

IaaS Virtual Machines Security Baseline

The following security guidelines apply to IaaS VMs running on Windows or Linux. Although each operating system will have its own set of security settings, some general guidelines should be followed regardless of which operating system is being used.

- **Protect your virtual machines from viruses and malware:** The Microsoft Antimalware for Azure solution can be used by Windows users using Windows as a single agent for applications and tenant environments. It runs in the background without human intervention and is designed to run automatically. Depending on your application workload, you can deploy security by default or configure antimalware monitoring in an advanced manner. Microsoft Defender for Endpoint (MDE) can be used on Linux.

- **Encrypt your sensitive data:** Azure Disk Encryption is available for encrypting the disks of your virtual machines running Windows or Linux. A portion of Azure Disk Encryption's volume encryption service is provided by the industry-standard BitLocker feature of Windows and the dm-crypt feature of Linux. Integrating the solution with Azure Key Vault allows you to manage and control the disk encryption keys and secrets in your key vault subscription. In Azure Storage, all data stored on virtual machine disks is encrypted at rest.

- **Secure network traffic:** Azure virtual networks are logical constructs built on top of the physical Azure network fabric. Each logical Azure virtual network is separated from the other, and Azure virtual networks are isolated. By isolating your deployments, Microsoft Azure customers will not have access to the network traffic.

- **Identify and detect threats:** For Windows and Linux, you can use Microsoft Defender for Servers, which offers threat detection and integrates with Microsoft Deployment Engine (MDE).

Now, let's understand about the Azure security baseline for Windows virtual machines. You can use the Azure Security Benchmark to learn how to implement security controls for Windows virtual machines based on the security controls defined in the Azure Security Benchmark.

Azure Policy definitions can be found in the Regulatory Compliance section of the Microsoft Defender for Cloud dashboard. Microsoft Defender for Cloud allows you to monitor this security baseline and its recommendations.

Table 7.3 illustrates how the Microsoft Windows Virtual Machine completely maps to the Microsoft cloud security benchmark (also known as the Azure security baseline).

TABLE 7.3   Microsoft Windows Virtual Machine Mapping

Azure Control	Responsibility	Benchmark Recommendation
Network Security	Customer	Protect Azure resources within virtual networks.
Network Security	Customer	Monitor and log the configuration and traffic of virtual networks, subnets, and network interfaces.
Network Security	Customer	Protect critical web applications.
Network Security	Customer	Deny communications with known-malicious IP addresses.
Network Security	Customer	Record network packets.
Network Security	Customer	Deploy network-based intrusion detection/intrusion prevention systems (IDS/IPS).
Network Security	Customer	Manage traffic to web applications.
Network Security	Customer	Minimize complexity and administrative overhead of network security rules.
Network Security	Customer	Maintain standard security configurations for network devices.
Network Security	Customer	Document traffic configuration rules.
Network Security	Customer	Use automated tools to monitor network resource configurations and detect changes.
Logging and Monitoring	Microsoft	Use approved time synchronization sources.
Logging and Monitoring	Customer	Configure central security log management.

Azure Control	Responsibility	Benchmark Recommendation
Logging and Monitoring	Customer	Enable audit logging for Azure resources.
Logging and Monitoring	Customer	Collect security logs from operating systems.
Logging and Monitoring	Customer	Configure security log storage retention.
Logging and Monitoring	Customer	Monitor and review logs.
Logging and Monitoring	Customer	Enable alerts for anomalous activities.
Logging and Monitoring	Customer	Centralize antimalware logging.
Logging and Monitoring	Customer	Enable DNS query logging.
Logging and Monitoring	Customer	Enable command-line audit logging.
Identity and Access Control	Customer	Maintain an inventory of administrative accounts.
Identity and Access Control	Customer	Change default passwords where applicable.
Identity and Access Control	Customer	Use dedicated administrative accounts.
Identity and Access Control	Customer	Use Azure Active Directory single sign-on (SSO).
Identity and Access Control	Customer	Use multifactor authentication for all Azure Active Directory-based access.
Identity and Access Control	Customer	Use secure, Azure-managed workstations for administrative tasks.
Identity and Access Control	Customer	Log and alert on suspicious activities from administrative accounts.

TABLE 7.3   Microsoft Windows Virtual Machine Mapping *(continued)*

Azure Control	Responsibility	Benchmark Recommendation
Identity and Access Control	Customer	Manage Azure resources from only approved locations.
Identity and Access Control	Customer	Use Azure Active Directory.
Identity and Access Control	Customer	Regularly review and reconcile user access.
Identity and Access Control	Customer	Monitor attempts to access deactivated credentials.
Identity and Access Control	Customer	Alert on account sign-in behavior deviation.
Identity and Access Control	Customer	Provide Microsoft with access to relevant customer data during support scenarios.
Data Protection	Customer	Maintain an inventory of sensitive Information.
Data Protection	Customer	Isolate systems storing or processing sensitive information.
Data Protection	Customer	Monitor and block unauthorized transfer of sensitive information.
Data Protection	Shared	Encrypt all sensitive information in transit.
Data Protection	Customer	Use an active discovery tool to identify sensitive data.
Data Protection	Customer	Use role-based access control to control access to resources.
Data Protection	Customer	Use host-based data loss prevention to enforce access control.
Data Protection	Shared	Encrypt sensitive information at rest.
Data Protection	Customer	Log and alert on changes to critical Azure resources.
Vulnerability Management	Customer	Run automated vulnerability scanning tools.

Azure Control	Responsibility	Benchmark Recommendation
Vulnerability Management	Customer	Deploy an automated operating system patch management solution.
Vulnerability Management	Customer	Deploy an automated patch management solution for third-party software titles.
Vulnerability Management	Customer	Compare back-to-back vulnerability scans.
Vulnerability Management	Customer	Use a risk-rating process to prioritize the remediation of discovered vulnerabilities.
Inventory and Asset Management	Customer	Use automated asset discovery solution.
Inventory and Asset Management	Customer	Maintain asset metadata.
Inventory and Asset Management	Customer	Delete unauthorized Azure resources.
Inventory and Asset Management	Customer	Define and maintain an inventory of approved Azure resources.
Inventory and Asset Management	Customer	Monitor for unapproved Azure resources.
Inventory and Asset Management	Customer	Monitor for unapproved software applications within compute resources.
Inventory and Asset Management	Customer	Remove unapproved Azure resources and software applications.
Inventory and Asset Management	Customer	Use only approved applications.
Inventory and Asset Management	Customer	Use only approved Azure services.
Inventory and Asset Management	Customer	Limit users' ability to interact with Azure Resource Manager.
Inventory and Asset Management	Customer	Limit users' ability to execute scripts within compute resources.

TABLE 7.3 Microsoft Windows Virtual Machine Mapping *(continued)*

Azure Control	Responsibility	Benchmark Recommendation
Inventory and Asset Management	Customer	Physically or logically segregate high-risk applications.
Secure Configuration	Customer	Establish secure configurations for all Azure resources.
Secure Configuration	Customer	Establish secure operating system configurations.
Secure Configuration	Customer	Maintain secure Azure resource configurations.
Secure Configuration	Customer	Maintain secure operating system configurations.
Secure Configuration	Customer	Securely store configuration of Azure resources.
Secure Configuration	Customer	Securely store custom operating system images.
Secure Configuration	Customer	Deploy configuration management tools for Azure resources.
Secure Configuration	Customer	Deploy configuration management tools for operating systems.
Secure Configuration	Customer	Implement automated configuration monitoring for Azure resources.
Secure Configuration	Customer	Implement automated configuration monitoring for operating systems.
Secure Configuration	Customer	Manage Azure secrets securely.
Secure Configuration	Customer	Manage identities securely and automatically.
Secure Configuration	Customer	Eliminate unintended credential exposure.
Malware Defense	Customer	Use centrally managed antimalware software.
Malware Defense	Not applicable	Pre-scan files to be uploaded to non-compute Azure resources.
Malware Defense	Customer	Ensure antimalware software and signatures are updated.

Azure Control	Responsibility	Benchmark Recommendation
Data Recovery	Customer	Ensure regular automated backups.
Data Recovery	Customer	Perform complete system backups and back up any customer-managed keys.
Data Recovery	Customer	Validate all backups including customer-managed keys.
Data Recovery	Customer	Ensure protection of backups and customer-managed keys.
Incident Response	Customer	Create an incident response guide.
Incident Response	Customer	Create an incident scoring and prioritization procedure.
Incident Response	Customer	Test security response procedures.
Incident Response	Customer	Provide security incident contact details and configure alert notifications for security incidents.
Incident Response	Customer	Incorporate security alerts into your incident response system.
Incident Response	Customer	Automate the response to security alerts.
Penetration Tests and Red Team Exercises	Shared	Conduct regular penetration testing of your Azure resources and ensure remediation of all critical security findings.
Inventory and Asset Management	Customer	Maintain an inventory of approved software titles.

For references and more information, visit the following page:

```
github.com/MicrosoftDocs/SecurityBenchmarks/blob/master/
Azure%20Offer%20Security%20Baselines/1.1/windows-virtual-
machines-security-baseline-v1.1.xlsx
```

Visit the following page for how Linux Virtual Machine completely maps to the Microsoft cloud security benchmark (also known as Azure security baseline):

```
github.com/MicrosoftDocs/SecurityBenchmarks/raw/master/
Azure%20Offer%20Security%20Baselines/1.1/linux-virtual-
machines-security-baseline-v1.1.xlsx.
```

To help you strengthen organization security through improved tooling, tracking, and security features, Azure security baselines provide standardized documents that describe the available security capabilities and the optimal security configurations for each of its product offerings.

Currently, service baselines are available only for Microsoft Azure.

Cloud-centric control areas are the focus of Azure security baselines. These controls are based on well-known industry standards, such as CIS or NIST, which are well-established. Our baselines guide the control areas in the Microsoft cloud security benchmark v1.

Establish Security Requirements for IoT Workloads

In the Internet of Things (IoT), billions of connected devices use operational technology (OT) networks to communicate. The IoT/OT network and devices are often constructed without security in mind and, therefore, cannot be protected by traditional security systems. The risk to IoT devices and OT networks increases with each new wave of innovation.

Using the IoT, organizations can better understand the complex relationships between people, systems, and data. But securing a variety of device-based solutions with little or no direct interaction with each other is also a challenge.

The design and architecture of an IoT solution should consider potential threats and add defense in depth along the way. Understanding how an attacker might compromise a system is essential to ensure appropriate mitigations are in place, so it's crucial to design the solution with security in mind from the start.

A rigorous security-in-depth approach is required for the successful security of an IoT infrastructure. The strategy involves the following:

- Securing data in the cloud
- Protecting data integrity while traveling over the public Internet
- Securely provisioning devices

Each layer increases the overall level of security assurance.

To develop and implement this security-in-depth strategy, various stakeholders involved with manufacturing, developing, and deploying IoT infrastructure and devices will need to be actively engaged.

Zero Trust security begins with non-IoT-specific requirements: securing identities and devices and limiting their access is the first step. In addition to explicitly verifying users, seeing what devices users are bringing onto the network, and using real-time risk detections, dynamic access decisions can be made.

Using this method, users are limited in their ability to gain unauthorized access to IoT services and data on-premises or in the cloud, preventing both mass information disclosure (such as leaked factory production data) and potential elevation of privilege for command and control (for instance, halting the factory's production line).

Multiple personas are involved in the life cycle of an IoT solution, such as IoT device builders, IoT application developers, and IoT solution operators.

Table 7.4 provides a high-level outline of these roles and security requirements.

TABLE 7.4   Roles and Security Requirements

Role	Role Description	Security Requirements
IoT hardware manufacturer/ integrator	Often, these players are either manufacturers of IoT hardware, integrators who assemble hardware from various manufacturers, or suppliers who provide hardware for IoT deployments that are manufactured or integrated by other suppliers.	Determine the minimum requirements for hardware. Protect hardware from tampering. Ensure the security of upgrades.
IoT solution developer	Solution developers are typically responsible for developing IoT solutions. These developers may be part of an in-house team or work for a system integrator (SI) specializing in this field. In addition to developing various components of the IoT solution from scratch, the developer can integrate various off-the-shelf or open-source components into the IoT solution.	Develop software in a secure manner. Choose open-source software carefully. Ensure that security flows are avoided by integrating.
IoT solution deployer	To deploy an IoT solution in the field, hardware needs to be deployed, devices need to be connected, and solutions must be deployed on hardware or in the cloud.	Ensure the secure deployment of hardware. Ensure the safety of authentication keys.
IoT solution operator	Operating, monitoring, upgrading, and maintaining the IoT solution for the long term after deployment is necessary. Several in-house teams can perform these tasks, including information technology specialists, hardware operations and maintenance teams, and domain specialists who monitor the correct behavior of the IoT infrastructure as a whole.	Maintain an up-to-date system. Ensure that malicious activities are prevented. Regularly conduct audits. Credential protection in the cloud.

A framework for securing digital access to connected special-purpose devices requires consideration of a significant number of interactions, surface areas, and interaction patterns that occur on these devices. In this context, "digital access" distinguishes operations involving direct device interaction from physical access control. For example, place the device in a room with a lock on its door. Physical access cannot be denied using software or hardware, but measures can be taken to prevent interference with the system caused by physical access.

Look at both "device control" and "device data" as you examine the interaction patterns. Any information provided to a device by any party to change or influence its behavior in relation to its state or its environment can be classified as a *device control*. The term *device data* describes any information a device transmits to any other party regarding its state and the observed state of its environment.

During the threat modeling exercise, it is recommended that a typical IoT architecture be divided into several components/zones to optimize security best practices. These components/zones are as follows:

- Device
- Field gateway
- Cloud gateways
- Services

The *device and field gateway zones* are the primary physical space around the device and gateway where physical and peer-to-peer digital access is achievable. Many industrial companies use the Purdue model included in the ISA 95 standard to ensure their process control networks protect both the limited bandwidth of the network and the ability to offer real-time deterministic behavior. In recent years, with cybersecurity events being ascended from internal and external parties, cybersecurity teams have looked at the Purdue model as an extra layer of the defense-in-depth methodology.

The *cloud gateway and services zones* are any software component or module running in the cloud that is interfacing with devices and gateways for data collection and analysis and command and control.

It has been found that zones provide a broad means of segmenting a solution; each zone often has its own needs for data, authentication, and authorization. In addition to isolating damage, zones can also limit the impact of low-trust zones on higher-trust zones. Trust boundaries separate each zone, representing transitions from one source of information to another. During this process, the data/information may be susceptible to spoofing, tampering, repudiation, information disclosure, denial of service, and elevation of privilege (STRIDE).

IoT workloads require an ongoing security assessment to improve the overall security posture, as any other cloud workload does. Additionally, threat detection is necessary to understand current attack vectors and strategies for responding to them. Adopting a solution that provides security posture management and threat detection is critical to IoT security requirements.

Microsoft Defender for IoT offers a unified security solution that enables users to identify and manage IoT devices, vulnerabilities, and threats. Figure 7.1 depicts the integrated view.

FIGURE 7.1   Microsoft Defender for IoT

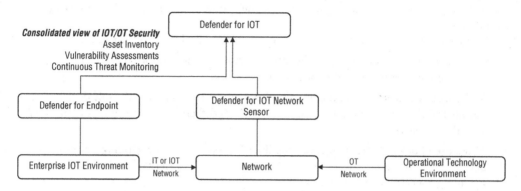

The Defender for IoT system offers connectivity with both cloud and on-premises elements and is designed to scale in large and geographically dispersed environments. The Defender for IoT system includes the following components:

- Azure Portal, which allows you to manage and integrate your cloud, such as Microsoft Sentinel, with other Microsoft services.

- A network sensor can be deployed in a virtual machine or as a physical appliance. An OT sensor can be configured to be cloud-connected or fully on-premises.

- A critical component is the availability of a cloud-connected or a local, air-gapped management console on-premises.

- The presence of an embedded security agent is optional.

Defender for IoT will surface security recommendations in the Defender for Cloud dashboard, as shown in Figure 7.2.

FIGURE 7.2   Security best practices

As part of your security IoT solution, it is also necessary to integrate the threat detection information generated by the system with your SIEM system. In addition to bridging the gap across IT and OT security problems, Microsoft Sentinel and Microsoft Defender for IoT provide SOC teams with out-of-the-box abilities to analyze, detect, and respond to OT threats efficiently and effectively. By integrating Microsoft Defender for IoT and Microsoft Sentinel, organizations can quickly detect multistage attacks that frequently cross IT and OT boundaries.

The following are the key best practices recommended by Microsoft for Azure IoT:

- **Keep up-to-date:** Ensure you use the latest versions of the supported platforms, programming languages, protocols, and frameworks.

- **Make sure you keep your authentication keys safe:** To prevent a malicious device from masquerading as registered, keep the device IDs and their authentication keys physically safe after deployment.

- **Make use of device SDKs whenever possible:** To assist you in developing a robust and secure device application, device SDKs implement a variety of security features, including encryption and authentication.

- **Hub access control should be defined:** Based on the functionality of each component, determine how much access each member has to the IoT Hub. Four permissions can be granted: Registry Read, RegistryReadWrite, ServiceConnect, and DeviceConnect. A default shared access policy can also define permissions based on a component's role within your IoT Hub.

- **Back-end access control should be defined:** In addition to the IoT Hub, Azure Cosmos DB, Stream Analytics, App Service, Logic Apps, and Blob storage can consume the data ingested by your IoT Hub solution.

- **Secure device authentication:** You will ensure secure communication between your IoT Hub and your devices by using security tokens based on the protocol you choose (MQTT, AMQP, or HTTPS).

- **Secure device communication:** Since IoT Hub supports versions 1.2 and 1.0 of Transport Layer Security (TLS), it is recommended to use version 1.2.

- **Secure service communication:** Through IoT Hub, endpoints can connect to services such as Azure Storage and Event Hubs via the TLS protocol, so no endpoints are exposed through an unencrypted channel. Once this data reaches these back-end services for storage or analysis, ensure they use appropriate encryption and security methods, and protect sensitive information there.

- **Make sure your devices are protected from unauthorized access:** Build mechanisms to prevent or detect physical tampering with your devices. Keep hardware ports at a minimum to avoid unwanted access.

- **Build secure hardware:** Secure devices and infrastructure by incorporating encryption or a Trusted Platform Module (TPM) security feature. Install antivirus and antimalware software if space permits, and ensure that the operating system and drivers are up-to-date.

- **Monitor unauthorized access to your devices:** Monitor any security breaches or physical tampering of the device or its ports using the logging features of your device operating system.

- **Monitor your IoT solution from the cloud:** Azure Monitor metrics provide an overview of your IoT Hub solution's health.
- **Set up diagnostics:** To get visibility into the performance of your solution, log events in your solution and send them to Azure Monitor.

The acronym STRIDE stands for spoofing identity, tampering with data, repudiation threats, information disclosure, denial of service, and elevation of privileges. In the late 1990s, Loren Kohnfelder and Praerit Garg developed STRIDE at Microsoft.

An app or system can be checked for threats during design using the STRIDE threat model. Using a proactive approach, the first step identifies potential threats, and a system's design forms the basis for spotting threats. To close gaps, the next step is to identify inherent risks in how the system has been implemented.

Establish Security Requirements for Data Workloads, Including SQL Server, Azure SQL, Azure Synapse, and Azure Cosmos DB

Microsoft recommends protecting your data on-premises and in the cloud from unauthorized and unintentional access. Unintentional access occurs when a user gains access to data that they shouldn't be able to access based on their position. In the case of unauthorized access, a malicious insider or external attacker intentionally attempts to access data, resulting in data leakage, data destruction, or data security and privacy violations. In addition to malicious insiders, superficial attackers can erase, modify, exfiltrate, and encrypt your most sensitive data, making you less secure against ransomware attacks.

Identifying your data, protecting it, preventing its destruction or exfiltration, and ensuring that only users with a business purpose have access to it are necessary for both attacks. Protecting your data is essential as part of Zero Trust's assume-breach principle. Despite your organization's protections for user accounts and devices, you should anticipate that an attacker may find their way in and begin exploring your environment, seeking out valuable company information.

Understanding your data landscape and identifying important information across your cloud and on-premises environment is the first step in defining the security requirements for data workloads. To achieve a better understanding of your data, you can take the steps shown in Table 7.5.

TABLE 7.5 Steps to Identify Data

Step	Owner
1. Differentiate data classification levels.	Data Security Architect
2. Differentiate built-in and custom sensitive information types.	Data Security Architect
3. Differentiate the use of pre-trained and custom trainable classifiers.	Data Security Architect
4. Discover and differentiate sensitive data.	Data Security Architect and/or Data Security Engineer

You can establish essential requirements once you have a clear understanding of your data, including the following:

- Protect sensitive data throughout its life cycle by applying sensitivity labels associated with protection actions such as encryption, access restrictions, visual markings, and so on.

- Monitor, prevent, and remediate risky activities with sensitive data in the cloud, on-premises environments, and endpoints by applying consistent data loss prevention policies.

- To meet business and productivity requirements, use least privilege access: restrict access to data to only those who have the right to access it and what they may do with it.

Security Posture Management for Data

Similarly, to other cloud workloads, data workloads require a continuous security assessment to improve their overall security posture. You can use Azure Microsoft Purview to manage and govern your on-premises, multi-cloud, and SaaS data across multiple clouds. Provide data curators with a comprehensive, up-to-date view of your data landscape by automating data discovery, classifying sensitive data, and tracking data lineage from beginning to end. Data consumers should be able to find valuable, trustworthy data with the assistance of data providers. Figure 7.3 depicts security poster management for data.

With the integration of Microsoft Defender for Cloud with Azure Purview, you can access a vital layer of metadata derived from Azure Purview and use that information to create alerts and recommendations with information about potentially sensitive data. As a result of this knowledge, security professionals can focus their attention on threats to sensitive data and solve the triage challenge. Figure 7.4 shows an example of a SQL database status in Defender for Cloud with data enrichment provided by Azure Purview in the lower-left corner.

FIGURE 7.3 Security posture management for data

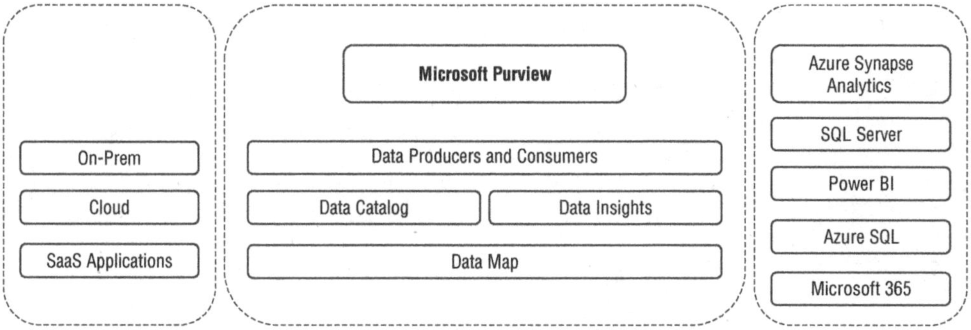

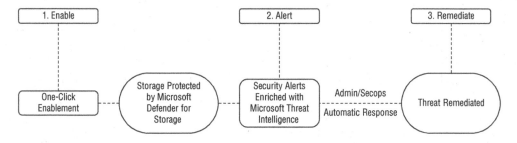

FIGURE 7.4 Microsoft Defender for Azure SQL database servers

Databases

Among the data workloads are databases, and Microsoft Defender for SQL can be utilized to manage the security posture for databases. Microsoft Defender for Cloud supports
Azure SQL Database, Azure SQL Managed Instances, and Azure Synapse Analytics. As part
of this functionality, potential database vulnerabilities can be identified and mitigated, and
abnormal activities can be detected that could indicate a database threat. Defender for Cloud
provides a single access point for enabling and managing these capabilities. Figure 7.5 shows
security recommendations for SQL databases.

By providing advanced threat protection, you continuously monitor your SQL servers for
threats such as SQL injections, brute-force attacks, and privilege abuse. As part of this service, Microsoft Defender for Cloud alerts you to suspicious activity, offers guidance on mitigating the threats, and allows you to continue your investigation using Microsoft Sentinel.

The Azure Cosmos DB cloud-native database is also necessary in addition to SQL. Using
Microsoft Threat Intelligence, Microsoft Defender for Azure Cosmos DB detects SQL injections, known bad actors, suspicious access patterns, and the possibility that compromised
individuals or malicious insiders may exploit your database through compromised identities.
Defender for Azure Cosmos DB utilizes advanced threat detection capabilities and Microsoft Threat Intelligence data to provide contextual security alerts. As part of those alerts,
steps are also included that can be taken to mitigate the detected threats and prevent future
attacks.

FIGURE 7.5 Security recommendations for SQL databases

Azure offers unique advantages derived from global security intelligence, sophisticated customer-facing controls, and a hardened, secure infra-structure that integrates security into every aspect.

For Azure data security and encryption best practices, recommendations focus on these states of data when determining how to protect your data in the cloud:

- Encryption controls are built into services from virtual machines to storage and SQL databases.
- Using industry-standard encryption protocols, data can be protected as it moves between clouds and customers.
- Cloud applications and services can securely store cryptographic keys, passwords, connection strings, and certificates in Azure Key Vault.
- Azure Information Protection will categorize, label, and protect your sensitive data.

Define the Security Requirements for Web Workloads

The security requirements for your web workloads must be considered when evaluating Azure App Service. Azure App Service is a web application, REST API, and mobile back-end service based on HTTP. Both Windows and Linux-based environments are compatible with these applications.

As part of the Azure App Service platform, you will have access to Azure VMs, storage, network connections, web frameworks, management, and integration functionality. Azure App Service has the following security requirements:

- **Ensure that you secure your apps with HTTPS:** It is already possible to access your app through HTTPS once it has been created (*app_name*.azurewebsites.net). For clients to make secure HTTPS connections to your custom domain, you should configure the custom domain with a TLS/SSL certificate.

- **Disable insecure protocols:** The App Service provides a one-click configuration to enforce HTTPS, which means unencrypted (HTTP) traffic is turned away before it ever reaches your application code.

- **Create static IP restrictions:** Default settings allow your App Service application to accept requests from any IP address on the Internet, but you can restrict this access to a subset of IP addresses. For example, App Service on Windows allows you to define a list of IP addresses permitted to access your application.

- **Enable client authentication and authorization:** The Azure App Service provides a turn-key authentication and authorization service for clients and users. The user and client app can sign in with little or no application code. You may use App Service to handle the authentication and authorization process or implement your own solution.

- **Don't store application secrets:** There is a commonly accepted method for accessing application secrets, such as database credentials, API tokens, and private keys, by referencing them as environment variables.

- **Implement network isolation:** Isolated tiers provide complete network isolation by deploying your applications within a dedicated App Service environment hosted in your Azure Virtual Network instance.

Security Posture Management for App Service

The overall security posture of web workloads needs to be continually assessed, just as it does for any cloud workload. Defender for App Service utilizes the cloud scale to identify attacks targeting applications running over App Service. Attackers probe web application weaknesses to find and exploit them—requests to applications running in Azure pass through several gateways before they are routed to specific environments. After collecting data, exploits and attackers can be identified, and new patterns can be learned.

This Defender plan offers the following services when you enable Microsoft Defender for App Service:

- Defender for App Service assesses the resources covered by your App Service plan and generates security recommendations based on its findings. Use the detailed instructions in these recommendations to harden your App Service resources.

- Defender for App Service detects a multitude of threats to your App Service resources by monitoring the following:

  - The VM instance in which your App Service is running and its management interface

  - The requests and responses sent to and from your App Service apps

  - The underlying sandboxes and VMs

  - App Service internal logs—available thanks to the visibility that Azure has as a cloud provider

- In Defense for App Service, your App Service plan's resources are assessed for security vulnerabilities, and security recommendations are generated based on the assessment results. Use the detailed instructions in the recommendations to harden your App Service plan's resources.

Because of Defender's cloud-native nature, it can identify attack methods that apply to multiple targets. For example, a single host might not be able to distinguish a distributed attack from small subsets of IP addresses crawling various hosts.

It may be necessary to include the following requirements in a cloud-native policy for network and web traffic controls:

- Cloud-native policies might not allow hybrid connections to on-premises resources. A robust enterprise security policy sample would be a better reference should a hybrid connection prove necessary.

- Azure virtual networks and network security groups allow users to establish secure connections.

- By blocking or not enabling direct access to a virtual machine over SSH/RDP, the Windows Azure Firewall protects hosts against malicious network traffic.

- Services such as Azure Application Gateway, Web Application Firewall (WAF), and Azure DDoS Protection safeguard applications and ensure virtual machine availability.

Determine the Security Requirements for Storage Workloads

Azure Storage accounts are ideal for workloads that require fast and consistent response times or involve many input-output operations (IOPs). Storage accounts contain all your Azure Storage data objects, such as the following:

- Blobs
- File shares
- Queues
- Tables
- Disks

Optimize your Azure Storage account's security by following these recommendations:

- Enable soft deletion for blobs.
- To authorize access to blob data, use Azure AD.
- Consider the principle of least privilege when assigning permissions to an Azure AD security principal using Azure RBAC.
- To store business-critical data, use blob versioning or immutable blobs.
- Storage accounts should be restricted from accessing the Internet by default.
- Limit access to your storage account by configuring firewall rules.
- Network access should be limited to specific networks.
- Access the storage account only with trusted Microsoft services.
- Make sure all your storage accounts have the Secure Transfer required option enabled.
- SAS tokens should be used only with HTTPS connections.
- Avoid and prevent storage accounts with Shared Key authorization.
- Make sure you regenerate your account keys regularly.
- If you issue SAS to clients, create a revocation plan.

Security Posture Management for Storage

To improve the overall security posture of web workloads, they need to undergo an ongoing security assessment, just like any other cloud workload. Azure Defender for Storage detects distinctive and potentially destructive attempts to access and exploit your storage account using Azure-native security intelligence. Security alerts are provided contextually based on Microsoft Threat Intelligence data and advanced threat detection capabilities. As part of those alerts, steps are also outlined for mitigating the threats and preventing future attacks.

Defender for Storage can be enabled at the subscription (recommended) or resource (optional) level. The Azure Blob Storage and Azure Files services generate telemetry streams that Defender continuously analyzes for storage. Security alerts are generated when potentially malicious activities are detected. As well as the details of the suspicious activity and the appropriate investigation steps, remediation actions, and security recommendations, Microsoft Defender for Cloud displays these alerts in its alert pane. Figure 7.6 illustrates Defender for Storage's two significant actions.

FIGURE 7.6   Defender for Storage two-action view

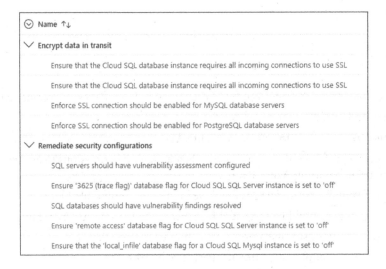

Using the dashboard of Defender for Cloud, enable Defender for Cloud with a single click. As soon as Defender for Cloud is enabled, it will monitor the storage account and generate security recommendations. If it detects suspicious activity, Defender for Cloud will alert users. Defender for Cloud dashboards or Microsoft Sentinel dashboards can facilitate the alert.

It may be necessary to include the following requirements in a cloud-native policy for network and web traffic controls:

- Cloud-native policies might not allow hybrid connections to on-premises resources. A robust enterprise security policy sample would be a better reference should a hybrid connection prove necessary.

- Azure virtual networks and network security groups allow users to establish secure connections.

- By blocking or not enabling direct access to a virtual machine over SSH/RDP, the Windows Azure Firewall protects hosts against malicious network traffic.
- Services such as Azure Application Gateway, Web Application Firewall (WAF), and Azure DDoS Protection safeguard applications and ensure virtual machine availability.

Define Container Security Requirements

Using a container, an application can run on a host operating system in an isolated, lightweight silo. In a container, only apps and some lightweight APIs and services of the operating system that run in user mode are stored on top of the kernel (which can be viewed as the buried plumbing of the operating system). Even though containers share the kernel of their hosts, they do not have full access. In some cases, the container receives a virtualized view of the system instead of an isolated view. In the example of a virtualized file system and registry, a container can access them, but the changes affect only the container and are discarded after it stops. A container can mount persistent storage (such as Azure Disks or Azure Files) to store data.

Images are containers built from images stored in repositories. Public repositories, such as Docker Hub, can be joined with private repositories, such as Docker Trusted Registry, which can be hosted either on-premises or in a virtual private cloud. Additionally, Azure Container Registry operates as a private container registry based in the cloud.

Publicly available container images do not guarantee security, and container images have multiple software layers that may have vulnerabilities. Images should be stored and retrieved from a private registry, such as Azure Container Registry or Docker Trusted Registry, to reduce the threat of attacks. Additionally, Azure Container Registry provides basic authentication flows based on service principals through Azure Active Directory. In addition to read-only (pull) and write-only (push), this authentication allows for role-based access.

It is important to understand how deep threat detection is provided by the different solutions when scanning container images in a private registry and identifying potential vulnerabilities. In Azure Container Registry, all Linux images pushed to the registry are automatically scanned by Microsoft Defender for Cloud, for example. An integrated Qualys scanner detects, categorizes, and provides remediation guidance for image vulnerabilities with Microsoft Defender for Cloud.

As containers can be distributed across various clusters and regions in Azure, you must secure credentials such as passwords or tokens for logins and API access. Ensure that only privileged users can access them in transit and at rest. Ensure all credential secrets are inventoried; developers must use container platform-specific tools for managing secrets. A reliable solution should include encrypted databases, TLS encryption for encrypted data in transit, and least privilege access control. For containerized applications, Azure Key Vault protects encryption keys and secrets (such as certificates, connection strings, and passwords). Keeping access to your key vaults secure is important because this data is sensitive and business critical.

Allow only approved container images. There is enough change and volatility in the container ecosystem without allowing unknown containers as well. Monitor for and prevent unapproved container images with tools and processes in place. Controlling the flow of container images into your development environment is an effective way to reduce the attack surface and prevent developers from making critical security mistakes.

Security Posture Management for Containers

Web workloads must undergo an ongoing security assessment to improve their overall security posture. Defender for Containers assists with all aspects of container security, including the following:

- **Environment hardening:** No matter where your Kubernetes clusters are hosted, Defender for Containers protects them. By continuously assessing clusters, Defender for Containers provides insight into misconfigurations and guidelines for mitigating identified threats.

- **Vulnerability assessment:** Tools for managing images that are stored in ACR registries and running in Azure Kubernetes Service.

- **Runtime threat protection for nodes and clusters:** Threat protection for clusters and Linux nodes generates security alerts for suspicious activities.

In Defender for Cloud, your clusters' configurations are continuously assessed and compared to your subscription initiatives. Upon discovering misconfigurations, Defender for Cloud generates security recommendations. To view and remediate recommendations, use Defender for Cloud's recommendations page.

Container security should be focused on the following security domain areas: control domain, identity management, asset management, endpoint security, posture and vulnerability management, backup and recovery, privileged access data protection, logging threat detection, and network security.

Adopt the following key best practices in container security:

- Utilize a centralized identity and authentication system.
- Utilize only approved applications in a virtual machine.
- Credentials and secrets should not be exposed.
- Utilize modern antimalware software.
- Make sure antimalware software and signatures are up-to-date.
- Define and establish secure configurations for compute resources.
- Rapidly and automatically remediate vulnerabilities.

- Backups should be automated on a regular basis.
- Make sure only approved services are used.
- Follow the just-enough-administration principle (least privilege).
- Utilize a secure certificate management process.
- Restrict resource access based on conditions.
- Choose the approval process for third-party support.
- Utilize the customer-managed key option in data at-rest encryption when required.
- Data-at-rest encryption should be enabled by default.
- Data in transit should be encrypted.
- Monitor anomalies and threats targeting sensitive data.
- Enable threat detection capabilities.
- Secure cloud services with network controls.
- Utilize endpoint detection and response (EDR).
- Utilize a secure key management process.
- Separate and limit highly privileged/administrative users.
- Automate and secure application identity management.
- Establish boundaries for network segmentation.
- Enable network logging for security investigation.
- Discover, classify, and label sensitive data.
- Assess vulnerabilities.

Define Container Orchestration Security Requirements

In container management, an application called a *container orchestrator* manages the containers. Typically, orchestration involves tooling that automates all aspects of application management, such as placements, scheduling, and deployments, as well as steady-state activities, such as deployments, updates, and health monitoring, that support scaling.

As one of the fastest-growing open-source projects in history, Kubernetes has become an integral part of many companies' compute stacks. Kubernetes clusters can be deployed and managed easily on the Azure platform using three services: Azure Kubernetes Service (AKS), Azure Container Service Engine (ACS-Engine), and Azure Container Instance. Kubernetes is a popular solution and is supported by a large developer community. There are several other orchestrators out there that offer cloud-provider integration. Still, this is the only one that integrates natively with public clouds such as Microsoft Azure, Amazon Web Services, and Google Cloud Platform.

In addition to its many advantages, Kubernetes also brings several security challenges that must be addressed. Therefore, understanding the various security risks in containerized environments is crucial.

Azure Kubernetes Service clusters and Azure Arc–enabled Kubernetes clusters (Preview) are protected by default when you enable Microsoft Defender for Containers. The security recommendations appear in the Defender for Cloud dashboard when you enable Microsoft Defender for Containers, as depicted in Figure 7.7.

FIGURE 7.7 Microsoft Defender for Containers

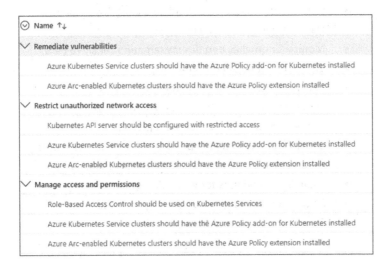

Defender for Cloud provides runtime protections and collects node signals for Azure Kubernetes Service clusters without the need for agent software. Defender profiles are deployed on each node, providing runtime protections and collecting node signals. Azure Policy's Kubernetes add-on includes clusters and workload configurations for admission control policies. Figure 7.8 depcits Azure kubernetes service cluster.

- The Defender profile incorporates a DaemonSet, a set of containers focused on collecting inventory and security events.
- The open Policy Agent (OPA)'s Gatekeeper is the admission controller webhook, which implements at-scale enforcement and safeguarding at scale on clusters.

FIGURE 7.8   Azure Kubernetes Service clusters

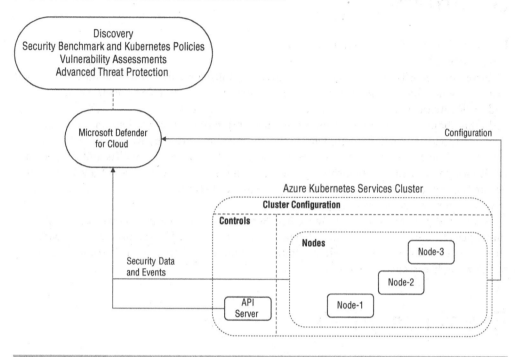

Pod security standards and secrets are security components of Kubernetes. On the other hand, Azure's security components include Active Directory, Microsoft Defender for Containers, Azure Policy, Azure Key Vaults, network security groups, and orchestrated cluster upgrades.

The following security component is combined with AKS to provide the following:

- An authenticating and authorizing story is provided.

- You can secure your applications using AKS's Azure Policy.

- With Microsoft Defender for Containers, you can get end-to-end insight from development to deployment.

- Update your AKS cluster's OS security and Kubernetes releases regularly.

- Access sensitive credentials and pod traffic securely.

Summary

Understanding the classification of security responsibilities among organizations and Microsoft is essential.

Increasing security coverage can be achieved by shifting security responsibilities to a cloud provider, which allows organizations to devote their attention to other business priorities and reallocate their security resources.

In this chapter, you learned about a brief description of the security baselines for Azure PaaS workloads and which Azure PaaS workloads are supported by Microsoft Defender for Cloud. You also learned how to specify a security baseline for IaaS VMs and the general guidelines you can enforce regardless of the operating system. We discussed how Microsoft Secure Score could be used to track the improvement of security postures over time in SaaS environments and the security requirements for IoT workloads.

Additionally, you learned how Azure App Service provides posture management and threat detection by using Microsoft Defender for App Service. The requirements for data and storage workloads were discussed. In addition, container orchestration and security requirements were discussed.

Exam Essentials

Know to identify security baselines for SaaS, PaaS, and IaaS services.   The security baselines are standardized documents that describe Azure product capabilities and the best configurations to enhance security through improved tools, tracking, and security features.

For IaaS, SaaS, and PaaS, you need to consider that different cloud services will have additional security requirements when designing the security strategy for your cloud workloads.

The physical infrastructure is at the bottom of the stack, where Microsoft mitigates common risks and responsibilities. Since Microsoft constantly monitors the Microsoft cloud, it makes little sense for an attacker to attempt to attack it. An attacker is unlikely to pursue the Microsoft cloud unless they have a lot of funds and resources.

Identify security requirements for IoT workloads.   OT networks are used to connect billions of connected devices using the Internet of Things (IoT). Because of the lack of priority placed on security, IoT and OT networks can't be protected by traditional systems. IoT devices and OT networks are increasingly vulnerable to attack surfaces as a result of each new wave of innovation.

A security-in-depth strategy is critical to securing Internet of Things (IoT) infrastructure. Additionally, it is crucial to integrate your SIEM solution with your security IoT solution for threat detection.

Know to identify security requirements for data workloads, including SQL Server, Azure SQL, Azure Synapse, and Azure Cosmos DB.   Both on-premises and cloud data must be protected from inadvertent and malicious access. Inadvertent access occurs when a user gets access to data they shouldn't. A malicious insider or an external attacker intentionally attempting to access data can lead to unintended data leakage, data destruction, and violations of data security and privacy regulations. Malicious insiders can misuse data or be impacted by external attackers who can delete, alter, exfiltrate, and encrypt your sensitive data.

Microsoft Defender for SQL can manage databases' security posture, so you can use it for data workloads. SQL Database, SQL Managed Instance, and Azure Synapse Analytics are all compatible with Microsoft Defender for Cloud. This product can identify database vulnerabilities and mitigate them as well as detect anomalous activities that might indicate a database security threat.

Know to identify security requirements for web workloads, including Azure App Service.   Azure App Service is an HTTP-based service for deploying web applications, REST APIs, and mobile back ends. When considering Azure App Service, you need to consider the security requirements for your web workloads. Both Windows and Linux-based environments are compatible with applications.

To improve the overall security posture of web workloads, just like any other cloud workload, ongoing security assessments are required. With the scale of the cloud, Microsoft Defender for App Service can identify attacks targeting web applications. Attackers probe web applications for weaknesses and exploit them. Requests for Azure applications go through several gateways, where they are inspected and recorded before they are routed to specific environments.

Know to identify security requirements for storage workloads, including Azure Storage.   Input-output (IOP) operations per second are ideal for workloads requiring fast and consistent response times. An Azure Storage account contains all the data objects you use in your Azure Storage account, including blobs, file shares, queues, tables, and disks.

To improve the overall security posture of web workloads, ongoing security assessments are required, like for any other cloud workload.

Know to identify security requirements for containers.   Containers are lightweight, isolated silos for running applications on host systems. Containers are built on top of a host operating system's kernel (the buried plumbing of the operating system), and they contain only applications and some lightweight APIs and services. Even though a container shares the kernel with its host, it does not get full access to it, and the container gets an isolated—and sometimes virtualized—view of the system instead.

You can view Defender for Cloud's recommendations page and remediate issues if it finds misconfigurations in your clusters by comparing them with the initiatives applied to your subscriptions. Defender for Cloud generates security recommendations when it finds misconfigurations.

Know to identify security requirements for container orchestration.   The container orchestration system Kubernetes has become a significant part of many organizations' compute stacks. Kubernetes clusters can be deployed and managed easily on Azure using three services. Kubernetes is a popular solution and has a strong developer community. Azure Kubernetes Service (AKS), Azure Container Service Engine (ACS-Engine), and Azure Container Instance are available.

Defender for Cloud collects audit log data that is agentless and frictionless when it protects clusters hosted in Azure Kubernetes Service.

Review Questions

1. Which of the following components of the cloud landscape is protected and mitigated by Microsoft's 100 percent standard risks and obligations beginning at the bottom of the shared responsibilities stack?

   A. Physical infrastructure

   B. Data management

   C. Application and platform

   D. None of the above

2. As a Cybersecurity Architect, you need to address data governance and rights management at the top of the stack in your design to defend against risk. Which of the following mitigation solution will you adopt?

   A. Data management

   B. Certificate management

   C. Key management.

   D. None of the above

3. As a Cybersecurity Architect, you must adopt a process to strengthen security through improved tooling, tracking, and security features for your organization. Which solution will you adopt in your design and deployment?

   A. Azure Security baselines

   B. Secure Score

   C. PaaS and SaaS CIS standards

   D. None of the above

4. As a Cybersecurity Architect, you must take the first step in protecting the virtual machine part of IaaS workloads for your organization; which solution will you adopt in your design and deployment?

   A. Deploy Azure Security baseline.

   B. Enable remote access.

   C. Provide access to authorized users only.

   D. None of the above.

5. As a Cybersecurity Architect, how will you control and enforce access policies for your Linux workloads for your organization? Which solution will you adopt in your design and deployment?

   A. Integrate with Microsoft LDAP over AD running in on-prem.

   B. Integrate with Microsoft Active Directory running in on-prem.

   C. Integrate with Azure AD.

   D. None of the above.

6. As a Cybersecurity Architect, you want to encrypt using the BitLocker feature of Windows and the dm-crypt feature of Linux workloads for your organization; which Azure services will you adopt in your design and deployment?

   A. Azure Disk Encryption

   B. Storage Encryption

   C. File-Level Encryption

   D. None of the above

7. From which centralized dashboard can you monitor your organization and work on securing your 365 identities, apps, and devices?

   A. Microsoft Azure Portal

   B. Microsoft 365 Portal

   C. Microsoft 365 Defender

   D. None of the above

8. Which of following is the feature from Microsoft 365 that helps with the security posture of your SaaS environment?

   A. Microsoft Secure Score

   B. Microsoft 365 Portal

   C. Microsoft 365 Defender

   D. None of the above

9. Microsoft's recommended IoT architecture is divided into several components/zones as part of the threat modeling exercise. Which of the following are valid?

   A. Device, network gateway, services

   B. Device, field gateway, cloud gateways, services

   C. Device, network gateway, function

   D. None of the above

10. The transition of data/information from one source to another could be subject to STRIDE. What is STRIDE?

   A. Spoofing, threat, risk, information disclosure, denial of service, and elevation of privilege

   B. Searching, threat, risk, information disclosure, denial of service, and elevation of privilege

   C. Spoofing, tampering, repudiation, information disclosure, denial of service, and elevation of privilege

   D. None of the above

11. Which of the following is the best security solution that identifies IoT devices, vulnerabilities, and threats and manages them from one location?

   A. Microsoft Defender for IoT

   B. Azure Security Center

   C. Azure Sentinel

   D. None of the above

12. Which of the following Azure services help to close the gap between IT and OT security issues and to entrust security operations teams with built-in abilities to detect and respond to OT threats efficiently and effectively?

   A. Microsoft Sentinel and Microsoft Defender for IoT

   B. Microsoft Security Center and Microsoft Defender for IoT

   C. Microsoft Defender for Cloud and Microsoft Defender for IoT

   D. None of the above

13. As a Cybersecurity Architect, you need choose one of the Azure services that allows you to deploy a unified data governance service for managing and governing SaaS, multi-cloud, and on-premises data. Which one do you choose?

   A. Microsoft Defender for IoT

   B. Microsoft Purview

   C. Microsoft Sentinel

   D. None of the above

14. What Azure service allows you to use Microsoft Purview metadata for alerts and recommendations with information about potentially sensitive data?

   A. Microsoft Defender for Cloud with Microsoft Purview

   B. Microsoft Defender for IOT with Microsoft Purview

   C. Microsoft 365 Defender with Microsoft Purview

   D. None of the above

15. Which Azure services are available for Azure SQL Database, Azure SQL Managed Instance, and Azure Synapse Analytics?

   A. Microsoft Defender for Cloud

   B. Azure Security Center

   C. Azure Sentinel

   D. None of the above

16. What Azure service allows a one-click HTTPS configuration to secure your app against all unencrypted HTTP connections?

   A. Azure VMs

   B. App Service

   C. Azure function

   D. None of the above

17. What Azure service provides turnkey authentication and authorization of users or client apps?

    A. App Service

    B. Azure function

    C. Azure VMs

    D. None of the above

18. As soon as you enable Microsoft Defender for App Service, you can immediately take advantage of which of the following features? (Choose two.)

    A. Security assessment

    B. Threat detection

    C. Threat protection

    D. Security automation

19. Which of the following does Microsoft use to analyze threats and mitigations?

    A. STRIDE

    B. PASTA

    C. LINDDUN

    D. None of the above

20. As a Cybersecurity Architect, you need to reduce the attack surface of container images because images consist of several layers. Every layer is highly vulnerable; which Azure service will you consider in your design and deployment?

    A. Docker Trusted Registry

    B. Azure Container Registry

    C. Public available images

    D. Both A and B

Chapter

8

Define a Strategy and Requirements for Applications and Data

THE MICROSOFT SC-100 EXAM OBJECTIVES COVERED IN THIS CHAPTER INCLUDE:

✓ Specify priorities for mitigating threats to applications

✓ Specify a security standard for onboarding a new application

✓ Specify a security strategy for applications and APIs

✓ Specify priorities for mitigating threats to data

✓ Design a strategy to identify and protect sensitive data

✓ Specify an encryption standard for data at rest and in motion

In this chapter, we will read about the insights and design a strategy for applications and data.

Cloud platforms ultimately store business value in applications and data associated with them. Applications play a significant role in the security environment because of business processes and business data, even though platform components like identity and storage are essential.

Design and functional specifications must be established during the design phase. Additionally, design assists in mitigating issues related to security and privacy throughout a project.

A secure design concept and requirements can help you avoid or minimize security flaws. After your application is released, a security flaw might allow a user to perform malicious or unexpected actions.

Think about how you can layer your security during the design phase; more than one level of protection may be needed. What will happen if an attacker manages to get past your web application firewall (WAF)? Defending against such an attack requires another security measure.

As you finish this chapter, you will learn about specifying priorities for mitigating threats to applications, defining a security standard for onboarding a new application, defining a security strategy for applications and APIs, identifying sensitive data and protecting it, designing a strategy to mitigate threats to data, and defining the encryption standard for data at rest and in motion.

Knowing the Application Threat Intelligence Model

Let's get started with a basic understanding of the Application Threat Intelligence Model. It allows you to determine threats, attacks, vulnerabilities, and countermeasures by performing a comprehensive analysis. An application can be protected from its threats if the information is available. You can identify potential risks by asking simple questions and then proceed to advanced threat modeling techniques.

Microsoft's Threat Modeling Tool is a core component of Microsoft's Security Development Lifecycle (SDL). Early detection and mitigation of potential security issues allows software architects to reduce costs and ensure their products' security, significantly reducing the total development costs. Microsoft also designed the tool with nonexperts in security in mind so that threat modeling is easier for all developers.

It facilitates communication about security design and analysis of security issues for their systems, as well as managing mitigations for those issues.

You will gather information about the basic security controls. Microsoft Azure provides a report of all threats identified by a threat modeling tool. Developers typically upload this report into a tracking tool or convert it to work items that can be validated and addressed. As new features are added to the solution, the threat model should be updated and incorporated into the code management process. When a security issue is found, there should be a process for triaging its severity and determining how and when to fix it (for example, in the next release cycle).

You will gather information about each component of the application in your environment. As a result of answering these questions (listed in Table 8.1), gaps in basic protection will be identified, and attack vectors will be clarified.

TABLE 8.1 Questions to Ask

Raise the Question	To Detect the Control Applied
Can connections be authenticated using Azure AD, TLS (with mutual authentication), or another modern security protocol?	Ensure that unauthorized individuals do not access application components and data.
Is access to the application limited to those accounts that need to write or modify data?	Protect data from unauthorized modification or tampering.
Using Azure Monitor or a similar solution, is application activity logged and fed into a security information and event management (SIEM) system?	Respond quickly to attacks by detecting and investigating them.
Can critical data be protected with encryption that the security team has approved?	Ensure that data at rest is not copied unauthorized.
Need to encrypt inbound and outbound network traffic using TLS?	Data in transit should be protected from unauthorized copying.
Can Azure DDoS protection protect the application from distributed denial-of-service (DDoS) attacks?	Detect attacks that overload an application and prevent it from working.
Is the application capable of storing logon credentials or keys to access other applications, databases, or services?	Determine whether your application can be used to attack other systems.
Can you meet regulatory requirements with the application controls?	Ensure the privacy of users and avoid fines for noncompliance.

Analyze the Application Design Progressively

Analyze the relationships between application components and connections. In threat modeling, security requirements are defined, threats are identified and mitigated, and the mitigations are validated. Regardless of where an application is in development or production, this technique is most effective when new functionality is being designed.

A tool is provided to assist with Microsoft's SDL, which uses STRIDE. The tool is free of charge.

Developing a threat model is integral to the Microsoft SDL. This engineering technique helps you identify threats, attacks, vulnerabilities, and countermeasures that could affect your application. By using threat modeling, you can improve the security of your application, meet your company's security objectives, and reduce risks.

By visualizing system components, data flow, and security boundaries in a standard notation, the Microsoft Threat Modeling Tool makes threat modeling easier for all developers. By analyzing the structure of software designs, threat modelers can also identify the classes of threats they should consider. Through clear guidance on creating and analyzing threat models, Microsoft designed the tool with nonexperts in security in mind.

By identifying and mitigating potential security issues early, the Microsoft Threat Modeling Tool makes resolving those issues relatively simple and cost-effective. Doing so dramatically reduces the overall development cost. The tool also provides clear guidance on creating and analyzing threat models so they can be used by developers who are not security experts.

Mitigation Categories

Based on the Web Application Security Framework, the Microsoft Threat Modeling Tool mitigations are categorized in Table 8.2.

TABLE 8.2 Microsoft Threat Modeling Tool Mitigations

Category	Description
Auditing and Logging	What was done, when, and by whom? Logging and auditing refer to the way in which your application records security-related information.
	The following are recommendations from Microsoft for specific products/services from an auditing and logging standpoint.
	Dynamics CRM
	■ Implement change auditing in your solution to identify sensitive entities.
	Web Application
	■ Make sure the application is audited and logged.
	■ Make sure logs are rotated and separated.
	■ Make sure sensitive user data isn't logged by the application.
	■ Restrict access to audit and log files.

Category	Description
	▪ Make sure user management events are logged. ▪ Anti-misuse measures should be built into the system. ▪ Using the Azure App Service, enable diagnostics logging for web apps. ▪ Make sure the database is audited and logged. ▪ Make sure SQL Server is configured to audit logins. ▪ Enable Azure SQL threat detection.
Authentication	Who are you? Credentials, such as a username and password, are typically used to prove an entity's identity during authentication. The following are recommendations from Microsoft for specific products/services from an authentication standpoint. **Web Application** ▪ Authenticating a web application should be done using a standard authentication mechanism. ▪ Authentication failure scenarios must be handled securely by applications. ▪ Adaptive authentication or step-up authentication can be enabled. ▪ Ensure that administrative interfaces are appropriately secured. ▪ Ensure that forget password functionality is implemented securely. ▪ Implement password and account policies. ▪ Prevent username enumeration by implementing controls. **Database** ▪ Connect to SQL Server using Windows Authentication whenever possible. ▪ Use Azure Active Directory authentication whenever possible when connecting to SQL databases. ▪ Ensure that SQL server account and password policies are enforced when SQL authentication mode is used. ▪ Databases contained within a container should not use SQL authentication.

TABLE 8.2   Microsoft Threat Modeling Tool Mitigations *(continued)*

Category	Description
Authorization	What can you do? Resource and operation access is controlled by authorization within your application.

Authorization

What can you do? Resource and operation access is controlled by authorization within your application.

The following are recommendations from Microsoft for specific products/services from an authorization standpoint.

Web Application

- Ensure that business logic flows are processed sequentially.
- To prevent enumeration, implement a rate limiting mechanism.
- Follow the principle of least privilege and ensure proper authorization.
- Request parameters should not be used to determine business logic and authorization decisions for resource access.
- Don't allow forceful browsing or enumeration of content and resources.

Database

- When connecting to a database server, use the least-privileged account.
- Data access by tenants can be prevented by implementing row-level security (RLS).
- There should be only valid users in the sysadmin role.

Communication Security

Who are you talking to? All communication is secured using communication security.

The following are recommendations from Microsoft for specific products/services from a communication security standpoint.

Web Application

- SSL, TLS, and DTLS connections are authenticated with X.509 certificates.
- In Azure App Service, configure TLS/SSL certificates for custom domains.
- Traffic to Azure App Service should be sent over HTTPS.
- HTTP Strict Transport Security (HSTS) should be enabled.

Database

- Ensure that SQL Server connections are encrypted, and certificates are validated.
- Communication with the SQL Server must be encrypted.

Category	Description
Configuration Management	Who does your application run as? What databases does it connect to? How is your application administered? What are security measures in place to protect these settings? The configuration management of your application refers to how these operational issues are handled.

The following are recommendations from Microsoft for specific products/services from a configuration management standpoint.

Web Application

- Ensure that Content Security Policy (CSP) is implemented, and disable inline JavaScript.
- Turn on the XSS filter in your browser.
- Tracing and debugging must be disabled before deploying ASP.NET applications.
- Use only trusted third-party JavaScript code.
- Implement UI redressing and click-jacking defenses on authenticated ASP.NET pages.
- ASP.NET Web Applications should allow only trusted origins if Cross-Origin Resource Sharing (CORS) is enabled. CORS is a mechanism by which application, data, or any other resource of a website could be shared to a third-party website when there is a need.
- The ValidateRequest attribute should be enabled on ASP.NET pages.
- JavaScript libraries should be hosted locally.
- MIME sniffing should be disabled.
- Avoid fingerprinting by removing standard server headers on Windows Azure websites.

Database

- Ensure that the database engine is protected by a Windows firewall.

TABLE 8.2   Microsoft Threat Modeling Tool Mitigations *(continued)*

Category	Description
Cryptography	What methods do you use to keep secrets (confidentiality)? What are you doing to protect your data and libraries from tampering (integrity)? Can we provide cryptographically strong seeds for random values? Using cryptography, you can ensure the integrity and confidentiality of your application. The following are recommendations from Microsoft for specific products/ services from a cryptography standpoint. **Web Application** ■ The key length and symmetric block ciphers must be approved. ■ When using symmetric ciphers, use block cipher modes and initialization vectors that have been approved. ■ Ensure key lengths, padding, and asymmetric algorithms are approved. ■ Generators that are approved should be used. ■ Symmetric stream ciphers should not be used. ■ Algorithms for MACs, HMACs, and keyed hashes should be approved. ■ Use cryptographic hashes that have been approved only. **Database** ■ Encrypt data in the database with robust encryption algorithms. ■ Encrypted and digitally signed SQL Server Integration Services (SSIS) packages are recommended. Microsoft SSIS is a data migration and integration tool that ships with the Microsoft SQL Server database that can be used to extract, integrate, and transform data. SSIS is an extract, transform, and load (ETL) solution. ■ Secure critical database information with digital signatures. ■ Protect encryption keys with SQL Server Extensible Key Management (EKM). ■ To prevent encryption keys from being revealed to the database engine, use the AlwaysEncrypted feature.
Exception Management	What happens when a method call in your application fails? What is the extent of your disclosure? Can you provide end users with friendly error information? Are you passing valuable exception information back to the caller? Are you able to handle failures gracefully in your application? The following are recommendations from Microsoft for specific products/ services from an exception management standpoint. **Web Application** ■ Security details should not be exposed in error messages. ■ A default error handling page should be implemented. ■ Specify Retail as the deployment method in IIS. ■ Safe exception handling is essential.

Category	Description
Input Validation	What is the best way to verify that the input your application receives is safe and valid? Your application validates input before it is further processed by filtering, scrubbing, or rejecting it. Encode output through exit points and constrain input through entry points. Are databases and file shares reliable sources of data? The following are recommendations from Microsoft for specific products/services from an input validation standpoint. **Web Application** ▪ Untrusted style sheets should not be used for Extensible Stylesheet Language Transformations (XSLT) scripting. ▪ Make sure all pages that could contain user-controllable content opt out of automatic Multipurpose Internet Mail Extensions (MIME) sniffing. ▪ Resolving XML entities in a hardened or disabled manner. ▪ The URL canonicalization verification process is performed by applications that utilize `http.sys`. ▪ Accepting files from users should be controlled appropriately. ▪ Type-safe parameters should be used for data access in web applications. ▪ To prevent Model View Controller (MVC) mass assignment vulnerability, separate model binding classes or binding filter lists should be used. ▪ Prior to rendering, encode untrusted web output. ▪ All string type model properties should be validated and filtered. ▪ Rich text editors, for instance, should be sanitized since they accept all characters. ▪ Sinks without built-in encoding should not be assigned DOM elements. ▪ Make sure all redirects within the application are closed or done safely. ▪ Validate all string types accepted by controller methods. ▪ To prevent DoS due to bad regular expressions, set an upper limit time-out for regular expression processing. ▪ Razor views should not use `Html.Raw`. **Database** ▪ Stored procedures should not use dynamic queries.

TABLE 8.2   Microsoft Threat Modeling Tool Mitigations *(continued)*

Category	Description
Sensitive Data	What is your application's approach to handling sensitive data? Any data in memory, over the network, or in persistent storage that must be protected is sensitive data.

The following are recommendations from Microsoft for specific products/services from a sensitive data standpoint.

Web Application

- Browser caches should not contain sensitive content.
- Ensure that sensitive data in web app configuration files is encrypted.
- Forms and inputs containing sensitive information should be explicitly disabled from using the autocomplete HTML attribute.
- Mask-sensitive data displayed on the user's screen.

Database

- Limit sensitive data exposure to nonprivileged users by implementing dynamic data masking.
- Passwords should be stored in salted hash format.
- Encrypt sensitive data in database columns.
- Make sure that database-level encryption such as transparent data encryption (TDE) is enabled.
- Encrypt database backups.

Category	Description
Session Management	What steps does your application take to ensure that user sessions are protected? Your web application responds to a series of related interactions with a user during a session.

The following are recommendations from Microsoft for specific products/services from a session management standpoint.

Web Application

- Secure cookies must be used by applications accessible over HTTPS.
- For cookie definitions, all HTTP-based applications should specify HTTP only.
- ASP.NET web pages should be protected from Cross-Site Request Forgery (CSRF) attacks.
- Configure the inactivity lifetime for the session.
- The application should be able to log out properly.

Mitigate the Identified Threats

Using the Threat Modeling Tool, all threats are identified, and a report is generated. As soon as a potential threat is identified, determine how to detect and respond to it. Establish a process and timeline to minimize exposure to any identified vulnerabilities in the workload so they cannot go unaddressed.

Defense in depth is a technique that uses numerous security measures to safeguard an organization's assets. The consideration is that if one line of defense is compromised, added layers exist as a blockage to ensure that threats are stopped along the way. Defense in depth manages the security vulnerabilities ingrained not only with hardware and software but also with people, as delinquency or human error often generates a security breach.

As a result, it is possible to determine what controls are needed in the design to mitigate risk if a primary security control fails. Analyze how likely it is that the primary control will fail. In this case, what are the potential risks for the organization? In addition, how effective is the additional control (especially when it causes the primary control to fail)? Address potential security control failures using defense-in-depth measures based on the evaluation.

Defense in depth can be implemented using the principle of least privilege. One account cannot cause as much damage as another. Ensure that accounts are granted the least number of privileges necessary to achieve the required permissions within a reasonable amount of time. Access to the account mitigates the damage caused by an attacker compromising security assurances.

In the Microsoft SDL, the Threat Modeling Tool plays a crucial role. As a result, software architects can identify and mitigate potential security issues early when their resolution is relatively simple and cost-effective. Therefore, it dramatically reduces development costs.

Specify Priorities for Mitigating Threats to Applications

The application portfolio of enterprise organizations is typically extensive, but only some applications are equally important. Monitoring, time, and resources should be appropriately directed for applications with business-critical information-regulated data and high visibility, value, and criticality. A significant amount of access to systems or applications may allow control over other critical systems.

Identify and Classify Applications

Analyze your portfolio to identify and classify critical business applications. The effectiveness of your security program can be enhanced if you prioritize your time and effort in manual and resource-intensive tasks like threat modeling.

Assess the potential impact or risk of applications. Analyze your portfolio to identify and classify critical business applications. The effectiveness of your security program can be enhanced if you prioritize your time and effort in manual and resource-intensive tasks like threat modeling.

Assess the Potential Impact or Risk of Applications

The following are critical areas to assess the potential impact or risk of applications:

- **Business critical data:** Applications that process or store information must provide security, integrity, and availability assurances.

- **Regulated data:** This is a software application that handles sensitive personal information and monetary instruments, such as are governed by a Payment Card Industry (PCI), General Data Protection Regulation (GDPR), or Health Insurance Portability and Accountability Act (HIPAA) regulation.

- **Business critical availability:** There are several types of applications that are critical to the business mission, such as production lines that generate revenue, devices or services that are vital to life and safety, and other functions.

- **Significant access:** Through technical means, applications with high impact are able to access systems such as the following:

  - Access credentials, keys, or certificates stored on the server.

  - ACLs and other methods of granting permissions.

- **High exposure to attacks:** Web applications on the public Internet, for example, are easily accessible to attackers. A legacy application can also be more vulnerable, since attackers (and penetration testers) frequently target them since these legacy applications often have vulnerabilities that are hard to fix.

Determine which applications have the greatest potential to impact or to expose the organization to threats (see Table 8.3).

TABLE 8.3   Risky Applications

Risk	Mitigation	Examples
High-potential impact	Identify applications with a significant impact on the business in the event of a compromise.	A business-critical application is one that processes or stores data that would have a severe negative impact on business operations or the mission if security, integrity, and availability were compromised.
		The handling of sensitive information and monetary instruments is regulated by standards. Among them are PCI and HIPAA, which protects health information.
		A critical application, such as a production line earning revenue, a device or service that is critical to life and safety, or another critical application, must be available at all times for the organization's business mission to be accomplished.
		By storing credentials or obtaining permissions through access control lists, or other technical means, applications that have significant access to systems with a high-potential impact can have significant impact on the systems.

Risk	Mitigation	Examples
High exposure to attacks	A web application on the open Internet is easily accessible by attackers.	Not applicable

Typical enterprise organizations have an extensive application portfolio, but only some are equally significant. Monitoring, time, and resources should be appropriately directed toward applications that contain business-critical data, contain regulated data, and have high business value, visibility, or criticality. Assess each application that is easily accessible to attackers, such as an open Internet web application. Assess each applications that could have a significant impact on the business in the event of a compromise.

Specify a Security Standard for Onboarding a New Application

Business value on a cloud platform is ultimately stored in applications and their data. Applications play an outsized role in business risks despite the importance of platform components like identity and storage.

- **Business processes:** Applications encapsulate and execute business processes, and services must be accessible and reliable.
- **Business data:** The confidentiality, integrity, and availability of business data are essential to application workloads.

There is a difference between applications written by you or others on your behalf and those installed on IaaS VMs that are SaaS or commercially available.

Modern cloud platforms like Azure can host both legacy and modern generations of applications.

- **Legacy:** A legacy application runs on a virtual machine that includes all OS, middleware, and other dependencies as part of the infrastructure as a service (IaaS).
- **Modern:** PaaS applications, which are sometimes fully serverless and built using functions as a service, don't require the application owner to manage and secure underlying server operating systems.
- **Hybrid:** There are many forms of hybrid applications, but the most common is an IaaS-plus state in which legacy applications migrate into modern architecture, and modern services replace or add to legacy components.

Three types of components must be secured when securing an application:

- **Application code:** Application code is the logic that defines your custom application. Including any open-source snippets or components in the code, the application owners are responsible for the security of this code in all generations of application architecture. Designing and implementing an application must be secure, and risks must be identified and mitigated. Including components in the supply chain also requires assessing their risk.

- **Application services:** Application services include databases, identity providers, event hubs, IoT device management, and other standardized components.

- **Application hosting platform:** An application executes and runs in this computing environment. It is possible for the application hosting platform in a company where applications are hosted on-premises, in Azure, or in third-party clouds like Amazon Web Services (AWS) to take many forms, and there are also significant differences in who is responsible for security.

Onboarding New Applications

Register your business application with Azure AD. Downtime or compromise can result from any misconfiguration or lapse in hygiene. The following properties are security best practices:

- **Redirect URI:** Maintaining your application's redirect URIs is meaningful. An application compromise can occur if an owner of one of the redirect URIs lapses. Regularly monitor DNS records for changes and update them as necessary. Ensure that all URIs are owned, and do not use wildcard reply URLs or non-secure URI schemes like HTTP.

- **Implicit grant flow for an access token:** It is now possible to reduce the risk of compromise associated with implicit grant flow misuse by using Auth code flow in scenarios that require implicit flow. For security reasons, we recommend you turn off the setting if you do not actively use implicit flow to obtain access tokens for your application.

- **Credential:** Applications used as confidential clients require credentials for registration. Ensure that you do not have any credentials stored on your app if it is used only as a public client app (which allows users to sign in using a public endpoint).

- **AppId URI:** A tenant's AppId URI can be used to identify a resource exposed by a certain application (via WebAPI). To avoid URI collisions in your organization, Microsoft recommends using API or HTTPS URI schemes and setting the AppId URI in the following formats below:
    - URI formats
    - api://<appId>
    - api://<tenantId>/<appId>
    - api://<tenantId>/<string>

- api://<string>/<appId>
- https://<tenantInitialDomain>.onmicrosoft.com/<string>
- https://<verifiedCustomDomain>/<string>
- https://<string>.<verifiedCustomDomain>
- https://<string>.<verifiedCustomDomain>/<string>

- A verified customer-owned domain must be used for the AppId URI to prefix scopes in the API's code. Additionally, the value must be globally unique for multi-tenant applications.

- **Application ownership:** Keep the number of people who own apps within the organization to a minimum. To maintain ownership of the application registration, Microsoft recommends checking the owner's list once every few months.

- **Checklist:** A checklist is available in the Azure Portal to guide app developers in ensuring their app registration meets a high-quality bar. When combined with the Microsoft identity platform, the integration assistant highlights best practices and recommendations that help bypass oversights.

Security Standards for Onboarding Applications

Organizations should use guidance and automation tools from external sources to secure cloud applications rather than starting from scratch.

- Organizations can improve their security posture by using resources and lessons learned from external organizations that have already adopted these models more quickly.

- Rather than writing custom versions of well-established functions like databases, encryption, identity directory, and authentication, developers should use the services provided by your cloud provider.

- Using native security features built into cloud services should be preferred over adding external security components (such as data encryption, network traffic filtering, threat detection, and so on).

- Use identity services rather than cryptographic keys to authenticate.

- Implement web application firewalls (WAFs) to prevent attackers from exploiting common security vulnerabilities.

- The following guidelines are intended to help you manage this new application architecture type:

  - Enforce security for applications hosted in containers, general application best practices, and some specific guidelines.

  - Two popular threat model standards are STRIDE and Open Web Application Security Project (OWASP), which enable the identification of more potential risks.

Because of potential security implications, several capabilities should be prioritized first.

- **Identity:** Security assurances can be achieved only by developing user directories and other authentication functions. Instead of using homegrown authentication solutions, choose mature capabilities such as Using Azure Active Directory (Azure AD), AAD B2B for Azure, and a B2C version of Azure AD. Users, partners, customers, applications, services, and other entities can be authenticated and granted permission through third-party solutions.

- **Data protection:** To encrypt and protect data, developers should use cloud services that include native encryption. There are many examples in the security world of failed attempts to protect data or passwords that cannot withstand attacks. Developers should only attempt to create their own cryptographic algorithms if they can directly use cryptography.

- **Key management:** Instead of directly handling keys, prefer identity authentication. A key management service, such as Azure Key Vault or AWS Key Management Service, can access services requiring keys. As opposed to attempting to handle keys in application code safely, this will help you manage and secure these keys.

- **Application configurations:** Inconsistent configurations can create security risks for applications. The Azure App Configuration service helps mitigate this risk by centrally managing application settings and feature flags.

From the SC-100 exam standpoint, remember that two popular standards, STRIDE and OWASP, can identify more potential risks. When designing an app or system, developers can spot threats using the STRIDE threat model. OWASP is a nonprofit organization dedicated to improving software security.

Specify a Security Strategy for Applications and APIs

Continuous integration/continuous delivery (CI/CD) for applications and API development should be incorporated into the DevOps life cycle as rapidly as possible to avoid a waterfall development cycle.

What is a waterfall model? The *waterfall model* was the first process model to be introduced. It is also referred to as a *linear-sequential life-cycle model* and is very simple to understand and use. In a waterfall model, each phase must be completed before the next step can begin, and there is no overlapping of the stages.

Continuous delivery of value to end users is enabled by the union of people, processes, and tools in DevOps. As a result of the merging of Dev and Ops, multidisciplinary teams from development and operations collaborate using tools and practices that are shared and efficient.

In a DevOps environment, security concerns can be addressed quickly without waiting for a waterfall model's longer planning and testing schedule. Application and API life cycles are influenced by DevOps throughout the planning, development, delivery, and operation phases. Phases do not have specific roles, but they all depend on each other. To some extent, all roles are involved in each phase in a true DevOps culture. Table 8.4 describes the phases of a DevOps culture.

TABLE 8.4   DevOps Phases and Tasks

Phase	Task
Plan	A DevOps team imagines, defines, and describes the features and capabilities of applications and systems they are building. A single-product task can be tracked at a low level of granularity, and a multiproduct portfolio task can be tracked at a high level of granularity. DevOps teams plan with agility and visibility by creating backlogs, tracking bugs, managing agile software development with Scrum, using Kanban boards, and visualizing progress.
Develop	This includes all aspects of coding, such as writing, testing, reviewing, integrating, and packaging code for deployment into various environments by team members. Teams use version control software to collaborate on code and work in parallel, usually Git. Furthermore, they aim to innovate rapidly without compromising quality, stability, or productivity. Through automated testing and continuous integration, they iterate in small increments using highly productive tools, automate mundane and manual steps, and use highly effective tools.
Deliver	Deploying applications consistently and reliably into production environments, ideally via continuous delivery. In addition to the delivery phase, the infrastructure that underpins those environments must also be deployed and configured. Containers, microservices, and infrastructure as code (IaC) are commonly used in these environments.
Operate	In this phase you maintain, monitor, and troubleshoot production applications in public and hybrid clouds. DevOps practices ensure that systems are reliable and highly available and aim for zero downtime while reinforcing security and governance.

Enforcing Security for DevOps

Teams that don't have a standard DevSecOps strategy are urged to begin the preparations as soon as possible. Initially, team members may be reluctant to accept the existing threats because they don't fully appreciate them. Some may consider a unique investment wasteful, as they believe that the team needs to be equipped to take on the challenge. As a first step, the team needs to build consensus on the nature of the risks, how to mitigate them, and whether they need additional resources they do not have right now.

There are a few common arguments skeptics will raise, including the following:

- **What is the level of threat?** Data and services that teams are charged with protecting are often undervalued.

- **Is our team good?** Security discussions may be perceived as doubt about the team's ability to build a secure system.

- **This is not possible.** Junior engineers often make this argument, and experienced individuals usually know better.

- **We have never been breached.** How do you know? Can you tell us how?

- **Value debates are endless.** It may be perceived that DevSecOps is a distraction from core feature development. Although security investments must be balanced with other priorities, they cannot be ignored.

Security Strategy Components

Many techniques can be applied in the quest for more secure systems. Table 8.5 demonstrates the security strategy components.

TABLE 8.5   Security Strategy Components

Preventing Breaches	Assuming Breaches
Threat models	War game exercises
Code reviews	Central security monitors
Security testing	Live site penetration tests

There should already be some practices in place in every team to prevent breaches. Static analysis tools and other security testing features are increasingly available free of charge, and most developers have become accustomed to writing secure code.

In a world where breaches are a given, many teams need a strategy for dealing with them. The admission of this can be challenging, especially when dealing with complex management situations. Practice techniques that assume breaches will help the team answer questions about their security on their own time, so they don't have to figure it all out during an actual security emergency.

Team members should consider the following questions:

- Is there a way to detect an attack?

- If you are attacked or penetrated, how will you respond?

- Is there a way to recover from an attack, such as when data is leaked or tampered with?

Strategies for Mitigating Threats

Identifying every possible threat to a system is impossible because the list is so long. In some cases, security holes are caused by dependency issues, such as outdated operating systems and libraries. Maintaining these dependencies is crucial.

The majority of modern web applications make APIs available for clients to use. A well-designed web API should support the following:

- **Platform independence:** No matter how the API is implemented internally, any client should be able to call it. For this to work, standard protocols must be used, and an agreement must be reached on the data format to be exchanged between the client and web service.

- **Service evolution:** Client applications should not depend on the web API to evolve and add functionality, and the API should be able to support existing client applications without requiring any modifications. All functionality must be discoverable so that client applications can fully use it.

Focus on the web API's business entities. An e-commerce system, for instance, might have customers and orders as its primary entities. The process of creating an order involves sending an HTTP POST request that contains the order information. HTTP responses indicate whether the order has been placed successfully. Nouns (the resource) should be used as resource URIs whenever possible rather than verbs (the operations on the resource).

From the SC-100 exam standpoint, remember that a security strategy's critical components for preventing breaches are threat models, code reviews, security testing, and SDLs.

Specify Priorities for Mitigating Threats to Data

Microsoft maps cybersecurity weaknesses in your organization to actionable security recommendations, prioritizing them according to their impact. Mitigating or remediating vulnerabilities is easier with prioritized recommendations.

Within the security industry, attacks follow a process referred to as the *kill chain*. An attack follows a basic pattern and progresses from one step to the next. Security measures can be implemented at choke points in the chain to prevent this step-wise process. Various exploitation techniques can bypass any stage, so the most effective strategies build defenses at every level.

During the content inspection, you can use firewalls, email gateways, and proxies on-premises. In addition to mobile devices, tablets, and cloud assets, that boundary now includes mobile devices, tablets, and cloud assets. In many cases, companies lightly manage or do not manage the devices that access their data. Mobile device management (MDM) solutions may help companies enforce security measures, such as encryption and remote wipes, in the case of a stolen device. When data on these devices leaves its controlled environment, the solutions still do not have any control over it.

Today's cloud-centric world presents organizations with both the unregulated (such as files stored on cloud services) and the unknown (such as advanced threats targeting users' email). As a result, it is harder to protect data from all sources—on-premises, on PCs, on phones, and in the cloud.

Table 8.6 describes Microsoft's recommended methods to protect data.

TABLE 8.6   Method to Protect Data

Product/Service	Description
Machine Trust Boundary	Binaries containing sensitive information should be obfuscated.
	Protect confidential user-specific data with an encrypted file system (EFS).
	A file system must be encrypted before sensitive data can be stored by the application.
Web application	Make sure sensitive content is not cached in the browser.
	Ensure sensitive data in web app configuration files is encrypted.
	Forms and inputs containing sensitive information should be explicitly disabled from using the autocomplete HTML attribute.
	The user screen should be masked when it displays sensitive data.
Database	Limit sensitive data exposure to nonprivileged users by implementing dynamic data masking.
	Passwords should be stored in salted hash format.
	Data in database columns should be encrypted to protect sensitive information.

Product/Service	Description
	Table-level encryption (TDE) must be enabled in the database.
	The backups of your database should be encrypted.
Web API	Don't store sensitive data in the browser related to the Web API.
Azure Document DB	Using Azure Cosmos DB, you can encrypt sensitive data.
Azure IaaS VM Trust Boundary	You can encrypt disks used by virtual machines using Azure Disk Encryption.
Service Fabric Trust Boundary	Apps that use Service Fabric should encrypt secrets. Azure Service Fabric is a PaaS solution designed to enable the development, deployment, and management of highly scalable and customizable applications from the Microsoft Azure cloud platform.
Dynamics CRM	Utilize business units and teams where appropriate for security modeling.
	Reduce access to critical entities' Share feature.
	The Dynamics CRM Share feature comes with some risks, so users should be trained about the risks and how to avoid them.
	In the exception management standard, include a rule that prohibits showing configuration details.
Azure Storage	Use data-at-rest encryption with Azure Storage Service Encryption (Preview).
	Azure Storage can be encrypted using client-side encryption.
Mobile Client	Data that contains sensitive or personally identifiable information (PII) should be encrypted before being stored on a phone's local storage.
	Distribute obfuscated binary files.
WCF	Certificates or Windows credentials should be set as clientCredentialType.
	WCF-Security configuration isn't enabled.

Ransomware Protection

The high impact of ransomware and extortion attacks, as well as the likelihood that an organization will be targeted, makes preventing them an urgent priority for organizations. An example of ransomware is an extortion attack that encrypts files and folders, preventing access to important information. Typically, ransomware extorts money from victims through the demand for cryptocurrency in exchange for a decryption key. The Dark Web and the public Internet are often used as a means of extorting money from victims through ransomware.

Business operations can be severely damaged by these attacks, which are difficult to clean up, requiring complete adversary eviction to prevent future attacks. Human-operated ransomware poses a far greater threat to your business operations than early forms of ransomware that only required malware remediation.

Ransomware: Preventing and Recovering

Ransomware prevention and recovering is classified into three phases as described following:

First phase: Your recovery plan should be prepared.   By making it impossible for ransomware attackers to make money, this phase minimizes the monetary incentive they receive.

- Accessing and disrupting systems and encrypting or damaging key organization data is much more complicated.
- Your organization will be able to recover more quickly from an attack without paying a ransom.

Second phase: Damages should be limited.   By restricting access to privileged access roles, attackers will have a more challenging time gaining access to multiple business-critical systems. The attacker will have a more difficult time profiting from an attack on your organization when they can't get privileged access, so it's more likely they will give up.

Third phase: Increase the difficulty of getting in.   In addition to raising friction for entry, this last set of tasks will take time to complete as part of a more significant security endeavor. Attackers will have to work much harder at these common entry points to access your on-premises or cloud infrastructure. Because of the many tasks here, it's essential to prioritize your work based on how fast you can accomplish it with the available resources.

Key security recommendations to mitigate threats to data include storing sensitive data in Azure Storage using Azure Storage Service Encryption (SSE) and client-side encryption, encrypting disks used by virtual machines with Azure Disk Encryption, enabling database-level encryption (TDE), and not caching sensitive content on browsers.

Design a Strategy to Identify and Protect Sensitive Data

If everything went smoothly, all your employees would understand the importance of protecting information and adhering to your policies. But your business partner may inadvertently upload a sensitive document with incorrect permissions to your Box repository if they frequently work with accounting information. Imagine if your business's confidential data is leaked to your competitors a week later.

Identifying and protecting data requires consideration of the following elements. Some concepts might be more important than others, depending on the product you are using.

- **Data discovery:** Inventory all of your organization's data stores and knowledge bases.
- **Data classification:** Determine which data is sensitive for your organization.
- **Data protection:** Apply flexible protection measures, including encryption, access restrictions, and visual markings to control access to and sharing of data.
- **Usage monitoring:** Record and audit data access activity.
- **Data loss prevention:** Prevent sensitive information from being accidentally shared.

Data Discovery: Know Your Data

Organizations must identify the type and amount of sensitive data to protect and govern it. It would be best if you had a detailed understanding of where the sensitive data is stored and how it is protected. To develop your strategy for protecting and governing your data, you need to discover and classify essential data in your environment and use this information to assess your overall risk. This process involves answering questions such as these:

- What types of data do you have?
- Who owns my data?
- Where is my data?
- Why is it a risk?
- What methods can I use to classify my data?
- Where can I classify my data?
- How can I see what happens to my data over its life cycle?

Data Classification

In data classification, you identify and classify content using the methods described in Table 8.7 to gain a better understanding of your data landscape.

TABLE 8.7   Data Classification

Capability	What Problems Does It Solve?
Sensitive information types	Uses regular expressions or functions to identify sensitive data. Corroborating evidence consists of keywords, confidence levels, and proximity.
Trainable classifiers	You can train a classifier yourself with your own content or use built-in classifiers to identify sensitive data.
Data classification	This can help you gain insight into how your users are acting on items that have sensitivity labels, have retention labels, or have been classified in your organization.
Policies	Inputs to policies include sensitive information types, trainable classifiers, sensitivity labels, and retention labels. A policy defines behaviors, such as whether a default label is applied, whether labeling is mandatory, where the label will be applied, and under what circumstances.

What Is a Data Classification Framework?

The data classification framework (also called a *data classification policy*) typically consists of three classification levels: a name, a description, and a real-world example.

To keep the user interface (UI) manageable, Microsoft recommends five top-level parent labels, each with five sublabels (25 total).

- Public.
- Internal.
- Confidential.
- Highly confidential.
- Restricted, Unrestricted, and Consumer Protected are some examples of level name variations you may encounter as a final choice.

Microsoft recommends that label names be self-descriptive and indicate their relative sensitivity. Confidential and Restricted, for example, may leave users wondering which is more sensitive, while Confidential and Highly Confidential make it clear which is more sensitive.

The controls associated with each level are another critical component of a data classification framework. Data classification levels indicate the content's value or sensitivity. Data classification frameworks specify the controls you need to implement for each classification level to protect your data. These controls include the following:

- Storage type and location
- Encryption
- Access control

- Data destruction
- Data loss prevention
- Public disclosure
- Logging and tracking access
- Other control objectives, as needed

Custom Sensitive Data Types

By identifying sensitive information types, sensitive items can be prevented from being accidentally shared or inappropriately shared, relevant information can be found in eDiscovery, and governance actions can be enforced on certain types of information through the use of sensitive information types. It is essential to consider the following factors when defining sensitive information types (SITs):

- Patterns
- Keyword evidence such as employee Social Security number, or ID
- Character proximity to proof in a particular pattern
- Confidence levels

Is it reasonable to have a SIT that matches exact or nearly exact data values instead of one that uses generic patterns to find matches? A sensitive information type can be created using exact data match (EDM) classification and be designed to do the following:

- Be dynamic and quickly refreshed.
- Be more scalable.
- Result in fewer false positives.
- Work with structured sensitive data.
- Handle sensitive information more securely, not sharing it with anyone, including Microsoft.
- Be used with several Microsoft cloud services.

Millions of data feed can inform a DLP or MCAS policy of pieces of data like SSNs or credit card numbers using EDM. Dynamically updating the database is possible, and this exact-match database can contain as many as 100 million rows of data. When a retailer wants to set rules around sensitive information like credit card numbers with strict rules about those numbers it has for its customers and less stringent rules for credit card numbers derived from out-of-the-box classifiers, this is a good solution.

Data Protection

As a result of the data protection component, different types of sensitive information are accessed and shared according to the policies established throughout the data estate.

A *data estate* refers to all an organization's data, no matter where it is stored. When you migrate this data to the cloud or modernize your environment on-premises, you can gain vital insights to fuel innovation.

Processes and Capabilities of Microsoft Information Protection

Different products can be used for information protection, so there are different phases.

- **Defender for Cloud Apps:** Discover, classify, protect, and monitor with this tool. You can protect your organization's data leak points with Microsoft Defender for Cloud Apps, which provides an extensive suite of DLP capabilities.

- **Microsoft Purview:** Microsoft Purview helps you to know your data, protect your data, prevent data loss, and manage your data. Microsoft Purview is a unified data governance service that enables you to govern and manage your on-premises, multi-cloud, and software-as-a-service (SaaS) data.

    Microsoft purview is classified into the following phases.

Purview Phase 1: Know Your Data   Microsoft Purview automates the discovery and classification of data.

Data discovery and classification are merged under the "Know your data" pillar of Microsoft Purview. The capabilities listed in Table 8.8 can help you understand your data landscape and identify sensitive data across your hybrid environment.

TABLE 8.8   Purview Capabilities

Capability	What Problems Does It Solve?	Get Started
Sensitive information types	A regular expression or function is used to identify sensitive data. In addition to keywords and confidence levels, proximity is a form of corroboration.	Customize a built-in sensitive information type.
Trainable classifiers	Instead of identifying elements in the item (pattern matching), this function determines sensitive data using examples. A classifier can be trained using your own content or with built-in classifiers.	Get started with trainable classifiers.
Data classification	Graphically identify items in your organization with sensitivity, retention, or classification labels. This information can also be used to gain insight into your users' actions.	Get started with content explorer.

Defender Phase 1: Discover Your Data   Automate data discovery with Defender for Cloud Apps.

- **Connect apps:** The first step in discovering which data is being used in your organization is to connect cloud apps used in your organization to Defender for Cloud Apps. Once connected, Defender for Cloud Apps can scan data, add classifications, and enforce policies and controls. How apps are connected affects how and when scans and controls are applied. You can connect your apps in one of the following ways:

- **Use an app connector:** Microsoft app connectors use the APIs supplied by app providers. They provide greater visibility into and control over the apps used in your organization. Scans are performed periodically (every 12 hours) and in real time (triggered each time a change is detected).

- **Use a conditional access App Control solution:** A conditional access App Control solution uses a reverse proxy architecture that is uniquely integrated with Azure Active Directory (AD) conditional access. Once configured in Azure AD, users will be routed to Defender for Cloud Apps where access and session policies are enforced to protect the data apps attempt to use. This connection method allows you to apply controls to any app.

- **Investigate:** After you connect an app to Defender for Cloud Apps using its API connector, Defender for Cloud Apps scans all the files it uses. You can then go to the file investigation page by selecting Investigate ➤ Files to get an overview of the files shared by your cloud apps, their accessibility, and their status.

Defender Phase 2: Classify Sensitive Information   Microsoft Information Protection and Defender for Cloud Apps are natively integrated with data classification.

Purview Phase 2: Protect Your Data (Phase 3 Defender)   Table 8.9 lists the comprehensive set of data protection capabilities included with Microsoft Purview (including Defender for Cloud Apps as a capability).

TABLE 8.9   Data Protection Capabilities

Capability	What Problems Does It Solve?
Sensitivity labels	Protect your data inside and outside your organization with a single labeling solution across apps, services, and devices.
Azure Information Protection unified labeling client	With additional features for Office apps if you need them, extend labeling to File Explorer and PowerShell for Windows computers.
Double Key Encryption	It would be best to keep encryption keys within a geographical area for regulatory requirements. Only your organization can ever decrypt protected content.
Office 365 Message Encryption (OME)	Provides encryption so authorized recipients can only read email messages and attached documents.
Service encryption with Customer Key	In Microsoft data centers, BitLocker disk encryption complements this feature by protecting data from being viewed by unauthorized systems or personnel.
SharePoint Information Rights Management (IRM)	Ensures that only authorized people can view and use downloaded files from SharePoint lists and libraries when a user checks out a document.

TABLE 8.9   Data Protection Capabilities *(continued)*

Capability	What Problems Does It Solve?
Rights Management connector	Use only for existing on-premises deployments of Exchange, SharePoint, or File Classification Infrastructure (FCI) installations.
Information protection scanner	Provides sensitive data discovery, labeling, and protection services for on-premises data storage.
Microsoft Defender for Cloud Apps	Provides secure access to cloud-based data stores by discovering, labeling, and protecting sensitive information.
Microsoft Purview Data Map	Analyzes Microsoft Purview Data Map assets and applies automatic labeling to sensitive content. Azure Cosmos DB and Azure SQL DB support storing schematized data such as files and columns.
Microsoft Information Protection SDK	Third-party apps and services can now be tagged with sensitivity labels.

Defender Phase 4: Monitor and Report on Your Data   With Defender for Cloud Apps, monitoring and reporting are emphasized more. Data inspection and protection policies are all in place. You will need to check your dashboard daily to see whether any new alerts have been triggered. Keep an eye on your cloud environment's health here. You can see what's happening in your dashboard and, if necessary, launch an investigation.

You can monitor sensitive file incidents most effectively by going to the Policies page and reviewing the matches for the policies you have configured. Also, consider regularly monitoring file alerts if you have configured alerts. Go to the Alerts page, specify DLP as the category, and review which file-related policies are being triggered. As a result of reviewing these incidents, you can fine-tune your policies to target threats of interest to your organization.

Therefore, when sensitive information is managed this way, cloud data is protected from infiltration and exfiltration by malicious parties. In addition, only authorized users can access files that have been shared or lost.

Purview Phase 4: Govern Your Data   In Microsoft Purview, governance consists of the following:

- Data life-cycle management
  - Retention policies for workloads
  - Inactive and archive mailboxes
- Records management
  - Retention labels for items
  - Disposition review

Microsoft Purview Data Life-Cycle Management

To keep what you need and delete what you don't, refer to Table 8.10.

TABLE 8.10   Purview Data Life-Cycle Management Capabilities

Capability	What Problems Does It Solve?
Microsoft 365 retention policies, with labels for exceptions	Emails, documents, Teams, and Yammer messages can be retained or deleted with policy management.
Inactive mailboxes	Provides administrators, compliance officers, and records managers with access to mailbox content after employees leave the organization.
Archive mailboxes	Allows users to store more information in their mailboxes.
Import service for PST files	Bulk import PST files to Exchange Online mailboxes is supported to retain and search email messages for compliance or regulatory requirements.

Microsoft Purview Records Management

For business, legal, or regulatory record-keeping purposes, manage high-value items as described in Table 8.11.

TABLE 8.11   Records Management

Capability	What Problems Does It Solve?
File plan.	Retention labels can be created interactively or imported in bulk and exported for analysis. The labels allow for additional administrative information (optional) to assist you in identifying and tracking business or regulatory requirements.
If required, retention policies for baseline retention should be developed for individual items.	With labels, you can create flexible retention and deletion schedules, which can be applied manually or automatically, along with records declarations as needed.
Proof of disposition and review of disposition.	Proof of disposition of records is required before content can be permanently deleted.

Best Practices

The following are best practices:

Separate production environments from non-production environments.   Especially when you have different instances of data for each environment, you should deploy separate instances of Microsoft Purview accounts. A Microsoft Purview instance can register and scan production and nonproduction data sources. Microsoft Purview allows you to register data sources in multiple cases if necessary.

Enforce compliance requirements.   Imagine your organization has data across multiple geographies and you need to keep metadata in the same region as the actual data. Microsoft Purview must be deployed separately per geography in such a case. The Microsoft Purview account corresponding to the data source region or geography will need to be registered and scanned with data sources from each region.

Best Practices for Data Protection

The following are best practices:

DP-1: Discover sensitive data, classify it, and label it.   A Microsoft privacy review and SDL process cover all data flow within Microsoft Defender for Cloud Apps. There is no control over the data by the customer,

DP-2: Protect sensitive information.   Using Azure Active Directory (Azure AD) roles, Microsoft Defender for Cloud Apps manages sensitive data.

DP-3: Detect unauthorized data transfer.   Monitor the transfer of data to locations outside the visibility and control of the enterprise. Data exfiltration is typically detected by monitoring abnormal activities (large or unusual transfers).

DP-4: Encrypt sensitive data during transit.   Data in transit is encrypted with TLS v1.2 or greater using Microsoft Defender for Cloud Apps. For traffic on external and public networks, this is optional but crucial. If you are using HTTP traffic to connect to Azure resources, please ensure that the client can negotiate TLS v1.2 or higher. Use SSH (for Linux) or RDP/TLS (for Windows) instead of an unencrypted protocol when remote managing. Weak ciphers and obsolete SSL, TLS, and SSH protocols should be disabled.

Organizations need to identify the types and amounts of data they have in their environment. By identifying and labeling content within your organization, the classification process helps them better understand their data landscape. A data protection component acts as a point of enforcement for policies relating to accessing and sharing sensitive data across the organization.

Specify an Encryption Standard for Data at Rest and in Motion

By encrypting data at rest, Microsoft Defender for Cloud Apps protects against out-of-band attacks (such as accessing underlying storage). The data is thus protected from being read or modified by attackers. The following are critical areas for adopting encryption standards for data at rest and motion.

- Security and privacy for Cloud Apps with Microsoft Defender.

- Understand how Azure encryption at rest works.

- In Azure, data at rest is double encrypted.

It would help to consider the possible states where your data may occur and what controls are available for each state. The following are best practices for Azure data security and encryption:

At Rest The term *at rest* refers to all physical media, whether magnetic or optical, that house information storage objects, containers, and types.

In Transit When data is in transit, it is transferred between components, locations, or programs. Typical examples include transfers over the network, across a service bus (from on-premises to cloud and vice versa, including hybrid connections such as ExpressRoute), or during input and output operations.

Data in transit and at rest is encrypted in Azure. Double encryption involves two or more independently encrypting layers to prevent compromises of any encryption layer. The threat of data encryption compromise is mitigated when two layers of encryption are used.

Encryption of Data at Rest

From Microsoft Azure, a variety of cloud-based services are available with data encryption at rest, including SaaS, PaaS, and IaaS.

Information at rest refers to information stored on physical media in any digital format. Archived data, magnetic or optical media, and data backups can be included in the media. With Microsoft Azure, you can store your data in various ways, including files, disks, blobs, and tables. Aside from Azure SQL Database, Azure Cosmos DB, and Azure Data Lake, Microsoft also provides encryption.

Data Encryption Models in Azure

With Azure, you can use server-side encryption with service-managed keys, customer-managed keys in Key Vault, or customer-managed keys on hardware that the customer controls. Client-side encryption allows you to store and manage keys locally or in another secure location.

Encryption performed on the client side occurs outside of Azure. It includes the following:

- An application running in the customer's data center or a service application encrypts data.
- Azure receives data that is already encrypted.

You keep the encryption keys, so cloud service providers cannot decrypt your data with client-side encryption.

Server-Side Encryption   Different key management characteristics are offered by the three server-side encryption models, which you can select based on your needs.

- **Service-managed key:** Control and convenience are combined with a low overhead with service-managed keys.
- **Customer-managed key:** This allows you to manage your keys, including bring your own keys, or create new ones.
- **Service-managed key in customer-controlled hardware:** Managing keys in your proprietary repository, outside of Microsoft control, is possible with service-managed keys on customer-controlled hardware. This feature is called Host Your Key. As a result, most Azure services do not support this configuration.

Azure Disk Encryption   DM-Crypt and Windows BitLocker are two methods of protecting the operating system disk and the data disk with full volume encryption with Azure Disk Encryption.

Your Azure Key Vault subscription safeguards encryption keys and secrets. Key Encryption Key (KEK)–configured virtual machines (VMs) can be backed up and restored using Azure Backup.

Encryption of Data in Transit

When moving data from one location to another, Azure offers many mechanisms for ensuring privacy.

Data-Link Layer Encryption in Azure

A data-link layer encryption method is applied across the underlying network hardware whenever Azure Customer traffic moves between data centers outside physical boundaries not controlled by Microsoft (or on behalf of Microsoft). This method is known as MACsec. A physical man-in-the-middle attack, also known as an *on-path attack* or *snooping/wiretapping attack*, is prevented by encrypted packets and decrypted on the devices before they are sent. In addition to providing line rate encryption on the network hardware itself, this technology also increases link latency in no measurable way. All Azure traffic traveling within or between regions is encrypted with MACsec by default, so customers do not need to take any action to enable it.

TLS Encryption in Azure

Microsoft uses Transport Layer Security (TLS) when data travels between cloud services and customers. Azure services are connected to Microsoft data centers via TLS connections. The TLS protocol provides strong authentication, message privacy, and integrity (enabling the detection of tampering, interception, and forgery), interoperability, algorithm flexibility, and ease of deployment.

Perfect Forward Secrecy

Perfect forward secrecy combination makes it difficult to intercept and access data in transit if a unique key secures a customer's client system. RSA-based 2,048-bit keys also encrypt Microsoft cloud services.

Azure Storage Transactions

In addition to using the Azure Portal, you can interact with Azure Storage through the Storage REST API over HTTPS. All transactions with Azure Storage take place over HTTPS. By enabling the secure transfer required for the storage account, you can force HTTPS when you use REST APIs to access objects in storage accounts.

Shared Access Signatures

When used to delegate access to Azure Storage objects, Shared Access Signatures (SAS) allow you to specify that only the HTTPS protocol can be used. This ensures that SAS tokens are sent over HTTPS only.

The Azure file share access protocol, SMB 3.0, supports encryption. It is available in Windows Server 2012 R2, Windows 8, Windows 8.1, and Windows 10.

The client-side encryption secures the data and protects it as it travels across the network before it arrives at your Azure Storage instance.

SMB Encryption Over Azure Virtual Networks

It is possible to encrypt data in transit over Azure virtual networks by using SMB 3.0 in VMs running Windows Server 2012 or later. Administrators can enable SMB encryption for the entire server or specific shares to protect data against tampering and eavesdropping attacks. Encryption protects data from tampering and eavesdropping.

Shares and servers that are encrypted with SMB are accessible only by SMB 3.0 clients by default.

Point-to-Site VPNs

With point-to-site VPNs, clients can access Azure virtual networks using the Secure Socket Tunneling Protocol (SSTP), which can pass through firewalls (the tunnel appears as an HTTPS connection). Point-to-site connectivity can be achieved with your internal public key infrastructure (PKI) root certificate authority (CA).

Site-to-Site VPNs

Through an IPsec/IKE (IKEv1 or IKEv2) VPN tunnel, you can connect your on-premises network to an Azure virtual network via a site-to-site VPN gateway connection. An external-facing public IP address must be assigned to the on-premises VPN device to perform this type of connection.

Azure Data Security and Encryption Best Practices

The following are critical best practices for Azure Data Security and Encryption.

Choose a Key Management Solution

Using Key Vault, you can create several secure containers called *vaults*, which hardware security modules (HSMs) back.

An HSM is a hardware unit that stores cryptographic keys to keep them private while they are unrestricted to those privileged to use. The immediate purpose of HSM security is to handle which people have access to an organization's digital security keys.

With HSM encryption, you allow your employees to operate your private keys without giving them direct access.

Vaults help reduce the risk of accidental loss of security information by centralizing application secrets. In addition to controlling and logging access to anything stored in key vaults, Azure Key Vault also handles issuing and renewing Transport Layer Security (TLS) certificates. Certificate life-cycle management has been simplified with this robust solution.

> **Best practice: Set up a specific scope for accessing users, groups, and applications.** A user would be granted access to key vaults by assigning Key Vault Contributor's predefined role to them at a specific scope if you used Azure RBAC predefined roles. If the predefined roles don't meet your needs, you can define your own roles. The scope, in this case would be a subscription, resource group, or key vault.

> **Best practice: Make sure users have access to only what they need.** Access to a key vault is controlled independently by management plane and data plane access controls.

> **Best practice: Ensure the security of your application and your data is maintained by keeping certificates in a key vault.** Your certificates are of high value, and if they fall into the wrong hands, the security of your application or data could be compromised. Azure Resource Manager securely deploys certificates stored in Azure Key Vault to Azure VMs when deployed. Managing all your certificates is also easy with Azure Key Vault. You can also control who has access to your certificates by setting appropriate access policies.

> **Best practice: Make sure you can recover deleted key vault objects or key vaults.** It is possible to delete a key vault or key vault object inadvertently or maliciously, especially for keys that encrypt data at rest, enabling soft delete and purge protection features in Key Vault. Deleting these keys is equivalent to data loss, so you can recover lost vaults and vault objects. Practice Key Vault recovery operations frequently.

Manage with Secure Workstations

A compromise of an endpoint can allow an attacker to gain access to the organization's data by using the user's credentials. Because the vast majority of attacks target the end user, the endpoint becomes one of the primary points of attack. Endpoint attacks typically take advantage of users' local administrators.

Best practice: Ensure the security of sensitive accounts, tasks, and data by using a secure management workstation. Reduce the attack surface on your workstations by using privileged access workstations. These secure management workstations can help mitigate some of these attacks and keep your data safe.

Best practice: Ensure endpoint security. Implement security policies across all devices that consume data, regardless of the location of the data (cloud or on-premises).

Protect Data at Rest

For example, unauthorized or rogue users might steal data from compromised accounts or gain unauthorized access to data coded in Clear Format in organizations that don't enforce data encryption. For companies to comply with industry regulations, they must also demonstrate that they are diligent and implementing the appropriate security controls to secure their data.

Best practice: Encrypt your disks to ensure that your data is protected. The Azure Disk Encryption feature allows administrators to encrypt disks in both Windows and Linux virtual machines. It combines Windows BitLocker's volume encryption utility with Linux's dm-crypt. By default, Azure Storage and Azure SQL Database encrypt data at rest. You can also use Azure Key Vault to control the keys used to access and encrypt your data.

Best practice: Implement encryption to mitigate risks associated with unauthorized data access. Make sure your drives are encrypted before you write sensitive data on them.

Protect Data in Transit

Best practice: Provide secure access to Azure virtual networks from multiple on-premises workstations. It is essential for your data protection strategy to protect data in transit. SSL/TLS protocols should always be used to exchange data across multiple locations since data moves back and forth between many locations. In some circumstances, you might want to isolate the entire communication channel between your on-premises and cloud infrastructures by using a VPN.

Use a Site-to-Site VPN

Best practice: On-premises workstations must have secure access to Azure virtual networks.   To provide secure communication between the end user or admin workstation to Azure secure virtual network need to be designed and deployed, aligning with organization requirements and standards.

Use a Point-to-Site VPN

These are the best practices:

Best practice: Use high-speed WAN links for larger datasets.   To provide additional protection, you can use ExpressRoute with SSL/TLS or another protocol to encrypt data at the application level.

Best practice: Use the Azure Portal to interact with Azure Storage.   To interact with Azure Storage, use the Storage REST API over HTTPS. All transactions occur over HTTPS.

Key Management with Key Vault

A cloud service can function effectively only if its encryption keys are adequately protected and managed. Key Vault is Microsoft's recommended way of working and controlling access to encryption keys. Azure Active Directory accounts can be used to assign permissions to services or users to access keys. HSMs and key management software no longer need to be configured, patched, and maintained with Key Vault.

Azure Key Vault helps solve the following problems:

- **Secrets Management:** Azure Key Vault allows token storage, password storage, certificate storage, and API keys management in a secure and tightly controlled way.

- **Key Management:** Key Management can be accomplished using Azure Key Vault. With Azure Key Vault, you can easily manage and create encryption keys.

- **Certificate Management:** Azure Key Vault makes it easy to provision, manage, and deploy TLS/SSL certificates for Azure and your internal connected resources.

Azure supports a variety of encryption models, including server-side encryption using service-managed keys, customer-managed keys in Key Vault, and customer-managed keys on customer-controlled hardware. Client-side encryption is performed outside of Azure.

From the SC-100 exam standpoint, remember that to prevent out-of-band attacks (such as accessing underlying storage), Microsoft Defender for Cloud Apps encrypts data at rest.

Summary

This chapter guides planning and designing an overall application and data security strategy. An organizational application security strategy and architecture were designed, defined, and recommended using different strategies.

With Microsoft Sentinel, you can quickly access threat intelligence from various sources thanks to its cloud-native security information and event management (SIEM) solution.

The Microsoft SDL includes the Threat Modeling Tool. Early detection of potential security issues enables software architects to mitigate them cost-effectively and efficiently. Thus, development costs are greatly reduced.

Microsoft 365 Defender now includes Microsoft Defender for Cloud Apps (previously known as Microsoft Cloud App Security). Security admins can manage their security tasks in one place with the Microsoft 365 Defender portal. In addition to simplifying workflows, Microsoft 365 Defender adds new functionality. You can monitor and manage security across your Microsoft identities, data, devices, apps, and infrastructure with Microsoft 365 Defender.

In this chapter, you read about methods for specifying priorities for mitigating threats to applications, defining a security standard for onboarding a new application, defining a security strategy for applications and APIs, identifying sensitive data and protecting it, designing a strategy to mitigate threats to data, and defining the encryption standard for data at rest and in motion.

Exam Essentials

Know to set priorities for mitigating threats to applications.　The Threat Modeling Tool is an integral part of the Microsoft Security Development Lifecycle. By identifying and mitigating potential security issues early, you can resolve them relatively easily and cost-effectively. Therefore, the total development cost is greatly reduced. By providing clear guidance on creating and analyzing threat models, we designed the tool to be easy to use even for nonexperts in security.

Anyone can use this tool to communicate about their security design, analyze those designs for potential weaknesses, and suggest mitigations for those weaknesses.
Prioritize applications based on identification and classification to ensure proper monitoring, time, and resource allocation.

Know to specify a security standard for onboarding a new application.　Instead of starting from scratch, organizations should use guidance and automation from external sources to secure applications in the cloud. To begin with, you can adopt the following standards using resources and lessons learned by external organizations that are early adopters of these models to accelerate the improvement of an organization's security posture with less effort and fewer resources. Following that, developers should use services from your cloud provider for well-established functions such as databases, encryption, identity directory, and authentication instead of writing custom versions. Use a more comprehensive threat model standard that identifies more potential risks; two popular standards are STRIDE and OWASP. Finally, use native security capabilities built into cloud services instead of adding external security components (data encryption, network traffic filtering, threat detection, and other functions).

Know to specify a security strategy for applications and APIs.   Especially in developing APIs and applications, organizations should move as quickly as possible from a waterfall-based development process to a DevOps approach involving continuous integration, delivery, and deployment. Continuous delivery of value to end users is enabled by the union of human resources, processes, and tools in DevOps.

The Microsoft Defender for Cloud security baseline and its recommendations can be monitored. The Microsoft Defender for Cloud dashboard will list Azure Policy definitions under Regulatory Compliance.

Be able to specify priorities for mitigating threats to data.   Today's cloud-centric world presents organizations with both the unregulated (such as files stored on cloud services) and the unknown (such as advanced threats targeting users' email). As a result, it is harder to protect data from all sources: on-premises, on PCs, on phones, and in the cloud. The high impact of ransomware and extortion attacks and the likelihood that an organization will be targeted makes preventing them an urgent priority for organizations. Deploy Microsoft's recommended remediation plan.

Understand methods to design a strategy to identify and protect sensitive data.   An enforcement points to sensitive information access and sharing across the data estate; the data protection component enforces policies on accessing and sharing sensitive information.

Depending on the product being used, protection of information can be divided into different phases. With Defender for Cloud Apps, you can discover, classify, protect, and monitor your cloud applications. A comprehensive suite of data leak prevention capabilities is available with Microsoft Defender for Cloud Apps, covering a wide range of data leak points across organizations.

You can govern your data, protect your data, and prevent data loss with Microsoft Purview. Data governance is the practice of managing and governing your on-premises, multi-cloud, and SaaS data in one place.

Especially when you have different instances of data for each environment, you should deploy separate instances of Microsoft Purview accounts.

Know to specify an encryption standard for data at rest and in motion.   To keep your data safe in the cloud, you need to consider possible states where your data may occur and what controls are available in those states. Data in transit and at rest is encrypted in Azure. A double encryption system uses two or more independent layers of encryption to protect against compromises of any of the layers. When data is encrypted using two layers, it mitigates threats that come with it. Various encryption models are supported by Azure, including server-side encryption using service-managed keys, key management in Key Vault, or key management on customer-controlled hardware. Keys can be managed and stored securely on-premises or at another secure location using client-side encryption.

Review Questions

1. When it comes to recording security-related events in your application, which of the following applies?

    A. Communication security

    B. Auditing and logging

    C. Authorization

    D. Exception management

2. Which one of the services confirms an entity's identity, usually through credentials, such as a username and password?

    A. Input validation

    B. Authentication

    C. Authorization

    D. Exception management

3. Which one of the services confirms how your application handles access controls for Azure resources and operations?

    A. Input validation

    B. Authentication

    C. Authorization

    D. Exception management

4. Which category defines the risk for applications that process or store information that must provide security, integrity, and availability assurances?

    A. Regulated data

    B. Business-critical data

    C. Business-critical availability

    D. High exposure to attack

5. Which category defines the risk for applications critical to the business mission, such as production lines that generate revenue, devices, or services that are vital to life and safety, and other functions?

    A. Regulated data

    B. Business-critical data

    C. Business critical availability

    D. High exposure to attack

6. Which category defines the risk of a web application on the public Internet being easily accessible to attackers?

   A. Regulated data

   B. Business-critical data

   C. Business-critical availability

   D. High exposure to attack

7. Which of the following methods is defined as hosting applications on virtual machines that include all required dependencies, including OS, middleware, and so on?

   A. Modern

   B. Legacy

   C. Hybrid

   D. Replatform

8. Applications such as platform as a service (PaaS) don't require the application owner to manage and secure the underlying server operating systems and are sometimes fully serverless and built nearly exclusively with functions as a service. In which category do they get classified?

   A. Modern

   B. Legacy

   C. Hybrid

   D. Replatform

9. Which solution should you consider deploying to mitigate the risks associated with an attacker being able to exploit commonly known security issues?

   A. Azure WAF

   B. Azure NSG

   C. Azure Firewall

   D. None of the above

10. Which processes affect the application and API life cycle throughout planning, developing, delivering, and operating?

   A. DevOps

   B. Togaf

   C. SRE

   D. None of the above

11. Organizations should shift from which development cycle to the DevOps life cycle of continuous integration/continuous delivery (CI/CD) for applications, and API development as quickly as possible?

   A. Waterfall

   B. Togaf

   C. SRE

   D. None of the above

12. As a Cybersecurity Architect, you have to adopt a security standard or model to secure modern applications in your organization; which standard or model will you adopt from the following?

   A. STRIDE

   B. Togaf

   C. NIST SP 800-63-1

   D. None of the above

13. Which of the following is a type of extortion attack that encrypts files and folders, preventing access to essential data?

   A. Malware attack

   B. Phishing attack

   C. Password attack

   D. Ransomware attack

14. Which part of data identification and protection creates a list of all your organization's data stores and knowledge bases?

   A. Data creation

   B. Data discovery

   C. Data classification

   D. Data loss prevention

15. In which part of data identification and protection should data sharing and access policies be defined, implementing flexible protection measures such as encryption, access restrictions, and visual markings?

   A. Data create

   B. Data discovery

   C. Data protection

   D. Data loss prevention

16. Which of the following Azure services offers comprehensive data leak prevention capabilities such as discover, classify, protect, and monitor?

   A. Defender for Cloud Apps

   B. Defender for Identity

   C. Defender 365

   D. None of the above

17. You can manage and govern your data across on-premises, multi-cloud, and software as a service (SaaS) with which of the following?

   A. Defender 365

   B. Defender for Identity

   C. Defender for Cloud Apps

   D. Microsoft Purview

18. Defender for Cloud Apps' data classification features are natively integrated with Microsoft Purview services by which services?

   A. Microsoft Information Protection

   B. Defender 365

   C. Defender for Cloud Apps

   D. Microsoft Purview

19. Sensitive data is managed by Microsoft Defender for Cloud Apps; all data flows are governed by which process?

   A. Microsoft privacy review and SDL process

   B. Microsoft compliance review and SDL process

   C. Microsoft DevOps review and SRE process

   D. Microsoft DevSecOps review and SRE process

20. Which of the following will allow you to provision, manage, and deploy public and private Transport Layer Security/Secure Sockets Layer (TLS/SSL) certificates for Azure and for your internal resources?

   A. Microsoft CA Server

   B. Azure Key Vault Certificate Management

   C. Azure WAF

   D. None of the above

Chapter

9

Recommend Security Best Practices and Priorities

THE MICROSOFT SC-100 EXAM OBJECTIVES COVERED IN THIS CHAPTER INCLUDE:

✓ Recommend best practices for cybersecurity capabilities and controls

✓ Recommend best practices for protecting from insider and external attacks

✓ Recommend best practices for Zero Trust security

✓ Recommend best practices for Zero Trust Rapid Modernization Plan

✓ Recommend a DevSecOps process

✓ Recommend a methodology for asset protection

✓ Recommend strategies for managing and minimizing risk

✓ Plan for ransomware protection and extortion-based attacks

✓ Protect assets from ransomware attacks

✓ Recommend Microsoft ransomware best practice

In this chapter, you will read about the best practices and priorities for Azure security.

With the volume and complexity of threats, organizations face many challenges when securing their data centers, including recruiting and retaining security experts. With Azure, organizations can overcome these challenges.

As you read this chapter, you will learn about best practices for cybersecurity capabilities and controls, best practices for protecting from insider and external attacks, best practices for Zero Trust security, and recommended best practices for a Zero Trust rapid modernization plan.

As well, you will read about the DevSecOps process, methodology for asset protection, strategies for managing and minimizing risk, plans for ransomware protection, protecting assets from ransomware attacks, and recommended Microsoft ransomware best practices.

Recommend Best Practices for Cybersecurity Capabilities and Controls

Microsoft Azure products and services include a comprehensive set of security features and configuration settings. Their main benefit is that they can be customized (up to a point), so your organization can develop a security posture that fits its needs. The value goes beyond just turning on the proper settings to adopt and maintain a good security posture.

When developing best practices, it is essential to focus on controls and technical capabilities. Technology does not improve security on its own and does not replace the need for security experts, but it automates processes and allows people to focus on other tasks.

Microsoft recommends that each organization focus on the following areas under four domains (people, process, technology, and architecture):

- **People:** Educate teams about the cloud security journey.
- **People:** Educate teams on cloud security technology.
- **Process:** Assign accountability for cloud security decisions.
- **Process:** Update incident response (IR) processes for the cloud.

- **Process:** Establish security posture management.
- **Technology:** Require passwordless or multifactor authentication.
- **Technology:** Integrate native firewall and network security.
- **Technology:** Integrate native threat detection.
- **Architecture:** Standardize on a single directory and identity.
- **Architecture:** Use identity-based access control (instead of keys).
- **Architecture:** Establish a single unified security strategy.

It is possible to find best practices and capabilities in the Microsoft Cybersecurity Reference Architecture (MCRA) and the Microsoft Cloud Security Benchmarks (MCSBs). Some are embedded in MCRA architecture diagrams (explained in Chapter 1, "Define and Implement an Overall Security Strategy and Architecture"), others are in other MCRA sections, and others are explicitly stated in MCSBs.

The detailed technical diagrams are an integral part of Microsoft Cybersecurity Reference Architecture. They describe Microsoft cybersecurity capabilities, Zero Trust user access, security operations, operational technology (OT), multi-cloud and cross-platform capabilities, attack chain coverage, Azure native security controls, and security organizational functions.

Essential Best Practices in the MCRA

Essential best practices in the MCRA consist of the following:

- **Find out what resources are available to you:** Know what security controls and capabilities you have access to and use the resources.
- **Apply the right tool for the job:** Use a multi-technology approach rather than relying solely on one technology, such as a network firewall or a SIEM.
  - **Security of the data and management planes:** Ensure that both security controls on the data plane (which are available since the days of pre-cloud on-premises data centers) and security controls on the management plane (which can be embedded within the cloud platform to enable additional visibility and control) are included.
  - **Platform and infrastructure security and workload security:** Ensure you have controls to protect specific workloads (such as web application firewalls [WAFs]) and the overall infrastructure and development environment.
  - **Adopt cloud-native controls:** Ensure that native cloud controls protect your cloud assets.
  - **Adopt consistent tooling:** Use consistent tooling across cloud providers to ensure effective control deployment across your infrastructure and platforms. You can accomplish more security with the available resources by reducing the time and effort required to implement and monitor controls.
- **Consider security holistically:** It is essential to have visibility and control over the entire life cycle of an asset to ensure its security. In the case of a cloud-hosted resource, the following would be included:

- The number of people who access it
- User accounts and groups to access the system
- The devices end users use to access those accounts
- A resource access interface (Azure Portal, command-line interface, application programming interface, and so on)
- As a whole, the resource
- Storage, virtual machines, containers, and other cloud/application services that interact with the resource
- The resources that are accessible by all devices and customer accounts

- **Security and productivity:** Make sure that security enables productivity, as well as reduces risk. When designing or operating a system, security should provide healthy friction that encourages people to think critically about risk. Security mustn't create unhealthy friction that hinders productivity or fails to reduce risk effectively.

- **Maintain privileged access protection:** Ensure elevated security measures, monitoring, and response are in place for privileged accounts and systems. As a result of compromised privileged access, an attacker can shut down business operations across the organization through a ransomware/extortion attack. Because of the rapid and efficient compromise of many systems at once that can be achieved with such a level of access, attackers frequently target highly privileged accounts. Several enhanced protections should be implemented by organizations, including the following:

  - Protect privileged user accounts with strong multifactor authentication, threat detection, and tagging to ensure rapid response to anomalous events.

  - Ensure that the workstations and devices associated with these accounts are protected by using privileged access workstations (PAWs) and additional monitoring and response.

  - Enhanced protections, security policy monitoring, threat detection, and more can benefit intermediaries handling privileged accounts and sessions, such as virtual private networks (VPNs), privileged identity management (PIM)/privileged access management (PAM) solutions, domain controllers, and more.

- **Plan for ransomware and extortion attacks:** Ensure you prepare for ransomware and extortion attacks by implementing the most comprehensive security controls.

- **Validate BC/DR process:** Make sure your business continuity and disaster recovery (BC/DR) process considers all business-critical systems and a ransomware/extortion attack scenario. Furthermore, it would be best if you exercise this scenario recently. If you have yet to, you may be unable to recover all business-critical systems from such an attack.

- **Secure backups against sabotage:** Ensure that backups are protected from deliberate erasure or encryption by attackers, a common tactic of attackers. You may not be able to recover critical business operations without paying the ransom/extortion payment if your backups are not secure. It is much slower, has no guarantee of success, and involves potential liability and other risks when paying a ransom.

Azure and multi-cloud environments can benefit from the MCSB, which provides prescriptive best practices and recommendations to improve the security of workloads, data, and services. As part of this benchmark, Microsoft and industry security guidance is incorporated into a set of cloud-centric control areas, including the following:

- Guidelines on cloud adoption, including security strategy, roles and responsibilities, and the Azure top 10 security best practices.

- Guidelines for securing your workloads on Azure using the Azure Well-Architected Framework.

- In the CISO workshop, CISOs will discuss guidelines and reference strategies that will help them accelerate security modernization using Zero Trust principles.

- In addition to Amazon Web Services' Well-Architected Framework and Center for Internet Security Controls, the National Institute of Standards and Technology (NIST) and Payment Card Industry Data Security Standard (PCI-DSS) are among the best practice standards and frameworks available to industry organizations and cloud service providers.

Several best practices related to cybersecurity are included in the MCSB security controls. These include both technical and nontechnical capabilities and controls, such as processes.

MCSBs focus on the following three areas:

- Security framework for multi-cloud environments

- Microsoft Defender for Cloud, which provides automated control monitoring for Amazon Web Services

- A refresh of the already available Azure security principles, identified in the following list

Network Security (NS)   The concept of network security refers to measures taken to secure and protect networks, including the creation of virtual networks, the establishment of private connections, the prevention and mitigation of external attacks, and the protection of DNS.

Identity Management (IM)   Identity management describes controls for creating a secure identity and access controls using identities and access management systems, such as single sign-on, strong authentication, managed identities (and service principals) for applications, conditional access, and monitoring of account anomalies.

Privileged Access (PA)   Protecting privileged access to your tenant and resources includes a range of controls to protect the administrative model, accounts, and privileged access workstations against deliberate and inadvertent misuse.

Data Protection (DP)   In addition to data protection control at rest, in transit, and via authorized access mechanisms, access control, encryption, key management, and certificate management are all used to detect, classify, protect, and monitor sensitive data assets.

Asset Management (AM)   Among the controls associated with asset management are recommendations on permissions for security personnel, security access to asset inventory, and approval management for services and resources (inventory, tracking, and correcting).

Logging and Threat Detection (LTD)   Logging and threat detection covers controls for detecting threats on the cloud and enabling, collecting, and storing audit logs for cloud services. In addition to allowing detection, investigation, and remediation processes with controls to generate high-quality alerts with native threat detection in cloud services, the system includes the following:

- The collection of logs through a cloud monitoring service
- Centralized security analysis through a SIEM
- Synchronization of time
- Retention of logs
- Incident response (IR)

Controls related to incident response include preparation, detection and analysis, containment, post-incident activities, and automating the incident response process through Azure services (for example, Microsoft Defender for Cloud and Sentinel).

Posture and Vulnerability (PV) Management   Managing posture and vulnerabilities within the cloud involves assessing and improving the security posture, including vulnerability scanning, penetration testing, remediation, and security configuration tracking, reporting, and correction.

Endpoint Security (ES)   In cloud environments, endpoint security includes endpoint detection and response (EDR) and antimalware services for endpoints.

Backup and Recovery (BR)   As a part of the backup and recovery process, controls are established to ensure that data and configuration backups are performed, validated, and protected at the different service tiers.

DevOps Security (DS)   In addition to addressing security engineering and operations in the DevOps process, DevOps security outlines measures to ensure security throughout the DevOps process, including the deployment of necessary security checks (such as static application security testing and vulnerability management). In addition to threat modeling and software supply security, it covers common topics.

Governance and Strategy (GS)   Governance and strategy guidance ensures a coherent security strategy and a documented governance approach to guide and maintain security assurance, including establishing roles and responsibilities for all cloud security functions, developing a unified technical strategy, and establishing supporting standards and policies.

For references and more information about Governance and Strategy guidance, see the following:

`learn.microsoft.com/en-us/security/benchmark/azure/`
`mcsb-governance-strategy`

Table 9.1 lists all high-level key best practices to apply in your organization. For references and more information, see the following:

`github.com/MicrosoftDocs/SecurityBenchmarks/blob/master/`
`Azure%20Security%20Benchmark/3.0/azure-security-benchmark-v3.0.xlsx`

TABLE 9.1   Microsoft Azure Security Benchmark Key bestpratices across various workloads

Security Controls

DP-1: Discover, classify, and label sensitive data.

DP-2: Monitor anomalies and threats targeting sensitive data.

DP-3: Encrypt sensitive data in transit.

DP-4: Enable data at rest encryption by default.

DP-5: Use customer-managed key option in data at rest encryption when required.

DP-6: Use a secure key management process.

DP-7: Use a secure certificate management process.

DP-8: Ensure security of key and certificate repository.

AM-1: Track asset inventory and their risks.

AM-2: Use only approved services.

AM-3: Ensure security of asset life cycle management.

AM-4: Limit access to asset management.

AM-5: Use only approved applications in virtual machine.

PV-1: Define and establish secure configurations.

PV-2: Audit and enforce secure configurations.

PV-3: Define and establish secure configurations for compute resources.

PV-4: Audit and enforce secure configurations for compute resources.

PV-5: Perform vulnerability assessments.

PV-6: Rapidly and automatically remediate vulnerabilities.

PV-7: Conduct regular red team operations.

ES-1: Use endpoint detection and response (EDR).

ES-2: Use modern antimalware software.

ES-3: Ensure antimalware software and signatures are updated.

TABLE 9.1 Microsoft Azure Security Benchmark Key bestpratices across various workloads *(continued)*

Security Controls

BR-1: Ensure regular automated backups.

BR-2: Protect backup and recovery data.

BR-3: Monitor backups.

BR-4: Regularly test backup.

DS-1: Conduct threat modeling.

DS-2: Ensure software supply chain security.

DS-3: Secure DevOps infrastructure.

DS-4: Integrate static application security testing into the DevOps pipeline.

DS-5: Integrate dynamic application security testing into the DevOps pipeline.

DS-6: Enforce security of workload throughout the DevOps life cycle.

DS-7: Enable logging and monitoring in DevOps.

GS-1: Align organization roles, responsibilities and accountabilities.

GS-2: Define and implement enterprise segmentation/separation of duties strategy.

GS-3: Define and implement data protection strategy.

GS-4: Define and implement network security strategy.

GS-5: Define and implement security posture management strategy.

GS-6: Define and implement identity and privileged access strategy.

GS-7: Define and implement logging, threat detection, and incident response strategy.

GS-8: Define and implement backup and recovery strategy.

GS-9: Define and implement endpoint security strategy.

GS-10: Define and implement DevOps security strategy.

There are numerous cybersecurity best practices that MCSBs contain, both technical and nontechnical capabilities, and controls such as processes. The MCSBs include a set of high-impact security recommendations in a single or multi-cloud environment. In addition to security controls, MCSB offers include service baselines. In contrast to a baseline, a control describes a feature or activity in a high-level way. It does not specify the technology or implementation of the activity, while a baseline describes how the control is implemented on the individual Azure services. In Azure, service baselines are available only for Azure currently. Each organization dictates benchmark recommendations.

Recommend Best Practices for Protecting from Insider and External Attacks

Throughout the MCRA and MCSB, you can find best practices for both insider risk and external threats. The purpose of this section is to examine primarily insider risk and external attack security operations aspects of security controls. All security controls should reduce risk in one or both of these scenarios.

In an attack chain, an adversary or insider takes technical and nontechnical actions to damage an organization. It is important to note that there is no linear path for insider risk or external attacks. Each attack can take its own unique path, but all attacks have many common elements.

As shown in Figure 9.1, the MCRA includes an attack chain diagram that illustrates standard external and insider attack techniques.

In Figure 9.1, the top portion illustrates the steps common to many external attacks, as well as the Microsoft capabilities corresponding to each step. In the bottom part, you will find information about leading insider risk indicators and how Microsoft Purview Insider Risk Management helps you quickly identify, triage, and act on risky user activity.

Several common steps and patterns are involved in external attacks, which can be seen in Figure 9.1. The majority of external attack variation results from using different entry points. Furthermore, attacks may differ depending on the attackers' objectives, including stealing data, encrypting data, or disrupting business operations.

An external attack that results in a significant incident typically involves some form of privilege escalation using credential theft, which can be mitigated by safeguarding privileged access.

An early adaptation of the military concept of kill chain to cybersecurity was created by Lockheed Martin. As a result of this concept of a cybersecurity attack chain, organizations have evolved their understanding of attacks and security controls by viewing attacks as a sequential sequence of events. For detailed control planning, such as threat detection coverage, many organizations today utilize the MITRE ATT&CK framework.

Figure 9.2 illustrates how these are related to a simple prepare-enter-traverse-execute (PETE) model developed by Microsoft to improve communication with nonsecurity professionals and business leaders.

Attackers can use different techniques to achieve their objectives of preparing, entering, traversing, and executing. They can also combine various techniques or use the same process repeatedly to accomplish their goals.

FIGURE 9.1 Microsoft Cybersecurity Reference Architecture

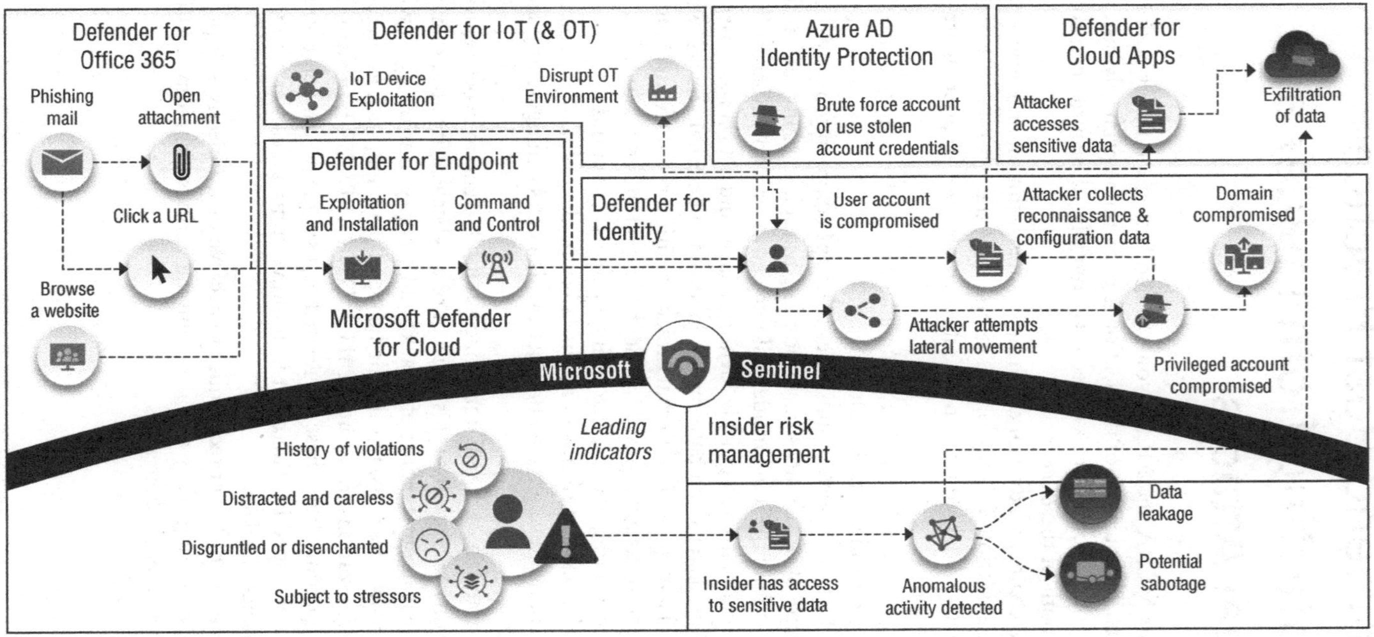

FIGURE 9.2   Prepare-enter-traverse-execute

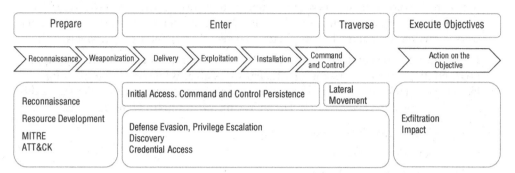

The MCRA and MCSB security best practices are all intended to minimize the risk of attackers succeeding. The MCRA best practices primarily focus on detecting, responding, and recovering from external attacks. Key best practices include the following:

- **Continual improvement toward complete coverage:** Ensure that areas with no visibility and highly vulnerable areas without any preventative measures are continuously improved.

- **Balanced control investments:** Invest in security controls across the entire life cycle of identifying, protecting, detecting, responding, and recovering.

- **From SIEM for everything to XDR + SIEM:** SIEM has been the primary tool for detecting attacks and responding to them for many security operations. From SIEM for everything to XDR and SIEM, security information and event management (SIEM) has been the primary tool for detecting and responding to attacks. Because of their rapid reduction in false positives, extended detection and response (XDR) tools quickly became indispensable for the platforms they monitor (starting with endpoint detection and response [EDR] for endpoints). These tools protect a different breadth of sources than the SIEM for technologies covered by XDR, but they significantly simplify and enhance detection and response. The security best practices then evolved to reflect the strengths of SIEM (comprehensive visibility and correlation across all tools and technology) and XDR (simple, high-quality threat detection of covered assets), as well as the collective need for both types of tooling in security operations.

- **Modern analytics and SOAR Automation:** Integrate the use of security orchestration, automation, and response (SOAR), machine learning (ML), and user entity behavioral analytics (UEBA) technologies to reduce the amount of manual effort involved in security operations. By automating manual actions, SOAR technology reduces distractions and fatigue for human analysts during detection, investigation, and response procedures. Machine learning significantly improves detection by extending human expertise over large data sets and detecting anomalies that may indicate malicious activity. In contrast to attempting to find patterns in the full set of raw log data, UEBA improves detection and investigation by profiling the individual accounts and entities compromised by attackers.

- **OT adaptation:** Adjust your tools and processes as you integrate them with OT environments. It is common for these environments to prioritize safety and to have older systems that still need patches available and may crash after an active scan. Passive network detection is often the best approach to detect threats and isolate systems.

- **Deploy appropriate controls for insider risk as a distinct focus area:** Developing appropriate controls for insider risk is a particular focus area. While some objectives for insider risk attacks are similar to those for external attacks, reducing insider risk is different from lowering external risk. The following are examples of insider risks:

  - Leaks of sensitive data and data spillage
  - Confidentiality violations
  - Intellectual property (IP) theft
  - Fraud
  - Insider trading
  - Regulatory compliance violations

There are many best practices included in the Microsoft Cloud Security Benchmark that help prevent insider and external attacks, including the security controls listed in Table 9.2 that are focused on security operations.

TABLE 9.2   Microsoft Security benchmark for Incident response and logging perspective

Security Controls

IR-1: Preparation: update incident response plan and handling process.

IR-2: Preparation: set up incident notification.

IR-3: Detection and analysis: create incidents based on high-quality alerts.

IR-4: Detection and analysis: investigate an incident.

IR-5: Detection and analysis: prioritize incidents.

IR-6: Containment, eradication, and recovery: automate the incident handling.

IR-7: Post-incident activity: conduct lessons learned and retain evidence.

LT-1: Enable threat detection capabilities.

LT-2: Enable threat detection for identity and access management.

LT-3: Enable logging for security investigation.

LT-4: Enable network logging for security investigation.

LT-5: Centralize security log management and analysis.

LT-6: Configure log storage retention.

LT-7: Use approved time synchronization sources.

For references and more information, visit the following:

github.com/MicrosoftDocs/SecurityBenchmarks/blob/master/
Azure%20Security%20Benchmark/3.0/azure-security-benchmark-v3.0.xlsx

You can use these best practices in MCRA and MCSB to improve your security program effectiveness against both insider and external threats.

> Your security program can be more effective against insider threats and attacks from outside threats by following best practices in MCRA and MCSB. As part of the MCRA and MCSB, several security best practices are directed at reducing the risk of attackers succeeding. Several MCRA best practices focus on the security operations aspects of external attacks: detecting, responding, and recovering.

Recommend Best Practices for Zero Trust Security

To keep up with threats, changes in cloud platforms, and changes in business models as the world rapidly evolves, a Zero Trust approach to security is required. You can find best practices for adopting a Zero Trust approach to security in the MCRA and MCSBs. This section will cover best practices related to a Zero Trust strategy's first and most visible priority, modernizing access controls.

Three principles guide Microsoft's Zero Trust approach to security: assume breach, verify explicitly, and exercise the least privilege. These principles are typically applied to Zero Trust transformations across the technical estate through a series of modernization initiatives. The initiatives include secure identities and access; modern security operations; infrastructure and development security; OT and Internet of Things (IoT) security; data security; and governance, risk, and compliance.

Secure Identities and Access   Through this initiative, users can securely access resources from anywhere in the world by modernizing access control. In contrast to traditional access control based on network location, modern access control explicitly validates trust signals on users and devices. Furthermore, this applies the general mindset that assumes breach/compromise and implements the least privileges for limiting access to resources (defining permissions, just-in-time permissions, and so on).

Modern Security Operations   By reducing attacker dwell time, this initiative aims to reduce organizational risk. Developing modern detection for attackers who try to remain hidden requires reducing dwell time by utilizing the assume breach principle. Dwell time is associated with the length of time an attacker has access to resources before they are detected and removed.

Infrastructure and Development Security   A vital goal of this task is to integrate security into infrastructure, platforms, and applications. Security should be integrated into related initiatives, such as migrating existing workloads to the cloud and developing new workloads using DevOps techniques.

OT and IoT Security   A key goal of this task is to modernize OT and IoT security and adopt Zero Trust principles within constraints imposed by older technologies that have limited processing power, limited connectivity, stringent safety regulations, and operational uptime requirements.

Data Security   This initiative aims to enable an organization to identify, classify, protect, and monitor critical business data.

Governance, Risk, and Compliance   Using Zero Trust principles as the foundation for processes, practices, and policies, this initiative aims to modernize the functions that ensure that the organization adheres to security and compliance requirements.

As part of the initiative to modernize access control, the MCRA includes many best practices.

Prioritize privileged access.   Provide elevated security for privileged resources.

To modernize access control, implement Zero Trust principles.   Implement and validate telemetry and signals during access requests and authorized sessions, and limit access to accounts based on least privilege. Conditional Access brings signals together, to make decisions, and enforce organizational policies. Azure AD conditional access is at the heart of the new identity-driven control plane.

Make sure that multifactor authentication (MFA) combines multiple types of authentication and that the claimant is who they say they are.

You can validate trust signals on users and their sessions using Azure AD Identity Protection and Azure AD conditional access.

Explicitly validate device trust signals.   Device trust signals indicate if a user's device is configured correctly and patched and if an attacker has compromised it. Microsoft Defender for Endpoint, Azure AD Conditional Access, and Microsoft Intune can be used to implement this. As attackers discover new ways to evade existing controls, continuously improve signal coverage and fidelity. Ensure consistent authentication policies are enforced across all access requests, including direct access to cloud applications, remote network access through virtual private networks, remote access to legacy and on-premise applications via application proxies, and local wireless and wired networks. People can work securely from anywhere with this technology.

Integrate security operations signals with access decisions.   Integrating current information on compromised devices, users, and other assets into access decisions is important. Access should be blocked to and from compromised assets while security operations are cleaning them up. Once the integrity of the asset has been restored, access should be granted.

Simplify identity and access management architecture.   Complexity can degrade security, resulting in human error during manual tasks and automation deployment. It is essential to simplify the experience of general users, IT personnel, and security engineers so that attackers can exploit gaps and inconsistencies. Using a single identity and implementing single sign-on, for instance, will simplify the user experience and reduce friction and complexity in security operations workflows, administrator workflows, and more. Architecture, operations, and security operations will be simplified using a single directory.

Go beyond VPNs to modernize access to on-premises applications.   With this concept, people can work from home without experiencing a slowdown or experiencing the extra steps that VPNs introduce. This concept is included in adopting secure access service edge (SASE) architectures, which emphasize identity-enabled network access options.

Several Zero Trust best practices are included in the MCSB security controls, including those in Table 9.3 relating to access control modernization. Table 9.3 lists all high-level key best practices to apply in your organization from identity management, privileged access, and network security perspectives.

For references and more information, visit the following:

```
github.com/MicrosoftDocs/SecurityBenchmarks/blob/master/
Azure%20Security%20Benchmark/3.0/azure-security-benchmark-v3.0.xlsx
```

TABLE 9.3   Best Practices for Identity Management, Privileged Access, and Network Security

Security Controls

IM-1: Use a centralized identity and authentication system.

IM-2: Protect identity and authentication systems.

IM-3: Manage application identities securely and automatically.

IM-4: Authenticate server and services.

IM-5: Use single sign-on (SSO) for application access.

IM-6: Use strong authentication controls.

IM-7: Restrict resource access based on conditions.

IM-8: Restrict the exposure of credential and secrets.

IM-9: Secure user access to existing applications.

PA-1: Separate and limit highly privileged/administrative users.

PA-2: Avoid standing access for user accounts and permissions.

PA-3: Manage the life cycle of identities and entitlements.

PA-4: Review and reconcile user access regularly.

PA-5: Set up emergency access.

PA-6: Use privileged access workstations.

PA-7: Follow the just enough administration (least privilege) principle.

PA-8: Determine the access process for cloud provider support.

TABLE 9.3 Best Practices for Identity Management, Privileged Access, and Network Security *(continued)*

Security Controls

NS-1: Establish network segmentation boundaries.

NS-2: Secure cloud services with network controls.

NS-3: Deploy a firewall at the edge of an enterprise network.

NS-4: Deploy intrusion detection/intrusion prevention systems (IDS/IPS).

NS-5: Deploy DDOS protection.

NS-6: Deploy a web application firewall.

NS-7: Simplify network security configuration.

NS-8: Detect and disable insecure services and protocols.

NS-9: Connect on-premises or cloud networks privately.

NS-10: Ensure domain name system (DNS) security.

As threats, cloud platforms, and business models evolve rapidly, a Zero Trust approach to security is required to keep up. Throughout the MCRA and MCSBs, you can find best practices for adopting a Zero Trust approach to security.

Recommend Best Practices for Zero Trust Rapid Modernization Plan

To achieve the most excellent security and productivity gains with the least time and effort, you need to start with Zero Trust, a significant security program transformation.

The Zero Trust Rapid Modernization Plan (RaMP) is included in the MCRA and provides best practices that help you prioritize your security modernization. In the RaMP, Microsoft identifies the most effective controls for the most relevant and common attacks with the least amount of time, effort, and resources required.

Among the recommended security modernization initiatives in the Zero Trust RaMP are as follows:

- **Secure identities and access:** Using cloud-based security solutions such as Azure AD, Intune, Microsoft Defender for Endpoints, and Azure AD App Proxy, these quick wins modernize access control to improve productivity and security.

- **Data security goverance, risk, compliance (GRC):** This quick win addresses securing business-critical data and rapidly recovering from ransomware/extortion attacks.

- **Modern security operations:** These quick wins aim to streamline responses to standard attacks, get enterprise-wide visibility, and automate manual tasks that fatigue analysts.
- **Infrastructure and development security:** Deployment of microsegmentation concepts for identity and network access control, as well as reducing legacy risk, are among the quick wins in this area.
- **OT and IoT security:** This quick win aims to detect, protect, and monitor these systems quickly.

 You can prioritize your security modernization by following the Zero Trust RaMP, which is included in the MCRA. As a result of this RaMP, the most effective controls are identified for the most common and relevant attacks with the least amount of time, effort, and resources.

Recommend a DevSecOps Process

Using DevSecOps processes and tools, innovation security is applied to DevOps development processes. DevSecOps must understand and thoughtfully integrate security into the development process since DevOps itself is an emerging discipline with many process variations. Low-friction changes to the code, development processes, and infrastructure that hosts the workload should be the first step toward adding security. Invest in changes that have the most significant positive impact on security while putting a low burden on DevOps skills and processes.

Continuous integration and continuous delivery (CI/CD) DevOps processes are discussed in this section, along with which security controls Microsoft recommends integrating first.

Plan and Develop

Modern development typically uses an agile development methodology. Security should be integrated into this process in the following ways:

- Modeling threats to view the application from the point of view of a potential attacker
- Using a lightweight static analysis plug-in for integrated development environments (IDEs)
- Establishing security coding standards, peer review processes, and pre-commit hooks through peer reviews

Each of these steps isn't mandatory, but each helps uncover security issues early when they can be fixed much more efficiently and at a lower cost.

Threat Modeling

A threat model is one of the most critical security practices because it delivers immediate results and helps developers develop a security mindset to improve security in future projects.

A threat model is simple, though it can be complicated if necessary. Its purpose is to provide your application with a realistic security view that includes the following:

- How can attackers exploit the application's design?

- How can vulnerabilities be fixed?

- How important is it to fix issues?

It lets you see an application from an attacker's perspective, putting yourself in the attacker's shoes. You learn how to block attacks before attackers can execute them. The attacker can be treated as a hostile user persona if your team uses user personas in the design.

There are various threat modeling approaches, from simple question-and-answer approaches to detailed tool-based analyses, such as the STRIDE model, the DREAD model, or the OWASP threat model.

Starting Simple with Threat Modeling

Using basic questions as a starting point for threat modeling is recommended since some approaches can be time-consuming and skill-intensive. Though more straightforward methods provide less detail, they start the critical thinking process and help you identify major security issues quickly.

The simple questions method from Microsoft asks specific technical questions designed to highlight common security design errors.

The following questions should be asked and answered for each application or component:

- Is Azure AD, TLS (with mutual authentication), or another modern security protocol used to authenticate connections? This prevents unauthorized access to the application and data. Your security team recommends using Azure Active Directory, TLS (with mutual authentication), or another modern security protocol to protect your application and data against unauthorized access.

  - Application and users (if applicable)

  - Interactions between different application components and services (if applicable)

- Does your application limit access to data to only those who need it? This prevents unauthorized alteration or tampering with data.

- The security team can detect and investigate attacks faster if application activity is logged and fed into a security information and event management (SIEM) via Azure Monitor or a similar solution.

- Ensure that business-critical data is encrypted with a security team-approved method. This prevents unauthorized copying of data at rest.

- TLS helps prevent unauthorized copying of data during inbound and outbound network traffic.

- Is the application protected against distributed denial-of-service (DDoS) attacks using a service like Azure DDoS protection, Akamai, or similar?

- The application may store authentication credentials for accessing other applications, databases, or services, which can help identify if an attacker can use it to attack other systems.

- What security and privacy requirements must you meet in the localities you operate in? (This helps protect your users' private information and avoid compliance fines.)

The OWASP threat modeling method also begins the threat modeling process by asking simple, nontechnical questions.

You can choose either or both approaches based on your team's needs.

The team will be able to apply advanced techniques from the Microsoft Security Development Lifecycle as they become more comfortable with the process. They can also integrate threat modeling tools like Microsoft's Threat Modeling Tool to gain deeper insights and automate the process.

Pre-Commit Hooks and Security Plug-Ins for the IDE

Developers need to focus on the speed of delivery so that security checks don't slow down the process. When security checks start at the pipeline, a slowdown occurs. Adding steps such as IDE security plug-ins and pre-commit hooks is essential to speed up the process and provide immediate feedback. Developers learn about potential vulnerabilities after pushing the code to the repository. Pushing the code means moving or publishing the content for production or end-user usage.

In the developer's familiar IDE environment, IDE security plug-ins identify different security issues during the development process. In addition to providing immediate feedback on security risks in the developer's code, plug-ins can also reveal security risks in third-party libraries and packages. Depending on your IDE, many open-source and commercial plug-ins are available and provided by security companies.

If your version control system allows it, consider using a pre-commit framework. Pre-commit frameworks are Git hook scripts that help identify issues before a developer submits code for review.

A Git hook is a script that runs automatically whenever a particular event occurs.

For instance, you can use GitHub's pre-commit feature.

Secure Coding Standards and Peer Review

Pull requests are standard in the development process. Often, peer reviews reveal undiscovered defects, bugs, or issues caused by human error during the pull request process. Before creating a pull request, it's good practice to have a security champion or knowledgeable security teammate to guide you through the peer review process.

The OWASP secure coding practices can be integrated with general coding techniques to help developers learn certain coding principles and how to apply them.

Commit the Code

Developers manage, share, and create their code in repositories like GitHub or Azure Repos. This approach allows developers to collaborate easily on a central, version-controlled library of code. However, enabling many collaborators on one codebase also runs the risk of introducing changes. It is possible to introduce vulnerabilities or unintentionally include credentials and tokens in commits due to this risk.

Development teams should evaluate and implement a repository scanning capability to address this risk. Repository scanning tools analyze source code within repositories for vulnerabilities and credential changes and flag any issues for remediation. This capability protects against human error and is helpful for distributed teams where many people collaborate in the same repository.

Dependency Management

Most software code in current applications contains elements from external packages and libraries or is based on them. As a result of the adoption of dependencies in source code, potential risks must be addressed. There are serious security issues with third-party libraries and developers who must follow the best life cycles and update dependencies consistently.

Ensure that your development team knows what components to include in their applications. You can use tools such as OWASP Dependency-Check, WhiteSource, and others to download secure and up-to-date versions from known sources. Your team will also need a process for keeping versions up-to-date.

The security of package feeds is also essential, and the focus is not just on dependency vulnerabilities or their life cycles. A responsible package management administration must address these risks because known attack vectors target package management systems, including typosquatting, compromising existing packages, substitution attacks, and others.

Typosquatting is a social engineering attack targeting Internet users who erroneously type a URL into their web browser, preferably using a search engine. Commonly, it concerns tricking users into visiting malicious websites with URLs that are common misspellings of reputable websites. End users may be tricked into entering sensitive details into these fake sites. These sites can do significant reputational damage to organizations victimized by these attackers.

Compromising existing packages, an attacker uploaded a malicious script to modify the existing packages, so all developers who used the package embedded in their code unwittingly infected end users' PCs with malware.

A substitution attack can target internally developed packages and packages obtained from public repositories. Typically, malicious code is published in a package with a high version number in shared package repositories. The attackers identify internal package names and place malicious code with the same name in shared package repositories.

Static Application Security Testing

In addition to third-party libraries and package management, your team should focus on code security. Different ways can be used to improve code security, and a comprehensive source code scan can also help catch mistakes missed by previous steps. As we discussed previously, you can use IDE security plug-ins or wire incremental static analysis pre-commit and commit checks. The result of this approach is that development can be slowed down, and a burden may be introduced.

If a team wants to implement static code scanning practices, one way is to integrate static code analysis into continuous integration, which verifies security as soon as changes are made. SonarCloud is a good example. SonarCloud wraps multiple static application security testing (SAST) tools for different languages, assessing and tracking technical debt while focusing on maintainability. It also has security-specific checkers for code quality and style. Commercial and open-source tools are also available.

You want to minimize false positives and provide clear, actionable feedback about problems to fix to ensure the feedback loop is effective. It's also a good idea to implement a workflow to prevent code commits to the default branch if there are any findings. Unit testing as well as quality becomes part of security.

Secure Pipelines

In DevOps, automation is taken to a new level because everything is built into a pipeline. Continuous integration and delivery (CI/CD) are integral to modern development processes. CI/CD involves regularly merging developer code into a central codebase and automatically performing standard builds and tests.

A pipeline is a crucial part of development. But using it to run scripts or deploy code can pose unique security risks. You want to ensure your CI/CD pipelines do not become avenues for running malicious code, stealing credentials, or giving attackers any surface area for access.

Additionally, your team should only deploy the code that will be released. There are different guidelines for addressing the risks related to other platforms used by DevOps teams.

Build and Test

Iterative changes to sections of code can be made quickly and at scale with release pipelines. Many organizations use build-and-release pipelines to automate and standardize the development process. The teams will only need to spend a little time redeploying or upgrading existing environments.

The release pipelines allow teams to promote code from development environments to testing environments and finally into production. In addition to automation, development teams should include security tools that perform scripted, automated tests when deploying code into testing environments. Unit testing should be conducted on application features to check for vulnerabilities and public endpoints, and testing ensures intentional access.

Dynamic Application Security Testing

As part of a waterfall development model, security is usually introduced at the end, right before going into production. Penetration (pen) testing is one of the most popular security approaches. During penetration testing, a team can examine the application from an attacker's point of view or the black-box perspective.

Dynamic application security testing (DAST) is one of the action points of a penetration test. The DAST test is a web application security test that examines how the application responds to specially crafted requests to find security issues. DAST tools are also known as web application vulnerability scanners. One example is an open-source tool, OWASP Zed Attack Proxy (ZAP). It finds vulnerabilities in a running web application. OWASP ZAP can perform a passive baseline or full scan based on the configuration.

Pen testing has the disadvantage that it takes time, and since DevOps development moves rapidly, that time frame might not be feasible. Pen testing is still worthwhile to uncover issues that SAST and other steps might have missed during the development process, and DAST tools like OWASP ZAP can assist.

The OWASP ZAP scanner spins up in the container during the run, does its scanning, and then publishes the results. OWASP ZAP is integrated into the pipeline as a task. Even though it's not a complete penetration test, it is still a valuable quality measure in the development cycle for improving security posture.

Cloud Configuration Validation and Infrastructure Scanning

Ensure you secure the code for your applications and the environments into which they are deployed. Organizations that want to move quickly, innovate, and utilize new technologies require secure environments, allowing teams to experiment rapidly in new environments.

Organizations can create security standards using Azure capabilities, including Azure Policy, and teams can create policy sets using Azure Policy. As a result of the policy sets, certain workload types and configuration items, such as public IP addresses, cannot be created. Teams can experiment within a safe and controlled environment using these guardrails, which balance innovation and governance.

As part of its efforts to bring developers and operations closer together, DevOps supports migrating existing infrastructure to infrastructure as code.

As part of infrastructure as code (IaC), infrastructure (networks, virtual machines, load balancers, and connection topologies) is managed descriptively. IaC uses the same versioning model as the DevOps team uses for source code. Similar to the principle that the exact source code yields the same binary, an IaC model creates the same environment every time it is utilized. IaC is a crucial DevOps practice used in continuous delivery.

DevSecOps shifts security left and emphasizes that security isn't just about application security but infrastructure security. As part of DevSecOps, infrastructure security is supported by incorporating security scanning before deployment. You would then apply the same security actions to infrastructure as to application security as infrastructure became code. Depending on the IaC strategy you have chosen, there are security tools that can be used to conduct infrastructure security scanning.

Teams increasingly utilize containerization as part of application architecture decisions due to cloud adoption—some container repositories scan images for packages with known vulnerabilities. However, there is still a risk that a container may contain outdated software.

Because of this risk, scanning the container for security risks is vital. There are several open-source and commercial security tools aimed at this area that are highly integrated into the CD process and target this area. In addition to enabling teams to adopt DevSecOps for infrastructure as code, the security tools assist them in learning how to use containers more specifically.

Go to Production and Operate

After the production period, the security state must continue to be monitored and managed. At this point, attention must be paid to the cloud infrastructure and widespread applications.

Configuration and Infrastructure Scanning

Azure tenant security from (The Azure Tenant Security Solution) AzSK provides visibility into cloud subscriptions and resource configuration across multiple subscriptions.

Monitoring and security capabilities are included in Azure. These capabilities are designed to detect and alert any abnormal events or configurations that require investigation and potential remediation.

Several first-party tools, such as Microsoft Defender for Cloud and Microsoft Sentinel, are natively integrated into Azure environments and complement environment and code security tools. Additionally, the technologies provide comprehensive security monitoring so organizations can experiment and innovate safely and securely.

Penetration Testing

Microsoft recommends performing penetration testing to determine whether the infrastructure or application configuration contains any vulnerabilities that attackers could exploit.

Microsoft guides penetration testing in Azure, as do many products and partners. Several types of testing are typically conducted.

- Tests are shown on your endpoints to identify vulnerabilities.

- You can test your endpoints for fuzz errors by providing malformed input data.

- The fuzz testing method finds functional bugs and security flaws in code and applications. An error discovered in fuzz testing is named a *fuzz error*.

- Your endpoints should be scanned for ports.

A key element of DevSecOps is the use of data-driven, event-driven processes. Providing organizations with an integrated security model allows them to move quickly and experiment with new technologies that will drive innovation.

Many organizations integrate alerts and usage data into their IT service management (ITSM) platforms as part of these processes. These processes assist teams in identifying, evaluating, and responding to potential risks. Therefore, security events can be handled using the same structured workflow that is used for other incidents and requests.

Feedback Loops

Through all of these techniques and tools, teams can identify and flag potential risks and vulnerabilities that require further investigation and resolution. A route back to the development team is necessary for operations teams who receive alerts or discover potential issues when investigating support tickets. A smooth, collaborative feedback loop addresses problems quickly and minimizes vulnerabilities.

Integrating feedback into a developer work management system, such as Azure DevOps or GitHub, is common. It is possible to link alerts or incidents to work items that developers can manage. As a result, developers can cost-effectively resolve issues within the context of their standard workflow, including development, testing, and release.

A DevSecOps approach prioritizes security during development and operations. DevSecOps help developers write more secure code, embracing security best practices, respond quickly to software supply chain vulnerabilities, and release code faster and more securely by collaborating and embracing security best practices. It's essential to understand and thoughtfully integrate security into the development process because DevOps is an emerging discipline with a high degree of process variation.

Recommend a Methodology for Asset Protection

An asset can be either physical or virtual, such as a laptop, a database, a file, and an account for virtual storage. The security of business-critical assets often rests on the performance of underlying systems, such as storage, data, endpoint devices, and application components. As a general rule, the most valuable technical assets are data and the availability of applications, such as business websites, production lines, and communication tools.

Asset protection controls support a security architecture, standards, or policy. Asset types and security requirements differ, and the security standards for any asset type should be consistently applied to all instances.

Protection of assets is the responsibility of an asset protection team. The team collaborates with other disciplines, such as governance, architecture, security operations, and workload management.

As a result of gaps in the application of standards and policies, threat actors are persistent and seek out vulnerabilities. Attackers can directly target data and applications that are critical to the business. They can also target the infrastructure that grants them access to business-critical data and applications. In access control, the focus is on managing authorized access to resources. As part of asset protection, consideration is given to all other possible ways to gain access or control resources out of the band. Together, these two disciplines complement each other and should be designed following your architectural, policy, and standard needs.

Get Secure

Our goal at Get Secure is to bring your organization's resources up-to-date with the current security standards, policies, and architecture. Activities can be divided into two categories.

- **Brownfield:** Enhance the security of existing assets by retrofitting current security standards and controls. IT environments may be designed and operated by organizations with security as a low priority. As a result of this approach, a significant amount of technical debt is created: weak security configurations, outdated software, unencrypted communication and storage, legacy software and protocols, and more. Bring your security controls up-to-date. As attackers continually enhance their capabilities to exploit these opportunities, this improvement is critical to mitigating risk.

- Greenfield: Maintain standards for the configuration of new assets and asset types. This process is crucial to avoid continuously creating an instant legacy, brownfield systems, or systems that do not comply with current standards. A more significant expense will be associated with this technical debt, which will increase risk exposure until it is resolved.

Typically, getting secure corresponds to a one-time investment in capital expenditures (CAPEX). For new software projects, major software upgrades, or overall cloud adoption initiatives, security budgets should be allocated as closely as possible to the creation of the asset.

Stay Secure

As time passes, everything degrades. Items made of physical materials wear out over time. Virtual things like virtual machines, SaaS, security controls, and security are changing in the environment. They may not meet changing requirements in the future. Because of the following changes, these shifts occur rapidly today:

- Business requirements are influenced by digital transformation.

- Updates to technology requirements result from rapid advancements in cloud platforms and new features.

- Attacker innovations and the rapid advancement of native cloud security capabilities necessitate updates to security requirements.

DevSecOps in innovation security is impacted by this dynamic, as well as security operations, access control, and DevSecOps in security.

There are many aspects to staying secure. Protect your assets by focusing on these two areas:

- **Continuous cloud improvement:** Take advantage of the continuous improvements in security capabilities that the cloud offers. In recent years, many Azure services, such as Azure Storage and Azure SQL Database, have added security features to protect against attackers.

- **Software end of life:** If security updates are no longer provided for any software, including operating systems, business-critical data and applications may be vulnerable to cheap and easy attacks. Cloud providers typically maintain software as a service (SaaS) and infrastructure and platforms in the cloud, but enterprises typically install, author, and maintain a significant amount of software themselves. Consider upgrading or retiring end-of-life software.

Investing in your security posture will reduce the risk of a significant security incident. Investments require ongoing security maintenance as part of their operational expenditures (OPEX).

Dilemmas Surrounding Patches

The support of IT and security leaders and teams is of paramount importance to business leaders. A hostile environment poses inherent risks when running complex software. Managing operational risks and security risks is a constant challenge for IT and security leaders.

- **Operational risk:** A change to the software where the system runs could disrupt business processes. Such changes affect the assumptions made when the system was customized for the organization. This fact creates pressure to avoid changing the system.

- **Security risk:** In the event of an attack, the business is at risk of experiencing downtime. Security updates are analyzed by attackers as soon as they are released. Within 24 to 48 hours, they can develop a working exploit to attack organizations that have not updated their security software.

Because of the continual evolution of technology and attack techniques, your organization may face this dilemma frequently. Stakeholders of the businesses should be aware of the risks associated with using complex software. Consider the following examples of updating business processes:

- **Integrating software maintenance:** With IT business operational assumptions, schedules, forecasts, and other business processes, software maintenance needs to be planned and executed.

- **Investing in architectures:** Make a commitment to architectures that simplify maintenance and minimize the impact on business operations. Implementing a service-oriented architecture or migrating to cloud services could involve updating existing architectures or creating a new architecture entirely.

IT and security leaders can support essential business goals only with the support of business leaders. Constantly needing to manage corporate politics to ensure security in the IT environment creates a no-win situation.

Network Isolation

Isolating the network may be a viable solution to protect older assets that are no longer secure but cannot be immediately retired. It is typical for end-of-life operating systems and applications to encounter this scenario, which is common in OT environments and legacy systems.

Even though asset protection is concerned with protecting assets that cannot be secured, isolation is considered an access control measure.

In some cases, it is difficult to disconnect and isolate end-of-life systems completely. These insecure systems should not be fully connected to a production network, because attackers can compromise such configurations and gain access to the organization's assets.

Technology that has worked well for a decade or more is never cheap or easy to upgrade or replace; nonetheless, the potential business impact of losing control over multiple critical assets is often more significant than the cost of upgrading or replacing them. When it comes to assets that cannot be isolated, organizations find that modernizing the workload with cloud technology and analytics can create new business value that can offset or justify the cost of upgrading or replacing the asset.

Security is a challenge in a world that is constantly changing. Maintaining a constant awareness of what assets need to be modernized and what assets need to be secured is critical. Evaluation should be based on business risks and business priorities.

Getting Started

Microsoft recommends that organizations follow these steps to begin protecting their assets:

- **Focus on well-known resources first:** Consider virtual machines, networks, and identities in the cloud that the team is already familiar with. By using native cloud tools such as Microsoft Defender for Cloud, you can make immediate progress, and the assets are often easier to manage and secure.

- **Start with vendor/industry baselines:** Consider implementing a proven and well-known security solution, such as the following:

  - Security baselines in the Microsoft cloud security benchmark. For each Azure service, Microsoft provides security configuration guidance. Based on these baselines, Azure security benchmarks are applied to each service's unique characteristics. Security teams can use this approach to secure each service and refine configurations as necessary.

  - Microsoft security baselines. Microsoft provides security configuration guidance for Microsoft products, such as Windows, Microsoft Office, and Microsoft Edge.

  - Center for Internet Security (CIS) benchmarks. There are specific configuration guidelines provided by the CIS for many products and vendors.

Key Information

The following sections act as a guide to support your asset protection process.

Accountable and Responsible Teams

Security is always the responsibility of the ultimate resource owner in the business, that is, the individual responsible for all other risks and benefits. In addition to advising the accountable owner on the risks, any mitigations, and how to perform the actual deployment, the security teams and subject-matter experts are collectively accountable.

Asset protection responsibilities may be carried out by IT operations that manage enterprise-wide assets, by DevOps and DevSecOps teams responsible for the assets of their workloads, or by security teams collaborating with IT and DevOps and DevSecOps teams.

Cloud computing allows organizations to transfer many of these responsibilities to the cloud provider, such as updating firmware and virtualization solutions, or make them more accessible, such as scanning and remediating security configurations.

Cloud Elasticity

The life span of cloud resources may be shorter than that of on-premises resources. To accomplish a task, workloads can create additional instances of servers, Azure Functions, and other resources as needed. After the resource has been removed, Azure removes it. In some cases, this scenario can occur within months, while in others, it can happen within minutes or hours. Ensure that your asset protection processes and measurements account for this possibility.

Many processes must be adjusted to take advantage of cloud elasticity. You will be able to see your inventory on demand rather than having static reports, improving your visibility. Additionally, cloud elasticity enhances your ability to resolve problems.

Exception Management

The best practice should be applied consistently to all instances of an asset once identified. Exceptions may need to be made temporarily, but they should be managed with specific expiration dates. Make sure that temporary exceptions do not become permanent business risks.

Challenges with Measuring Value

Often, it is difficult to determine the business value of asset protection, and a problem is apparent only once it results in a real-world failure. In the absence of security updates, vulnerabilities are silent and invisible.

Prefer Automated Policy

Consider automated enforcement and remediation mechanisms such as Azure Policy for asset protection. By avoiding repetitive manual tasks, cost and morale issues can be avoided. Human error is also reduced as a result of this technology.

In Azure Policy, central teams can specify which configurations should be used across all cloud-based assets.

Design Controls as a Team

Stakeholders should be involved in the design of all controls:

- In addition, the asset protection team provides subject-matter expertise related to the assets, the controls available for them, and the feasibility of implementing those controls.

- The governance team provides context regarding how the controls fit within the security architecture, policies, and standards, as well as regulatory compliance requirements.

- It is the responsibility of security operations to advise on detective controls. Security operations tools, processes, and training are integrated with alerts and logs.

- In addition, vendors and cloud providers are able to provide deep subject-matter expertise on systems and components to avoid issues that are commonly experienced by their customers.

Asset protection aims to implement controls to support security architecture, standards, and policies. Each asset type and security requirement are unique, and security standards should be applied consistently to every instance of the asset type. Preventive, detective, and other types of controls are aligned to meet the policies, standards, and architecture of asset protection.

Recommend Strategies for Managing and Minimizing Risk

Business operations involve risks. Security teams provide information and advice to decision-makers to address security risks. After learning about your business, security professionals use their expertise to identify threats to your goals and assets. Your security team evaluates each risk, and acceptable risks are recommended to your decision-makers. The following information is provided with the understanding that the owner must make decisions regarding the asset or process.

A mature security policy exposes, mitigates, and empowers the business to make changes with the least risk. To achieve that maturity level, you must deeply understand risk and integrate security. Regardless of your organization's maturity level, the top security risks should be included in your risk register, and those risks are then reduced to a manageable level.

What Is Cybersecurity Risk?

Human attackers attempt to steal technology, money, or information to damage or destroy business assets, revenue, and reputation.

Cybersecurity risks should be aligned with your risk measurement, tracking, and mitigation framework, even though they occur in the technical environment. Although these attacks happen in the technological environment, they often pose a risk to your entire organization. It is still common for organizations to view cybersecurity risks as technical problems that must be fixed. The wrong conclusions are drawn from this perception that fails to mitigate the strategic business impact of cybersecurity risks.

A typical technical-oriented program becomes a business framework in Figure 9.3 as per Microsoft's recommendation.

FIGURE 9.3   Technical-oriented program

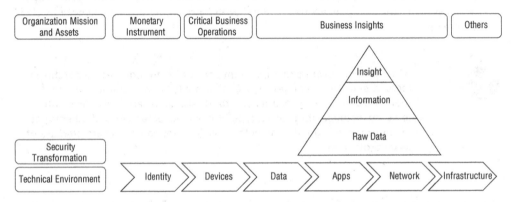

Rather than focusing on the technical aspects of security, security leaders should learn what assets and data matter to business leaders. Organize teams according to business importance in spending time, attention, and budgets. While working through solutions, the security and IT teams apply the technical lens. Cybersecurity risks can be solved incorrectly if viewed purely as a technological problem.

Align Your Security Risk Management

Maintain a strong connection between your organization's leadership and cybersecurity. In addition to human relationships, this concept also applies to explicit processes. Business opportunities are always changing, as is the nature of security risk, and maintaining and improving this relationship is essential to reducing security risks.

Understanding how business value relates to specific technical assets is key to this relationship. Without this direction, your security team cannot determine what's most important to your organization, and the most important assets can be protected only with lucky guesses.

The process should begin as soon as possible. Understanding your organization's sensitive and business-critical assets is an excellent place to start. A typical process would proceed as follows:

- Communicate in the language of the part of the organization you are dealing with when explaining security threats. In this way, the risk and impact on the overall mission and strategy of the organization can be quantified.

- Talk to people across the organization to actively listen and learn. Understand what impact a compromise or breach would have on essential business services and information. By understanding this, your security team can see how important it is to invest in policies, standards, training, and security controls.

- Implement concrete, sustainable actions based on learnings about business priorities and risks, including the following:
  - Priority-oriented short-term planning.
    - Ensure your critical assets and high-value information are protected with appropriate security controls. These controls enhance business productivity while security is increased.
    - The most likely threats to cause business impact are immediate and emerging.
    - Maintain alignment with business strategies and initiatives.
  - Setting long-term goals to improve the overall security posture by making steady progress over time.

- Create a Zero Trust strategy, plan, and architecture for reducing risks within your organization by aligning them with Zero Trust principles such as assuming breach, least privilege, and detailed verification. By adopting these principles, static controls are replaced by dynamic risk-based decisions. These decisions are made based on real-time detections of unusual behavior regardless of where the threat originated.

- Operate security best practices throughout the organization to pay off technical debt. Security patches, retirement or isolation of legacy systems, and replacing password-based authentication with passwordless and multifactor authentication are examples of ways to reduce technical debt. You must make steady payments to realize your investments' full benefits and value, just like paying off a mortgage.

- To protect data from loss or compromise throughout its life cycle, use data classifications, sensitivity labels, and role-based access controls. It is impossible to capture the business context's dynamic, prosperous nature, and insight into these efforts. However, these methods guide information governance and protection, limiting the impact of an attack.

The culture should emphasize open collaboration between business, IT, and security colleagues. Practice, communicate, and publicly model the correct behavior to establish a healthy security culture. Applying this behavior in a growth mindset of continuous learning is essential. Changes in culture should focus on eliminating silos across security, IT, and the larger business organization to increase knowledge sharing and resilience.

Knowing Cybersecurity Risk

Cybersecurity risk comes from human attackers trying to steal money, information, or technology. It is essential to understand their motivations and behavior patterns.

Reasons for Motivation

Organizations with legitimate motivations and incentives mirror those of attackers. As long as you understand the attacker's motivations, you can determine the likelihood and potential impact of different attacks. Security strategies and the most critical technical controls are similar across organizations, but this context helps you prioritize security investments.

A Pattern of Behavior

Human attackers influence organizations' behavior in a variety of ways.

- **ROI:** For-profit attackers are most likely to pose the most threats to organizations because they seek a financial return on investment (ROI). These attackers tend to use the cheapest and most effective tools and techniques. Attacks (for example, stealth and tooling) typically become more sophisticated as new methods are proven and made available for large-scale adoption.

- **The long game:** An attack group that has a leading edge is driven by long-term mission outcomes and has funding available to pursue innovation. Innovative tactics might include investing in supply chain attacks to hinder detection and investigation or changing tactics within an attack campaign to hinder detection and investigation.

  - **Flexible:** The attack vectors they use to enter the network are flexible.

  - **Objective-driven:** They achieve a defined purpose by accessing your environment. The goals may be specific to your people, data, or applications, or you may fit into a particular class of targets. For example, you may be seen as a profitable business that will pay to restore data access.

  - **Stealthy:** They remove evidence and hide their tracks, usually with varying levels of investment and priority.

  - **Patient:** To understand your infrastructure, application, data, and business environment, they must be patient.

  - **Well-resourced and skilled:** Their skills and resources are well-suited to the technologies they target, though the depth of their expertise can vary.

  - **Experienced:** Their experience allows them to gain access or control of different aspects of the estate using established techniques and tools.

It is important to understand the motivations and behavior patterns of these attackers so that you can minimize cybersecurity risks. Human attackers steal money, information, or technology. Typically, attackers are flexible, objective-driven, stealthy, patient, well-resourced, skilled, and experienced.

Plan for Ransomware Protection and Extortion-Based Attacks

The biggest security challenge facing businesses today is ransomware attacks, which have risen at a high percentage per year in recent years. While the best strategy is to prevent ransomware attacks from happening in the first place, you can never be sure your data won't be held hostage. Therefore, a ransomware response plan is essential. Microsoft classified the ransomware plan into three phases.

Developing a recovery plan is phase 1 of ransomware protection. Ransomware attacks can be limited by phase 2 of ransomware protection: keeping the scope of damage to a minimum. They can be rendered impossible by phase 3: preventing ransomware attacks from happening in the first place.

Let's start with phase 1 of ransomware protection, building a recovery plan.

If you're facing such attacks, preparing your organization for an alternative to paying the ransom is important. While hackers have a variety of ways to force you into paying, they mainly focus on two things.

- Letting you regain access for a fee
- Letting you avoid disclosure by paying

Regain Access for a Fee

By encrypting your systems and data and demanding payment for the decryption key, attackers usually threaten not to give you back access to your systems and data.

Ransom payment isn't as straightforward as it appears. It is uncertain whether paying the ransom will work because you are dealing with criminals who are interested only in payment (and often amateur operators using a toolkit provided by others). If they fail to provide you with a key that decrypts 100 percent of your systems and data, they are not required to provide a key. In many cases, homegrown attacker tools are used to decrypt these systems.

Avoid Disclosure by Paying

Payment is demanded so that your data will not be released to the Dark Web (other criminals) or the public.

Your organization needs to ensure that its entire enterprise can be restored from immutable storage, which neither the attacker nor you can alter, to avoid being forced into paying (the most profitable situation for attackers). Identifying the most sensitive assets and ensuring their protection at a higher level of assurance is also critical, but this is a more complex and a longer process. In phases 1 and 2, we recommend bringing together business, IT, and security stakeholders to ask and answer questions like the following:

- When our business assets are compromised, which could be the most devastating? For example, what assets are we willing to pay an extortion demand for if attackers control them?

- What are the IT assets associated with these business assets (such as files, applications, databases, servers, and control systems)?
- To prevent attackers with access to the general IT environment from accessing these assets, how can we protect or isolate these assets?

Secure Backups

To force you into paying extortion demands, attackers frequently target backups and critical documentation required for recovery. Most organizations' backup and restoration procedures don't protect this level of intentional targeting. To prevent an attacker from deliberately erasing or encrypting backups of critical systems and data, you should always back up essential systems and their data.

As a result of this preparation, the organization is more resilient to natural disasters and rapid attacks such as WannaCry.

Accountabilities of Members of Programs and Projects

To determine and drive results, Table 9.4 shows how to protect your data from ransomware through sponsorship/program management/project management.

TABLE 9.4   Protecting Against Ransomware

Lead	Implementor	Accountability
Central IT operations or CIO		Executive sponsorship
Program lead from central IT infrastructure	Central IT infrastructure/ backup	Drive results and cross-team collaboration
	Central IT productivity/end user	Enable infrastructure backup
	Security architecture	Enable OneDrive backup
	Security policy and standards	Advise on configuration and standards
	Security compliance management	Update standards and policy documents
		Monitor to ensure compliance

Deployment Checklist

Apply the best practices shown in Table 9.5 to secure your backup infrastructure.

TABLE 9.5   Securing Your Backup Infrastructure

Task	Description
Maintain a regular backup schedule for all critical data.	Ensure that you can recover data up to the point of the last backup.
Practice business continuity/disaster recovery (BC/DR) regularly.	Provides rapid recovery of business operations during ransomware or extortion attacks.
Protect backups against deliberate erasure and encryption via strong protection such as the following: ■ Require out-of-band steps (MFA or PIN) before modifying online backups (such as Azure Backup). ■ Backups can be stored in immutable online storage (like Azure Blob) or completely off-site.	Businesses may be unable to recover their data if backups are accessible by attackers. Improve backup security and make it impossible to alter backup data.
Make sure you protect your configuration management database (CMDB) and network diagrams, as well as your restoration procedure documents, to make sure you will be able to recover.	Ensure these resources survive a ransomware attack because attackers target them intentionally.

Deployment Results and Timelines

Ensure that the mean time to recover (MTTR) meets your BC/DR goal, as measured during simulations and real-world operations.

Data Protection

For rapid and reliable recovery from ransomware attacks, it is essential to implement data protection.

A ransomware attack can be recovered rapidly and reliably if you implement data protection. For example, you can block some of the attack techniques utilized by the attackers by implementing data protection.

It is only possible for ransomware to extort data and destroy systems when all legitimate access has been lost. Suppose attackers are unable to remove your ability to resume operations without payment. In that case, your business will be protected, and the monetary incentive for attackers to attack your business will be undermined.

Accountabilities of Members of Programs and Projects

According to the sponsorship/program management/project management hierarchy, Table 9.6 provides an overview of how your data will be protected from ransomware.

TABLE 9.6   Protecting from Ransomware

Lead	Implementor	Accountability
Central IT operations or CIO		Executive sponsorship.
Program lead from central IT infrastructure	Central IT infrastructure/backup	Drive results and cross-team collaboration.
	Central IT productivity/end user	Enable infrastructure backup.
	Business/application	Analyze critical business assets.
	Security architecture	Enable OneDrive Backup.
	Security policy and standards	Advise on configuration and standards.
	Security compliance management	Update standards and policy documents. Monitor to ensure compliance.
	User Education	Update guidance for users based on policy changes.

Deployment Checklist

Apply the best practices in Table 9.7 to protect your organization's data.

TABLE 9.7 Protecting Organization Data

Task	Description
Embrace the cloud by migrating your organization: ■ Use cloud solutions such as OneDrive/ SharePoint to manage user data and do versioning. ■ Make sure that the users are taught how to recover their files independently to reduce the cost and time of the recovery process.	User data in the Microsoft cloud can be protected by built-in security and data management features.
Set up protected folders.	Makes it more difficult for unauthorized applications to modify the data in these folders.
Make sure you have the right permissions. A broad write/delete permission is defined as the number of users with write/delete permissions for business-critical data on file shares, SharePoint, and other solutions. Reduce broad permissions for critical data locations while meeting business collaboration requirements. Audit and monitor critical data locations to ensure broad permissions are not reapplied.	Reduces risk from ransomware activities that rely on broad access.

Ransomware is a cybersecurity attack that encrypts or destroys files and folders, preventing users from accessing their data. The first thing you should do for these attacks is to prepare your organization so that it has an alternative to paying the ransom. Even though attackers control your organization by using various methods to pressure you into paying, the most common demands are to pay to regain access and avoid disclosure.

Protect Assets from Ransomware Attacks

Keeping the scope of damage to a minimum is the second phase of ransomware protection. This phase involves protecting privileged roles to prevent attackers from gaining access to sensitive data and systems.

Strategy for Privileged Access

It is essential that you implement a comprehensive strategy for reducing the risks associated with privileged access compromises. The attacker with privileged access can easily invalidate all other security controls in your environment. Ransomware attackers use privileged access to control all critical assets in the organization.

Accountabilities of Members of Programs and Projects

Table 9.8 provides an overview of how your data will be protected from ransomware specifically from a privileged access perspective, according to the sponsorship/program management/project management hierarchy.

TABLE 9.8   Privileged Access Perspective

Lead	Implementor	Accountability
CISO or CIO		Executive sponsorship.
Program lead		Drive results and cross-team collaboration.
	IT and security architects	Prioritize components to integrate into architectures.
	Identity and key management	Implement identity changes.
	Central IT productivity/end-user team	Implement changes to devices and Office 365 tenant.
	Security policy and standards	Update standards and policy documents.
	Security compliance management	Monitor to ensure compliance.
	User education team	Update any password guidance.

Deployment Checklist

Build a multipart strategy using the guidance at aka.ms/SPA that includes the checklist shown in Table 9.9.

TABLE 9.9 Deployment Checklist

Task	Description
Enforce end-to-end session security.	Access to administrative interfaces is explicitly validated (using Azure Active Directory conditional access) before users and devices are granted access.
Protect and monitor identity systems.	Protects directories, identities, administrator accounts, groups, and consent grant configurations from privilege escalation attacks.
Mitigate lateral traversal.	A single compromised device does not immediately lead to the control of many or all other devices using local account passwords, service account passwords, or other secret information.
Ensure rapid threat response.	Limits adversary access and time.

Deployment Results and Timelines

Within 30 to 90 days, try to achieve the following results:

- All administrators must be using secure workstations.
- All passwords on local workstations/servers are randomized.
- A 100 percent privilege escalation mitigation is in place.

Detection and Response

To limit the attacker's ability to make their way around your organization laterally, you must quickly detect and remediate common attacks on endpoints, email, and identities—minutes matter.

Accountabilities of Members of Programs and Projects

Table 9.10 provides an overview of how your data will be protected from ransomware specifically from a detection and response time perspective, according to the sponsorship/program management/project management hierarchy.

TABLE 9.10   Detection and Response Time Perspective

Lead	Implementor	Accountability
CISO or CIO		Executive sponsorship.
Program lead from security operations		Drive results and cross-team collaboration.
	Central IT infrastructure team	Implement client and server agents/features.
	Security operations	Integrate any new tools into security operations processes.
	Central IT productivity/ end-user team	Enable features for Defender for Endpoint, Defender for Office 365, Defender for Identity, and Defender for Cloud Apps.
	Central IT identity team	Implement Azure AD security and Defender for Identity.
	Security architects	Advise on configuration, standards, and tooling.
	Security policy and standards	Update standards and policy documents.
	Security compliance management	Monitor to ensure compliance.

Deployment Checklist

Apply the best practices shown in Table 9.11 for improving your detection and response.

TABLE 9.11   Deployment Checklist

Task	Description
Put the following entry points at the top of the priority list: • Monitor for brute-force attacks like password spraying using integrated Extended Detection and Response (XDR) tools like Microsoft 365 Defender. • Password spraying is an example of a brute-force attack.	Ransomware operators prefer endpoints, email, identity, and RDP as entry points.

Task	Description
Monitoring for adversaries disabling security (often as part of an attack chain) includes the following: ■ The PowerShell Operational log and the Security Event log must be cleared. ■ Tool and control disabling.	For a safer attack, attackers target security detection facilities.
The threat of commodity malware should not be ignored.	From dark markets, ransomware attackers regularly purchase access to target organizations.
The Microsoft Detection and Response Team (DART) can be integrated into processes to complement expertise.	To detect and recover, experience is crucial.
With Defender for Endpoint, you can quickly isolate compromised computers.	It's easy to do this with Windows 11 and 10.

Security must be a top priority for organizations to protect privileged access due to the significant potential business impact of hackers compromising this level of access. Strategy requires a Holistic approach combining multiple technologies to protect and monitor those authorized escalation paths using Zero Trust principles, including explicit validation, least privilege and assumed breach from ransomware attacks.

Recommend Microsoft Ransomware Best Practices

To protect against ransomware, phase 3 makes it hard for attackers to gain access. This phase involves incrementally removing the risks at the entry points of your on-premises or cloud infrastructure to make the attackers work much harder.

A ransomware attack can be prevented by hardening your infrastructure in four main areas.

■ Remote access

■ Email and collaboration

■ Endpoints

■ Accounts

Remote Access

A ransomware attacker may access your organization's intranet through a remote access connection. The Colonial Pipeline cyberattack in 2021 is an excellent example of an attacker roaming on an intranet to gather intelligence, elevate privileges, and install ransomware once a user account is compromised.

Accountabilities of Members of Programs and Projects

Table 9.12 provides an overview of how your data will be protected from ransomware specifically from a remote access perspective, according to the sponsorship/program management/project management hierarchy.

TABLE 9.12   Remote Access Perspective

Lead	Implementor	Accountability
CISO or CIO		Executive sponsorship.
Program lead on the central IT infrastructure/network team		Drive results and cross-team collaboration.
	IT and security architects	Prioritize component integration into architectures.
	Central IT identity team	Configure Azure AD and conditional access policies.
	Central IT operations	Implement changes to the environment.
	Workload owners	Assist with RBAC permissions for app publishing.
	Security policy and standards	Update standards and policy documents.
	Security compliance management	Monitor to ensure compliance.
	User education team	Update any guidance on workflow changes and perform education and change management.

Deployment Checklist

Remote access ransomware attacks can be prevented by applying the best practices shown in Table 9.13.

TABLE 9.13 Deployment Checklist

Task	Description
Ensure that software applications and appliances are up-to-date. Avoid missing or neglecting manufacturer protections (security updates, support status).	A well-known vulnerability that has not yet been patched is often used by attackers as an attack vector.
Enforce Zero Trust user and device validation with conditional access in Azure Active Directory (Azure AD) to support existing remote access.	With Zero Trust, your organization is protected on multiple levels.
Install and configure security for existing third-party VPN solutions (such as Cisco AnyConnect, Palo Alto Networks GlobalProtect and Captive Portal, Fortinet FortiGate SSL VPN, Citrix NetScaler, Zscaler Private Access [ZPA], and so on).	Your remote access solution comes with built-in security.
Provide remote access using Azure Point-to-Site (P2S) VPN.	Utilize your existing Azure subscriptions and Azure AD integration.
With Azure AD Application Proxy, you can publish on-premises web applications.	Remote access is not required for apps published through Azure AD Application Proxy.
Azure Bastion provides secure access to Azure resources.	Connect to your Azure virtual machines securely and seamlessly over SSL.
Finding deviations from baselines and potential attacks (See Detection and Response in Chapter 9 and Page 39) should be audited and monitored.	Protect baseline security features and settings from ransomware attacks.

Email and Collaboration

Attackers can transfer malicious content into an environment via email or file sharing with the help of authorized collaboration tools. Implement best practices for email and collaboration solutions so that your workers can access external content easily. Microsoft has made enhanced mitigations to prevent these attacks.

Accountabilities of Members of Programs and Projects

Table 9.14 provides an overview of how your data will be protected from ransomware specifically from an email and collaboration perspective, according to the sponsorship/program management/project management hierarchy.

TABLE 9.14 Email and Collaboration Perspective

Lead	Implementor	Accountability
CISO, CIO, or identity director		Executive sponsorship.
Program lead from the security architecture team		Drive results and cross-team collaboration.
	IT architects	Prioritize component integration into architectures.
	Cloud productivity or end-user team	Enable Defender for Office 365, ASR, and AMSI.
	Security Architecture/ infrastructure + endpoint	Configuration assistance.
	User education team	Update guidance on workflow changes.
	Security policy and standards	Update standards and policy documents.
	Security compliance management	Monitor to ensure compliance.

Deployment Checklist

To prevent ransomware attacks on your email and collaboration solutions, follow the best practices shown in Table 9.15.

TABLE 9.15 Deployment Checklist

Task	Description
Allow Office VBA to use AMSI.	Defender for Endpoint prevents Office macro attacks.
The use of Defender for Office 365 or a similar solution is recommended for advanced email security.	A common entry point for attackers is via email.

Task	Description
ASR rules can be used to block common attack techniques, such as the following: ■ Theft of credentials, ransomware, and suspicious use of PsExec and WMI. ■ Injection of processes initiated by Office applications, including macros and executables. **Key Note:** Consider deploying these rules in audit mode first, then assessing any negative impacts, and then deploying them in block mode.	In addition to providing additional layers of protection, ASR is specifically designed to mitigate the common attack methods.
To detect and fix deviations from baseline and potential attacks, perform audits and monitors.	As a result, ransomware activities that probe baseline security settings and features are reduced.

Endpoints

The deployment of relevant security features and best practices for software maintenance should be prioritized for endpoints (devices) and applications directly exposed to Internet traffic.

Endpoints that are exposed to the Internet are a common entry point for attackers to gain access to an organization's assets. Prioritize blocking standard OS and application vulnerabilities with preventative controls to slow or stop them from executing further attacks.

Accountabilities of Members of Programs and Projects

Table 9.16 provides an overview of how your data will be protected from ransomware specifically from an endpoints perspective, according to the sponsorship/program management/project management hierarchy.

TABLE 9.16 Endpoints Perspective

Lead	Implementor	Accountability
Business leadership accountable for business impact of both downtime and attack damage		Executive sponsorship (maintenance).
Central IT operations or CIO		Executive sponsorship (others).

TABLE 9.16   Endpoints Perspective *(continued)*

Lead	Implementor	Accountability
Program lead from the central IT infrastructure team		Drive results and cross-team collaboration.
	IT and security architects	Prioritize component integration into architectures.
	Central IT operations	Implement changes to the environment.
	Cloud productivity or end-user team	Enable attack surface reduction.
	Workload/app owners	Identify maintenance windows for changes.
	Security policy and standards	Update standards and policy documents.
	Security compliance management	Monitor to ensure compliance.

Deployment Checklist

Ensure that the best practices shown in Table 9.17 are applied to all Windows, Linux, macOS, Android, and iOS devices.

TABLE 9.17   Deployment Checklist

Task	Description
All known threats can be blocked by reducing attack surfaces, providing tamper protection, and securing the source.	Avoid letting this lack of use be the reason for an attacker's entry into your organization.
Install security baselines on Windows servers, clients exposed to the Internet, and Office applications.	Build security into your organization starting with the minimum level.

Task	Description
Ensure that your software is: • *Updated*: Rapidly deploy critical security updates for operating systems, browsers, and email clients. • *Upgraded*: Upgrade your operating system and software to the latest version. • Unsupported operating systems and legacy protocols should be isolated, disabled, or retired.	You must stay up-to-date with manufacturer updates and upgrades to avoid becoming a target for attackers.
Isolate, disable, or retire insecure systems and protocols, including unsupported operating systems and legacy protocols.	Attackers exploit known vulnerabilities in legacy devices, systems, and protocols to gain access to your organization.
Firewalls and network defenses can block unexpected traffic.	To make a connection for an attack, malware attacks sometimes use unsolicited inbound traffic.
The audit and monitoring process is used to identify deviations from baseline and potential attacks (see the "Detection and Response" section).	Assists in reducing the risk of ransomware activities that probe baseline security features and settings.

Accounts

It is impossible to protect accounts from common attacks we see today with passwords, just as antique skeleton keys will not protect a house from a modern-day burglar. Passwordless authentication improves the sign-in experience by eliminating the need for your users to remember or type a password. MFA was once a burdensome extra step. Furthermore, trusted devices are stored in a Zero Trust infrastructure, thus preventing annoying out-of-band MFA prompts.

Using passwordless or multifactor authentication for high-privilege administrator accounts is a best practice.

Accountabilities of Members of Programs and Projects

Table 9.18 provides an overview of how your data will be protected from ransomware specifically from an accounts perspective, according to the sponsorship/program management/project management hierarchy.

TABLE 9.18   Accounts Perspective

Lead	Implementor	Accountability
CISO, CIO, or identity director		Executive sponsorship.
Program lead from identity and key management or security architecture teams		Drive results and cross-team collaboration.
	IT and security architects	Prioritize component integration into architectures.
	Identity and key management or central IT operations	Deploy configuration changes.
	Security policy and standards	Update standards and policy documents.
	Security compliance management	Monitor to ensure compliance.
	User education team	Update password or sign-in guidance and perform education and change management.

Deployment Checklist

To prevent ransomware attacks, follow the best practices shown in Table 9.19.

TABLE 9.19   Deployment Checklist

Task	Description
Engage strong multifactor authentication for all users. Start with administrator and priority accounts using one or more of the following: • Passwordless authentication with Windows Hello or the Microsoft Authenticator app. • Azure multifactor authentication. • Implement an independent multifactor authentication service.	By determining the password for the user account, an attacker will have difficulty compromising credentials.

Task	Description
Azure AD Password Protection detects and blocks known weak passwords and additional weak terms specific to your organization so that you can increase password security. Extend Azure AD Password Protection to on-premises Active Directory Domain Services (AD DS) accounts.	Passwords based on your organization's name or common passwords should be protected against brute-force attacks.
Finding and fixing deviations from baselines and potential attacks through auditing and monitoring.	As a result, ransomware activities that probe baseline security settings and features are reduced.

Microsoft ransomware best practices make it essential to make it hard to get into your on-premises or cloud infrastructures during phase 3 of ransomware protection. During this phase, you incrementally remove the risks at the points of entry, making attackers work much harder to get into your infrastructure. There are four main areas where best practices can be applied to harden your infrastructure against ransomware attacks: remote access, email and collaboration, endpoints, and accounts.

Summary

This chapter has exposed you to various recommendation security best practices and priorities across Azure services and environments.

The best practices are the most effective or efficient ways of doing things. Best practices help you avoid errors and ensure that your resources and effort are well-spent. Best practices can be found in Microsoft reference materials such as the Microsoft Cybersecurity Reference Architectures (MCRA), Microsoft cloud security benchmark, and the Cloud Adoption Framework (CAF).

Among the many topics covered by the MCRA, Zero Trust user access, security operations, cross-platform capabilities, multi-cloud capabilities, operational technology, attack chains, technical capability coverage, Azure native security controls, and security roles and responsibilities are all vital resources for security best practices.

For a hybrid environment of Microsoft Azure, on-premises data centers, and other cloud providers that you have read about, the MCSBs provide the security best practices that are in this chapter.

You have explored security best practices for capabilities and controls, security best practices for Zero Trust, security best practices for insider risk and external attacks, and the Zero Trust rapid modernization plan (RaMP).

Followed by that, you read how to recommend a DevSecOps process, recommend a risk management methodology, and recommend strategies for managing and minimizing risk, as well as prepare for ransomware protection and extortion-based attacks, protect assets from ransomware attacks, and recommend best practices for Windows ransomware.

Exam Essentials

Know how to develop recommendations for cybersecurity capability and control best practices. The role of security is to ensure confidentiality, integrity, and availability in a business. Security efforts help to protect operations from malicious and unintentional internal and external activities. Best practices for capabilities and control are found within the Microsoft Cybersecurity Reference Architecture and Microsoft Cloud Security Benchmarks. The Microsoft Cloud Security Program recommends that you adhere to four domains when setting up a cloud strategy: people, process, technology, and architectural decision-making.

Four areas are further classified under each category such as People (educate teams about the cloud security journey and educate teams on cloud security technology), Process (relegate accountability for cloud security decisions, update incident response methods for cloud, and develop security posture management), and Technology (enforce passwordless or multifactor authentication). Provide native firewall and network security, and provide native threat detection and fundamental architecture recommendations. Standardize on a single directory and identity, use identity-based access control (in place of keys), and establish a single unified security strategy.

Know to establish best practices for protecting from insider attacks and external attacks. In addition to protecting against insider risk, adequate security programs must also protect from external threats. The Microsoft Cybersecurity Reference Architecture (MCRA) and Microsoft Cloud Security Benchmarks (MCSBs) provide best practices for both. This section focuses primarily on insider risk aspects and the security operations elements of external attacks, even though all security controls should reduce risk in one or both of these scenarios.

The attacker can choose different techniques to achieve each of the four objectives: preparing, entering, traversing, and executing. The attacker can also combine techniques or use the same process over and over iteratively.

Detect, respond, and recover from external attacks by applying all best practices in the MCRA, and the MCSBs are intended to reduce the risk of attackers succeeding.

Understand the method to provide recommendations for Zero Trust security practices. Using security best practices for Zero Trust today is imperative to stay ahead of evolving threats, cloud platforms, and business models.

Microsoft Zero Trust's security is based on three principles: assume breach, verify explicitly, and use the least privilege. A series of modernization initiatives are typically used to implement a Zero Trust transformation by applying these principles across the technical estate.

The initiatives include secure identities and access; modern security operations; infrastructure security; security of the Internet of Things; data security; and governance, risk, and compliance.

Know how to develop a Zero Trust rapid modernization plan based on best practices. Investing the least amount of time and resources into the most impactful items is crucial when implementing Zero Trust, which transforms a security program dramatically.

In the Microsoft Cybersecurity Reference Architecture (MCRA), the Zero Trust rapid modernization plan (RaMP) provides best practices for prioritizing security modernization. Based on the most relevant and common attacks, this RaMP identifies the most effective controls that require the least amount of effort and resources.

You can prioritize your security modernization with the Zero Trust RaMP. MCRA includes this RaMP because it identifies the most effective controls for the most common and relevant attacks requiring the least amount of time, effort, and resources.

A checklist-based approach is taken by RaMP guidance such as first the mapping of key stakeholders, implementers, and their accountabilities can help you organize an internal project more quickly and define the tasks and owners, and second is to make it easier to see the bigger picture of infrastructure requirements when you have a checklist of deployment objectives and implementation steps.

Know how to provide recommendations for DevSecOps. Integrating security early in the development cycle can harden your development environment and supply chain against new types of cybersecurity attacks. With DevSecOps, DevOps and SecOps teams can collaborate with GitHub and Azure products and services to build secure, innovative apps faster than ever.

Build solutions for managing and interacting with client or custom data with security in mind if your business stores this data. DevSecOps utilizes security best practices from the beginning of development rather than auditing at the end.

To succeed with DevSecOps, you must understand and thoughtfully integrate security into the development process since it is an emerging discipline with a high level of process variation. Starting with low-friction changes to the code, development processes, and infrastructure, hosting the workload is the best way to improve security. Put the least burden on DevOps processes and skills while focusing on changes that will positively impact security.

Know how to protect assets by recommending a methodology. The asset protection process implements controls to comply with security architecture, standards, and policies. These standards should be consistent for each asset type and should apply to all instances.

Policies, standards, and architecture are aligned to ensure efficient and effective asset protection.

The two-step asset protection process can be followed in one or two steps, depending on the organization's needs. Focus on well-known resources first, and begin with vendor and industry baselines.

Know how to manage and minimize risk by recommending strategies.   Cyberattacks can damage business assets, revenue, and reputation. Human attackers attempt to steal information, money, and technology.

Even though these attacks occur in the technical environment, they often pose a threat to your entire organization. Cybersecurity risk should be integrated into your risk management, tracking, and mitigation framework. Many organizations still view cybersecurity risk as a technical issue to be solved, and this perception leads to the wrong conclusions that don't mitigate the risk's strategic business impact.

Maintain a strong relationship between cybersecurity and your organization's leadership. This concept applies to both human relationships and explicit processes. Security risk and business opportunities are constantly changing, and building and improving this relationship is essential to reducing security risk sources.

Understand what ransomware protection is and be able to create an extortion-based attacks plan.   An encrypting or destroying of files and folders are known as *ransomware*, and it prevents the owner of an affected device from accessing it. In exchange for unlocking the encrypted data, cybercriminals may need to extort money from the business owner. Still, even if paid, they may need to return the key to restore access to the business owner.

Human-operated ransomware is the result of active cybercrime attacks targeting on-premises or cloud IT infrastructures, elevating privileges, and deploying ransomware.

In most cases, these ransomware attacks are automated, spreading like a virus, infecting devices through methods such as phishing emails and malware delivery, and requiring a malware removal program to remove them.

To quickly configure your IT infrastructure for the most effective protection, follow the three phases of exploiting attack weaknesses to protect your organization against ransomware and extortion solutions: start with ensuring your organization is prepared to recover from an attack without paying a ransom, then protect privileged roles from ransomware attacks to limit their impact, and finally remove risks one by one to make it more difficult for an attacker to get into your environment.

Understand that ransomware attacks must be prevented.   As per Microsoft's recommendation, it would help if you implemented a comprehensive strategy for reducing the risks associated with privileged access compromises.

The attacker with privileged access can quickly invalidate all other security controls in your environment. Ransomware attackers use privileged access to control all critical assets in the organization.

Detecting and remediating common attacks on endpoints, emails, and identities must be done quickly, and minutes matter. By rapidly remediating common attack entry points, you will limit the attacker's time traversing your organization laterally.

Know how to recommend Microsoft's best practices for fighting ransomware. Ransomware attacks are generally classified into four categories: remote access, email and collaboration, endpoints, and accounts.

The possibility of ransomware attackers accessing your organization's intranet via a remote access connection is a potential attack vector. An attacker can roam an intranet once an on-premises user account has been compromised, gaining intelligence, elevating privileges, and installing ransomware.

Keep your workers safe and secure by implementing best practices for email and collaboration solutions.

Maintain software maintenance best practices for endpoints (devices) and applications, prioritizing applications and operating systems directly exposed to Internet traffic.

Similarly, passwords can't protect accounts against the kind of attacks we see today, just as antique skeleton keys can't stop modern-day burglars.

Review Questions

1. Security best practices can be useful only if they're applied in practice. Which of the following elements must be integrated into security best practices?

   A. Habits and skills of people

   B. The processes in your organization

   C. The architecture of technology

   D. All of the above

2. Capabilities and control best practices can be found throughout which of Microsoft's offerings? (Choose two.)

   A. Microsoft Cybersecurity Reference Architecture (MCRA)

   B. Microsoft Cloud Security Benchmarks (MCSBs)

   C. Public Cloud Security Benchmarks (PCSBs)

   D. All of the above

3. The compromise of this type of account can shut down business operations across an organization in a ransomware/extortion attack if it is not properly protected, monitored, and responded to. Which type of account will you prioritize in your cybersecurity solution?

   A. Privileged and systems accounts

   B. Personal accounts with MFA

   C. End-user account with only a password

   D. A and B

4. Which of the following Microsoft Azure services help your SOC team to monitor platforms and quickly reduce false positives?

   A. Azure EDR

   B. Azure XDR

   C. Azure Monitor

   D. A and B

5. During detection, investigation, and other responses tasks, which of the following Microsoft Azure services can automate manual efforts that distract and tire human analysts?

   A. Azure EDR

   B. Azure XDR

   C. Azure SOAR

   D. A and B

6. As part of a Zero Trust architecture, which of the following components enables an organization to discover, classify, protect, and monitor critical business information?

   A. Operational technology (OT) and Internet of Things (IoT) security

   B. Infrastructure and development security

    C. Data security

    D. Application data

7. Which is arguably the most important security practice? This helps developers establish a security mindset for all future projects and delivers immediate results.

    A. SDLCS

    B. Threat modeling

    C. IDE plugin

    D. None of the above

8. How can you find web application security issues by observing how the application responds to specially crafted requests?

    A. Dynamic application security testing

    B. Static application security testing

    C. User acceptance testing

    D. None of the above

9. Which approach defines the operation of infrastructure (networks, virtual machines, load balancers, and connection topology) in a descriptive model?

    A. Infrastructure as a code

    B. SRE

    C. DevOps

    D. None of the above

10. What plug-ins identify security issues during the development process in the developer's familiar integrated development environment?

    A. VSS security plug-ins

    B. IDE security plug-ins

    C. Azure information protection plug-ins

    D. None of the above

11. Which of the following is the Microsoft-recommended procedure for checking for applications or infrastructure vulnerabilities that could lead to an attack?

    A. Vulnerability assessment

    B. Penetration testing

    C. IT audit

    D. IT risk assessment

12. Which of the following asset protection controls is implemented to support asset protection?

    A. Security architecture

    B. Standards

    C. Policy penetration testing

    D. All the above

13. For older assets that cannot be secured but cannot be immediately retired, what might be a viable securing method?

    A. Network isolation

    B. Data only isolation

    C. Application only isolation

    D. None of the above

14. To avoid risks and impacts, security accountability should remain with whom?

    A. Resource owner

    B. Application user

    C. Application developer

    D. System administrator

15. Which services provide subject-matter expertise on the assets, the controls available for them, and the feasibility of deployment of the controls?

    A. Security operations

    B. Governance team

    C. Asset protection

    D. CISO

16. When it comes to asset protection, what should be the first step?

    A. Choose resources that are well known.

    B. Identify responsible and accountable teams.

    C. Baseline industry measurements are a good place to start.

    D. Baseline security for Azure is a great place to start.

17. Which services provide context about how the controls fit into the security architecture, policies, and standards?

    A. Security operations

    B. Governance team

    C. Asset protection

    D. CISO

18. Which services advise on detective controls and integrate alerts and logs into security operations tools, processes, and training?

    A. Security operations

    B. Governance team

    C. Asset protection

    D. CISO

19. Which risk is classified as "By stealing money, information, or technology, human attackers may damage business assets, revenue, or reputation"?

  A. Cybersecurity risk

  B. Residual risk

  C. Undefined risk

  D. None of the above

20. Which of the following should be the goal of a mature security program for you as a Cybersecurity Architect?

  A. Identify and eliminate risks.

  B. Expose and mitigate risks.

  C. Ensure that risks are prevented.

  D. With the CISO, define a baseline.

Appendix

Answers to Review Questions

Chapter 1: Define and Implement an Overall Security Strategy and Architecture

1. A, B, D. A cloud computing service deployment model lets you decide how much control you want over your information and what type of services you need to provide. A cloud computing service can be classified as infrastructure as a service, platform as a service, or software as a service.

2. A. In a private cloud, multiple users (for example, business units) can use the infrastructure exclusively. An organization may own, manage, and operate it, or a third party may do so, and it may be based on- or off-premises.

3. C. The community cloud is a cloud service that permits multiple organizations to share IT resources and services based on common requirements (for example, objective, task, security, and compliance concerns). One or more community organizations, third parties, or some combination of these may own, manage, and operate it depending on its ownership, management, and operation.

4. B. Cloud computing is commonly deployed in public clouds. The cloud resources (such as servers and storage) are managed and owned by a third-party cloud service provider. The cloud provider owns and manages all the hardware, software, and other infrastructure in a public cloud, and Microsoft Azure is a good example. Customers can use some public cloud computing resources for free, while other resources can be purchased through subscription or pay-per-usage pricing models.

5. A. Using Azure Firewall, you can protect your Azure Virtual Network resources. It is highly available, easy to deploy, and requires zero maintenance. You can create, enforce, and log policies across subscriptions and virtual networks by using the Azure Firewall.

6. A. Under Zero Trust, they must be authenticated, authorized, and continuously validated for security configuration and posture, whether inside or outside the organization's network. As Zero Trust assumes, there are no traditional network edges; networks may be local, in the cloud, or hybrid, with resources located anywhere and workers anywhere.

7. A. Zero Trust is an essential aspect of security. Microsoft defines Zero Trust as following three fundamental principles: verify explicitly, apply least privilege access, and assume breach.

8. B. By extending the Azure platform, Azure Arc helps you build applications and services that can run across data centers, at the edge, and in multi-cloud environments.

9. B. Using Active Directory signals, Microsoft Defender for Identity (aka Azure Advanced Threat Protection) identifies, detects, and investigates advanced threats, compromised identities, and malicious insider actions aimed at your organization.

10. D. By connecting a virtual network to Azure platform as a service, customer-owned services, or Microsoft partner services, Azure Private Link provides private connectivity. Eliminating the exposure of data to the public Internet simplifies the network architecture and secures Azure endpoint connections.

11. A. Microsoft describes its cybersecurity capabilities and how they can be integrated with existing security mechanisms in the Microsoft Cybersecurity Reference Architecture. A reference architecture consists mainly of detailed technical diagrams for Microsoft cybersecurity capabilities, Zero Trust user access, SecOps, operational technology (OT), hybrid cloud and cross-platform capabilities, attack chain scope, Azure native security management, and security organizational procedures.

12. C. By collecting, analyzing, and acting on telemetry from your cloud and on-premises environments, Azure Monitor helps you maximize the availability and performance of your applications and services. Using this information, you can determine how well your applications are performing and identify problems affecting them and the resources they depend on proactively.

13. C. You can access virtual machines from your browser or your local computer using Azure Bastion with native SSH or RDP clients installed already. It is an Azure PaaS service that you provision inside your virtual network that is fully platform-managed.

14. A, B. Azure Arc extends the Azure platform so that you can develop applications and services that can run across data centers, at the edge, and in multiple clouds. Organizational standards can be enforced at scale, and compliance can be assessed. Providing an aggregated view of the environment allows an organization to drill down to a per-resource, per-policy level of granularity.

15. A, B, C. Planning workload resources based on security, getting familiar with the types of protection offered by cloud services, and evaluating service enablement using a framework are some of Microsoft's recommendations for Cybersecurity Architects regarding resource planning and hardening.

16. A, B. By automating and applying the least privileges, Microsoft's recommendations for Cybersecurity Architects can be avoided, including data exfiltration and malicious actor scenarios. By automating and minimizing human interaction, DevSecOps can be used to implement the least privilege at every level of the application and control plane.

17. A, B, C. Microsoft's recommendations for protecting against code-level vulnerabilities include identifying and mitigating cross-site scripting and SQL injection vulnerabilities. A security fix and a patch for codebases and dependencies should be regularly incorporated into the operational life cycle.

18. A, B. Among Microsoft's recommendations for Cybersecurity Architects regarding data protection, classification, and encryption is to categorize data according to its level of risk, and to securely store and manage keys and certificates for both the storage and transmission of the data.

19. A. The Azure Key Vault cloud service allows you to store and access secrets securely. A secret is anything you want to control tightly, including API keys, passwords, certificates, or cryptographic keys. Using Key Vault, you can store software, keys, secrets, certificates, and managed hardware security modules (HSMs). Managed HSM pools support only HSM-backed keys.

20. B, C. A multi-tenant solution refers to a solution used by multiple organizations, companies, groups, or departments. As per Microsoft, multi-tenancy has two standard models: business-to-business (B2B) and business-to-consumer (B2C). In addition to accounting software and work tracking, software-as-a-service (SaaS) products are available for business-to-business (B2B). Social networking, photo sharing, and music streaming are business-to-consumer (B2C) solutions.

Chapter 2: Define a Security Operations Strategy

1. A. Cybersecurity technologies are selected, operated, and maintained in a security operations center, and threat data is continuously analyzed for improvement.

2. D. In general, traditional environments categorize SOC activities and responsibilities into three categories, such as preparation, planning, and prevention; monitoring, detection, and response; and recovery, refinement, and compliance.

3. A. To manage threats, your SOC team needs tools that support reactive and proactive detection.

4. D. A Microsoft Cybersecurity Architect should consider the Microsoft security operations strategy in the following scenario: multiple engineering teams working in Microsoft Azure, multiple subscriptions having to be managed and secure, regulatory requirements having to be enforced, standards have to be followed for all cloud resources, and a defined logging and auditing security process required.

5. A. Microsoft defines that the SOC functions need to address three critical objectives: incident management, incident preparation, and threat intelligence.

6. D. SOC metrics directly influence organizational risk such as mean time to acknowledge (MTTA), mean time to remediate (MTTR), incidents remediated (manually or via automation), and escalations among each tier.

7. D. Malicious code is being run by the adversary in the execution phase of the MITRE ATT&CK framework.

8. C. To plan future operations, the adversary gathers information in the reconnaissance phase of the MITRE ATT&CK Framework.

9. D. Microsoft recommends the following design considerations for logging and auditing that aligns with the enterprise cloud security strategy: Make everything observable, use a tool for monitoring, use a tool for root-cause analysis, use distributed tracing, standardize logs and metrics, automate management tasks, treat the configuration as code, and align the logging and auditing with the Cyber Kill Chain.

10. D. You can gain insights into your applications by logging data from cloud applications, which can be complex with many moving parts. Microsoft Azure offers log types such as control/management logs, data plane logs, and processed events.

11. A. Azure resource logs provide detailed insight about resource operations in Microsoft Azure Cloud.

12. D. Azure Active Directory reporting provides detailed insight about users and group management activity, including sign-ins and system activity.

13. B. Azure Storage Analytics logs and provides metrics about all storage services in your Azure account and the blob, queue, and table logs. Azure Storage Analytics reporting provides detailed insight about the analysis of usage trends, insight into trace requests, and diagnosis of storage account issues.

14. B. Application insight service provides monitoring of web applications (APM) across multiple platforms.

15. B. Azure Monitor collects managed data sources, and centralized data stores are used to store them. Events, performance data, or custom data provided through APIs can be included. Data can be analyzed, alerted, and exported after it is collected.

16. A. Azure Automation automates manual, long-running, error-prone, and frequently repeated tasks in a cloud and enterprise environment. In addition to saving time, it improves the reliability of administrative tasks.

17. C. You can back up (or protect) and restore your Azure data using Azure Backup. This cloud-based backup solution that's reliable, secure, and cost-effective replaces existing on-premises or off-site backup solutions.

18. C. Your imported threat intelligence can be visualized in the threat intelligence workbook in Microsoft Sentinel.

19. A. Microsoft Defender for IoT can be deployed in many environments and has native threat intelligence capabilities and support for Azure-connected environments, hybrid environments, and on-premises deployments.

20. B. A Defender for Cloud incident is correlated with alerts and contextual signals. Correlation analyzes alerts and combines security knowledge and artificial intelligence to discover new attack patterns by analyzing different signals across resources. In the event of a threat being detected, Defender for Cloud will send you an alert with detailed information about the event, including suggestions for resolving the issue.

Chapter 3: Define an Identity Security Strategy

1. A. Users, apps, and data can be protected on-premises and in the cloud using Azure Active Directory (Azure AD). With Azure AD Application Proxy, IT professionals can publish on-premises web applications (for instance, SharePoint sites, Outlook Web Apps, and IIS-based) accessible via the Internet. As a result, remote end users can securely access internal applications outside the corporate network.

2. B. Multifactor authentication adds a critical second layer of security to user sign-ins and transactions by requiring more than one verification method. While meeting user demand for a simple sign-in process, multifactor authentication secures access to data and applications. Various options are available for strong authentication, including phone calls, text messages, app notifications, and verification codes from third parties.

3. C. With single sign-on (SSO), all the applications and resources you need are accessible through a single user account, so you only have to sign in once. You do not need to authenticate (for example, type a password) again once you have signed in to all applications.

4. D. The Azure Active Directory device identity provides administrators with the information they can use to manage access and configurations. Like users, groups, and applications, the device identity helps administrators decide what access should be granted and what configurations should be made. Conditions such as device-based conditional access policies and mobile device management with Endpoint Manager demand device identities. Security administrators can use access controls within conditional access policies to grant or block resource access.

5. A. Microsoft analyzes trillions of signals daily to identify and protect customers from threats. Identity Protection enables organizations to perform three essential tasks. Risks associated with identity can be detected and remedied automatically. Using data from the portal, investigating risks and data can be exported to other tools for risk detection. So, Azure AD Identity Protection can protect your organization's identities by providing a consolidated view of risk detections and potential vulnerabilities.

6. A. Azure Active Directory is Microsoft's cloud-based identity and access management service. Enterprises can protect and automate identity processes at scale with single sign-on authentication, conditional access, passwordless and multifactor authentication, automated user provisioning, and many other features.

7. B, C. In a hybrid identity solutions scenario, Azure AD supports cloud authentication and federated authentication.

8. A, C. This authentication method uses Azure AD to handle users' sign-in process. Coupled with seamless single sign-on (SSO), users can sign in to cloud apps without re-entering their credentials with two options: Azure AD password hash synchronization and Azure AD pass-through authentication.

9. A. Customer identity and access management (CIAM) in Azure Active Directory B2C supports millions of users and billions of daily authentications. This solution enables branded web and mobile applications to blend seamlessly with white-label authentication experiences.

10. A. Azure AD passes the authentication process to an external authentication system, such as Active Directory Federation Services (AD FS).

11. A. Your users can use the same passwords to sign in both to on-premises and cloud-based applications with Azure Active Directory (Azure AD) pass-through authentication.

12. C. Azure AD Connect Health is the health monitoring solution available when you adopt federation with AD FS in your solution.

13. D. Based on conditional access, Microsoft recommends creating a Zero Trust access model that aligns with these three principles: verify explicitly, use least privilege access, and assume breach.

14. A, B. Windows Hello for Business supports both the key trust model and the hybrid cloud trust assume breach method. However, both require the Windows Server 2016 Domain functional level.

15. A, B. The purpose of access reviews is to ensure only the right people have access to your organization's administrators. Regular auditing of your administrators is crucial for several reasons. For example, a malicious actor can compromise an account and, without auditing, people can accrue unnecessary access over time as they move between teams.

16. D. There are three levels of security recommended by Microsoft (enterprise security, specialized security, and privileged security), which provide clear guidance and flexibility and enable progressive security improvement. The security levels are consistent across all devices, accounts, intermediaries, and interfaces.

17. A, B. Working with clients across various industries gave Microsoft rich experience with cyberattack incidents and response management. At a very high level, following is the objective of each stage: in the first stage (24–48 hours), Microsoft recommends that you take care of critical items right away, the second stage is to mitigate the most commonly used attacks (2–4 weeks), the third stage (1–3 months) involves building visibility and controlling administrator activity, and the fourth stage (six months and beyond) involves further hardening your security platform. Microsoft does not have the fifth stage in the Microsoft framework.

18. B, C. To ensure that business-sensitive systems can be accessed only by trustworthy "clean" devices, accounts, and intermediaries, Microsoft recommends incrementally building a closed-loop system for privileged access. A secure privileged access system has two simple objectives: limit access to privileged actions to a few authorized paths and protect and closely monitor those pathways.

19. A, B. Establish privileged identity strategies that work. Combining the following methods will be helpful: the rapid modernization plan (RAMP) and Zero Trust access control are described throughout this recommendation and asset protection safeguards against direct asset attacks by applying good security hygiene practices to systems.

20. A. Through Azure Active Directory entitlement management, organizations can automate access request workflows, assign and review access for users, and expire access at scale.

Chapter 4: Identify a Regulatory Compliance Strategy

1. **A.** With Microsoft Defender for Cloud, you can protect your resources directly from Azure and extend protection to on-premises and multi-cloud environments.

2. **D.** By using Azure Automation, you can manage operating system updates across physical machines, virtual machines, and on-premises machines.

3. **A.** At scale, Azure Policy helps organizations enforce standards and assess compliance. Its compliance dashboard provides an aggregated view of the environment's state, with the option to drill down to per-resource, per-policy details. Bulk remediating existing and automating new resources also helps bring your resources to compliance.

4. **B.** An organization's standard, patterns, compliance for core services and requirements can be implemented and adhered to using Azure Blueprints, which makes it easy for cloud architects to create repeatable Azure resources.

5. **C.** Updates are made as needed to support enhancements and new capabilities delivered by Azure Desired State Configuration (DSC) VM extensions.

6. **B.** With Microsoft Defender for Cloud Apps, you can operate across multiple clouds as a Cloud Access Security Broker (CASB). With these tools, your organization's governance decisions are enforced and automated. They provide rich visibility, control over data travel, and sophisticated analytics.

7. **A.** Microsoft Defender for Cloud protects Azure, whether on-premises and in other clouds. The solution protects hybrid data, cloud-native services, and servers from ransomware and other threats; and it integrates with existing security workflows such as SIEM solutions.

8. **A.** Defender for Cloud services protects a host of Azure PaaS services. You can detect anomalies in your Azure activity logs by integrating with Microsoft Defender for Cloud apps.

9. **A.** In addition to Defender for Cloud's CSPM features, your AWS resources are assessed based on AWS-specific security recommendations, which are included in your secure score. Additionally, AWS built-in security standards (AWS CIS, AWS PCI DSS, and AWS Foundational Security Best Practices) will be evaluated. Asset inventory in Defender for Cloud is a multi-cloud feature that lets you manage your AWS resources alongside your Azure resources.

10. **B.** Remediating all of the recommendations in the security control will result in a potential score increase. The percentage points listed for security control are increased when you remediate all its recommendations.

11. **A.** A metadata property in the policy definition classifies the definition based on its area of focus.

12. **B.** Using enforcement mode, policies can be configured so that certain policy effects can be enabled or disabled.

13. A. Event Grid can be used to integrate an incident or outcome when something changes in Azure Policy.

14. C. By setting guardrails throughout your resources, Azure Policy can help you ensure cloud compliance, avoid misconfigurations, and practice consistent resource governance throughout your organization.

15. B. Data that persists on physical media is always encrypted using FIPS 140-2 compliant encryption protocols by default with Microsoft Managed Keys.

16. A. The traffic between data centers is protected by IEEE 802.1AE MAC Security Standards, preventing physical man-in-the-middle attacks.

17. A. As soon as customer data is written to Azure Storage, including Azure Managed Disks, Azure Blobs, Queues, and Table Storage, it is automatically encrypted. The Azure Storage data is encrypted using 256-bit AES encryption, in addition to being FIPS 140-2 compliant.

18. A. In Azure Disk Encryption, full-volume encryption is provided for operating system disks and data disks using BitLocker on Windows and DM-Crypt on Linux for infrastructure-as-a-service (IaaS) VM disks.

19. D. Virtual machines, storage, and SQL databases are some of the Azure services that can be deployed regionally and assigned to a specific region.

20. C. Cloud-based Intel SGX and virtualization-based security protect customer data during processing with Azure Confidential Computing. Confidential Computing protects data when it needs to be processed in the open (unencrypted) within a Trusted Execution Environment (TEE).

Chapter 5: Identify Security Posture and Recommend Technical Strategies to Manage Risk

1. A, B, C. In general, security posture describes how a company's identities, endpoints, users, applications, and infrastructure are protected. A security posture management strategy consists of three pillars: Protect, Detect, and Respond.

2. A. You can secure your cloud solutions on Azure by following the recommendations in the Azure Security Benchmark. Azure Security Benchmark groups content by security and compliance standards and requirements.

3. A. Rapid Modernization Plan (RaMP) helps you with your security posture, and it can be improved rapidly with the least number of challenges.

4. A. Defender for Cloud monitors your subscriptions, resources, and organization for security threats. Afterward, the results of all the analyses are aggregated into a score, which indicates your current security situation at a glance: the higher the score, the lower the level of risk identified.

5. C. You can create campaigns for remediating recommendations using MITRE ATT&CK when assessing your security posture based on the various phases of the MITRE ATT&CK framework. By implementing recommendations that correspond to the early stages of the MITRE ATT&CK framework, you can mitigate a threat actor from gaining further access to your systems.

6. C. For workload owners to be notified when security recommendations need to be resolved, a ticket must be opened and assigned to them. Upon review of the ticket, the workload owner determines that a quick fix is available for this recommendation. The workflow owner begins a change management process to schedule and deploys the remediation as soon as they feel comfortable with the changes.

7. A. Azure Security Center is a Microsoft cloud security posture management solution that continuously assesses Azure Resources for achieving Security Hygiene and recommends solutions based on Azure Security Benchmarks for hybrid workloads, whether on-premises or in the cloud. It is significant to note that different cloud vendors have developed tools in support of this cloud security solution.

8. C. Azure Defender, a cloud workload protection platform, provides an advanced level of protection for hybrid and Azure resources. With Defender enabled, you have access to additional policies, regulatory standards, and Azure Security Benchmarks to customize your compliance analysis.

9. B. As a result of a multisubscription Azure environment, Azure landing zones are a result of scaling, security governance, networking, and identity considerations. Using Azure landing zones, applications can be migrated, modernized, and innovated at an enterprise scale.

10. D. The technical cloud estate of an organization must be transparent to the organization. Security monitoring and audit logging are essential components of a scalable framework for Azure platform services. It is important to review the following guidelines when designing security operations: security alerts, logs, security controls, vulnerability management, shared responsibility, and encryption keys.

11. B, C. Various technical environments require different solutions. There are, however, several Azure landing zone implementation options that can assist you in meeting your growing cloud infrastructure's deployment and operation's needs. The scalable and modular method helps to achieve it.

12. D. Considerations and recommendations in the security design area govern landing zone decisions. As part of the Cloud Adoption Framework, the Secure methodology provides further guidance for holistic security tools and processes. This design area aims to provide a foundation for security across Azure, hybrid, and multi-cloud environments. Using the Secure methodology of the Cloud Adoption Framework, you can enhance this foundation in the future. There is a ready-made deployment experience called the Azure landing zone accelerator for organizations that use this conceptual architecture with their operating model and resource structure. For Cybersecurity Architects, Microsoft recommends considering all of the elements listed.

13. D. The following default tool sets are included in the Azure landing zone accelerator: Microsoft Defender for Cloud, standard or free tier, Microsoft Sentinel, Azure DDoS standard

protection plan (optional), Azure Firewall, Web Application Firewall (WAF), and Privileged Identity Management (PIM).

14. C. The effective use of threat intelligence is to monitor threats and mitigate risks. As a result of threat intelligence, context, relevance, and priority are provided.

15. B. With Microsoft Sentinel, malicious cyber activity can be detected, responded to, and contextualized in cyber threat intelligence (CTI). Microsoft Sentinel can also import threat indicators from Structured Threat Information Expressions (STIX), Trusted Automated Exchange of Intelligence Information (TAXII), or any threat intelligence platform (TIP).

16. A. Identifying, assessing, responding, and monitoring and reporting are the major phases of risk management.

17. B. The Microsoft Defender for Cloud product also uses threat intelligence. With Defender for Cloud, you can monitor security information from Azure resources, the network, and connected partner solutions to combat threats. For identifying threats, this information is analyzed, often correlating data from multiple sources.

18. A. You should review Defender for Cloud's recommendations page and implement the remediation instructions for each recommendation to improve your security. The recommendations are categorized according to security controls. In addition, each control represents a logical group of related security recommendations and reflects the vulnerability of your attack surface.

19. A. Defender for Cloud can assist with the governance of azure workloads by using Azure Policy to enforce secure configuration following specific recommendations.

20. D. Most users behave predictably, so allowing them to sign in could be risky if they deviate from this pattern. The user may need to be blocked, or perhaps you should ask them to perform multifactor authentication to ensure that the end user is who they declare to be.

The sign-in risk is the likelihood that the identity owner will not authorize a given authentication request. The Azure AD Premium P2 license enables organizations to create conditional access policies incorporating Azure AD Identity Protection sign-in risk detections.

Chapter 6: Define a Strategy for Securing Infrastructure

1. B. The field of people security focuses on educating people, protecting them, and protecting the organization from insider threats.

2. D. The security of a business helps ensure its confidentiality, integrity, safety, and availability. Internal and external malicious and unintentional acts can significantly impact operations if not protected against. Security strategy processes that are successful align closely with business strategies and modernize security strategies.

3. B. When Microsoft Defender for Cloud is deployed, your organization can continuously assess its security posture. Defender for Cloud strengthens your cloud security posture by protecting workloads in Azure, hybrid cloud platforms, and other platforms integrated with Microsoft Defender.

4. A, B. An organization's security posture is measured by Microsoft Secure Score, with a higher number indicating more recommended actions. Microsoft recommends scorecard metrics in four areas: business enablement, security improvement, security posture, and security response.

5. B. The CIA triad principles (confidentiality, integrity, and availability) guide a business's information security policies. To operate a business successfully, the confidentiality, integrity, and availability of information are crucial. The CIA triad breaks these three ideas down into different focuses. Differentiating security concerns helps security teams pinpoint the approaches they can take to address them. Redundancy is not part of this CIA triad.

6. B. A viable option is to use the Security Compliance Toolkit (SCT), a collection of tools for downloading, analyzing, testing, editing, and storing Microsoft-recommended security configuration baselines for Windows and other Microsoft products. Administrators can use the SCT to manage their enterprise's Group Policy Objects (GPOs). This toolkit allows administrators to compare their current GPO with Microsoft-recommended GPO baselines, edit them, save them as GPO backup files, and apply them through Active Directory or individually.

7. C. For servers, Azure Security Benchmark (ASB) can be used to apply Azure security baselines to machines. Windows and Linux security baseline documents have been developed based on ASB guidance on OS hardening.

8. A. In addition, ensuring a more secure communication method and disabling legacy protocols are crucial for server security. Network protocol Server Message Block (SMB) is used mainly for sharing files. Aside from file sharing, printers, scanners, and email servers also frequently use it. There is no encryption support in SMB 1.0, the original version of SMB; version 3.0 of SMB introduced encryption.

9. A. Using Local Administrator Password Solution (LAPS), you can manage the passwords for local accounts on domain-joined computers. There is a version of LAPS for every version of Windows Server and client that is currently supported.

10. A. Microsoft Intune is used for MDM and app protection policies to protect your work files when enrolling a device in Intune. App protection policies can also secure employee-owned devices not enrolled in Intune for management. It is still essential to ensure the safety of work files and resources, even if your organization does not manage the device.

11. B. Work emails, calendars, contacts, and documents can be accessed from smartphones and tablets, allowing employees to do their work anytime and anywhere. When people use devices in your organization, you need to protect their information. Access rules and device security policies can be set using Basic Mobility and Security, and mobile devices can also be wiped if they are lost or stolen with it.

12. C. Many environments use Active Directory (AD) on-premises. Devices that are AD domain-joined and also joined to Azure AD are called hybrid Azure AD joined devices. With Windows Autopilot, you can enroll hybrid Azure AD-joined devices in Intune. A Domain Join configuration profile is also required to enroll.

13. C. Using Windows events directly from your domain controllers and capturing network traffic, Microsoft Defender for Identity monitors and analyzes your domain controllers to identify attacks.

14. A. Azure Key Vault allows you to store encryption keys, certificates, and server-side tokens in the cloud. By providing secure access, permission control, and access logging, Key Vault helps ensure that your applications' secrets remain safe. Vaults, keys, and secrets are the main concepts in an Azure Key Vault.

15. C. Users and apps trying to access a vault are authenticated using Azure Active Directory (Azure AD). Any authentication request is authenticated by associating the user or app's authenticated identity with the Azure AD tenant of the subscription containing the Key Vault. Key Vaults cannot be accessed anonymously.

16. A. A comprehensive desktop and app virtualization service is available in Azure via Azure Virtual Desktop. Virtual desktop infrastructure (VDI) with simplified management, Windows 10/11 multisession support, Microsoft 365 app optimizations, and Remote Desktop Services (RDS) support are the only VDI parts that deliver all these features.

17. C. Using the Azure Bastion solution, the remote worker could access resources deployed in Azure without requiring public IP addresses on the VMs being accessed instead of a VPN connection, providing secure shell access using RDP or SSH.

18. C. With Azure Bastion, you won't need to worry about hardening each VM in your virtual network, as it sits at the perimeter of your virtual network and is hardened internally to ensure secure RDP/SSH connectivity. Azure Bastion is a managed PaaS service from Microsoft Azure that's hardened internally to provide secure RDP/SSH connectivity. As part of the Azure platform, the Azure Bastion is hardened and kept up-to-date to protect you from zero-day exploits.

19. A. You can establish a secure connection to your virtual network from an individual computer using a Point-to-site (P2S) VPN gateway. Client computers establish P2S connections.

20. B. Site-to-site VPN may connect two sites, for example, the main offices and remote location. It uses IPsec/IKE (IKEv1 or IKEv2) VPN tunnels to secure two sites. In hybrid and cross-premises configurations, S2S connections can be used. On-premises VPN devices with public IP addresses are required for S2S connections.

Chapter 7: Define a Strategy and Requirements for Securing PaaS, IaaS, and SaaS Services

1. A. Microsoft mitigates risks and responsibilities, beginning at the bottom with the physical infrastructure. The Microsoft cloud is not a good target for attackers because Microsoft continually monitors it, so attacking it makes no sense.

2. C. Key management mitigates one of the risks associated with data governance and rights management at the top of the stack. While key management is an extra responsibility, you have spots in a PaaS deployment that you don't have to handle so that you can move resources to key management.

3. A. Azure Security baselines strengthen security by improving your organization's tooling, tracking, and security features. They also deliver a constant background of knowledge when securing your environment.

4. C. As per the Microsoft recommendation, setting up new virtual machines in Microsoft Azure and granting access to them to only authorized users is the first step in protecting your virtual machine.

5. C. To enhance the security of Linux workloads on Microsoft Azure, you can combine them with Azure AD authentication. When you use Azure AD authentication for Linux workloads, you centrally manage and enforce policies that permit or restrict access to the Linux workloads.

6. A. You can encrypt your Windows and Linux virtual machine disks with Azure Disk Encryption. Disk encryption for Windows and Linux OSs is provided by Azure Disk Encryption, which uses BitLocker and dm-crypt features.

7. C. Monitoring and securing Microsoft 365 identities, apps, and devices from a centralized Microsoft 365 Defender portal dashboard. In a central place, the Microsoft 365 Defender portal combines protection, detection, investigation, and response to the email, collaboration, identity, device, and cloud app threats.

8. A. Microsoft Defender for Cloud has a Secure Score that helps you improve the security posture of Azure workloads, and Microsoft 365 has a Secure Score that assists SaaS systems in improving their security posture.

9. B. In the threat modeling exercise, Microsoft recommended dividing a typical IoT architecture into four zones: devices, field gateways, cloud gateways, and services.

10. C. Typically, a solution is segmented by zones; each zone has its own authentication, authorization, and data requirements. Trust boundaries separate zones, representing the transfer of information and data between them. Spoofing, tampering, repudiation, information disclosure, denial of service, and elevation of privilege (STRIDE) could occur during this transition.

11. A. IoT devices, vulnerabilities, and threats can be identified and managed by Microsoft Defender for IoT through a single interface.

12. A. By bridging the gap between IT and OT security challenges and empowering SOC teams with out-of-the-box capabilities to detect and respond to OT threats, Microsoft Sentinel and Microsoft Defender for IoT work effectively and efficiently. Detecting multistage attacks that often cross IT/OT boundaries is made easier through the integration between Microsoft Defender for IoT and Microsoft Sentinel.

13. B. Microsoft Purview services help you manage and govern your data across on-premises, multi-cloud, and software as a service. Identify sensitive data, classify it, and trace it from end to end for a holistic picture of your data landscape.

14. A. Integrating Microsoft Defender for Cloud with Microsoft Purview allows you to obtain a vital layer of data from Microsoft Purview for alerts and recommendations with information about any potentially sensitive data.

15. A. Data workloads include databases, and Microsoft Defender for SQL can manage security postures for databases. In addition to Azure SQL Database and Azure SQL Managed Instance, Microsoft Defender for Cloud is available for Azure Synapse Analytics as well as Azure SQL Database.

16. B. App Service allows you to enforce HTTPS by one click to secure your app from all unencrypted (HTTP) connections. Before reaching your application code, unsecure requests are rejected.

17. A. Users and clients can authenticate and authorize themselves using Azure App Service. Using it, clients and users can sign in without writing any code.

18. A, B. You immediately benefit from the security assessment and threat detection services when you enable Microsoft Defender for App Service.

19. A. STRIDE is a model for threat modeling used by Microsoft as part of the Security Development Lifecycle (SDL). Threat modeling allows software architects to detect and mitigate security issues early when they can be resolved relatively quickly and economically.

20. D. If you want to reduce the risk of attacks, you should use a private registry, such as Azure Container Registry or Docker Trusted Registry.

Chapter 8: Define a Strategy and Requirements for Applications and Data

1. B. For identifying gaps in your security policies and procedures, Azure provides a wide range of configurable auditing and logging options. Security-related events are recorded by your application through auditing and logging.

2. B. Credentials, such as usernames and passwords, are typically used in authentication to verify an entity's identity. The process of authentication involves proving that you are who you claim to be. A person or device's identity is verified.

3. C. An application's authorization controls access to resources and operations. Authenticated parties are authorized to do something when they are granted permission. In it, you are given access to specific data and are allowed to do certain things with that data. AuthZ is sometimes used to shorten authorization. Authorization is handled by the Microsoft identity platform using the OAuth 2.0 protocol.

4. B. Applications that process and store information must provide security, integrity, and availability assurances for business-critical data.

5. C. Applications that are critical to the business mission, such as production lines that generate revenue, devices, or services that are vital to life and safety, and other functions are defined as business-critical availability.

6. D. High exposure to attacks defined the category of risk for public Internet web applications that are easily accessible to attackers. It is also common for attackers (and penetration testers) to target legacy applications because they often have hard-to-fix vulnerabilities.

7. B. In legacy applications, operating systems, middleware, and other components are typically included on infrastructure as a service (IaaS) virtual machines.

8. A. Modern: Platform as a service (PaaS) application doesn't need to manage and secure the underlying server operating system and can be fully serverless and built primarily using functions.

9. A. Use web application firewalls (WAFs) to reduce the likelihood that an attacker will be able to exploit commonly seen security vulnerabilities.

10. A. DevOps influences the planning, developing, delivering, and operating phases of an API or application life cycle. There is no role specificity to the phases, as each one relies on the others. DevOps cultures involve each role in each phase to some extent.

11. A. Continuous integration/continuous delivery (CI/CD) and API development should be moved from the waterfall development cycle into the DevOps life cycle.

12. A. The STRIDE model should be adopted for securing modern applications as per Microsoft's recommendation. Praerit Garg and Loren Kohnfelder developed STRIDE at Microsoft to identify computer security threats.

13. D. As an extortion attack, ransomware encrypts files and folders, making it impossible to access important documents. Typically, ransomware is used by criminals to extort money from victims by requesting cryptocurrency in exchange for a decryption key. The Dark Web or the public Internet is also frequently used by criminals to extort money from their victims in exchange for a promise not to release sensitive information.

14. B. Your organization's data stores and knowledge bases should be inventoried during the data discovery part of the data identification and protection strategy definition.

15. C. Data protection is the answer. Create policies that control access and sharing of data using encryption, access restrictions, and visual markings to provide flexible protection.

16. A. Microsoft Defender for Cloud offers comprehensive data leak prevention capabilities such as discover, classify, protect, and monitor.

17. D. Data governance is about knowing, protecting, preventing, and governing your data. Microsoft Purview is a unified data governance service for managing and governing on-premises, multi-cloud, and SaaS data.

18. A. Microsoft Information Protection, part of Microsoft Purview, is natively integrated with Data Classification with Defender for Cloud Apps.

19. A. A privacy review and SDL process are in place to protect sensitive data in Microsoft Defender for Cloud Apps. The data is not under the control of the customer.

20. B. For Azure and internal connected resources, Azure Key Vault makes it easy to provision, manage, and deploy public or private Transport Layer Security/Secure Sockets Layer (TLS/SSL) certificates.

Chapter 9: Recommend Security Best Practices and Priorities

1. D. A Cybersecurity Architect must ensure that best practices are applied and integrated. Security best practices must be integrated into people's skills, habits, organizational processes, and technology architecture.

2. A, B. Microsoft Cybersecurity Reference Architectures (MCRA) and Microsoft Cloud Security Benchmarks (MCSBs) contain capabilities and control best practices. Some are embedded in MCRA diagrams, others in MCSB guidelines.

3. A. Microsoft recommends that a compromise of privileged access could result in the shutdown of business operations across the organization in a ransomware/extortion attack if higher security protections, monitoring, and response are required for privileged and systems accounts.

4. B. The primary tool for security operations to detect and respond to attacks has been the security information and event management (SIEM) capability. After extended detection and response (XDR) tools were introduced, they quickly became indispensable for monitoring platforms (starting with endpoint detection and response [EDR] for endpoints) since false positives are reduced rapidly. For technologies covered by XDR, these tools simplify and improve detection and response in a way that the SIEM cannot.

5. C. Using security orchestration, automation, and response technologies (SOAR), machine learning (ML), and user entity behavioral analytics (UEBA) can reduce the amount of manual effort in security operations. By automating manual efforts, SOAR technology relieves human analysts of distractions and fatigue during detection, investigation, and response activities.

6. C. An organization's critical business data must be discovered, classified, protected, and monitored through this initiative. So, it is data security.

7. B. One of the essential security practices is threat modeling. As a result, developers develop a security mindset that will lead to improved security in all their future projects. Threat modeling is a straightforward concept but can be pretty detailed and technical if needed.

8. A. There are several action points in a penetration test, including dynamic application security testing (DAST). By looking at how the application responds to specially crafted requests, DAST tools detect security issues in the running application. They are also called *web application vulnerability scanners*.

9. A. In infrastructure as code (IaC), infrastructure (networks, virtual machines, load balancers, and connection topology) is managed using a descriptive model. The same versioning model used by DevOps teams for source code is used for infrastructure as code. Like the principle of generating the same binary with the same source code, the same environment is generated every time it is applied.

10. B. Developers can identify security issues in their familiar, integrated development environment (IDE) with security plug-ins during the development process. Plug-ins can provide immediate feedback if the developer's code contains a potential security risk. You can also use plug-ins to find threats in third-party libraries or packages. Many open-source and commercial plug-ins are available and provided by security companies depending on the IDE you use.

11. B. A penetration test is a recommended practice to identify vulnerabilities in an application's configuration or infrastructure that may be exploitable by attackers. In Azure, Microsoft provides guidance on penetration testing. Many products and partners offer penetration testing services.

12. D. The controls in asset protection support security architectures, standards, and policies. Security standards should be consistently applied to all instances of every asset type and security requirement. Asset protection focuses on consistent execution across all control types. Preventive, detective, and other control types align to meet policy, standards, and architecture.

13. A. When an asset cannot be secured anymore but cannot be immediately retired, network isolation may be a valid option. A scenario like this can occur with end-of-life operating systems and applications. It occurs often in legacy systems and operational technology (OT) environments.

14. A. A company's ultimate resource owner who owns all other risks and benefits should always be held accountable for security. It is the responsibility of the security teams and subject-matter experts to advise the accountable owner about risks, mitigations, and implementation.

15. C. Subject-matter experts in asset protection provide knowledge about assets, their controls, and how to implement them.

16. A. Take a look at well-known resources first. Consider virtual machines, networks, and identities that the team is already familiar with. With native cloud tools like Microsoft Defender for Cloud, you can make immediate progress, and they are often easier to manage and secure.

17. B. The governance team provides context on how the controls relate to the security architecture, policies and standards, and regulatory requirements.

18. A. As part of security operations, alerts and logs are integrated into security operations tools, processes, and training.

19. A. The risk associated with cybersecurity is the potential damage to a business's assets, revenue, and reputation due to human attackers stealing money or information. While these attacks occur in the technical environment, they often represent a risk to your entire organization. Your risk measurement, tracking, and mitigation framework should be aligned with your cybersecurity risk. Cybersecurity risks are still considered technical problems, and this perception leads to incorrect conclusions that do not mitigate the risk's strategic business impact.

20. B. As security matures, the goal is to expose and mitigate risks and empower the business to change with minimal risk. This requires insight into security risks and deep security integration. Your organization's top security risks should appear on its risk register at any maturity level. Those risks are then managed down to an acceptable level for your organization.

Index

Online Test Bank

To help you study for your MCE Cybersecurity Architect certification exam, register to gain one year of FREE access after activation to the online interactive test bank—included with your purchase of this book! All of the practice questions in this book are included in the online test bank so you can study in a timed and graded setting.

Register and Access the Online Test Bank

To register your book and get access to the online test bank, follow these steps:

1. Go to www.wiley.com/go/sybextestprep. You'll see the "**How to Register Your Book for Online Access**" instructions.
2. Click "here to register" and then select your book from the list.
3. Complete the required registration information, including answering the security verification to prove book ownership. You will be emailed a pin code.
4. Follow the directions in the email or go to www.wiley.com/go/sybextestprep.
5. Find your book on that page and click the "Register or Login" link with it. Then enter the pin code you received and click the "Activate PIN" button.
6. On the Create an Account or Login page, enter your username and password, and click Login or, if you don't have an account already, create a new account.
7. At this point, you should be in the test bank site with your new test bank listed at the top of the page. If you do not see it there, please refresh the page or log out and log back in.